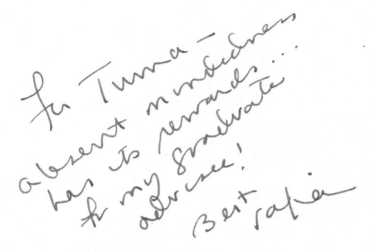

for Tunma —
absent mindedness...
has its rewards...
to my graduate
advisee!
Best Rafia

BLACK MASCULINITY AND THE U.S. SOUTH

BLACK
MASCULINITY
FROM AND THE
UNCLE TOM U.S. SOUTH
TO
GANGSTA

RICHÉ RICHARDSON

The University of Georgia Press | Athens and London

© 2007 by the University of Georgia Press
Athens, Georgia 30602
www.ugapress.org
All rights reserved
Set in 10.5/13.5 Adobe Caslon by Bookcomp

Printed digitally in the United States of America

Library of Congress Cataloging-in-Publication Data

Richardson, Riché, 1971–
Black masculinity and the U.S. South : from Uncle Tom
to gangsta / Riché Richardson.
xi, 296 p. ; 23 cm.—(The new southern studies)
Includes bibliographical references (p. 265–284) and index.
ISBN-13: 978-0-8203-2609-2 (hardcover : alk. paper)
ISBN-10: 0-8203-2609-7 (hardcover : alk. paper)
ISBN-13: 978-0-8203-2890-4 (pbk.   )
ISBN-10: 0-8203-2890-1 (pbk.   )
1. African American men in popular culture—Southern
States. 2. African American men in literature. 3. African
American men in motion pictures. 4. Popular music—
Southern States. 5. Popular culture—Southern States.
6. Masculinity—Southern States. 7. Sex role—Southern
States. 8. Regionalism—Southern States. 9. Southern
States—Intellectual life. 10. Southern States—Social
conditions. I. Title.
E185.86 .R537 2007
305.38'896073075—dc22   2006023814

British Library Cataloging-in-Publication Data available

For Emma Jenkins Richardson, my grandmother,
and in loving memory of Joe Richardson, my grandfather

CONTENTS

ACKNOWLEDGMENTS

I have been supported at various junctures of this book's development by people in and beyond the academy. It has been a privilege to live and work in intellectual community at the University of California, Davis, with such interlocutors as Elizabeth Freeman, Gayatri Gopinath, Gregory Dobbins, Jon Rossini, Michael Ziser, Desirée Martín, Seeta Chaganti, Claire Waters, Katherine Sugg, and Bishnupriya Ghosh, all of whom I owe thanks for their thoughtful and incisive readings of sections of this book. Other colleagues at UC Davis whose ideas and suggestions at various junctures undoubtedly helped to make this a better book include Patricia A. Turner, Clarence E. Walker, Jacob Olupona, Carl Jorgensen, Clarence Major, David Van Leer, Karl Zender, David Simpson, and Linda Morris. Peter Hays reminded me early on to confront the example of the black rapist as a historical stereotype of black masculinity in the South. This book has benefited from the diligent and methodical research skills of Eden Osucha, Tara Pedersen, and Hana Fujimoto. I appreciate Kara Thompson's compilation of the index. I have also found intellectual stimulation and support in ongoing dialogues with Roy Kamada and Andrew Strombeck.

I am thankful for the support and advice that Georges Van Den Abbeele and Ron Saufley at the Davis Humanities Institute gave so freely as I drafted research proposals and made applications for fellowships; their support of the project, particularly in its early phases when I was a new faculty member, was heartening. I also extend thanks to them and to John Van Den Heuvel and the 2002–3 DHI fellows for such a stimulating year of discussion on "The Poetics and Politics of Place." I am grateful for the opportunity to have participated in an interdisciplinary research cluster on masculinity for a year at UC Davis, which allowed me to dissect and digest some of the most interesting and innovative scholarship in the field with scholars who were also developing projects on the topic. Judith Newton was particularly helpful as I developed the sections on the black-liberation movement, including the Black Panther Party and her namesake—Huey.

For support of this project from its early phases as a dissertation in the fabled English department at Duke University, I thank Karla FC Holloway, Cathy N. Davidson, Wahneema Lubiano, and Thomas Ferraro, whose counsel helped me as I searched out critical and theoretical foundations for this study and enabled me to stack the building blocks much more efficiently and creatively. I also appreciate Nahum Chandler's work on my dissertation committee as well as his sponsorship during the year that I spent at Johns Hopkins University in the Program for Comparative American Cultures. Furthermore, I owe thanks to Michael Moon, Lee Baker, David Barry Gaspar, and Paula Giddings. I cannot discuss the Duke roots of this project without mentioning various others working in and beyond the field of African American literary studies whose dialogues impacted my development as an intellectual. Among them are Shireen Lewis, Maurice Wallace, Ifeoma Nwankwo, Sarah Willburn, and Scott Trafton. I also appreciate the support and generosity of C. T. Woods-Powell and Richard Powell.

I've yet to see or experience intellectual community in the profession anywhere else in the way that I have experienced it among my colleagues and friends in southern studies. I particularly appreciate the support that I have been given by Jon Smith, Leigh Anne Duck, Scott Romine, Kathryn McKee, Annette Trefzer, George Handley, Deborah Cohn, Katherine Henninger, Robert Phillips, and John Lowe as I have completed this book. Houston A. Baker Jr.'s methodologies have widened the space for critical study of black masculinity and the U.S. South, and I have valued his support. The feedback of Marlon Ross and Richard Yarborough was also useful and arrived when I really needed it. I valued the opportunity to participate in a dialogue with Hortense Spillers about her rich body of work in psychoanalysis during my development of this study.

Funding from various sources enabled the development and completion of this project, including a Ford Foundation Postdoctoral Fellowship that gave me necessary leave time to write, a New Faculty Research Grant, a Faculty Development Award, a Davis Humanities Institute Fellowship, and a Faculty Research Grant. This book has been shaped inestimably over the years by conversations I've had in sessions at meetings sponsored by the Modern Language Association, the Collegium for African American Research, the American Studies Association, and the Society for the Study of Southern Literature. Conferences, workshops, and lectures at Duke University; the University of Florida, Gainesville; the University of Alabama, Tuscaloosa; UC Davis; Brewton-Parker College; Johns Hopkins University; and the University of California, Irvine, have given me opportunities to refine various aspects of my analysis. Finally, I have valued opportunities to dialogue with Martha Huie, the widow of William Bradford Huie, and have appreciated her encouragement and support of my work.

I thank Christine Wick Sizemore and Akiba Sullivan Harper for their diligent support and mentorship at Spelman College. I also appreciate the intellectual generosity of Beverly Guy-Sheftall and Gloria Wade-Gayles. Stephen A. Carey planted some of the earliest foundations for this project in his popular Modern Black Male Writers course at Morehouse and in his visionary scholarship on John Oliver Killens and southern masculinity. My four years of high school education at St. Jude Educational Institute—which was, in fact, the final camping ground for the Selma to Montgomery marchers in 1965—and eight years at St. John the Baptist Catholic School, primarily under the tutelage of the Sisters of the Blessed Sacrament, made a tremendous and unforgotten impact on my life and intellectual development.

Versions of chapters 1, 2, and 3 have appeared in essay form in the journals *Mississippi Quarterly* (Mississippi State University), *American Literature* (Duke University Press), and *Forum for Modern Language Studies* (Oxford University Press), respectively. I appreciate the permission to reprint them in extended and revised form in this book. Suggestions of anonymous readers at the University of Georgia Press were helpful, and Nancy Grayson has been a remarkable editor. I have appreciated the advice and encouragement of Rev. Janice Cooper. I thank Terrence Johnson, Denise Ross, Gvanit Efua Godare, and Palesa Mohajane for epic friendships, along with Adam Hotek. I'll always cherish the memory of Tangla Giles. Finally, Emma, Joanne, and Joseph Richardson and Pamela, Keri, and Megan Smith, along with George Baker, Sharon Frazier, and Lamar Landon, have encouraged me and cheered me on. My family—immediate, extended, and adopted—has been the most enabling force in my life on earth. I thank heaven for them and for this book!

BLACK MASCULINITY AND THE U.S. SOUTH

INTRODUCTION

Foundations and Frameworks

Sutton Griggs's first novel, *Imperium in Imperio: A Study of the Negro Race Problem* (1899), grapples with the contradictory models of leadership offered by the self-serving Bernard Belgrade and the progressive Belton Piedmont. In examining their conflicting strategies of racial uplift and the question of who is the better and truer "race man," the novel also points to distinctions and hierarchies that exist among African Americans on the basis of geography through a curious man simply referred to as "the Mississippian." Griggs's narrator informs us that

> There was a student in Stowe University who was noted for his immense height and for the size and scent of his feet. His feet perspired freely, summer and winter, and the smell was exceedingly offensive. On this account, he roomed to himself. Whenever other students called to see him he had a very effective way of getting rid of them, when he judged that they had stayed long enough. He would complain of a corn and forthwith pull off a shoe. If his room was crowded, this act invariably caused it to be empty. The fame of these feet spread to the teachers and young ladies, and, in fact, to the city. And the huge Mississippian seemed to relish the distinction. (69–70)

Belton, nearing the end of his days at the fictive Stowe University, has been named valedictorian and is preparing to give the speech of his life, as it were. When practicing before his roommate, Belton has become unusually emotional. Anticipating that such will be the case at the ceremony, he purchases an expensive silk handkerchief and places it in the tail pocket of his Prince Albert suit the night before. Unbeknownst to him, his roommate, who furtively witnesses his movements, is "insanely jealous" (69). After Belton goes to bed, the roommate steals the Mississippian's pungent socks and places them in Belton's suit pocket. The next day before the cheering audience, "Belton's head continued bowed in sadness, as he spoke parting words to his classmates, and lifted his supposed handkerchief to his eyes to wipe away the tears that were now coming freely. The socks had thus come close to Belton's nose and he stopped of a sudden and held them at arm's length to gaze at that terrible, terrible scent producer" (75). Attempting to recapture his composure before the laughing audience, he remarks the following: "Ladies and gentlemen, these socks are from Mississippi. I am from Virginia." Humor is Griggs's primary device for treating the Mississippian's absurdity. The sock incident undercuts the seriousness of tone in the passages of the staid baccalaureate sermon that opens the chapter. The chapter's title—"A Sermon, a Sock, and a Fight"—emphasizes the unlikely juxtaposition of such disparate and incongruent elements. That the narrator refers to this character as "the Mississippian" points to his namelessness and the ubiquity of place in defining him. Furthermore, the narrator's meticulous care in describing the positioning of characters suggests the extent to which place matters in these passages. That the narrator overviews the sermon word for word while omitting the content of Belton's valedictory address—which the roommate sabotages—foreshadows Bernard's foreclosure of his political mission that occurs later in the novel. Significantly, a speech by Belton also precedes this moment.

In these passages, Griggs establishes a stark contrast between Belton's meticulous care of his clothing and the Mississippian's slovenliness. Whereas Belton is the school's most distinguished student and aims to become a credit to his race, the Mississippian paradoxically takes pride in being distinguished for his body odor and seeks no higher purpose. His big, imposing body is a condition for his alienation and namelessness at the school and, in keeping with Cartesian logic, is the diametrical opposite of the intelligent mind that has earned Belton honor as valedictorian. Belton implies that he is not the same kind of southerner as the Mississippian and that this man is other to him. The larger conflict between Belton and Bernard easily obscures the Mississippian's role as a counterpoint to Belton, whom Griggs construes as the more ideal raced and gendered subject. This novel highlights a black southern male's body as pathological and abject because it is dirty, and describes its spatial alienation and role in the sabotage of a male hero who is striving for black racial uplift. These scenes in Griggs's novel, written over a century ago, are valuable not only because they point to hierarchies of black identity but also because they acknowledge ways in which southernness has sometimes functioned as a source of embarrassment in the African American context. Such perceptions of black southerners are by no means just a thing of the past.

Black Masculinity and the U.S. South examines the construal of black male southerners as inferior and undesirable models of black masculinity within such racial hierarchies based on geography. My main concern in this study is the role of geography in constituting difference and otherness within the category of African Americans, particularly among black men. The enduring and eponymous images of black masculinity that emerged in the South during the nineteenth century—the Uncle Tom and the black rapist—were paradigmatic, I suggest, in helping to establish foundations for the perennially complex politics of black masculine representation in the United States. The Uncle Tom, as a character on theatrical and minstrel circuits, epitomized an innocuous and neutered model of black masculine sexuality and came to be signified primarily in relation to an aged, black, masculine body. The image of him that most of us now know best is that of a shuffling older man with receding gray hair. This formulation was an outgrowth of reactionary sentiment in the South about slavery as an institution in the antebellum era. As critics have pointed out, it grossly contradicted Uncle Tom's original literary characterization in Harriet Beecher Stowe's *Uncle Tom's Cabin* (1852) as a strong, muscular man. Moreover, the several young children in his famed cabin made his virility quite evident. Wilson Jeremiah Moses has remarked, for instance, that "the racial symbolism personified in the character of Uncle Tom was not originally intended to be pejorative."[1] The central role that the mutually constitutive reconstruction of Uncle Tom's body and sexuality played in his eventual translation into what folklorist Patricia A. Turner has aptly identified as an epithet has seldom been considered.[2] Uncle Tom, who has been a figure of continuing fascination in American literature and culture, gained his initial popular salience in such contexts as advertising and theater, including the minstrel stage, and in one of the nation's earliest films. The reconstruction of his body and sexuality also served as the foundation for his national abstraction and later dispersal into a range of related types, from Old Black Joe to Uncle Remus. Similarly, the efficacy of mammy as an image, which was epitomized in the late nineteenth century with the emergence of the Aunt Jemima logo in 1889, was grounded in a visual representation of her black feminine body as plump and amply bosomed, characterizing this type as asexual. Like the Uncle Tom, her construction relied on an essentialist construction of the body and sexuality.

The myth of the black rapist that emerged in the South in the wake of Emancipation functioned in some ways as the obverse of the Uncle Tom and was rooted in even more explicitly perverse scripts of the black masculine body and sexuality. It was a myth that cast black men as sexually pathological, hyperbolized their phallic power, and construed them as inherently lustful and primitive. It was rooted in the growing panic about racial intermixture in the South that emerged after slavery ended, reflected the region's obsession with protecting white womanhood to ensure the purity of the race, and served as a primary rationale for lynching in the region. This myth in part drove the media fascination with the famous Scottsboro incident in 1931, in which nine young African American boys in Alabama were accused (but eventually acquitted) of raping two white women on a train. Raced and gendered historical images of black men as rapists continue to inform black masculine representations in contemporary media and popular culture, including the milder and more flattering associations of black men with sexual excess or know-how. Coupled with images of black men as violent and criminal, this mythology very likely informed the logic of Charles Stuart, a white man in Boston who falsely accused a black man of murdering his pregnant wife in 1989. While his statement led to a major manhunt in the city for any black men who fit the description of the attacker that he gave police, Stuart himself was later found to be the culprit. More recently, the vulnerability of black men to such stereotyping—and the shrewd manipulation of the public's propensity to believe it—was patently manifest in the attempt of the suspected abductors of Alabama teen Natalee Holloway to implicate three black men in her disappearance in Aruba in 2005. Whether they are guilty or not, the continuing efficacy of black-rapist mythology has made black men vulnerable to standing accused.

Both the Uncle Tom and the black rapist, this study suggests, link the South to some of the earliest national ideological scripts of black masculinity in the United States. These historical ideologies established foundations for a hermeneutics of black masculinity in the region as pathological, which continued to be evident in the twentieth century in such contexts as the military, black-liberation discourse, and aspects of black popular culture. Furthermore, it illustrates how constructions of the black male body as pathological in the late nineteenth century were in effect recast in the first decades of the twentieth century in several contexts. The Tuskegee Syphilis Study, for instance, is one of the most infamous and poignant historical examples of the confluence of science and medicine in constituting the black male body in the South as pathological in terms of sexuality and marking it as expendable. I shall illustrate how the military was instrumental in shaping a discourse of black men in the South as diseased and intellectually inferior combatants during World War I and generated regionally biased policies that had lasting effects. Though they have seldom been discussed, I also explore the raced, sexed, and gendered scripts of pathological black masculinity in the South that emerged as a byproduct of black-liberation discourse in the 1960s. I am interested in how such ideological models of black southern masculinity have helped maintain racial divisions and hierarchies within the national context and have helped formulate notions of African American identity, including notions of black authenticity.

My analysis reveals how these ideological models have at times impacted the development of racial discourses in the national context by counterbalancing formations of white masculinity and sexuality and obscuring race and gender distinctions within the category "white." Formulations of black masculinity in the South as pathological—particularly those rooted in sexuality—have also been invoked, for instance, to veil the white masculine pornographic imagination in the South. Alternatively, they have served as an instrument for displacing and unsettling notions of white pathology and forms of white sexual transgression. One must recognize the levels at which racial formations within and across black and white categories have been mutually constitutive. White masculinity in the South was historically defined by such concepts as chivalry, honor, and gentility that were upheld as the most cherished principles and values in white southern social life.[3] Their most perverse manifestations were patently evident after the end of slavery in sanctioning lynching and shaping the ideology of white supremacy that cast black men as rapists and stressed the necessity of defending and protecting the purity and sanctity of white womanhood. As Dana D. Nelson has argued, the foundational ideologies of white manhood in the United States were established during the Enlightenment. These frameworks are indispensable for understanding how ideologies of white masculinity in the South were consolidated by forcing black southerners to live under subjection while obstructing their claims to citizenship and by nationalizing a script of the black male body as pathological and bestial in the late nineteenth century.[4] During this time, this script complemented the caricatures of the black male body as an Uncle Tom, which also worked saliently in shaping a national discourse on race, masculinity, and sexuality.

Taken together, these images, which emerged in the final decades of the nineteenth century, mediated race, gender, and sexuality formations both within and beyond the African American context.

My critical endeavor seems necessary when we consider that beyond these familiar historical images of black masculinity in the South, many of the complex strategies through which the region has served as a backdrop for black masculine construction in the United States have yet to be acknowledged. How the South continued to shape the development of discourses on the black masculine body as perversely sexualized and pathological during the twentieth century, for instance, has seldom been recognized. Furthermore, my study uncovers a remarkably consistent imaging of black masculinity in the South as cowardly, counterrevolutionary, infantile, and emasculated. It examines the marking of black men in the South as other to authentic notions of blackness and masculinity and highlights instances in which southernness has been construed as an undesirable ingredient— even as a contaminant—in black masculine fashioning. I illustrate how such perceptions of black masculinity in the South have been related to class-inflected ideologies of uplift in the African American context and to urban-centered definitions of blackness and masculinity.

That black men from the South are sometimes perceived as inauthentic in terms of race and gender becomes understandable in light of Phillip Brian Harper's observation that "since the dominant view holds prideful self-respect as the very essence of healthy African-American identity, it also considers such identity to be fundamentally weakened whenever masculinity appears to be compromised. . . . Its primary effect is that all debates over and claims to 'authentic' African-American identity are largely animated by a profound anxiety about the status specifically of African-American *masculinity*."[5] Harper's remarks also well suggest *why* the topic of black masculinity is particularly useful to isolate and emphasize from a methodological standpoint when examining notions of racial authenticity, as formulated in the African American context, along with ideologies of black racial uplift.

The focus of this book rests primarily, then, on what might be regarded as more obviously pejorative representations of black men in the South. This investigation is important, I believe, because the familiar and relatively favorable ideological narratives construing black southern masculinities as romantic, genteel, traditional, morally upright, hardy, and hardworking have typically obscured the ideological strategies of constructing these identities as undesirable within and beyond the African American context. As an example, we might consider how the long-standing view of black men in the South as traditional (à la Booker T. Washington) fed the scripting of Supreme Court nominee Clarence Thomas as the grandson of a sharecropper from Georgia. Perhaps more than anything, it helped to authenticate Thomas as hardworking, loyal, and honest during the Senate Judiciary Committee hearings that resulted from law professor Anita Hill's allegations of sexual harassment in 1991. This narrative worked to similar effect when, after being nominated as national security advisor by President George W. Bush, Condoleezza Rice's lineage as the daughter of a longtime Republican preacher from Alabama was emphasized. In these instances, southern black men have been identified as part of the backbone of the African American community and as keepers of its time-honored values. Still, this study argues that the politics of black southern male representation are by no means so simple or straightforward and tries to throw into critical relief the economy of ideologies that subtend such romantic images. While scrutinizing these ideologies is not the main purpose of this study, I do believe they are as problematic as the more overtly ideological representations that I mainly consider. In recent years, such representations of black masculinity in the South have been hyperbolized in the public sphere and have served as a basis for reactionary agendas aimed at redirecting political dialogues in the African American context and instating a more conservative African American leadership in the nation's political realm. This fact alone is a strong indicator of their ideological potency.

This study stresses the indispensability of the U.S. South to critical dialogues about black masculinity and aims to clarify the role of geography in national politics of black masculine formation. The role of geography in formulating masculinity is increasingly necessary for thinking about such concepts as "black masculinity" and "black manhood" with originality, clarity, and depth. Furthermore, this work is necessary to the development of a more complex critical discourse on the intersections of masculinity and race. The project reflects my own critical investment in recognizing and studying black men as a historically differentiated and variegated raced, gendered, and sexed social category. When the ideologies that I am describing, such as the Uncle Tom and the black rapist, have been mentioned at all in contemporary scholarship, they have usually been shrouded in more generalized discussions of black masculinity. The impact of region and of the South in particular on race and gender formations has seldom been considered. *Black Masculinity and the U.S. South* aims to remedy these elisions within and beyond the burgeoning contemporary scholarship on masculinity, which provides some of the important critical and theoretical frameworks for the present study. This field of work has been elemental in the development of gender studies. It has become more attuned over the past decade to the impact of race in shaping masculinity to the point of having developed a veritable subfield of critical scholarship on black masculinity alone. Moreover, it has become less singularly and normatively invested in the study of white male subjectivity.[6]

In more recent years, some of the most significant critical developments in scholarship on black masculinity have increased our understanding of how sexuality helps create distinctions and hierarchies among black men. However, beyond the expanded conceptions of black masculinity yielded by the work on sexuality, black men frequently continue to be treated as an undifferentiated and monolithic racial and gender category. The distinctions among them based on geography are rarely mentioned. Serious questions have yet to be raised about hierarchical formulations of black masculinity rooted in distinctions on the basis of geography in part because region has been a neglected term in pondering primary variables that intersect in shaping identity such as race, gender, class, nationality, and sexuality.[7] My discussion of representations of black men in the South as unmanly and exterior to notions of authentic blackness and masculinity accords with critical work in black feminism and critical race theory that has contested reductive and exclusive definitions of blackness on the basis of gender and sexuality, which oftentimes narrowly shapes antiracist discourse.

As Houston A. Baker Jr. and Dana D. Nelson have pointed out, the South is often perceived as "America's abjected regional other."[8] Such critical perspectives have well suggested the utility of theories of abjection within psychoanalysis for studying the South. The psychoanalytic work on abjection, Julia Kristeva's in particular, provides important theoretical grounding for this study. Studies by such scholars as Patricia Yaeger, Anne Goodwyn Jones, and Susan Donaldson have theoretically expanded epistemologies of the South in feminism and gender studies while offering perspectives on southern abjection in relation to female subjectivity.[9] Furthermore, the status of the South as an "abject" region in the nation has been evident in the body of scholarship that has examined how the region has been constituted as a problem in this nation's history. As Larry J. Griffin and Don H. Doyle point out in the introduction to their anthology *The South as an American Problem*,

> The American South, more than any other region of the United States, has often been defined . . . as being at odds with the mainstream of American values or behavior and therefore has been constructed as a special problem. Because the fate of the nation was and remains unalterably bound to the fate of the region, however, the "problem of the South" has always been America's problem, understood most often as a blight on the broader cultural and political landscape and something that must be addressed and solved.[10]

By examining racial, legal, political, economic, and social frameworks, such scholarship has helped us understand why the South has so frequently registered as a "problem" in the United States, even if the South paradoxically remains pivotal in setting contemporary national political agendas that are frequently reactionary.[11] Many of the issues that have made the South a stigmatized region in the United States are well known: the adherence to slavery; the backlash against Reconstruction; the Supreme Court's legalization of the "Separate but Equal" doctrine in 1896, inaugurating an era of "Jim Crow" segregation that would only begin to be reversed with the *Brown v. Board of Education* case in 1954; the perpetration of white-supremacist ideologies, racial terror, and violence, particularly lynching; and of course, in more recent history, the opposition to black civil rights. Work that acknowledges the view of the South as a regional pariah in the nation is indispensable for examining ways in which subjects are construed as pathological, alienated, and subordinated within the category "white" through class-biased and racialist epithets with southern roots (such as "white trash"). We have increasingly come to understand how the South functions as a pariah region in the United States in which some white identities are excluded and viewed as socially undesirable on the basis of race and class. How black southerners have oftentimes been excluded from a southern category tacitly marked as "white" (a more metaphorical form of segregation) is also by now well understood. But there have been far fewer critical efforts to recognize how the prevailing ideological views of the South as inferior have been internalized and manifested *within* the category of African Americans and how southern identity has functioned as a basis on which blacks are maligned and excluded.

It almost goes without saying that the South has functioned historically as a site of ambivalent and conflicted identification for many African Americans in light of traumas associated with the region, which exacerbates the legacy of the South as politically, economically, and socially repressive. One goal of this study is to demonstrate ways in which the history of the South as a "problem" in the United States has inflected ideological scripts of black southerners. The critical work of Leigh Anne Duck, which clarifies in stunning detail how the South functions ideologically as "the nation's region," is a backdrop against which we might also understand the kinds of intramural conflicts about region among African Americans described in my study.

The South has played an organic role in shaping many of the prevailing ideologies of race in the United States. This fact was evident, for instance, in D. W. Griffith's 1915 film *Birth of a Nation*. Still, dialogues within academia that have focused on deconstructing the concept of race, which frequently signified this critical project with scare quotes (i.e., "race"), have been virtually silent about the South. This critical elision is curious in light of the increasingly central role that the region came to play following the late nineteenth century in constituting the nation's discourses of race. The South is one of the most fecund and historically appropriate sites on which to examine the intersection of race, gender, and sexuality. That the role of the South in shaping black masculinity has heretofore *not* been the subject of more widespread critical concern—especially within critical scholarship on black masculinity—is a bit ironic, too, in light of the status of the South as a key site in shaping some of the most dominant and influential conceptions of masculinity and femininity in the nation's history. For instance, ideologies of white female and male identity that emerged during the nineteenth century in relation to white elites, such as the "southern belle" and the "southern gentleman," have shaped the broader national grammar book on femininity and masculinity. They have complemented the South's range of racialist ideologies of black men and women as lascivious and deviant.

Toward New Southern Critical Horizons

The larger intellectual itinerary that I have pursued over the years has consistently focused on the historical and contemporary status of blacks in the South in constituting such concepts as the African American and the

American. Moreover, I have been highly committed to studying the status of the South in the development of discourses of race. Admittedly, my background as an African American born and raised in the South has partly fueled my passion to engage in systematic critical reflection on the region.[12] As an intellectual, in addition to teaching and studying African American literature, I have mainly worked in the fields of southern literature and southern studies, two other areas that inform this study. However, when I began to establish the early foundations for this project a decade ago in my dissertation, my investments in the methods of cultural studies, my critical and theoretical orientation, and my interest in texts beyond literature placed my work clearly beyond the pale of conventional studies of southern literature. I knew back then that I was trying to do something very different. As I worked, I walked by faith and often felt very alone as I attempted to examine the issues that were most critically interesting to me. It definitely helped to be in the Duke University English department, which had gained national recognition—and even inspired controversy—for its critical and theoretical innovation. The scholars with whom I worked in the program were tolerant of my need to be experimental in my methods. They respected and encouraged my efforts to think outside the box, so to speak. Back then, my approach was to draw on what was available in southern literature, along with southern history, as I attempted to develop a critical language that would enable me to formulate my research questions. Since then, changes have come about in the field of southern literature that I could not have ever imagined or anticipated. Furthermore, the face of the larger interdisciplinary and increasingly comparative field of southern studies looks very different from the way that it looked even just a few years ago when I began this project. Indeed, we are now in the midst of what some scholars working on the South, most notably Baker and Nelson, are referring to as a "new southern studies."[13] Even as I have recognized the urgency of these changes and have welcomed and tried in some ways to help shape them, I have also maintained my early belief in drawing methodologically on the best, and, for some purposes, the absolute worst of what more conventional fields such as southern literature and southern history have had to offer. In this study, this sensibility is particularly evident where I draw on writings in southern literature such as William Bradford Huie's 1967 novel *The Klansman* in combination with what has been classified as a "trash" film by that same name.

The current paradigm shift in southern studies is richly evident, of course, in critical efforts to examine the U.S. South in global perspective. Increasingly, efforts have been made in the field to unsettle the myopic racialist logic that construes the South as a fundamentally white region, along with binary formulations of the South that focus on such oppositions as North-South or black-white. An acknowledgment of the ethnic diversity of the region, in light of the growth of Asian, Mexican, Indian, and Latino populations over the past decade, has facilitated the move beyond this myopic historical lens when looking at racial dynamics in the region. Until quite recently, it seemed that matters concerning the U.S. South were of little concern in such fields as gay and lesbian and queer studies, which have tended to prioritize the role of urban contexts in shaping gay and lesbian identities. Nowadays, however, a substantial body of critical work is available that examines southern and rural contexts within studies of sexuality. The South has also emerged as a salient topic of interest in such fields as American literature, to the point that prominent journals like *American Literature* and *American Literary History* have devoted special issues to dialogues on the region. Journals that have been at the forefront in disseminating scholarship in southern literature, such as the *Mississippi Quarterly* and the *Southern Literary Journal,* are also helping to revolutionize southern literature and southern studies as well as American literary studies.

Amazingly, the current southern turns in academia have parallels in the national mainstream in the area of popular culture. They are perhaps most visibly evident among rap artists identifying themselves with the "dirty South" and proclaiming themselves to be "representin' the South." The genre of southern rap stands at the vanguard of contemporary hip-hop. In fact, the South, for better and for worse, has emerged as an epicenter for rap production in this nation. Southern rap's emergence has in effect collapsed the bicoastal logic that long alienated and excluded the South as a scene of rap production. The study of this phenomenon also reflects my interest in helping to expand the archive of conceivable textual objects in the fields of southern literature and southern studies.

Notwithstanding the expansion in southern scholarship in recent years, there have sometimes been challenges—and for some, even risks—in *representin'* the South in scholarship. This was particularly the case in the era before doing so became *kinda*—if not entirely—*cool;* I mean "cool" here in the sense that the singer Barbara Mandrell means it in the 1981 song "I Was

Country When Country Wasn't Cool." In other words, the historical status of the South as an "abject" region also impacts somewhat the extent to which the region is viewed in academia as a legitimate object of study. The region has therefore remained excluded or marginal as a topic of discussion in scholarly dialogues at times. These resistances are necessary and even urgent to reckon with in order for the South to become a less peripheral epistemology in contemporary scholarship. In fact, the historical salience of the South in shaping the nation's discourses of race, gender, and sexuality should make such elisions in scholarly dialogues unthinkable.

Black Studies / Southern Studies

This project brings together a range of texts in literature and culture. Its consideration of literature, films, speeches, and rap departs from conventional approaches in southern literature and southern studies and signals its cultural-studies orientation. To be sure, cultural studies methodologies that emphasize the deconstruction of the classic "high" and "low" binary seem appropriate for bringing such a perennially abject region as the U.S. South into bolder critical relief. Mae Gwendolyn Henderson's essay " 'Where by the Way Is This Train Going?': A Case for Black (Cultural) Studies," which emphasizes the importance of building upon conventional approaches to black studies in developing a black cultural studies, is, in fact, one of the critical works in cultural studies that has helped to establish foundations for the present study. Henderson reminds us of the utility in looking from Birmingham, England, to Birmingham, Alabama, in attempting to build a viable black cultural studies in the contemporary era. This inclusive strategy, she notes, permits an acknowledgment of the place of more conventional fields such as black studies within the genealogy of this newer field, which has seldom recognized or acknowledged these early foundations.[14] My own feeling—that a "new southern studies" can in some instances be enriched by building upon more conventional aspects of southern studies—parallels her outlook at this level.[15]

As a scholar working primarily in African American literature and southern studies, my main critical commitment has been to the development of methodologies for combining southern studies and black studies. One aspect of my work has examined how blackness functions as a salient framework for processing cultural flows and mediating a range of ethnic and racial formations in global contexts, even as black bodies remain invisible and abject in the global and national arena.[16] This phenomenon is strikingly reminiscent of the southern paradox in the United States. The mediative role of a historically abject and marginal blackness in the global arena is useful for theorizing ways in which the South in the United States, in light of its historical national abjection, is nevertheless serviceable as a paradigm for processing cultural formations within a global context. This insight can help push us closer to a more organic and comparative dialogue between such fields as black studies and southern studies. In general, the work of a range of African Americanist scholars whose work has addressed the South— including Trudier Harris, Henry Louis Gates Jr., Thadious Davis, Robin D. G. Kelley, Dolan Hubbard, Tera Hunter, William L. Andrews, Farah Jasmine Griffin, John Hope Franklin, Nell Irwin Painter, bell hooks, Jerry Ward, William J. Maxwell, and John Lowe—has helped my intellectual development in the field of southern studies over the years, along with the work of such newer scholars as Judith Jackson Fossett, Sharon Holland, Marla Frederick, Jacqueline Francis, Nicole Waligora-Davis, and Hasan Jeffries.[17]

In light of the issues related to the South's longstanding abjection and the politics of black southern devaluation within the African American context that I have outlined thus far, it may be true that topics related to black southerners are even *more* vulnerable to being excluded and overlooked in scholarship. The issues that I have been describing concerning black masculinity in the South have largely been neglected in black studies, a field in which few if any questions are ever raised about urban-centered paradigms for defining blackness and masculinity. These paradigms have consolidated all the more in recent years given the fascination with such topics as hip-hop. Alongside its emphasis on the importance of recognizing a more expansive and complex spectrum of black masculine formations, this study stresses the importance of unsettling these urban fetishisms. For like southern romanticisms, we need to understand how they reinforce essentialist definitions of black subjectivity within the discourses of race in the United States. As an example of this problematic, I consider the conventional binary logic about African American masculinity that links insurgency to black men in the urban North and accommodation to black men in the South in an essentialist way. Moses reveals that the roots of this ideology are traceable to the antebellum era, when the notion of the rebel slave in the figure of Nat Turner was contrasted with the Uncle Tom stereotype, yielding "a myth of slave servility and a myth of slave resistance." Highlighting the mythologizing of Stowe's Uncle Tom character, Moses points out that "Black Americans have found both the Uncle Tom and the Nat Turner myths useful. During the forty-year period of repression following the end of reconstruction, even such fiery militants as Frederick Douglass and Ida B. Wells would play on the image of the faithful, long-suffering, honest slave."[18] Indeed, we can trace the view of black masculinity in urban contexts (as more subversive and revolutionary) back to historical examples like Douglass, whose migration to the city of Baltimore played an important role in the development of his resistant sensibility. The same might be said of the reigning models of leadership in the African American context that emerged at the turn of the century—Booker T. Washington and W. E. B. Du Bois—who were situated in the South and urban North, respectively. Both men, as leaders, were frequently at odds over the issue of African American civil rights, and the latter was typically perceived to be the more radical of the two.

This study highlights the distinct regional contours of the Uncle Tom myth. Geography has sometimes played a salient, if typically unacknowledged, role in its critique. The stereotypical Uncle Tom or related types are frequently repackaged and redeemed through the eruption of a latent black militancy that abruptly and dramatically bursts forth. Such revisionist narratives have often implied that the most subversive forms of black masculinity and militancy have been urban, and they recurred in art of the 1960s black-liberation era. They have been manifest, for instance, in Robert Alexander's 1991 play *I Ain't Yo' Uncle: The New Jack Revisionist "Uncle Tom's Cabin,"* which combines the militancy of black-liberation discourse and "New Jack" and "gangsta" aesthetics to recast the Uncle Tom. That such narratives rely on an urban-oriented aesthetics to revise the codes that link the figure to the southern antebellum plantation points to Uncle Tom's geographical dimensions and to the role of geography in constructing identity among African Americans. The "Uncle Tom" now circulates as a general ideological descriptor for black men in the United States (it has most famously been attached to Supreme Court justice Clarence Thomas in recent years). This study acknowledges how the Uncle Tom has helped to produce specific narratives of black masculinity in the South as apolitical and counterinsurgent. Uncle Tom's marking as asexual and docile within the popular racial imaginary of the nineteenth century was recast, for instance, in black-liberation discourse's representations of him as homosexual, bisexual, or transvestite, representations that I consider in this study via an overview of Malcolm X's speech discourse. While southern rap challenges constructions of the "gangsta" as a fundamentally urban type, this study underscores the need to understand this concept as an outgrowth of other reigning ideologies of black masculinity steeped in southern history, like Uncle Tom and the black rapist.

The work of such critics as Henri Lefebvre and Edward Soja has expanded the critical possibilities for examining the impact of space on identity.[19] Their rethinking of time and space was revolutionary in a way similar to Jacques Derrida's critique of the conventional privileging of speech over writing. Still, critical regional studies—as it has developed within the framework of postmodern social theory—has not been an adequate terrain on which to engage problems of otherness related to southern subjectivity due to a fixation on urban geographies. As Barbara Ching and Gerald W. Creed have pointed out, "Postmodern social theory's stable reference point has been the city; it unquestioningly posits an urbanized subject without considering the extent to which such a subject is constructed by its conceptual opposition to the rustic. . . . In much postmodern social theory, the country as a vital place simply doesn't exist."[20] More generally, as Ching and Creed critique the hegemony of the urban in studies of identity and identity politics, it is useful that they highlight the pervasiveness of rural landscapes throughout the United States. Another drawback in postmodern social theory is that "urban" for theorists has almost exclusively meant urban places in the United States outside the South. Atlanta, Georgia, in spite of having hosted the 1996 Olympics, is far from the model "global city" in such dialogues, which have prioritized Los Angeles. Such reasoning has implicitly obscured the geographical complexity of the U.S. South, which is increasingly urban in its own right.

Of course, this "urban bias" in criticism and theory has reflected the modernization and globalization processes of the twentieth century. It is necessary to recognize its manifestations in the African American context, and its complements in such academic fields as black studies, as a byproduct of a range of historical phenomena, including the Great Migration to the urban North. (Current statistics show that the demography of the African American population has once again shifted back to the South, a phenomenon that is also helping produce more complex racial formations that defy the prevailing logic about race in the nation in and beyond the South.) The coming of modern life in the twentieth century and the impact of a modernist aesthetics made the urban foundational and dominant in the formation of racial subjectivity—and all aspects of social life—in much the same sense that globalization is now restructuring how we work and live. This study emphasizes the need to denaturalize and demystify logic that prioritizes the urban in the African American context and to recognize this category's complex regional dialectics. We need to recognize, for instance, how such logic creates hierarchies and distinctions among African Americans.

Postmodern social theory has also served as the backdrop against which cultural geographers the likes of David Sibley, Steve Pile, Doreen Massey, Gillian Rose, and Nancy Duncan have increasingly examined the impact of place in shaping identity over the past decade, frequently highlighting the role of space in shaping femininity and masculinity.[21] Such work has provided valuable critical and theoretical building blocks for this study. I have found the perspectives in cultural geography that highlight theories of abjection within psychoanalysis to be particularly useful in light of my investment in examining the problem of an abject black southern masculinity.

Theorizing Black Masculinity

Black men have been one of the most visible and topical categories in the nation's media for over a decade in light of a range of issues. They have included high rates of homicide and incarceration, the O. J. Simpson trial, the controversy over gangsta rap, and the historic Million Man March in Washington, D.C., led by Minister Louis Farrakhan and sponsored by the Nation of Islam. This political and social climate served as the backdrop against which the distinct and innovative body of scholarship in academia emerged on black masculinity, which has drawn on epistemologies in poststructuralism, cultural studies, queer studies, feminist studies, and whiteness studies. Developing a more complex critical and theoretical discourse on black masculinity seems all the more important and urgent in the contemporary era in light of a range of issues that have inordinately affected black men in the United States and limited or prevented opportunities for many of them to engage in community and civic life, including escalating HIV and AIDS infection rates, police brutality, homicides, and the privatization and exploitation of black male labor within the prison-industrial complex, which occurs even as black men experience astronomical rates of joblessness in a postindustrial and consumer-oriented global economy. Some contemporary "conservative" political agendas have been well-meaning in attempting to speak to these issues and need to be heeded and supported in areas where they can help. They perhaps fall shortest, however, in their typical presumption that such concepts as "family values" are alien to black men and that, with the right civilizing mission to make them more marriage-minded, poverty, the proverbial "female-headed households," and other perceived pathologies and social maladies in black communities might be eliminated. A better strategy might be to focus more on building the kind of economy that would give black men jobs instead of offering them these kinds of "lectures," if the goal is to make them more "marriageable," as it were. Furthermore, the most curious paradox of such agendas is that some who have propagated them in recent years have also supported reactionary "three strikes" laws, which have led to disproportionate incarceration rates of black men in the United States, or have failed to support gun-control measures. Moreover, they have endorsed a line of reactionary policymaking that was inaugurated with the notorious "southern strategy" after the Civil Rights era, which was designed in part to reverse the gains of the Civil Rights era that promised a more equitable society. That is to say, policies that we might read as an effect of the nationalization of this "southern strategy" in more recent years have helped to create the very climate in which many black men now experience so much despair and limited educational and work opportunities.

It is precisely because of this, I want to suggest, that an engagement of black men in the South is crucially relevant to the more general dialogue about black masculinity in the United States. For in some cases, just as ideologies that emerged in the South—such as the black rapist and Uncle Tom—eventually underwent nationalization, the South has also been the testing ground for the development of various policies that have proved to be inimical for black men in the nation at large in the contemporary era in such areas as labor, law enforcement, and education. For instance, the southern convict lease system that emerged during the late nineteenth century established some of the foundations for the contemporary prison-industrial complex. Paradigms that have largely limited the study of problems that black men face in contemporary society to contexts of the "inner city" have obscured such dynamics, which might become more apparent through a broader and more inclusive regional framework. Furthermore, this "urban" emphasis excludes a range of black men in the nation, including those in the South in nonurban contexts, and makes the struggles of such men invisible. Invisible, we might say, in a way akin to how critical approaches that focus on the circumstances and crises that relate to black men who are economically disadvantaged obscure black men in the middle class, who frequently find themselves grappling with their social privilege in self-destructive ways and face specific and unique challenges. While their struggles largely go unnoticed, they sometimes also internalize the issues that are overwhelmingly linked to black men who have often been described as "underclass." All this suggests the need to move away from "one size fits all" models for analyzing black masculinity.

In general, while I use such phrases as "black southern men" or "black southern masculinity" for convenience in this study, I do not mean to imply that those in this group have any unifying or intrinsic characteristics. Nor do I intend to romanticize or essentialize the South in the United States as a place where I refer to "black southerners" as a category, even as my methodology implies my recognition of historical distinctions between white southerners and black southerners. This is also one reason why such terms as "black South" are absent in this study. This study is by no means encompassing and does not aim to present a comprehensive examination of black men in the South. Moreover, I do not mean for this study to imply that black men in the South are actually less "masculine." Rather, the goal is to explore some typically unrecognized historical and contemporary aspects of black southern masculine representation, including scripts of them as alien or undesirable African Americans as they have been manifest in such contexts as literature and film.

Chapter 1 acknowledges the South as a historical framework for black masculine construction in this nation by examining the myth of the black rapist that emerged in the aftermath of the Civil War. Here I engage Terence Young's 1974 film *The Klansman* in relation to William Bradford Huie's novel by that same name, along with the film's and novel's primary frameworks in American literary and cinematic history—Thomas Dixon's 1905 novel *The Clansman* and Griffith's 1915 film *Birth of a Nation*. I consider why and how the film shifts its narrative focus to black male subjectivity and subordinates the trauma of black and white female rape highlighted in the novel, emphasizing the specter of black male lynching by "inventing"

Garth, a character portrayed by O. J. Simpson. This chapter suggests that these narrative shifts can be interpreted as a response to both black power and blaxploitation. Black power, which emerged in the late 1960s, reflected a more radical turn in the black-liberation movement of the decade and advocated very specific forms of black social and political empowerment and cultural appreciation. It was undermined in some ways in the early 1970s by the emergence of blaxploitation as a genre in popular film, which gave salience to many black actors and cast them heroically but often stereotypically. I acknowledge ways in which both the novel and the film production attempt to revise the raced, gendered, and sexed economy of Dixon's *The Clansman* and Griffith's *Birth of a Nation*. Additionally, I discuss the implications of this archive for the national discourse on O. J. Simpson that emerged in the wake of the murders of his ex-wife, Nicole Brown Simpson, and her friend Ronald Goldman. This film is particularly useful where it highlights the specificity of the black rapist as a product of the southern cultural imagination and attempts to chronicle the residual impact of this sexual ideology on black men in the South in the late twentieth century. Still, I discuss its limitations in making its model of a black southern male as defiant and resistant within a white-supremacist context reliant on urban forms of black militancy.

Chapter 2 acknowledges the military as a historical context for discourses on black masculinity as pathological in the South by drawing on Colonel E. D. Anderson's 1918 report, "Disposal of the Colored Drafted Men." In casting black southern men as pathological, diseased, and lacking in intelligence and expressing a preference for black soldiers from the North, this document foregrounded region and helped consolidate a hierarchy of black masculinity in the military early in the twentieth century. I ponder Charles Fuller's exploration of this black masculine hierarchy and such aspects of military history through his character from the Mississippi Black Belt named C. J. Memphis in *A Soldier's Play* (1981). Fuller's play powerfully critiques the politics of black southern masculine alienation and exclusion in the African American context. Yet I closely examine the plot structure and argue that he ultimately unsettles this statement by presenting C. J. as dead, disembodied, and without a voice and by using very conventional strategies in aestheticizing the urban captain, Richard Davenport, as the ideal model of black masculinity.

Chapter 3, which highlights the Tuskegee Syphilis Study as an extension of late-nineteenth-century scripts of black masculinity in the South as pathological, is also literarily oriented. It takes a deeper look at the politics of excluding identities deemed inferior in the African American context on the basis of geography through an examination of the negotiation of rural subjects like Trueblood in Ralph Ellison's novel *Invisible Man*. It argues that a more focused examination of the novel's rural geography is necessary for a deeper understanding of its discourse on masculinity and race. I consider ways in which Ellison clarifies Trueblood's status as an outsider by using geography as a structuring device and metaphor to plot spatially this character's otherness in terms of masculinity and race.

Chapter 4 begins by highlighting Malcolm X's formulation of a hierarchical discourse on black masculinity that was infused by ideologies of gender, sexuality, and geography. Within this hierarchy, I point out ways in which he reified urban black masculinities and, implicitly and explicitly, placed black southern masculinities at the bottom through his house Negro–field Negro metaphors along with his invocations of Uncle Tom. This rhetoric frequently invoked the Uncle Tom, who was sometimes cast as homosexual and linked to southern Civil Rights leadership. My main interest in this chapter is to examine how this strand of black-liberation ideology on the Uncle Tom has been recast in Spike Lee's films, including *School Daze*, *Get on the Bus*, and *Bamboozled*. Moreover, I consider Lee's recurrent casting of the black male revolutionary as quintessentially urban.

The fifth and final chapter of this study focuses on the genre of southern rap, including the invocations of the "dirty South" that have proliferated in the discourse in recent years. I argue that the rhetorical posturing of black southern rappers as "gangstas" and "playas"—in the process of "representin' the South"—began to occur not only because aspects of contemporary southern rap are an outgrowth of the gangsta genre but also as a defensive response to the exclusion of southern artists in the rap industry. I examine New Orleans rapper Joe Blakk's "Way Down South" (1995), a song that contests a litany of stereotypes about black men in the South and illustrates conflict between black men in the South and those from the North as well as the East and West coasts. In the song, Blakk's narrator confronts assumptions that southern guys pick cotton, ride on cows, spit tobacco, live on farms, play banjos, wear straw hats, and can't rap. Furthermore, this chapter considers the emergence of New Orleans as one of southern rap's major centers of production and overviews the roles of Master P of No Limit Records and Ronald "Baby" Williams and Brian "Slim" Williams of Cash Money Records in mainstreaming the genre.

Finally, I have found the range of texts that I examine in this study to be indispensable and valuable for considering the extent to which geography shapes identity in the African American context. I hope that my study demonstrates that works not ordinarily categorized as texts in southern literature perhaps should be in light of the important things that they say about the South. Above all, I hope this study promotes an understanding of why we should rarely, if ever, turn to the topic of black men in the United States—or to any topic, for that matter—without also turning to the South.

CHAPTER 1

Lessons from Thomas Dixon to *The Klansman*

No African American author writing in the post-Reconstruction era—beyond the obvious example of W. E. B. Du Bois—examined the issue of race and the status of blacks in the United States with an emphasis on the South more assertively, persistently, and prolifically than Charles Chesnutt. The founding of numerous historically black colleges; the rise of the black church as an institution; the election of black officials in proportions that even to this day remain unmatched in the nation's political arena; and substantial increases in rates of marriage, literacy, and property ownership, including businesses, were among the capstone achievements that bespoke the promise and hope of Reconstruction for many African Americans. If the Civil War and Reconstruction meant one thing for most blacks living in the

South, it meant another for the vast majority of whites. Increasing resentment and disquietude among whites, including poorer ones who had much to gain by such major reform initiatives as the Freedmen's Bureau (primarily designed to promote education, fair labor, and equitable land distribution in the region), meant that opportunities for black progress were drastically curtailed by the last decade of the nineteenth century. An age of reaction arose by the 1890s, marked by an upsurge of lynchings and a notable increase in caricatured images of blacks in American material culture in trade cards and other media. These representations frequently recuperated and romanticized images of the plantation South. They revealed the prevailing view of the black body in the white southern imagination, demonstrated the abject status of blacks within the nation more broadly, and served as reinforcement for minstrel characterizations that had already begun to gain widespread popularity during the antebellum era. It is also important to recognize that the inclination to caricature blacks in the post–Civil War era was already well established in journalism through portraits designed to discredit and malign blacks in and beyond politics.

The achievements that blacks had made during Reconstruction did little or nothing to deflect the racist historiography after the turn of the century of such figures as William Archibald Dunning, who depicted the period as a colossal failure in which corrupt and ignorant black politicians, carpetbaggers, and scalawags violated the rights of a noble and dispossessed white, Anglo-Saxon South. Thomas Dixon's novel *The Clansman* (1905) epitomized this view in fiction. In film, D. W. Griffith reinforced it in the epic *Birth of a Nation* (1915), which was based on Dixon's novel. It was also endorsed, if more sanguinely and romantically, by the 1939 epic film *Gone with the Wind* and the 1936 novel by Margaret Mitchell on which the film was based. While the ideological and political agenda of the latter film was by no means as bold and flagrantly racist as that of *Birth of a Nation* in endorsing the mythos of the Old South and the ideology of white supremacy, both films share common ground where they sanction lynching. Even in the present day, many critics of *Gone with the Wind* primarily view the film nostalgically and empathetically, as the film's original audiences were led to do, rarely considering the full implications of the "political meeting" of Ashley Wilkes and his other white male compatriots, who go to the shantytown at the Old Sullivan Place to defend Scarlett O'Hara's honor after her attack there. Several people are killed, and Scarlett's second husband,

Frank Kennedy, is a casualty. As the "Yankee" patroller cautions the remnants of this band, "It's about time you rebels learned that you can't take the law into your own hands." Though it is not said, they are members of the Ku Klux Klan, as Mitchell's novel ostensibly acknowledges. In film, as in a literary work, there is a risk in reading too much into the text or falling into the fallacy of analyzing characters as real people. Still, I want to suggest that this group may have conceivably lynched Big Sam, the black man who saves the day for Scarlett by rescuing her, and would have likely thought their actions entirely appropriate and justified had they presumed him to mean her harm in any way or if she had not recognized him as a "friend" and servant aware of his proper "place." In this film, Big Sam has the very body type that was consonant with the black rapist stereotype consolidating in the southern mind during the post–Civil War era in which this scene is set. The name "Big Sam" alone connotes the strength, power, and potential danger associated with such black men in the white southern imagination.

The Dunning school of thought received an assertive and at the time unprecedented challenge in Du Bois's monumental study *Black Reconstruction in America, 1860–1880*, which was published in 1935. The period has received comprehensive historical examination in more recent years in studies by Eric Foner and others.[1] Conventionally, 1877—the year in which the last federal troops stationed in the South in the aftermath of the war were withdrawn as part of the compromise between the North and South to restore national union and secure the election of Rutherford B. Hayes as president—has been regarded as the official end of Reconstruction. The dates of the Reconstruction era, as Du Bois's book title suggests, have been as debatable and subjective as other epochs in American cultural history. The *Plessy v. Ferguson* Supreme Court ruling in 1896, which legalized the "separate but equal" "Jim Crow" ethos in public facilities and sanctioned segregation, was the final sobering signal offered at the national level in the late nineteenth century that Reconstruction, regardless of whether it had succeeded or failed, was over; that democracy and the rights of citizenship in the South would not be extended to blacks; and that every effort would be made to keep blacks in the subordinate, subservient "place" that had been sanctioned by custom during slavery in the antebellum South.

The tide of racial violence against black southerners that began after the Civil War—with violently repressive vigilante activity and the formation of the Ku Klux Klan in 1866—would culminate in such incidents as the

Wilmington Riot of 1898 (fictively documented in Charles Chesnutt's 1901 novel *The Marrow of Tradition*) and in race riots in a range of cities (Atlanta, Chicago, Tulsa) in the first decades of the twentieth century that attempted to restore white social dominance. Chesnutt's emphasis on this issue reflects his interest in engaging history in his fiction. *The Marrow of Tradition* is useful to consider as one of the earliest examples of a novel situated in *both* African American *and* southern literature in the period after slavery.

Set in the fictive Wellington, North Carolina, *The Marrow of Tradition* foregrounds Dr. William Miller and his wife, Janet, as members of the rising black middle class in the South—a group that in some ways complemented Chesnutt's "Blue Veins" of the urban postbellum North in the short story "The Wife of His Youth" (1898)—whose accomplishments proved to be particularly incendiary for white southerners invested in maintaining the conventional, racially polarized social order. Janet's deceased father and white half-sister, Olivia Carteret, are her blood ties to the white southern ruling class in Wellington and Chesnutt's instrument for examining the history of racial intermixture in the region. Furthermore, he examines the social injunctions and taboos against interracial sex that obscured the more commonplace white male sexual abuse of black women through rape and other forms of sexual subjection during slavery and within the system of Jim Crow. The Millers' juxtaposition with faithful retainers who are antebellum plantation holdovers—such as Mammy Jane and her wily son Jerry—and the tension between "old" and "new" models of black identity anticipate debates over black subjectivity that would be prominent by the 1920s in the notion of the New Negro of the modernist era. At a linguistic level, Chesnutt's use of dialect in the novel for the latter characters in contradistinction to the standard English of the former also reinforces this juxtaposition.

The Marrow of Tradition addresses the fallout of the *Plessy v. Ferguson* decision, the North-South binary, and the problem of the color line in the relegation of the honorable and genteel Dr. Miller to a Jim Crow car once he enters the South. This dimension of the novel, like the riot, reflects Chesnutt's interest in developing a work of historical fiction. Tellingly, the chapter that addresses these issues introduces us to the character of Dr. Miller. Its very title, "A Journey Southward," signals the novel's North-South regional schema and the transition Dr. Miller makes as one of legal and symbolic significance entailing tremendous psychological challenges. He encounters a moral universe in the South so foreign and opposite to the northern one he is leaving that entering the South by train is the equivalent of undergoing a shift in cosmology as a human being.

Beyond the binary regional frameworks—and characteristically through the technique of foreshadowing—the novel outlines a series of raced, gendered, and classed oppositions that include Janet and Olivia, Dr. Miller and Major Carteret, and their respective boy children. However, the most provocative opposition in the novel is that of Dr. Miller, whose honor keeps him within the bounds of rationality, decorum, and law, and Josh Green, a poor black laborer driven by a family vendetta against the racist Captain George McBane. A clue early in the novel in the same chapter that introduces Dr. Miller suggests that Josh Green, a character entirely opposite in class and color, will shadow him and serve as a counterpoint. Green leads a group on a bold and defiant mission of self-defense against white rioters in Wellington while obviously outnumbered and outgunned. It is well known that perceived hedging between philosophies of nonviolence and self-defense is the main factor that garnered critical controversy for *The Marrow of Tradition* when it was published and curtailed the momentum of Chesnutt's prosperous literary career. This novel was a bold departure from the short-story genre in which Chesnutt had established his reputation as a writer, gained a substantial white readership, and demonstrated investment in local color while exploring the vexed color line. Still, as many of his critics have pointed out, Chesnutt's work was clearly revisionist and subversive of the plantation tradition and regionalism manifest in the work of a range of contemporary white authors such as Joel Chandler Harris and Thomas Nelson Page.

In a novel that illustrates the collusion of law and lawlessness in the foreclosure of black civil and human rights, it seems fitting that Chesnutt would invest some narrative energies in the making of a prototypical black outlaw figure in Josh Green and in drawing on the historical notion of the "bad Negro" or, more colloquially, the "bad nigger," as corollaries to the "badman" in African American cultural history. The folklorist John W. Roberts has traced the evolution of the black badman as an outlaw folk hero from the trickster tales that emerged within black slave communities and the economically, legally, and politically repressive social climate that blacks faced after Emancipation. As he points out in *From Trickster to Badman: The Black Folk Hero in Slavery and Freedom*, "The impact of white manipulations of the law on the economic and social life of African Americans in the late nineteenth century is crucial to an understanding of how and why African Americans transformed their conception of the trickster to create the badman as an outlaw hero."[2] Green, who flouts the value system of Chesnutt's black middle class, was one of the earliest examples of the "bad Negro" type in African American literature, though he was not entirely true to formulations of this type that are now familiar in light of the deep investments in family and community life that he maintained. That Chesnutt features the bad Negro in the novel is all the more significant in light of Chesnutt's established investment in folklore. He demonstrates an interest in exploring the impact of race and class in shaping a range of models of black masculinity in the late nineteenth century, an aspect of his work that needs more critical recognition.

Before I continue with my discussion in this chapter, I want to engage in some focused discussion of the Josh Green character and overview additional historical and literary contexts of the bad Negro, a prototype with southern roots. Chesnutt's binary contrasting of Dr. Miller and Josh Green complements the deconstructive analysis of white masculinity, including such ideologies as the southern gentleman. This latter work on "whiteness" is evident, for instance, in his examination of the hierarchical relationship of Major Carteret and Captain McBane. Chesnutt further deconstructs the color line by illustrating that such classic regional gender models as the "southern lady" and the "southern gentleman" could be accessibly and realistically embodied by or even revised by blacks. The Millers, in their social respectability, dignity, and erudition, represent the truest and noblest embodiments of these social ideals in the novel.

The pivotal chapter on the riot's beginning focuses on the three cohorts whom Dr. Miller encounters on the road as he struggles to return home to his wife and child. They include a group of poor blacks who are fleeing the town, Dr. Watson, a black lawyer who is also in flight, and, most significantly, Josh Green's band, who ask Watson and then Miller to lead their effort to mount some resistance against the white mob. In the exchange between them, the question of masculinity is resonant as Dr. Miller meditates on the group's initiative and the lack of potential for its success: "For Miller it was an agonizing moment. He was no coward, morally or physically. Every manly instinct urged him to go forward and take up the cause of these leaderless people, and if need be, to defend their lives and rights with his own,—but to what end?" (218). After this encounter, Dr.

Miller feels "shame" and "envy" that he does not accompany them. These anxieties are commingled with his concerns for the safety of his wife and son and intensify as he effectively "passes" for white in his buggy to escape the wrath of the mob. Implicit philosophical questions inflect these scenes related to what it means to be a man in this black community, how one might best serve and protect it, and how one might most effectively face the group of white men that has banded together on a mission to protect the interests of its own perceived community.

The novel reveals throughout these passages that not only lives in the community but manhood itself are very much at stake for such characters as Dr. Miller and Josh Green. This concern informs the choices they make and the physical and metaphysical struggles in which they engage. Rhetorically, Josh Green repeatedly invokes manhood as the rallying cry for his band to calm the growing fear among them that he senses as the angry white group, which by that time has grown into a veritable mob, pursues them. We learn from the third-person omniscient narrator that if there is a coward in their midst, it is not Dr. Miller or any of Josh's men but Jerry, whom Josh has forced to come along with the band and is told to "Shet up" and "ef you can't stan' up like a man, keep still, and don't interfere wid men w'at will fight!" (229). At every turn in the resistance, Josh Green's language and the intensity of his expression reveal manhood as a central frame for these scenes. His mission is not only to protect the black community but also to defend their manhood. Furthermore, his portrait is recognizably heroic and masculinist. The narrator draws attention to Green's size in these passages by characterizing him as "big Josh Green" (217) and elsewhere by referring to him as a "black giant" (112). He serves as an invincible physical emblem of masculinity, a rendering that aligns him with such personas as the folk figure John Henry. Green is ultimately the sole survivor of the volley of fire from the white mob. The awed gazes directed at Green's physicality recall the spectral image of black men's bodies and white male voyeurism that has been associated with the ghastly ritual of lynching. Green summons enough strength to withstand the assault of the mob and holds on to his life just long enough to make the brutal stab into Captain McBane (234).

It is significant that Chesnutt makes a direct association between Josh Green and the notion of the "bad Negro." As Dr. Miller warns Josh, "These are bad times for bad negroes. You'll get into a quarrel with a white man, and at the end of it ther'll be a lynching or a funeral. You'd better be peaceable and endure a little injustice, rather than run the risk of sudden and violent death" (112). The use of this term here well attests to its entrenchment in the African American lexicon by the end of the nineteenth century.

Chesnutt clearly has an investment in debunking pathologizing stereotypes of black men as the "beasts" and "rapists" with which readers might associate a man like Josh. The narrator highlights this character's deep sensitivity in Green's final request to Dr. Miller to see to it that his mother receive a decent burial. Provocatively, the novel implies that Dr. Miller and Josh Green are not entirely polar opposites. We must remember that he is the physician who heals Green's broken arm, which is used so powerfully in attacking McBane.

Chesnutt relates Josh's vendetta against McBane to the past trauma of an attack on his family by the Ku Klux Klan in the period following the group's origins as a vigilante secret society in Tennessee, an attack that occurred during his childhood in the post–Civil War era. The attack left his mother so frightened that she insanely wanders the streets and children refer to her as "Silly Milly." Through Josh's background, Chesnutt links the mob violence of Wellington to Klan violence that blacks experienced in the aftermath of the Civil War before federal efforts were made to suppress the group. The novel suggests that the mob is brutal, bestial, and utterly irrational, qualities ordinarily stereotypically associated with blacks in the white-supremacist mind.

In attempts to reconcile the dilemma between the bourgeois values of Dr. Miller and a revolutionary like Josh Green, it was likely not lost on Chesnutt that Wilmington, North Carolina, was the birthplace in 1785 of the abolitionist and orator David Walker, whose fiery condemnation of slavery and urge to violent resistance in the widely circulated tract published in 1829, *David Walker's Appeal in Four Articles; Together with a Preamble, to Coloured Citizens of the World*, helped establish foundations of black-nationalist thought and militant movement in the United States. In his youth, Walker had the opportunity to meet Denmark Vesey, one of the most successful slave insurrectionists in the history of the nation who, with Gabriel Prosser, led a band from one plantation to another in South Carolina, slaying fifty-seven whites before the resistance was suppressed. Walker migrated to Boston in the 1820s, married a woman named Eliza who had been a fugitive slave, and worked as a dealer of secondhand clothing. He gained recognition as he spoke out passionately against slavery and had an article on the subject published in *Freedom's Journal*, the nation's first black newspaper, in 1828. His *Appeal* was published a year later and released in three successive editions over the next two years, each of which amplified and extended his critique of slavery. Addressed mainly to an African American audience and modeled schematically on the Constitution, this pamphlet makes a scathing and unremitting critique of the nation's failure to recognize blacks as citizens or to accord them the basic protections and privileges of Americans. Moreover, it indicts the hypocrisy of white Christians. In his exhortation "Are we MEN!!—I ask you, O my brethren! are we Men?" Walker suggests that acquiescing to slavery compromises not only humanity but also the very possibility of black manhood and invokes a question that had been at play rhetorically in black masculinist discourse since the late eighteenth century. His message, which traveled widely, intensely alarmed slaveholders in the South and stoked their looming fears of insurrection. As a result of its publication, laws to repress incendiary literature were made in southern state legislatures. A bounty was placed on Walker himself by a cohort of white southern slaveholders. Upon his death in 1830, some abolitionists even suspected that he had been the victim of foul play.

Maroon communities and slave insurrections, forms of slave resistance viewed widely as the most radical ones, were rarer in the United States than other areas of the New World where slavery was practiced. Such factors as the ratio of the slave population to whites, planter absenteeism, the topography of the landscape, and the reliability and coherence of patrol systems played an important role in conditioning the opportunities for such resistance, though conspiracies and occasional uprisings were commonplace among slaves in the United States. A few became particularly well known. The plot of Nat Turner, who, like Vesey, became famous as an African American insurrectionist during the antebellum era, was uncovered before it could be carried out. Both men were executed, the former almost immediately and Turner after imprisonment and trial. Typically, slave rebellions were put down with swift and brutal punishments that mainly included hangings, and the mutilated bodies of the participants, especially leaders, were put on public display as "examples" for other slaves. The stories of Vesey and Turner quintessentially defined resistance during the antebellum era and forged the notion of the "rebel slave" in American cultural history, as would former slave Frederick Douglass in his vivid recounting of the confrontation with the notoriously cruel white slavebreaker Covey in his 1845 slave narrative, *The Narrative of the Life of Frederick Douglass*.

A slave rebellion was one of the most fearsome events that a slaveholder could imagine in the plantation South during the antebellum era. The panic was even greater in places where slaves outnumbered the master class. As historian Peter Wood has acknowledged, during the colonial era, the state of South Carolina was exceptional in its "black majority," where black slaves outnumbered whites roughly three to one. This ratio kept nerves on edge and is one reason that South Carolina stood at the vanguard in developing slave codes and laws to regulate slave behavior.[3] Fears of black rebellion did not necessarily subside with the end of slavery. The intensification of white-supremacist sentiment in the South during and after Reconstruction was intricately related to paranoia that whites were being oppressed and disfranchised by former slaves and allies of the freedman's cause. They felt a need to band together to protect and reclaim their communities and used lynching and other forms of terror and intimidation (like riots) to restore social control. In *The Marrow of Tradition*, this is precisely the attitude of the small group of elite white men in the community who see the rise of a bourgeois black professional class and black voting rights as a threat. In a town whose black population technically outnumbers the white one— as Josh acknowledges in pointing out that "Dere's two niggers in dis town ter eve'y w'ite man, an' ef we've got ter be killt, we'll take some wite folks 'long wid us" (217)—whites conspire to avert a takeover of the town and to disfranchise blacks before the next political election. Chesnutt illustrates well the irrationality and fear among white rioters in Wellington and their tendency to exaggerate the threat that blacks represented and to overreact, an attitude that leads to extreme and unwarranted reprisals for blacks in the town at every turn on the day of the riot and fuels the expansion of their mob. For Wellington whites, Josh Green and his band appear to be the heirs apparent of slave insurrectionists like Vesey and Turner who threatened to annihilate the white population, and rumors quickly spread that such a plan is in the works, which give a legitimate rationalization to the white riot and expands its supporters exponentially. In actuality, Green's group's agenda is self-defense, and they plan to respond only if they are attacked by whites first.

The trace of David Walker imprints Chesnutt's novel in a more direct way through the evocation of Walker's incendiary rhetorical style. For a bold and frank article in Wellington's *Afro-American Banner* sets plans for the riot in motion in the novel. The reaction to it by whites like Carteret closely parallels the historical outrage over Albert Manly's article on lynching in the *Wilmington Daily Record* (1898), which is thought to have been one of the main factors in catalyzing the riot. Manly's article addressed the white activist Rebecca Latimer Felton's stance that one thousand blacks be lynched a day to protect white southern women from black male rapists. Even more provocatively, Manly suggested that white women were attracted to black men in some instances, that rape was not as commonplace as it was thought to be, and that white men should be taught purity in light of their own dalliances with black women. Manly had been discouraged by prominent blacks from publishing the piece for fear of reprisals. Whatever its truth content, it struck nerves and feelings of indignation among whites. In the post-Reconstruction era, this kind of treatise on lynching was perceived as threatening and insubordinate in the way that black abolitionist writing such as Walker's bold attack on slavery had been perceived in the antebellum era.

A character like Josh Green points to the southern history of the concept of the bad Negro. The bad Negro was an outgrowth of the "rebel slave" with roots in African American folklore. One obvious question to consider, then, is that if the idea of the bad Negro had mythical origins in the South and was evident in folklore and literature, how did notions of revolutionary black masculinity, and the idea of the bad Negro itself, come to be so quintessentially identified with urban contexts?

In African American literary history, the fiction of Richard Wright has provided a compelling chronicling of and explanation for the urbanization of this type. It is revealing, for instance, that in Wright's repertoire, the resistant southern model of masculinity in the short story "Long Black Song," in which the sharecropper Silas kills a white salesman for sleeping with his wife and dies while boldly exchanging gunfire in a standoff with a mob of avenging white men, is complemented in the collection *Uncle Tom's Children* (1937) by "Big Boy Leaves Home," whose title character eventually flees to the North. In this latter tale, Big Boy, a black adolescent boy in the South, spends a day swimming nude with his friends on white property. The day begins innocently but takes a fateful turn when the owner and his wife discover them. Big Boy takes the owner's weapon and shoots him in self-defense, after the owner had already killed two of his three friends.

Under the cover of night, Big Boy and his remaining friend, Bobo, must hide from a mob that not only presumes them guilty of murder but also of rape. Big Boy witnesses the lynching of Bobo and escapes north on a truck in the wake of this trauma. In this story, the name "Big Boy," of course, suggests that this adolescent's very body type is perceived as intimidating and threatening by the white couple in the pivotal scene. But in Wright's work there is no more quintessential embodiment of the bad Negro than the character Bigger Thomas in the 1940 novel *Native Son*.

Native Son is significant for my purposes, like Chesnutt's *The Marrow of Tradition*, for the levels on which it explores the southern origins of the bad Negro. Set during the 1930s, the novel focuses on Bigger, a poor young black man living in an impoverished community in Chicago, who begins work as a chauffeur for a wealthy white family but, by twist of fate, accidentally suffocates their daughter Mary with a pillow when paralyzed by fear that he will be accused of rape if her blind mother discovers him in her bedroom. The novel goes on to recount the frenzy of his flight from the law through the city in the wake of murder and rape charges, the rape and murder of his girlfriend Bessie, and his eventual capture and imprisonment. In the reflective introduction to the novel entitled "How Bigger Was Born," Wright traces the type on which he bases his main character back to various personas that he encountered in his youth while growing up in Jackson, Mississippi, and relates them explicitly to the concept of the "bad nigger." The Bigger Thomases of Wright's youth were best known and envied for their refusal to submit to the ethos of Jim Crow, for utter fearlessness in the face of white intimidation, and for their rejection of family, community, and religion. Wright admits that he regarded these types with both fear and envy. As he recalls, "The Bigger Thomases were the only Negroes I know of who consistently violated the Jim Crow laws of the South and got away with it, at least for a sweet brief spell. Eventually, the whites who restricted their lives made them pay a terrible price. They were shot, hanged, maimed, lynched, and generally hounded until they were either dead or their spirits broken" (xi). Just as Chesnutt relates Josh's traumatized background in the South to his emergence as a bad Negro, so Wright makes it clear through Bigger that this type is not essentially "bad" so much as the fruit of the repressive southern Jim Crow ethos.[4]

While Wright's most primal memories of this type are in the deep South, upon moving to Chicago, his genealogy of this type extends to the urban

North, a context that makes the type even more volatile. As he points out, "The urban environment of Chicago, affording a more stimulating life, made the Negro Bigger Thomases react more violently than even in the South" (xv). Wright richly recalls his own personal metaphysical struggles and complex rites of passage to manhood within the Jim Crow South in his 1946 autobiography, *Black Boy*. In keeping with the realist and naturalist orientation of *Native Son*'s plot, Wright points to the role of region in shaping black masculinity, a phenomenon that has been seldom recognized or remarked upon but which my study aims to clarify. For Wright, the manifestations of this type in northern and southern climes exist in a continuum and, notwithstanding their relative distinctions, are two sides of the same coin. "So the concrete picture and the abstract linkages of relationships fed each other, each making the other more meaningful and affording my emotions an opportunity to react to them with success and understanding. The process was like a swinging pendulum, each to and fro motion throwing up its tiny bit of meaning and significance, each stroke helping to develop the dim negative which had been implanted in my mind in the South" (xvi).

Significantly, Wright links the police brutality that young black men in urban contexts experience—and the intimidation that often leads them to make false confessions under pressure—to the history of lynching and the mythology of the black male rapist in the South. In doing so, he points to the vulnerability and invisibility of black men under the law. Bigger very much operates with the understanding that he is condemned and guilty in the eyes of the law and knows before his trial begins that he will be presumed a rapist whether he raped Mary Dalton or not. He understands that the accidental character of her death will be irrelevant to his persecutors, even as his panic in the aftermath of his fateful encounter with her sets off a chain of events that leads him to rape and murder his girlfriend Bessie. Through Bigger Thomas, Wright provides a concrete literary illustration of the emergence of the bad Negro in the South and its development into an urban ideal.

Chesnutt's Josh Green and Wright's reflections on the origins of Bigger Thomas demonstrate the southern origins of this type and reveal the "bad Negro" as being among the conceivable range of black masculine models in the region. Selections in Sterling A. Brown's volume *Southern Road* (1932), like "Strong Men," exemplify an established aesthetic in which black men in the South were salient models of strength, courage, and tenacity in early decades of the twentieth century. More recently, the 1987 film adaptation of Ernest J. Gaines's novel *A Gathering of Old Men* (1983), which is set in Louisiana in the 1970s on a sugarcane plantation, depicts senior black southern men who take up arms and close ranks after one of their own shoots a Cajun farmer.

The "bad Negro" functioned as a prevailing trope in signifying black masculine insurgency by the turn of the century and, as a script of black masculinity more indigenous to the African American context, counterbalanced the dominant contemporary white-supremacist ideology of the black rapist. Like the black rapist myth, the roots of the bad Negro are traceable to the South. It is fascinating that the bad Negro's historical roots in folklore and primal connections to the South are sometimes obscured nowadays. This phenomenon has occurred in part because by the late twentieth century in popular and political contexts, the urban had become increasingly central in conceptualizations of black male insurgency and even of "authentic" black masculinity. One goal of this chapter is to demonstrate how linkages of black masculine authenticity to the urban became more widespread during the black-liberation movement of the 1960s.

The black rapist is one of the most virulently racist stereotypes of black masculinity in this nation's history. Revisiting it is useful for my purposes in this chapter because it is one of the earliest and most concrete examples of how a stereotype germinating in the South instated a national discourse on black masculinity and propagated a view of the black male body as intrinsically pathological. Darwinist scientific thought of the mid-nineteenth century—rooted in perceptions of blacks as primitive and racially inferior within the hierarchy of human beings—must be understood as a more general context for the development of the black rapist myth that congealed as racial propaganda later in the century. This myth was dehumanizing to the extent that it marked black men as predatory and bestial. It linked them to an inherently perverted sexuality. In the period after Emancipation, this script of black men as lustful and sexually insatiable further manifested the pornographic view of the black masculine body that had been established during slavery. That is to say, its content as a raced, sexed, and gendered ideology was fed on some levels by the material conditions of a slave system that had defined some black men as "bucks" and breeders and linked the black male body to sexual excess and licentiousness.[5]

Notwithstanding his eloquence and talent for treating questions of history from a literary standpoint, and particularly for assessing the controversial Reconstruction era and the development of the Ku Klux Klan, an author like Charles Chesnutt proved to be no match for a propagandist like Thomas Dixon. In the early twentieth century, such novels as *The Clansman* were decisive in shaping discourses of race in the South and the prevailing public perceptions of lynching, rioting, and rape. The cinematic adaptation of this novel in *Birth of a Nation*, which was famously praised by President Woodrow Wilson as "like writing history in lightning" after a showing at the White House, helped to revive and popularize the Ku Klux Klan among many whites in and beyond the South during and after World War I. Its showings in theaters across the nation incited violence against blacks and garnered protest, especially by organizations such as the National Association for the Advancement of Colored People (NAACP). *The Clansman* and *Birth of a Nation* have proved to be continuing sources of critical and ideological controversy and even vexation in later decades of the twentieth century. They received one of their boldest critiques and revisions in William Bradford Huie's novel *The Klansman* (1967), which highlights the reactionary racial and sexual ideological heritage in the Reconstruction-era South that was still evident during the Civil Rights era. *The Klansman* served as the basis of a 1974 film by the same name in which O. J. Simpson debuted as an actor and provided one of the most provocative exposés of the Ku Klux Klan during this period. Within a narrative schema that addresses the historical and contemporary politics of race, gender, and sexuality in the South, this novel, a work that draws to an extent on techniques of historiographic metafiction, engages the Ku Klux Klan's activity in the South and perpetration of violence against the black body through lynching and rape. It emphasizes the trauma of black female rape, a strategy that seems designed to explore the gendered particularities of southern violence against blacks. I begin with some discussion of this novel.

Intriguingly, the film that this novel inspired, whose screenplay was written by Millard Kaufman and Samuel Fuller, acknowledges yet ultimately subordinates the novel's concern with rape to focus on an examination of race, masculinity, and the specter of lynching. *The Klansman* is an interesting popular artifact to reconsider in light of its examination of the black rapist as a product of the southern cultural imagination and its attempt to chronicle the residual impact of this sexual ideology on black men in the South in the twentieth century. However, I am also intrigued by *why* the shifts to such a forthright and assertive engagement of this array of topics occur in the film. The obvious and decisive shift here suggests some of the inherent challenges in dialogues on lynching and rape. The hierarchy of oppression in the film is no more visionary than critical models in the contemporary era that posit rape and lynching as competing and even binary narratives in which one trauma narrows representational space for the other.

In this chapter, I suggest that we can understand the masculinist makeover of this film as a response to both the discourses of black power and blaxploitation that were the immediate backdrop for its production during the early 1970s. Furthermore, I argue that the particular strategies of historical revisionism which the film uses, in ways that both intersect with and diverge from those of Huie's novel, offer a means to critique and respond to D. W. Griffith's and Thomas Dixon's race and gender ideologies. At the time of its release, director Terence Young situated the film as "a denunciation of . . . crass, stupid bigotry and intolerance" and as "a cinematic statement against terrorism or counter-terrorism of any sort—black or white."[6] In spite of these intentions, *The Klansman*, which was filmed on site in Oroville, California, with an all-star cast that also included Linda Evans, Richard Burton, Lola Falana, and Lee Marvin, was a colossal failure, viewed as being too saturated with racial melodrama.[7] Vincent Canby of the *New York Times* remarked *The Klansman* as "one of those rare films that are not as bad as they seem when you're watching them" and as "a thoroughly clumsy adaptation of William Bradford Huie's novel" with a "primitively written script" and "easy movie melodrama." Roy Frumkes of *Films in Review* categorized *The Klansman* as the kind of film that "is so bad it's interesting." Most bitingly, A. D. Murphy of *Variety* described the film as "a perfect example of screen trash that almost invites derision" and as a "fetid carcass."[8] In spite of its critical shortcomings, *The Klansman* has much to teach us in light of its examination of race, gender, and sexuality in historical racialist narratives in film and literature. The analysis of a veritable trash film in this chapter reflects the intellectual agenda of cultural studies, which challenges us to look "high" and "low" as we engage texts in and beyond literature. Furthermore, the archive on which this chapter draws reaffirms the importance of continuing to expand our vision within southern literature beyond conventional "canons." Critical consideration of this film is necessary, too, because *The Klansman*, however problematic it may be, is one of the few popular sites on which a production as ubiquitous in American film history as *Birth of a Nation* has been engaged with so much directness and deliberateness.

In *Film and Fiction: The Dynamics of Exchange*, Keith Cohen acknowledges the "artistic hybrids" that inaugurated the twentieth century and situates cinema as a salient force in catalyzing these exchanges. His examination of the cross-fertilization between the novel and film as genres, which emphasizes their potential to share codes while remaining distinct sign systems, is a useful critical terrain on which to acknowledge the genealogical linkages of a film as paradigmatic as *Birth of a Nation* to its origins in Dixon's novels and to its later artistic dispersals in the twentieth century.[9] The film is also useful to the extent that it is shaped by and provides a commentary on black-liberation ideology, reflects its politics of gender (which stressed female subordination), and helps us recognize the seldom acknowledged impact of geography on black masculine fashioning during this period.

A further aim in this chapter is to address what is, of course, a white elephant in the room, so to speak. That is to say, I will examine some of the implications that the film holds for the discourse on O. J. Simpson that unfolded in the national media following the murders of his ex-wife, Nicole Brown Simpson, and her friend Ronald Goldman in 1994. It is quite stunning that the proliferation of critical work on what has been called "the trial of the century" interpreted the case in relation to a litany of literary and popular works (from *Uncle Tom's Cabin* to *Native Son*) but failed to reflect on the implications of a production such as *The Klansman* in which Simpson coincidentally performed.

Southern Shaft

William Bradford Huie has provided one of the Ku Klux Klan's boldest critiques in literature. The novel *The Klansman* draws on Huie's investigative research on the organization in the South, which he originally contemplated publishing as a historical study but finally opted to present in the form of fiction.[10] The title of Huie's novel echoes that of Dixon's *The Clansman* to acknowledge uses of the latter book in the region to recruit members during the Civil Rights era.

Born November 13, 1910, in Hartselle, Alabama, to John Bradford and Margaret Lois Huie, the author began his career in journalism at the *Birmingham Post* in 1932 and married Ruth Puckett in 1934. He moved on to *American Mercury*, a literary magazine, in 1941, and served as editor and publisher until 1952. His vehement opposition to white supremacy in the South and ongoing commitment to civil rights activism is evident throughout his body of writing. His twenty-one books of fiction and nonfiction, six of which were made into films, have sold more than 28 million copies and include additional novels such as *Mud on the Stars* (1942), *The Revolt of Mamie Stover* (1951), *The Americanization of Emily* (1959), and *In the Hours of the Night* (1975). He is best known and remembered for his controversial freelance work in support of the civil rights cause, which sometimes relied on the strategy of "checkbook journalism." Huie famously paid a large sum of money to secure a confession from Roy Bryant and J. W. Milam, the two alleged assailants of Emmett Till, the fourteen-year-old boy from Chicago murdered in Mississippi while visiting relatives for supposedly wolf-whistling at a white woman. He published the article in *Look* magazine in 1956. He used cash to extract stories from several Klan informants to get details on the disappearance and murders of civil rights workers Michael Schwerner, Andrew Goodman, and James Cheney. After publishing the article in the *New York Herald Tribune*, it served as the basis for his nonfiction book *Three Lives for Mississippi* (1965). These were, of course, radical achievements in an era when whites were unlikely to be held accountable or convicted for crimes against blacks. Huie continued this strategy in later years by interviewing James Earl Ray to secure information about the assassination of civil rights leader Martin Luther King Jr., the results of which were published in *He Slew the Dreamer: My Search with James Earl Ray for the Truth about the Murder of Martin Luther King*.[11] Huie, who consistently used his journalism as a tactic of civil rights activism, married Martha Hunt Robertson in 1977. He continued to write and lecture until his death in 1986.

The novel *The Klansman* opens with a description of the tall height, strength, and power of Korean War hero and Medal of Honor recipient Big Track Bascombe, the sheriff of fictive Ellenton, Alabama, who got his name as a teen because of a size fourteen foot. Successive short, declarative sentences in the opening paragraph, which all begin by referring to Big Track as "he," effectively establish the authority, insight, and credibility of Huie's narrator. Furthermore, the positioning of the chapter provides early clues about Big Track's significance to the development of the plot. The narrator describes Big Track's custom-designed Buick Wildcat, the build of his body, and his arsenal of weapons in vivid detail, one after the other, to suggest the kind of man that he is as well as to offer some insight into his family background. The novel suggests the car to be the most tangible symbol of Big Track's strength. The several testaments to his strength that the narrator cites in the voices of local citizens feature pronunciations and dialects, along with racist epithets, that mark the southern setting of the novel and its raced, classed, and gendered contours at a linguistic level, while references to sports, tourist sites, and Big Track's comparison to television character Marshal Dillon of *Gunsmoke* imply the popular impact of the national culture on Ellenton locals and Alabamians in general.

In this beginning section, Big Track and his son Allen, a high-school junior, are traveling through the state to transport a prisoner to a jail in Mobile and make stops along the way where they are shown photographs that construe the Selma to Montgomery march as having been licentious. In Montgomery, they meet and are photographed with Governor George Wallace, who describes the march as having been little more than a large public orgy for "Punks, whores, scum, degenerates, kooks, atheists and perverts, all controlled by Communists" (8).[12] Furthermore, the governor shows Big Track and Allen enlarged photographs of "the arms of white females around the necks of Negro males; the hands of Negro males on the rumps and breasts of white females; a Negro male and a white female kissing and 'sucking each other's tongues'; a Negro male and a white male kissing; and a Negro male and a white male lying under the tree with a hand in the other's crotch" (9). His mocking riffs on Martin Luther King's speeches and freedom songs, including Christian ones, signal his irreverence and outright derision for the event. In real life, Wallace, governor of Alabama, was notorious for his opposition to civil rights and stood in the door of the University of Alabama to bar the admittance of black students like Autherine Lucy, famously proclaiming, "Segregation today, segregation tomorrow, segregation forever." Huie's incorporation of characters like Wallace; key cities in Alabama that Big Track and Allen visit such as Montgomery, Selma, and Mobile; and events such as the march draws on strategies of historical novel writing.

The Klansman demonstrates how intricately sex and the project of civil rights were interlocked together in the southern cultural imagination. It provocatively hypothesizes that in the minds of white southerners, anxieties about the Civil Rights movement were at bottom fueled by a fear of and panic about interracial sex and racial intermixture. All the pictures that officials show Big Track and Allen are sexually provocative, evidence designed to expose the march's *real* agenda—promoting interracial sex. While white southern officials present the photographs as "the truth," Huie, always concerned about the theme of truth throughout his life and career (to the point of proclaiming himself to be "in the truth business"), unsettles these presumptions by suggesting their investments in propaganda to be a gross distortion and their photojournalism as ethically bankrupt. Big Track's admission to Allen that "A white man just naturally hates to think about a black hand on a white girl. The very thought of it makes him sick" and that "in a white man's mind all that this agitation comes down to is frigging" (14) poignantly reveals white masculine panic and anxiety about interracial sex as the main concern of the march's opponents. The photographs serve as a tangible, material manifestation of these fears and make them seem more valid. They appear to be all the more authoritative in light of a range of sworn affidavits that further testify to the sexual excesses of the march. Still, Huie suggests that such fears are animated by and would even be inconceivable without obsessive white male pornographic fantasies of interracial sex, particularly of sex between black men and white women, that enact such fears and reflect historical stereotypes in the South of black men as rapists. If the photos are "evidence" of anything, Huie contrarily suggests that their limited theme points to the sexual obsession of the march's detractors and indicts their "dirty minds." In the novel, it is also important to recognize that this perverse and fetishized photographic record threatens to displace and substitute for the kinds of video documentaries that were so effective in giving national exposure to the abuse and violence that black civil rights demonstrators encountered.

If we continue to read this scene carefully, however, we can recognize that, paradoxically, the photograph that makes the most lasting impression and generates the most anxieties is the one taken at the state capitol of Big Track, his son, and the governor. Big Track, while flattered, fears that its opportunistic staging and eventual publication will hurt his son's chances for admission to West Point and link his family to an unpopular racist ideology. This photograph brings into visual relief the contradictions in his public and private personas. Furthermore, the anxieties that the pictures of Selma to Montgomery marchers aim to generate about interracial sex come home to Big Track by the end of the day in the form of concerns that his son will have intercourse with his girlfriend too soon, which may make him a teen father and ruin his opportunity to go to college. Indeed, his bombardment with such explicit photographs for a day has in effect undermined and jeopardized Big Track's authority to influence him on matters of sexuality. That as a teen Big Track's sister paid black girls to have sex with their disabled father to avoid any incestuous encounters with him directly herself implicates the Bascomb family in the kinds of sexual pathologies these photographs attempt to displace onto blacks.

The attack on the white Detroit housewife Viola Liuzzo that Alabama state officials make in the novel is the most obvious illustration of the base effects of propaganda and an obsession with interracial sex. As Big Track travels to the spot where Liuzzo was slain, the novel suggests that a panic about sexual intermingling of black men and white women ultimately led to her murder by the Ku Klux Klan in the aftermath of the march (10–11).[13] Huie discredits such warped logic. Furthermore, the novel references Liuzzo's death when it invites us to recognize that the special hatred reserved for white priests suspected of using the cloth as a guise to establish intimate relations with black women also led to the murder of "one nigger, one white woman, and one white preacher . . . around Selma" (62).[14] Aspects of the novel that critique propaganda are all the more provocative to consider, of course, in light of Huie's status as a veteran journalist in his career and the propaganda charges that were sometimes leveled against him. For if his propaganda was meant for good, then the propaganda he presents in this novel was meant for evil.

Huie's main concern, however, is not only to illustrate the uses of propaganda in the present but also to critique its uses in southern history, particularly the propaganda that proliferated and gained widespread popular appeal in the film *Birth of a Nation* and the related novel. Huie's novel demonstrates how *Birth of a Nation* and *The Clansman* continued to be revered by Ku Klux Klan members in the 1960s and illustrates persisting Klan activity in the South. He titles all chapters for key characters, and his expository formulas rely on painstaking character development from beginning to end. Significantly, the second chapter, which focuses on sheriff's deputy Butt Cutt Cates, opens as Cates is reading a passage from *The Clansman*. Huie incorporates a didactic passage that conveys the history of this novel and the related film as well as their contemporary uses: "It was a passage from *The Clansman*, a novel published in 1905, from which a film was made. When released the film, too, was titled *The Clansman*, but this was changed to *Birth of a Nation*. In 1960–65 *Birth of a Nation* was the 'theme film' of the Ku Klux Klan. It was used to recruit new members

and reassure old ones. It was frequently shown in small town drive-in theaters, after which Klan recruiters said prayers, set fire to a cross, and led
the singing of 'Onward Christian Soldiers' and 'The Old Rugged Cross'"
(24). "Every day," the narrator reports, "Butt Cutt brought from the post
office an armload of revelations and exhortations" (26). Furthermore, he
is on the mailing list of twenty-four white-supremacist organizations that
spread racist propaganda and were designed to stoke paranoia about race
mixing and communism. In figuring the investments of the semiliterate
deputy, who has never actually read Dixon's novel—yet has an obsession
with posting its most incendiary passages in "whites only" sections around
town and views doing so as part of his civic duty—the novel critiques the
vile social and ideological uses of these works.

Huie's plot begins to advance and thicken when Loretta Sykes, a black
woman who grew up in a cabin on a mountain owned by cotton dynasty
heir Breck Stancill, returns home from Chicago to nurse her terminally ill
mother. She is almost immediately suspected of conspiring to help set up
a stronghold for "agitators" in the county on Stancill's mountain because
she allowed movement supporters to come into her home. The dialogue of
the novel intensifies in Butt Cutt's confrontation with Loretta. His paranoia about agitators convinces him the real reason that Loretta returned
to town is to join the movement. Furthermore, his internalization of racist
stereotypes of black women as promiscuous makes it impossible for him to
believe that Loretta did not have sex with the so-called agitators, leads him
to presume that she began an affair with Breck as a teenager, and makes the
fact of her virginity unthinkable. The "truth" that he is convinced he knows
about her leads him to arrest her.

Action squad members of the Ku Klux Klan choose rape to send a message to blacks in the county because it will not "show" and therefore be
possible to document in the media. In doing so, they agree to enact a specific form of violence for disciplining and violating the female body and
exploit the silence and invisibility that frequently surround the aftermath
of this trauma. They view the rape as an act that will "allow two niggers
the opportunity to prove again that niggers are bestial" and is necessary
"to help defend a Christian way of life" (64, 67). In these scenes, the novel
highlights and critiques the historical view in the South of the black body
as pathological and crystallizes the dehumanizing myth of its phallic power
in the character Lightning Rod. He is a black male brute who cannot talk

and is often paid to rape black women in the woods for the entertainment of white male spectators. This logic conforms to Angela Davis's observation that "the fictional image of the Black man as rapist has always strengthened its inseparable companion: the image of the Black woman as chronically promiscuous. For once the notion is accepted that Black men harbor irresistible and animal-like sexual urges, the entire race is invested with bestiality. . . . Viewed as 'loose women' and whores, Black women's cries of rape would necessarily lack legitimacy."[15] Similarly, as Paula Giddings has pointed out, black men were pathologized as rapists in the late nineteenth century in part because of black women's imagined sexual promiscuity and lasciviousness.[16]

In his thematic emphasis on Loretta's rape, Huie underscores the historical particularity of racial violence against the black female body in the South. He demonstrates the extreme results and consequences of propaganda circulated in *The Clansman* and *Birth of a Nation*, particularly when in the hands of someone as irrational and delusional as Butt Cutt. The citation of these works frames and rationalizes Loretta's rape and alludes to their historical role in fomenting violence and terror against blacks, along with the negative psychological consequences of these works and of all racist propaganda for whites. By illustrating white-supremacist ideologies that emerged in the Reconstruction South in the late nineteenth century and the panic against miscegenation in the Civil Rights era, Huie reveals the continuing impact of this history on the nation in the 1960s. His novel suggests that the kind of conspiratorial and violent riot activity Charles Chesnutt documents in the post-Reconstruction era is evident during the Civil Rights era in the South and that the black middle class continued to be viewed as a threat to a white-supremacist society.

That Big Track's resentful sister forces Loretta to strip and be hosed by the jailer evokes the graphic attacks on civil rights demonstrators frequently documented in the television and news media during the 1960s. The typewriter that Breck gives her as a teen, which ultimately allows her to escape the poverty of Ellenton for Chicago to become a secretary for Montgomery Ward and to enter the middle class, recasts the historical association of literacy and freedom in the African American context. Indeed, Breck informs her that the typewriter would spell "freedom" for her if she became the best typist in America. Butt Cutt's main motivations for helping his fellow Klan members orchestrate her rape lie in his resentment of her intelligence and educational attainment, which far exceed his own, and in his perception that she is "uppity." His outrage over her educational accomplishments is evident in his view that it would be most appropriate and humiliating for her to be raped by Lightning Rod.[17] Furthermore, Butt Cutt, whom the narrator describes as a "human bulldozer," sees hurting Loretta as a chance to strike back at Breck, his nemesis. That Loretta at one point cautions the demonstrators that allowing them into her home would "bring lightning" eerily anticipates the attack of Lightning Rod, who received his name because he was struck by lightning as a child. White men in the county relate this incident to his sexual proclivity. His name itself has phallic connotations and reduces him to his reputation as a sexual predator.

The novel highlights the Klan membership's sacralization of *Birth of a Nation* and *The Clansman* on a par with the Bible. Huie critiques Christian hypocrisy in the chapter that focuses on the rape of Loretta, which begins with a prayer by the minister Mark Alverson. Alverson heads the action squad of the Klan, endorses the rape, and finds a substitute for his evening service on Easter Sunday so that he will be able to witness it. Through the rape's timing, Huie casts the virgin Loretta as the innocent sacrificial lamb used to actualize a white-supremacist agenda. The novel's ordering of events is quite significant. For when Big Track and Allen are traveling to view the photographs, which demonstrate white women's vulnerability to violations by black men, a group of white men are literally plotting the rape of a black woman at home.

The lynching of a black man named Willie Washington for the rape of Nancy Poteet, a married and pregnant white woman, is an incident that drew national attention in the county the previous year. Contrasted with Loretta's rape, Nancy's rape becomes the instrument whereby Huie attempts to dismantle historical sexual stereotypes of white and black female identity. Furthermore, both rapes serve as his primary means for directly engaging *Birth of a Nation* and the Dixon novel. However, the rapes of Nancy Poteet and Loretta surface as competing narratives in the novel, a problem that the related film does not fully transcend in its representation of rape and lynching. A consideration of the film's points of departure from the novel in representing rape and lynching merits further attention.

It is well known that film adaptations of novels frequently alter or shift the meaning of the works on which they are based while adding or eliminating characters, and that the observable continuities and discontinuities from one genre to the other offer rich interpretive possibilities. A camera recession from the words of a sign that says "Drive Carefully, You are in Wallace Country," establishes the southern setting. The Staple Singers, in the soulful track "The Good Christian People," provide the first sound and allude to the irony of segregation in such a religious region. *The Klansman* presents Breck as a protagonist, emphasizing the struggle he endures as he attempts to live among and support blacks on his mountain within a racially polarized social order. These are choices that cause Stancill to be hated, regarded as a race traitor, and treated as an outcast in Ellenton. Richard Burton's attempt to portray this southern character was perceived as imperfect and awkward. The setting of events in a fictive place and the filming on location in California, as opposed to the South, also likely made *The Klansman* seem somewhat unrealistic in its depiction of southern life. Still, the vociferous critiques of this film, which in some cases amounted to downright ridicule, may have reflected in part critics' reluctance to grapple with the race and gender issues that it so boldly foregrounds. After all, incidents in *The Klansman* are by no means far-fetched or inconceivable for the time in which it is set.

The film begins with the public rape of a black woman in the county by the character Lightning Rod and goes on to depict Nancy Poteet's rape by a black man. The location of the black woman's attack in a rural setting, as she attempts to fight off Lightning Rod in the dirt, materializes racist associations of black sexuality with notions of the primitive, the bestial, and the savage. While the audience is led to presume that Big Track's priority when he drives up will be to disrupt this violent attack, his main concern is that the group is trespassing on private property. Furthermore, his payment of the dollar that Lightning Rod was promised reveals his indifference about black women as rape victims and the cheapness and expendability with which the black feminine body is viewed. The menacing dark hand that grabs the car door and the camera's emphasis on the body, while not revealing a face, give Nancy's rapist a phantom quality and establishes the mystery of his identity. This image ostensibly draws on black rapist mythology and establishes the grounds for its critique in the film. These two events set the plot in motion and establish rape as an important theme. The film depicts white men in the county facilitating and failing to recognize the rape of Loretta as wrong but passionately going out to avenge Nancy's because of their deep-seated white supremacy; hearing about the latter rape is sufficient evidence to compel them to lynch and maim. It dramatizes the vulnerability and devaluation of the black female body within a white racist context. The setting of the black woman's rape in a public place in broad daylight is also significant. The film suggests the sheer hypocrisy and absurdity in the fact that the black woman's attack is one that many people see but do not care about. The film confronts the moral bankruptcy in white supremacy's insistent obscuring of black humanity. Moreover, these rapes occur on the same day within the chronology of the film. Their timing, like the film's later shift from a figuration of Lightning Rod to Butt Cutt as Loretta's sexual assailant, effectively lays the groundwork for interracial rape as a parallel and interlocking theme.[18] The Klan's later rape of Loretta is recognizable, from an organizational standpoint, as the film's climactic scene.

It is important to recognize that such elements as character, plot, and narrative mean very different things in the contexts of film and literature. While *The Klansman* preserves most of the novel's characters, it invents a few of its own. Most notably, it adds Garth, whom O. J. Simpson portrays. The use of character in the film, and this one in particular, is the central device that foregrounds the theme of lynching, which, like rape, emerges toward the beginning of the film. While rape functions as a central narrative in the novel, lynching is the primary one in the film. The film introduces Garth in an early scene during which his ire is visibly raised as Big Track comes into the pool hall to arrest Willie Washington, a young black man, on circumstantial evidence for Nancy's rape. The next scene shows Garth walking along the road with his friend Henry as Klansmen in the county roam the county in search of black male prey. They spot Garth and Henry, and both men, sensing danger, run into the woods amid gunfire. The film uses dark lights and shadows to emphasize the danger that Garth and Henry face as they desperately run from the mob. Klan members eventually overtake Henry when he stumbles. As Garth looks on helplessly from a tree, they castrate Henry, who is crying out for mercy, and then take turns firing shots at him. The scene effectively reverses iconography of the black male body within white-supremacist discourse. For this group of white men, in its ritualized attack on the fallen Henry, comes across as violent and savage. Camera cuts back and forth from the pained and horrified look on Garth's face to Henry's body in the moments leading up to the latter's castration evoke empathy for Garth as well as the victim. They lead us to interpret the horror of the lynching from Garth's point of view. That the film confronts its audience with this graphic and brutal depiction of lynching underscores its investment in this theme. Ironically, Garth finds safety in a tree, ordinarily a primary setting for lynching. The film recurrently depicts Garth perched in trees with his gun. It is an image that strikingly contrasts with the image of him so powerless and helpless as he hides in the tree during Henry's lynching. The trees that punctuate the rural setting in the film, recurrent references to birds, along with the several shots of the tree on which Breck's great-grandfather was lynched during the antebellum era extend these allusions to the history of lynching. The last shot in this lynching scene is of Garth's pained face. The film intricately relates this trauma to the fact that Garth takes up a gun in subsequent days and murders Klan members.

The emphasis on lynching establishes a masculinist tone and thematic agenda in the film. One way to explain the emphasis on lynching and black male subjectivity is to recognize *The Klansman* as the product of a time during which the masculinist ideology of black power reigned. I would like to suggest that the discourse of black power primarily shapes constructions of race and gender in the film. Black power was heavily invested in a rhetoric that construed black women as "emasculating" and prone to sabotaging and betraying black men sexually and politically in the interests of white men. It is necessary to draw on this rhetoric in interpreting the film's revisionist portrayal of the character Loretta.[19] Like the novel, the film presents Loretta and Breck's friendship as platonic. But the film promotes a reading of her as apolitical and aligned with white patriarchy and invokes the historical myth of black female sexual complicity with white men. When she returns to town, reestablishing her relationship with Breck is one of her main priorities, even as she remains indifferent to the growing black social movement in Atoka County. Such terms as "handkerchiefhead" and "Uncle Tom" are linked to her several times. Furthermore, it is telling that Loretta's rape is the only event orchestrated by the Klan that Garth fails to show up and disrupt with gunfire, as he has done on several occasions in the wake of the lynching; it is an incident for which he shows little sympathy. These issues come to the fore in the scene in which Garth surprises Loretta at gunpoint in the back of Breck's truck as Breck transports her from the hospital. Garth attacks their liberal approaches to the race problem in the county. Space is particularly significant here. The triangulation of their bodies, with Garth in the back seat and Breck and Loretta in the front, and the several shots of Breck and Loretta together in opposition to Garth, gives further play to the longstanding myth of black female–white male collusion. Furthermore, that Garth has extensive dialogue as a character in this scene but is comparatively silent in most of the others lends assertion to his voice. His insensitivity to Loretta's rape and his view of her as apolitical are clear when he remarks to her that "If I was a honkey, I'd want all niggers to be just like you, marching them dumb ass marches and mouthing them dumb ass slogans. . . . What good is a peaceful meeting? That's for them bourgeois Negroes. When you gone learn anyway that all that marching is going to get you is what you got—screwed?" The film also seems to offer an equivocal statement on white female rape by never revealing the identity of Nancy Poteet's rapist. The film's investments in validating and vindicating black male subjectivity are perhaps most evident in its replacement of the Willie Washington described in the novel as a sexual philanderer who prefers sex with married women and who is revealed by the narrator as having committed the assault with a Willie Washington in the film who remains undeveloped as a character, who is never ascertained as the rapist, and who is released due to an alibi from his white lover. It is also significant that the film opts to foreground the lynching of an innocent black man. It makes its revisionist scripting of black male identity, which entails a destabilization of the myth of the black rapist, contingent on a signification of white and black female rape victimization as indeterminate, the constitution of rape and lynching as competing narratives, and the representation of a desexualized (and perhaps even asexual) black masculinity.

Whereas the film draws on discourses of black power to construct Loretta as an inauthentic black, it uses them to constitute the character of Garth as a quintessential embodiment of black masculinity. Though Garth, like Loretta, is external to the organized movement for black liberation in the county, the grounds on which he eschews official alignment with local activists are political and further underscore his racial authenticity. As he remarks to Loretta when asked if he is aware of his need for an organization: "I'm an organization of one, a headquarters, you might say, for the revolution in Atoka county." We can interpret his estrangement as an allusion to the tensions that were growing by the mid-1960s between the mainstream civil rights agenda that advocated nonviolent resistance and later strands of the black-liberation movement that espoused the ideology of black power and armed self-defense, the most salient example of which was the Black

Panther Party for Self-Defense founded in Oakland, California, by Huey P. Newton and Bobby Seale in 1966. It is clear that Garth's character endorses and is primarily modeled on the notions of militant black masculinity that were formulated within the latter movements. The film invokes these notions directly when Garth triumphantly raises his gun in a clenched fist, the sign of black power, after he has shot, sniper-style, one of the Ku Klux Klan members who is attempting to disrupt a civil rights demonstration in town; Garth has just run across the railroad tracks, just being missed by a train whose passing blocks the view of him and allows him to get away.

In the final scene, Loretta, once accused by Garth of being a sellout and buying into middle-class values, is shown also taking up the gun against Klan members and burning the tree on which Breck's ancestor was lynched. The film suggests that any potential for black male and black female reunification and for black female redemption lies in the mutual participation of black men and black women in the project of black revolution, violent revolution if necessary.[20] In one key scene, Garth asks Breck Stancill, who is an ineffectual "John Brown" in his view, "When you gone pick up the gun?"[21] With the death of Breck, the film seems to posit that white liberalism is an inadequate and dying ideology. In his aestheticization, Garth becomes everything and more in the film that Big Track is said to be in Huie's novel. As is the case with black and white women, the film's strategies for scripting white masculinity and black masculinity are binary and intertwined. A "weak" and emasculated white masculinity, which was a major premise of black power ideology, is implicit in *The Klansman*.

It is noteworthy that this film emphasizes the specificity of violence against the black male body in southern history and reveals the continuing manifestations of that abuse. Furthermore, the implication that Garth is a native southerner to a degree belies the culture's dominant images of the black male revolutionary of the 1960s as urban and northern. The media popularized these images and they became entrenched in the cultural imagination, notwithstanding the central historical role that organizations based in the South—such as the Mississippi Freedom Democratic Party (MFDP) of Jackson, Mississippi, and the Lowndes County Freedom Organization (LCFO) in Alabama—played in the origination and implementation of black power ideology. The formation of these groups was catalyzed by the Student Non-Violent Coordinating Committee (SNCC) under Stokely Carmichael's leadership for the purpose of advocating black voter registration and participation in electoral politics.[22] Through Garth, *The Klansman* points to the role of black southerners in advancing the strategy of armed self-defense within black-revolutionary thought. That the philosophy of armed self-defense advocated by the Black Panther Party was inspired in part by the LCFO and the Deacons for Defense, based in North Carolina, is a fact that has frequently been obscured, nor is it widely known that the black panther symbol originated in the LCFO and this organization was the source from which the Oakland Party derived it.[23] It is intriguing that few concerns have been raised about the ideological implications of the symbol's translation in this sense. For though the various organizations that adopted the black panther symbol were originally imagined as being loosely collective, we need to recognize that in its popularized form in the media, the symbol was far removed from its LCFO legacy in rural Alabama and instead registered as a benchmark of black urban political unrest. It is important to ponder the eventual obscuring of the symbol's black rural southern specificity because the Black Panther was arguably instrumental in helping to forge the black masculinist revolutionary sensibility of the era that leaders like Carmichael saliently embodied in the media and which produced regionally specific ideologies of gender that helped to construe notions of black masculinity in the South as counterrevolutionary and passive. While the critiques of the gender politics of the black-liberation movement of the 1960s have become familiar, we should also think more about the levels on which the movement produced ideologies of masculinity that were regionally oriented in order to recognize the alienation of black men in the South from notions of black activism.

That the black rural residents on Stancill's mountain are virtually unseen in the film until the final scenes is a cinematic strategy that points to their invisibility and lack of voice. Loretta, who stands apart because of her middle-class privileges, describes them as "mummified"; they are viewed as content as long as they have their shacks, relief checks, TV, and religion. Because they have Breck's patronage, they are a more privileged group than poor whites, which helps fuel racial tensions in the county, along with fears that black migration to the North will lead to a labor crisis in a county with a black majority. The film's characterization of Garth and the rural setting poignantly recall the historical Alabama and Mississippi origins of the black power movement. Yet the irony is that *The Klansman* evokes the urban manifestations of black power as a condition for its deployment in a southern context. The film seems limited in vision where it is only capable of representing a black and southern male as defiant and resistant within a white-supremacist context to the extent that he is linked to a discourse of urban black militancy, for Garth indicates that riots in such cities as Detroit have inspired his renegade activities. The film implies the most authentic and subversive forms of black masculinity to be urban and northern. As Robin D. G. Kelley observes in *Hammer and Hoe: Alabama Communists during the Great Depression*, the presumption has often been that black southerners are "unlikely radicals."[24]

If *The Klansman* draws on the discourse of black power in negotiating its narrative shift from the novel's emphasis on black female identity and rape to a highlighting of lynching and black masculinity, it also relies on conventions of blaxploitation film. This genre, which was heralded by productions such as Melvin Van Peebles's *Sweet Sweetback's Badasssss Song* (1971) and Gordon Parks's *Shaft* (1971), often drew on outdated Hollywood formulas from western, science fiction, and detective films and most typically highlighted black action heroes in conflict with an oppressive white establishment, against which they were ultimately triumphant. With over two hundred proliferating from the early to mid-1970s, the films in this genre had wide popular appeal for a while. They eventually came into ill repute for propagating stereotypes of black identity by glamorizing crime, violence, and sex in the urban "ghetto," including figures such as prostitutes and pimps.[25] This genre, with its emphasis on heroic models of black masculinity, is another key framework for developing the masculinist agenda in this film. The imprint of blaxploitation conventions is evident in Garth's one-man and ultimately victorious crusade against a white-supremacist system embodied in the Ku Klux Klan whose ideologies also help corrupt local law enforcement. Furthermore, it seems fitting to situate within the schema of blaxploitation the fiery climactic scene that reveals Garth battle worn but triumphant and unscathed as he walks into the darkness with his gun over his shoulder. Though he maintains a low profile in the film, he accomplishes his mission with the deliberateness and finesse of such eponymous blaxploitation heroes as John Shaft, the sexually insatiable, hip, confrontational, leather-clad New York detective portrayed by Richard Roundtree in Parks's film. The film's scant dialogue for Garth's character emphasizes his status as a man of action. *The Klansman* construes Garth as a hero by highlighting the various strategies that he deploys to outwit and subvert those in power. For instance, in one key scene, Garth dons a Klan robe and knocks on the window of a Klan action squad member to lure him outside, only to reveal a brown hand holding a gun. Here he plays the role of trickster in keeping with classic African American folkloric conventions. While some of his strategies are clandestine and under the cover of night and mirror tactics of the Klan, they are implied to be courageous and far more brazen in the sense that he works alone while they carry out attacks in groups.

That *The Klansman* offers a radical revision of the plot of Huie's novel and highlights Garth as a character in part reflected the fact that, by the early 1970s, the genre of blaxploitation film had come to play the most decisive role in fashioning popular notions of black masculinity. The attempt in *The Klansman* to present a southernized blaxploitation hero is provocative. Furthermore, it is noteworthy that *The Klansman*, with its rural southern settings, draws so intimately on blaxploitation formulas when we consider that the vast majority of these films were set in the urban North. The reliance on blaxploitation formulas reveals investments in an urban northern aesthetic of black masculinity. *The Klansman* suggests that the South is not a legitimate or fecund source for models of black masculinity or black militancy. The infusion of blaxploitation to enhance popular appeal draws on the generic cinematic formulas of the time and in effect contributes to a loss of the southern specificity of Huie's original story in translation.

Some reviewers of *The Klansman* were horrified by the stock quality of its characters and the predictability of its rape and lynching plot. Some of the campy elements of *The Klansman* are no doubt also attributable to blaxploitation. But we might also ponder these qualities as an allusion to and play on the sexual and stereotypical excessiveness of *Birth of a Nation* and the range of stock figures therein. When we consider that blaxploitation served as the dominant genre in consolidating a range of stereotypes of blacks during the 1970s, we can recognize that the reliance on such formulas in *The Klansman* ultimately revised and extended rather than unsettled the conventional stereotypical representations of African Americans in film.

The casting of *The Klansman* with a range of prominent stars, particularly O. J. Simpson, is also worth noting. At the time the film was released and Simpson made his debut and crossover into acting, he was of course best known in American culture as the 1968 winner of the coveted Heisman Trophy and then as the legendary running back for the Buffalo Bills in the NFL, a background that reinforced all the more the masculinism and heroism of his character in the film. African American athletes like Jim Brown and Bernie Casey were following similar paths to film stardom. In his discussion of the widespread fascination with the "jock" in 1970s film, Donald Bogle remarks that

> in American culture, the black athlete, powerful and seemingly of superhuman strength, has always been a double-sided social/political figure, both celebrated and feared because of his remarkable skills. The film industry, aware of this ambivalent attitude, has shrewdly learned how to manipulate the myth of the athlete and to alter his legend to fit the mood and tone of the times. The basic use of the black athlete has almost always been the same: if the "name" athlete, with strength and force enough to oppose the culture successfully, chooses instead to support it, his endorsement serves as a clue to all us mortal weaklings with thoughts of rebellion to cool it. Consequently, on screen athletes have traditionally been packaged to proclaim the pleasures of a great capitalistic society.[26]

If Simpson portrays a rebel with a cause in *The Klansman*, his character's radical philosophy is undercut and rendered ironic, perhaps by the very logic of his casting as an actor in the film, to the extent that it draws on his public and popular images as an African American who had achieved the American Dream.[27] There is some irony, too, in the casting of Lola Falana, who was one of the most prominent black sex symbols of the 1970s, as the virtuous Loretta Sykes. While the novel construes Loretta as an average-looking woman, the film, perhaps in light of the popular audience that it aims to draw, figures the character as a rather attractive woman and uses her as its aesthetic focal point. The costuming strategies for Loretta, in which she appears in tight-fitting pants and skirts, draw on Falana's star status. The featuring of Simpson and Falana and other major stars made the film's critical failure seem all the more abysmal. At this point, I shall turn to an examination of its contexts in American literary and cinematic history.

From *The Clansman* to *The Klansman*

The technological innovations that *Birth of a Nation* achieved as the first feature-length film ever made mean that it will always occupy a prominent place in the history of U.S. film. The term *national cinema* is frequently coded as a mainly "foreign" phenomenon within film studies, as a concept extraneous or irrelevant to the history of film production in the United

States. In a sense, it can be said that D. W. Griffith's *Birth of a Nation* gave rise to national cinema in the United States. The South as a region is ideologically dominant in shaping the narrative of national selfhood that the film offers. Even the title announces the film as one whose narrative holds national significance. Released during World War I, it framed the history of the Civil War against the contemporary reality of a nation at war. The film points to the importance of looking to the South in examining the evolution of U.S. popular culture. This artifact should make the region indispensable to dialogues about the foundations of film not only in the United States but in the global arena as well. *Birth of a Nation*, a paean to the Old South, recuperated and visualized a range of masculine and feminine antebellum models of whiteness such as the southern belle and the southern gentleman. Perhaps even more consequentially, it established a stereotypical paradigm in film for representing blacks. As Manthia Diawara points out,

> The release of D. W. Griffith's *The Birth of a Nation* in 1915 defined for the first time the side that Hollywood was to take in the war to represent Black people in America. In *The Birth of a Nation*, D. W. Griffith, later a founding member of United Artists, created and fixed an image of Blackness that was necessary for racist America's fight against Black people. *The Birth of a Nation* constitutes the grammar book for Hollywood's representation of Black manhood and womanhood, its obsession with miscegenation, and its fixing of Black people within certain spaces, such as kitchens, and into certain supporting roles, such as criminals, on the screen. . . . *The Birth of a Nation* is the master text that suppressed the real contours of Black history and culture on movie screens, screens monopolized by the major motion picture companies of America.[28]

As is the case in Huie's novel, one of the central aims of the film *The Klansman* is to critique and destabilize the litany of racial and gender ideologies advanced in *Birth of a Nation* and in the novel by Dixon.

There are a few obvious and significant parallels between *Birth of a Nation* and *The Klansman* in light of the ways in which the latter invests itself in a revision and critique of the former. *Birth of a Nation* is set in the period during and immediately following the Civil War, while *The Klansman*, which resonates and recuperates Dixon's title, is set during the Civil Rights era a century later. In both films, the Ku Klux Klan asserts itself to restore a white-supremacist social order in the South and, by extension, in a nation perceived to be in disrepair and under attack because of an unruly and upwardly mobile black population. In *Birth of a Nation*, the problems are perceived as stemming from Emancipation and Reconstruction agendas and, in *The Klansman*, from the social movement for integration and voting rights. White liberal patriarch Breck Stancill, who mobilizes his wealth for the sustenance of the black community in his county, is a rough analogue to Dixon and Griffith's Austin Stoneman. This parallel is sustained most directly through the allusion, in Breck's use of a cane after losing a leg during the Korean War, to Stoneman's crippling clubfoot: "His walk was a painful hobble. He was lame in both feet, and one of them was deformed. The left leg ended in a mere bunch of flesh, resembling more closely an elephant's hoof than the foot of a man" (Dixon 39).[29] Furthermore, like Stoneman, Breck is reputed to be having a relationship with a black woman.

From the outset, *The Klansman* acknowledges the view of black men as lascivious and rapacious in the southern cultural imagination as well as the logic in the southern mind that has historically deemed lynching the most natural and appropriate consequence for a black man's rape of a white female. In *Birth of a Nation*, the blackface character Gus, who chases Little Sister through the woods, is the most ostensible and graphic embodiment of the black rapist. The black rapist is also more subtly evident in the large and at times overbearing "mulatto" character Silas Lynch, who transgresses rigid social boundaries by pursuing and proposing marriage to the heroine, Elsie Stoneman. In this instance, the name "Lynch," coupled with a vile characterization, alludes to the idea of the black rapist and the punitive use of lynching to annihilate the black male body. His status as a product of racial miscegenation serves as a further marker of his deviance. Significantly, the chase sequence of Garth and Henry through the woods, which entails Henry's subsequent lynching and castration, purposefully revises the infamous chase in *Birth of a Nation* that features the brutish Gus. For in depicting the desperate run of Garth and Henry to protect their lives from the Ku Klux Klan members who are pursuing them, *The Klansman* highlights the vulnerability of the black male body to lynching, underscoring that the lynching of black men by white men was a more pervasive and truthful social phenomenon in the South than black male rape of white women. As Angela Davis remarks, "To be sure, there were some examples of Black men raping white women. But the number of actual rapes which occurred was minutely disproportionate to the allegations implied by the myth."[30]

In general, the film offers valuable historical connections when it acknowledges that lynching was used as a form of social terror against white abolitionists during the antebellum period even before it was used widely as a tactic for disciplining and annihilating the black body. *The Klansman* is equally revealing where it illustrates how white southern soldiers' xenophobia against Asians during the Korean War added fuel to segregationist ideologies and suggests that combat maneuvers learned during wartime led to violence and terror against blacks once these soldiers returned to the United States.

In addressing the ideologies through which black men have been construed as rapists, the film establishes a further bridge between the Civil War and Civil Rights eras, reminding us that this historical myth of black masculinity had its origin in the postwar South. Indeed, the black rapist myth was the historical basis on which the Ku Klux Klan emerged in the late 1860s, with its main goal being to protect white womanhood in the South from black male sexual violation and the threat of miscegenation. This myth served as the primary rationale for lynching, logic that is well illustrated in Dixon's and Griffith's respective works.

As Frederick Douglass noted, the idea of an inherent black male bestiality was belied and the excuse for lynching rendered weak by the failure of black male servants to take advantage of white male absence during the Civil War to rape white women who had been left alone on plantations. According to Robyn Wiegman, it was necessary to subtend the model of black male docility, which had been dominant within the white paternalism of antebellum plantation ideology and classically emblematized in popular representations of Uncle Tom, with the invention, in the late nineteenth century, of the rapacious black buck whose sexual pathology and depravity were an ever-looming threat to white female purity in the South.[31] While white femininity was exalted as the site of white racial purity within this ideology, it is ironic that the idea of the black rapist gained its force and authority precisely from the southern fantasy of a ravaged, traumatized, and potentially miscegenated white female body.

Lynching, whose victims were frequently male, functioned as the most legible cultural practice through which black bodies were disciplined, contained, and subordinated within the white-supremacist ideology dominant in the South. Though the black male body was scripted in post-Emancipation racialist thought as an imminent sexual threat to white femininity, the emergence of the black rapist myth during this time—along with its concomitant rationalization in the social terror of lynching—has been more accurately interpreted as less a reflection of the reality of white female rape than a public and ritualized manifestation of growing white panic about a shifting social order in the South that promised blacks education, property, political participation, and social inclusion.[32] Indeed, one of the key aims of *Birth of a Nation* is to depict mockingly the worst-case scenario in the South of a black political, economic, and social takeover and to endorse the view of the Reconstruction era that was already deeply entrenched in many white southern minds of black men as marauding rapists and inept politicians.

Similarly, *The Klansman* suggests that although white women may have been perceived as the only legitimate victims of rape in the South, the black female body has been more susceptible as the object of sexual brutality by white southern men. The film subtly emphasizes the sexual subjection and degradation of the black female body at a visual level in only depicting nudity in the scenes featuring the two black women rape victims. The positioning of the camera overhead and the high angle from which the scene of Loretta's rape is shot draws the attention of the viewer, stresses the dominance of Butt Cutt's body, and the subordination and subjection of Loretta's. He is enchanted by sexual myths of black femininity, lusts after the black female body, and rapes Loretta in part to prove that he is as sexually potent as a man like Lightning Rod. The face-to-face framing of Loretta and Butt Cutt in the film materializes the intensity of their dialogue in the novel. Butt Cutt is obviously titillated and even obsessed by the idea of sex between Loretta and a white man, arguing in the film that it will represent the height of degradation for her. The film's use of lighting in this scene, which occurs in the warehouse, contrasts dark shadows with lighted spaces and beige woodpiles in the background to further emphasize interracial rape. Butt Cutt emerges as the most vile and brutal rapist in the film. Big Track smears his face with Loretta's blood when he discovers what has happened. That Big Track forces Loretta to lie and say that a group of black men raped her as a condition of taking her to the hospital before she bleeds to death reveals his insensitivity and adds to her degradation. Furthermore, it reveals the accessibility and familiarity of the black rapist myth of masculinity in the county.

That Breck's white woman lover is the character who articulates the speculations about his past relationship with Loretta, who was supposedly a source for his "chocolate milk," foregrounds tensions and jealousies surrounding interracial sex. A close relationship to Breck Stancill positions Loretta as a rough analogue to Lydia Brown, Stoneman's mistress whom Dixon's novel describes as a "negress" with a "sleek tawny face" and "catlike eyes" (91, 94). Here, Lydia seems to embody a perverse and grotesque characterization of the "mulatto" legal or common-law wife to a white man, who appears in a host of novels ranging from Harriet Beecher Stowe's *Uncle Tom's Cabin* (1852) to Chesnutt's *The Marrow of Tradition* and who has been epitomized as a historical prototype by Sally Hemings. However, *The Klansman* enacts the most assertive revision of this type in Loretta when it underscores that there has been no sexual relationship between her and Breck—notwithstanding the widespread rumors in Ellenton of their sexual involvement—and stresses the avuncular character of his relationship with her. Instead, the film forges a romantic linkage between him and Nancy Poteet. Indeed, we might say that just as the film attempts to unsettle the myth of the black rapist by construing black masculinity as desexualized, it ultimately presents a similarly desexualized image of black femininity in an effort to destabilize the historical myth of black female sexual impurity and licentiousness. This myth is evident, for instance, in Big Track's remark that "every black girl has been popped by age thirteen" and in the widespread belief in the county that black women never mind "being raped a little."[33] The film also works to unsettle myths of black girls and women as loose and sexually available in revealing that the twenty-two-year-old Loretta was a virgin at the time of her rape.

Where the film works to establish narrative interplay between interracial rape of black and white women, we see how such ideologies also come to shape the view of Nancy Poteet, who is rebuked openly in the white community for attending a church service in the days after her rape and who is thought to be coming across as "too damned healthy" instead of "all broke up" as she should be, in the wake of being raped by a black man. Because her failure to offer a racist response to the violence that has been committed against her does not conform to the social expectations of white women in Ellenton, she is cast out, and her husband, who is already clearly abusive, deserts her (as well as their unborn child). For her protection, she is taken to Stancill's mountain. The film makes powerful use of setting in staging the most assertive and ostensible racism in the church. It highlights the irony in the minister's racist sermon and the cruelty in the question, "How can you push yourself on the good Christian folks after being in that nigger's foul embrace?" That repeated references are made in the film to Nancy's status as a "yellow-headed" girl acknowledges her blonde hair as the epitome of white femininity and makes her rape by a black man all the more unsettling and infuriating in the eyes of the white community. Nancy's husband is outraged that she seems to feel no shame over having been "screwed by a nigger." Her defiant dignity in the face of these rebukes reflects an emergent feminist sensibility, which is significant given this film's setting during the era of women's liberation in the 1970s. Just as he gives solace to poor blacks on his mountain, Breck's marriage proposal to Nancy redeems her and frustrates efforts in the white community to ostracize her. Furthermore, the futility in policing sex across racial boundaries is evident in a white woman named Martha's confession—in front of her husband—that she had consensual sex with Willie Washington on the night that Nancy was raped to offer an alibi and protect him from lynching. Having left her lonely and vulnerable as he is out roaming with the Klan, her husband is shocked and devastated by the betrayal of "the mother of my children."

As is the case with the film's negotiation of rape and lynching, the rapes of Loretta and Nancy are set forth as competing narratives, and the sexual redemption of black femininity is premised on a negation of white female sexual victimization. This logic is evident in the film's contrast of the serious medical crisis that Loretta faces in the wake of Butt Cutt's attack with Nancy's relative health following her rape. Such logic also seriously flaws Huie's novel. It is apparent when Breck and Clay Wilbanks compare Loretta's medical situation in the aftermath of her rape with Marian's from Dixon's *The Clansman* and discuss the suicide imperative in the South for white women who have been raped by black men: " 'Now note,' said Breck, 'that the victim of that rape, who was seventeen, was physically strong at 3 a.m. when she regained consciousness. She was as strong as Nancy Poteet was. She didn't need hospitalization. She wasn't even bleeding, as Loretta Sykes was. She was strong enough to bathe, dress, and go hurrying through the woods with her mother, who was thirty-five. Yet daughter and mother agreed suicide was necessary'" (158–159). There are also overtones of this logic when Breck remarks the hostile reaction of the Ellenton community to Nancy following her rape. This is a passage that merits quoting at length:

Well, since it was Sunday, ten hours after the rape and six hours after the lynching Nancy bathed and dressed herself and her child, and with her husband, she went to church as she was accustomed to doing. For her family's sake she wanted to carry on as though nothing catastrophic had happened. Bobby Poteet sat in the choir and joined in singing "Bringing in the Sheaves" and "What a Friend We Have in Jesus." Nancy sat in the congregation. All that she and Bobby needed were a few pats on the back, a few kind words. With their presence they were pleading for help. But they didn't get it. The church members were too shocked, too confused, too sickened to comfort Nancy and Bobby. I say "sickened" because one woman, sitting near Nancy, vomited during the sermon and had to be assisted out. The "nigger odor" which she smelled on Nancy had turned the woman's stomach. Several other women smelled the odor, but by holding perfumed handkerchiefs to their noses they managed not to throw up. To her fellow Christians Nancy had become loathsome . . . leprous . . . an Untouchable. (161)

Though Huie's novel is perhaps most revealing where it engages *Birth of a Nation* and *The Clansman* to examine the issue of rape in the South, and where it relates white panic about black male rape to a fear of miscegenation and to the continuation of racism, the novel is problematic when it construes the white female body as less sexually vulnerable. It is also significant that Wilbanks highlights the prevalence of sexual activity among white teenage girls in the county to challenge ideologies of an inherent white female sexual purity and black female promiscuity. In the film *The Klansman*, the difficulty of framing white and black female rape alongside each other reflects what Tara McPherson has theorized as a lenticular visual politics in the South's media representations throughout the twentieth century.[34] The same separatist logic, as the film demonstrates, often inflects narratives of rape and lynching.

The Klansman well suggests the extent to which Klan ideology infused politics and law in the South. For instance, as sheriff, Big Track has been ambivalent about the organization throughout the film and only decides to come down on the side of the law in the penultimate scenes after he takes Butt Cutt's badge for the rape of Loretta. Furthermore, the film points to the continuing viability of the Klan even during an era when many in the nation were assuming that the organization was virtually obsolete. In the film, dialogue between Big Track and Breck offers exposition on the Klan, acknowledges its distinguished members such as congressmen and senators, and intimates its national scope. However, *The Klansman* marks Klan members as a dying breed. The finale that presents Ku Klux Klan members lying wounded and dying on the battlefield of Stancill's mountain stands in striking contrast to their stampede to triumph in the climactic scenes of D. W. Griffith's film. In *The Klansman*, the Ku Klux Klan and white liberalism, as embodied in Breck, are figured as taking their last breaths together, so that the last man standing in the film is Garth, a symbol of the black revolution.

With regard to the interrogation of rape and lynching, the revisionist strategies of the film *The Klansman* echo those of the pioneering black filmmaker Oscar Micheaux's 1920 film, *Within Our Gates*, which was rediscovered in extant form in a repository in Spain in 1986. As film scholar Jane Gaines has observed, *Within Our Gates* offered a response to the racial logic of *Birth of a Nation* by depicting the attempted rape of a black woman by a white man—who is only deterred because he discovers that he is her father—and by highlighting the lynching of her adopted black family.[35] In doing so, Micheaux's film provocatively implies that black victimization at the hands of whites was the truer social reality.

In *The Klansman*, the irony in the narrative shift from an emphasis on black and white female rape to a spectacular emphasis on black male lynching to suture a sexed and gendered ideology of black male domination during the era of 1960s black liberation becomes clear, of course, if we recognize the historical role of the male-centered myth of the black rapist in consolidating a context of repression and disenfranchisement for African Americans in late-nineteenth-century America. While emerging a century apart, both ideologies were rooted in a pathological view of the black masculine body as hypersexual. The script of black men as potentially rapacious of the white feminine body during the era of black liberation was epitomized in Eldridge Cleaver's description of the "Supermasculine Menial" in *Soul on Ice*.[36]

The Bad White Woman and Other Fictions of Identity

I am also intrigued by the implications of the book and film versions of *The Klansman* for more contemporary public discourses, including O. J. Simpson's criminal trial during the mid-1990s. I want to turn to these matters before I conclude. While he serves as a radical contradiction to the black rapist myth, the character Garth is steeped, of course, in the folk mythology of the bad Negro. The film *The Klansman* illustrates how the politics of racial oppression and the trauma of lynching in the South give birth to an outlaw like Garth and reveals ways in which an ideology of black inferiority has been constituted in the national context from the Civil War to the Civil Rights era. Few in the 1970s would have anticipated that O. J. Simpson would face murder charges in the 1990s, fall from grace as a "hero" in the national context, and be transformed from the iconic advertising spokesperson for such products as Hertz rental cars into a persona non grata. As Toni Morrison points out, O. J. Simpson has literally emerged in the post–Civil Rights era as a poster boy for a national ideology scripting the black subject as criminal and violent.

> The official story has thrown Mr. Simpson into [a] representative role. He is not an individual who underwent and was acquitted from a murder trial. He has become the whole race, needing correction, incarceration, censoring, silencing; the race that needs its civil rights disassembled; the race that is sign and symbol of domestic violence; the race that has made trial by jury a luxury rather than a right and placed affirmative action legislation in even greater jeopardy. This is the consequence and function of official stories: to impose the will of a dominant culture. It is *Birth of a Nation* writ large—menacingly and pointedly for the 'hood.[37]

Here, Morrison acknowledges the view of blackness as pathological that was nationally abstracted through Simpson as a black masculine subject. This imaging was most obvious in the June 27, 1994, issue of *Time* magazine that featured a now infamous cover photograph of him with darkened skin. Simpson's portrait as a criminal, which belied his celebrity and the "colorblind" view of his identity that he had long maintained, emerged during the height of public discussions of black male homicide and incarceration owing to drug- and gang-related violence, during a time when the posturing of such rappers as Ice Cube, Tupac Shakur, and Snoop Doggy Dogg as "gangstas" reinforced the media view of black masculinity as violent. Morrison's clever wordplay in the title of her anthology *The Birth of a Nation'hood* draws on *Birth of a Nation* and links Simpson to the " 'hood." This is a black slang word that refers to the predominantly black urban communities that were by the early 1990s experiencing economic devastation and cast in the national imaginary as bastions of crime, violence, drugs, and gangs and, therefore, signified as "other" spaces in the national context. Her discussion acknowledges the translation of Simpson into a "thug" in U.S. culture as much as it recognizes his linkages to such black communities on the basis of his subjectivity as black and male, notwithstanding his class privilege. After the trial, the media further reinforced its characterization of blackness as pathological by highlighting the racially bifurcated reactions to the "not guilty" verdict for Simpson, with whites overwhelmingly believing in his guilt and blacks believing in his innocence. Simpson's place in the national consciousness as a metonym for black pathology, as Morrison points out, is in keeping with the historical ideological construction of blackness in the United States. Depictions of black masculinity such as *Time*'s may register now within the national pantheon of raced, sexed, and gendered stereotypes. However, one must recognize that the contemporary media's propagandistic representations of black men as criminal have a looming and paradigmatic precedent in the South's myth of the black rapist. This is one of the obvious reasons that it is important to recognize in critical scholarship on masculinity how contemporary black masculine representations continue to carry the burden of southern history. Representations of black men as gangstas in popular culture, for instance, which portray men as violent and threatening, lie to some extent along a continuum with the historical construction of black masculinity as pathological that is rooted in southern history.

Whether they thought him innocent or guilty, *The Klansman* has compelling implications for Simpson's supporters and detractors alike. For Garth, on the one hand, represents the quintessentially victimized and violable black male subject within a white-supremacist context whose protections even under the law are tenuous. On the other, that he goes on a killing spree, once finds refuge in the back of a sport-utility truck, and in the end gets away with murder are details that are surely not lost on those eager to identify ways in which Simpson's life may have imitated his art. If a jury vindicates Simpson, it is Big Track who ultimately vindicates Garth. At one point, during the climactic battle scene on Stancill's mountain, they turn their guns on each other, and the camera focuses on their intense stare for a moment. Both men drop their weapons, implicitly because they have been fighting the same enemy. Garth is released to go his way into the night, even though it is clear that Big Track suspects that he has committed the recent rash of Klan murders.

Historically, antimiscegenation law was in part designed to regulate white female sexuality and registered anxiety that some white women might transgress social decorum to marry across the color line or consent to sexual unions with black males. Nancy Poteet is alienated and becomes a "leper" and an "Untouchable" in the Ellenton community after her rape. White residents of the town eventually begin to perceive her as having had a consensual sexual encounter with a black man. What happens to Nancy Poteet in her exile to Stancill's mountain is not unlike the fate of Jean Toomer's Becky in *Cane* (1923).[38] Inscribed with the mark of Cain, Becky's ultimate fate— for having fallen from the pedestal on which white southern womanhood has been exalted within the historical racialist ideologies of the South— is burial under her cabin, which functions as a symbolic mound. In Harriet Wilson's novel *Our Nig* (1859), Mag Smith suffers a similar ostracism in light of perceived sexual improprieties with a black man, which results in her retreat to "her hovel again, with obstacles threefold insurmountable than before."[39] When considering the larger investments of this study in how difference and otherness are inscribed on the body through space and geography, it is telling that alienation from white communities for such characters is symbolized by their positioning in isolated and dilapidated homes. Their impugning is therefore connected to their resistance to conventional linkages between white femininity and domesticity. In the film *The Klansman*, Nancy Poteet is perceived to be "tainted," contaminated, and less pure as "white" by virtue of association with a black male body in much the same way that Viola Liuzzo was looked upon by her assailants for having dared to transport a black male in her car. Liuzzo's crime in their eyes was the sex that they fantasized her as having had with him and the attendant threat of miscegenation. In such instances, the view of black men as inherently bestial and oversexed is mapped onto white womanhood in a way similar to how Angela Davis describes this ideology's construction of black women as " 'loose women' and whores."[40] As Ruth Frankenberg points out, "white women who choose interracial relationships are presented as sexually 'loose,' sexually unsuccessful, or (at the least negative) sexually radical."[41]

In analyzing Daniel Defoe's poem "A True-Born Englishman" (1701), Jennifer DeVere Brody points out that "the female becomes the main vessel through which contamination [i.e., of whiteness] occurs" in England and is linked to impurity.[42] Though her discussion focuses on the instability in notions of racial purity in Victorian England, her observations are also useful for examining the discourse on whiteness and femininity in the U.S. South that emerged in the late nineteenth century. In the film *Birth of a Nation*, the panic regarding white female contamination through interracial rape and the link between white femininity and the conservation of white racial purity and homogeneity illustrate the perception of white females as the primary gatekeepers of whiteness. This construct in effect obscures the frequency of white male sexual intermixture with black women in the eras of slavery and Reconstruction and thereafter and casts the nation as feminine *and* southern in keeping with the logic of colonialist and imperialist discourses. The South centrally contributed to the development of the nation's discourses of race by constituting a gendered and sexed ideology of whiteness after slavery ended. The salience of the region in shaping the nation's discourses of race makes it both useful and necessary, from a critical standpoint, to bridge studies of the South and whiteness.[43]

The marking of a white femininity—or even a *perceived* white femininity—as "bad" when attached to a black masculine subject in an exogamous, amorous relationship was to some extent implicit, for instance, in one of the interview questions that talk-show host David Letterman posed to actress/singer/dancer Jennifer Lopez when she appeared on his show early in 2000, weeks after her boyfriend at the time, African American entertainer and rap mogul Sean Puffy Combs (now P. Diddy), was indicted for his alleged role in a New York nightclub shooting incident on New Year's: "What is a good girl like you doing with a bad guy like Puffy?" Letterman was clearly confused and shocked by Lopez's insistence on supporting Combs and on remaining in the relationship as well as by her obvious persisting affections for the rapper. The panic about her relationship with Combs perhaps becomes more understandable if we recognize that though Lopez herself is strongly invested in her Latino identity, because of her status as an entertainer widely admired by white men and her stylization (i.e., her relatively fair skin, her long, straightened blondish hair), she has perhaps undergone a symbolic whitening that is consistent with historical patterns of ethnic absorption and mainstreaming in the United States among Jewish and Irish populations that have been discussed by Noel Ignatiev and Karen Brodkin.[44] As is the case in *Time*'s portrait of Simpson, the implications of this statement about Combs cannot easily be dislodged from more general ideologies of black masculinity. They script Combs and, by extension, all black men (because, as Morrison points out, the logic of race in this culture typically makes the one black representative of all) as potentially corruptive, as something that contaminates and corrupts innocence. Interestingly, Lopez ended the relationship with Combs on February 14, 2001, partly at the behest of her family and managers, who feared that her association with his "bad boy" image would hurt her career.[45] While both artists have gone on to become more successful and are widely popular, this move on the part of Lopez was perceived by many to be a good riddance.

The film *The Klansman* has implications for the public discourse on O. J. Simpson, too, where it addresses the theme of interracial sex, the specter of which was arguably most significant in having made O. J. and Nicole objects of ongoing fascination in the national media during the course of the murder trial. Even more specifically, I want to suggest that the film, in its treatment of ways in which notions of fallen white womanhood are linked to interracial sex, can help us understand the politics of Nicole Brown Simpson's explicit and implicit raced, sexed, and gendered representation in the media during the course of the trial as a "bad girl." This imaging sometimes even obscured her status as a murder victim. Ann DuCille has related *Time* magazine's mug shot of O. J. Simpson to what she perceives to have been the "browning" that Nicole Brown Simpson underwent as a result of politics that construe white femininity as deviant when linked amorously to black masculinity:

Nicole Brown Simpson had ceased to be a white woman once she married a black man. . . . Her dead body may be worth millions in civil court, but Nicole Simpson had little surplus value in "real life," except perhaps her decorative female sexuality itself and the financial benefit for her marriage to a black man of means and property brought—indeed, continues to bring—her white family. Her awful murder can be appropriated for a national campaign against domestic abuse that figures a bestial black man as the signifier for all male violence, but she herself is a lost cause, a disappeared daughter, curiously written out of anything other than a metaphorical role in a national narrative that might well be called "The Rebirth of a Nation," in dubious tribute to D. W. Griffith's hugely successful 1915 film. In the film, as in *The Clansman*, the novel on which it is based, the need to protect white women from the sexual threat posed by lusty black bucks serves as the rationale for the rise of the Ku Klux Klan.[46]

Whiteness, in this instance, functions as a club to which one can belong as long as one plays by the rules. Like Morrison, DuCille cites the contexts of *Birth of a Nation* and *The Clansman*, suggesting that they continue to be didactic, if more implicitly so, in structuring the contemporary logic about race in this nation, whereas, nationally abstracted, now it is a racial logic fundamentally rooted in southern history in much the same sense as nationalized stereotypes like the black rapist. That such texts continue to be viable—if tacit—in shaping contemporary perceptions of race and gender, including white femininity, reveals that their social impact, as outlined by Huie through the character Butt Cutt Cates, continues to be felt. DuCille suggests that if the body of Nicole Brown Simpson was embraced and championed in death, it had been expendable, invisible, and stigmatized in life in the racial imaginary of the United States by virtue of Brown's exogamous marriage. Tellingly, a Guess Jeans ad that appeared during the 1995 trial featured look-alikes of O. J. and Nicole Brown Simpson in an erotic pose with the female looking vampish in black leather and the caption reading, "If you can't be good, be careful."[47]

On March 11, 2005, Brian Nichols, an African American male, was scheduled for a retrial in Atlanta, Georgia, for charges that included raping an ex-girlfriend, holding her hostage for days, and possession of a machine gun and large quantities of marijuana. A week after his mistrial for these allegations and the morning that the proceedings for a new trial were scheduled to begin at the Fulton County courthouse, he overpowered a female deputy, took her weapon, and killed the judge for his case, a court reporter, and wounded a deputy. He had attempted to bring a concealed weapon into the courtroom two days before this incident. While making his escape, Nichols attempted to hijack several vehicles, killed a man described as an immigration official, and became the target of a national manhunt. Pictures of Nichols, whom news reports described as a six-foot, two-hundred-pound black man, were circulated widely in the press. He was captured at the suburban apartment of Ashley Smith, a white woman he held hostage for hours. As she reported later, she gained his trust, told him about her life, calmly reasoned with him, cooked him pancakes, and read passages from Rick Warren's popular book *The Purpose-Driven Life*. The mother of a small child, Smith had lost her husband violently and mysteriously two years before and stressed to Smith that killing her would orphan her child. Her calm and self-possession during this terrifying ordeal, some reporters remarked, likely helped to save her life.

Nichols's actions evoke the historical profile of the "bad Negro." At the same time, his media imaging demonstrated the lingering presence of the black rapist myth in cultural memory. The Nichols ordeal, which entailed rape, the violent murder of whites, an "armed and dangerous" black male on the run, and, ultimately, the capture of a white female hostage, contained all the ingredients of classic racial melodrama in the South and, more broadly, in the nation. Though she was obviously traumatized, that Smith seemed to conscientiously avoid exaggerating or overstating her fears during her capture—and was in some ways even sympathetic to Nichols— demonstrates how much race relations in the South have advanced and moves us beyond conventional formulas about race, gender, and sexuality in the region. Furthermore, once Nichols was recaptured, religion was dominant in mediating the dialogue about Smith, Nichols, and Warren. Race and gender have not been factors at all. The historical contexts that I have engaged in this chapter can also help us understand in part how and why the rape charges of black male NBA star Kobe Bryant, who allegedly raped a white woman working at a Colorado resort, became such a media spectacle in the nation in more recent years.

While race problems in the South are clearly not what they used to be, some problems remain. The lingering effects of the racism birthed in the southern past have often been emphasized in films set in the South of the post–Civil Rights era. Like other films of its time such as *Tick Tick Tick* (1970), which starred Jim Brown, *The Klansman* highlights a small-town southern context in which corruption in law enforcement and vigilante violence persist along with racial bigotry and hostility. The film reminds us that though we may assume that the most egregious forms of racial terror are behind us, the black body has at times remained vulnerable in the South, as we see in the lynching of Henry and in the rape of Loretta. Furthermore, the rape of Loretta upon her return to Ellenton seems cautionary given the film's release at a time when rates of African American return migration to the South were beginning to escalate, inaugurating a reversal of the pattern of outward migration that had been dominant since the waves of the Great

Migration to the urban North earlier in the twentieth century. In more recent years, such films as *A Time to Kill* (1996) have addressed the seemingly anachronistic social polarities that have persisted in some areas of the South into the post–Civil Rights era, along with the continuing reality of racial terror, while acknowledging the Ku Klux Klan as a lingering specter and featuring a militant black male response to the organization. The horribly tragic death of James Byrd, a black man who, at the hands of three white men, was dragged to his death by a car in Jasper, Texas, in 1998, speaks for itself and serves as a reminder that we have not yet come to a day when we can regard lynching as a thing of the past in the South.

I have attempted to illustrate how much more we can learn about the ideological legacy of *The Clansman* and *Birth of a Nation* by placing Huie's novel and the related film in a historical continuum with these prior works and examining them together. In the end, the film *The Klansman* does little or no justice to the epic and richly complex proportions of Huie's novel. As Richard Combs notes, much of the compelling detail of the novel is omitted in the film.[48] Perhaps the film does the most extreme disservice to Huie's novel by making minimal and marginal references to Dixon's *The Clansman* and *Birth of a Nation*. However, at the very least, both the novel and the film versions of *The Klansman* give us more recent historical contexts in which to think about *Birth of a Nation* and *The Clansman* along with the public discourse on O. J. Simpson. Furthermore, this film and novel allow us to ponder further the historical role of the South in formulating raced and sexed pathologies of black masculinity and femininity.

It is important, of course, to acknowledge that we are living in a time when interracial relationships, including marriages, between blacks and whites have gained more widespread acceptance, even in the South. Indeed, if the cross-cultural appeal of a range of celebrities like Tiger Woods is any indication, race matters far less nowadays. Still, issues in more recent history, such as the fact that Taylor County High School in Butler, Georgia, sponsored its first integrated prom in 2002 (and in 2003 went back to segregated proms), attest to the lingering resistance in the South to the idea of dating and marriage across racial lines. Perhaps nowhere else have the persisting anxieties in the South about miscegenation been more evident in recent times than in how narrowly a 1901 constitutional ban on interracial marriage in the state of Alabama was defeated in the November 2000 election; the measure, which had been the last such law on the books in the South, was upheld by fully 40 percent of voters in the state and by twenty-four of the sixty-seven counties.

As a novelist, part of William Bradford Huie's mission in attempting to examine *Birth of a Nation* and *The Clansman* is to assess their ideological impact during the Civil Rights era and to disarm them during a time when they continued to serve as wellsprings of racial propaganda. By focusing on a setting a century after the post–Civil War era highlighted in these works, Huie has given us what has perhaps been their most provocative revision in literature. As Toni Morrison so ably underscores, because traces of these productions linger in the nation to this day, there can be no complex understanding of the interplay of race, sexuality, and gender in the United States without an understanding of southern history. Her critical work also suggests the importance of understanding the national ideology of black masculinity as rapacious and criminal that emerged after Emancipation as a converse to prevailing ideologies of white manhood, which have played the most decisive role in shaping notions of citizenship and belonging in the United States since the Enlightenment.[49]

Even though he had a career spanning more than four decades, during which he variously served as a reporter, editor, literary magazine publisher, lecturer, and freelance writer, most of Huie's books are now out of print, the amount of criticism that has been written on them is negligible, and he has yet to be the subject of a book-length biography.[50] We might take him to task for the politics of his investigative style, but William Bradford Huie deserves some credit for uncovering information as a journalist during the Civil Rights era that might not have come to light otherwise. He should go down in history as one of the most persistent and tireless cultural workers of the twentieth century. Often assuming the mantle of race traitor like his own Breck Stancill, Huie was never one to shy away from controversy, braving various forms of intimidation, including cross burnings, as a consequence of telling what he saw as the truth about the South. Interestingly, the novel *The Klansman* drew on Huie's investigative work and was originally begun as a nonfiction work, but Huie was persuaded by his attorneys and editors to fictionalize it as a condition for its publication.[51] We cannot afford to forget the lessons that he attempted to teach us through works such as *The Klansman*, a novel whose power is perhaps best exemplified in the myth of its Pulitzer Prize. To be sure, there is a lot more that we can learn from his legacy in southern literature and culture.

CHAPTER 2

Charles Fuller's
Southern Specter

William Faulkner's first novel, *Soldiers' Pay* (1926), provides a visionary treatment of race, region, masculinity, and the military as well as intricate and detailed portraits of the soldier, which make it a compelling counterpoint for a reading of Charles Fuller's *A Soldier's Play* (1981). I want to draw on it to help my critical effort of bringing into relief ideologies of black southern masculinity generated in the military in the first decades of the twentieth century. In their institutionalization and nationalization in the military, I contend, such ideologies extended and recast the pathological portraits of black masculinity in the South produced in the late nineteenth century that I discuss in chapter 1.

As Faulkner's *Soldiers' Pay* begins, the military and the impact of its hierarchy on masculinity are the main concerns. Set in Georgia after the end of World War I, *Soldiers' Pay* foregrounds complex portraits of three soldiers—Donald Mahon, Joe Gilligan, and Julian Lowe—that mediate and ground characterizations of such women as Cecily Saunders and Margaret Powers. The impact of postwar angst on southern subjectivity is a larger theme. Faulkner's literary style, characterized by such techniques as stream of consciousness, had not coalesced at the time of this novel's publication, and Yoknapatawpha County, Mississippi, had not emerged as the touchstone southern setting it would later become for him in his fiction. In retrospect, however, it is clear that Faulkner's grounding of a theme of postwar angst in southern geography—a theme that emerged as a primary concern of the modernist era—is just one of the qualities that made this novel more visionary, and even cutting edge, for its time than his early critics were able to recognize. Train rides that symbolically punctuate the beginning and end accentuate and center the novel's southern setting. The novel's structure is mainly linear, however. Lowe's extraneous placement in San Francisco, California, along with his epistolary and otherwise absent voice and body in the later chapters, further brings the South into relief as the primary setting in the novel while providing a pointed contrast with Mahon's present but wounded body and virtually absent voice.

The military's hierarchy feeds Lowe's and Gilligan's feelings of inadequacy as men. They associate Mahon's rank with maintaining racial privilege within the South's conventional social order, garnering favors with women, and being respected as a gentleman. Yet a plane crash has in effect neutralized the masculine virility that Mahon's eagle's wings symbolize. Fading from the first time that he makes an appearance in the novel, Mahon has been falsely reported as dead to his family and community. Once he returns to them, disfigured by his scar and going blind, he is virtually helpless, a ghost of his former self who speaks his name "like a parrot" (30).[1] Faulkner liberally evokes the image of the eye, precisely describing how all the characters look, stare, or gaze. Eyes clearly function as the window to the soul, are necessary and indispensable for understanding what characters truly think and feel, and draw attention to Mahon's disabling blindness.

Moreover, Faulkner establishes parallels between the military's hierarchy and the South's racial social order. The black porter on the train further helps to mark the South as a place in the novel—as well as its racial economy—through his language and voice. *Soldiers' Pay* reveals a portrait of the segregated racial landscape of the nation in the postwar period and demonstrates the acceptance of the South's social conventions in the North. This is a social hierarchy in which Gilligan desires more privilege. In Faulkner's novel, the alienation of blacks from American democracy is patently clear. To whatever degree that the raced, classed, and gendered ideology of the southern gentleman which had emerged in the antebellum era was attainable across the range of male subjects classed as white in the South, it wholly rejected and alienated black men. In some ways, this classic and coveted notion of the southern gentleman was contingent on the obverse of a degraded, disfranchised, and subjected black masculinity in the region. As the previous chapter suggests, that ideology nevertheless shaped the class and cultural ambitions of some elite black men, even if it was premised on their very exclusion. The desire among white men to be thus categorized typically signaled a yearning for the mythical Old South. The southern gentleman, like its white feminine analogue in the southern belle, was a typology that not only sustained the racial hierarchy in the South but also created distinctions and divisions among whites and demarcated some subjects as unwanted, undesirable, and inferior. *Soldiers' Pay* examines the lingering effects of subordination and subjection within the military on soldiers, particularly after the war, and the residual impact of war on the community, which is, in this case, mainly the South. But the conflicts and distinctions within the military relate to class and caste and, as they play out in the larger social world, exist exclusively among white men, the only soldiers represented. A view of blacks as a subordinate and excluded class in the South is evident in this novel. Blacks make marginal appearances as porters, maids, errand boys, and gardeners, and the novel emphasizes psychological struggles related to white masculinity. This theme recurs in several instances in Faulkner's fictional repertoire, perhaps most significantly in *Flags in the Dust*, where he highlights the Sartoris and Snopes clans to ponder class-based social disparities among whites and, through the use of flashback, provides a dialectical meditation on the Civil War and World War I. One would not imagine from a reading of *Soldiers' Pay* that black soldiers participated in the First World War. In considering Faulkner's scripting of black characters, his critics, of course, must be fair and recognize the particular society and world that shaped his vision. For instance, as Thadious Davis has pointed out, racial prejudices and blind spots in Faulkner's fiction, as well as his approaches to black characterization, mark the author as a product of his time and conditioning in a segregated, Jim Crow southern society in which blacks mainly occupied a servant class.[2] While the black male soldier is invisible and absent in the world that Faulkner creates, the complex psychic dramas that he relates to Mahon, Gilligan, and Lowe were quite conceivable among African American men in the military during and after the First World War and indeed, as Fuller's play reveals, did play out in ways that were similarly painful and tragic.

White malaise after the First World War was primarily related to fears of change in a modernizing and urbanizing nation and uncertainty about the future. It culminated in the poetics of a "lost generation" immortalized in fiction by such authors as Ernest Hemingway and F. Scott Fitzgerald. On the other hand, black postwar angst and disillusionment were in large measure fueled by continuing racism and Jim Crow inequalities and by the war's failure to expand the rights of blacks as citizens. Such leaders as W. E. B. Du Bois, as editor of the NAACP's *Crisis* magazine, encouraged African Americans to support the First World War to help ensure victory abroad and to expand democracy for blacks at home. African American soldiers carried a particularly onerous emotional, physical, and psychological burden both during and after the war. While they were drafted or enlisted as soldiers in spite of the opposition of white southern politicians to their participation in the war, they were typically limited to segregated units and commanded by white officers. The few blacks who became officers were not allowed to command white troops. The military's forced retirement of West Point graduate Colonel Charles Young from active service on the basis of a medical report suspected to be inaccurate, and designed to prevent his almost certain appointment to the rank of brigadier general, was the most infamous and notorious injustice suffered by a black officer during this time. Young rode his horse five hundred miles from home in Wilberforce, Ohio, to Washington, D.C., to demonstrate that he was in good health, an effort that was inspiring to many African Americans but futile in helping his case. If military doctors sabotaged the career of a northern man like Young, the health reports of black soldiers from the South had dire effects that have seldom been recognized. As I will illustrate in more detail later on, black southern soldiers were almost categorically marked as pathological by military officials. Moreover, the negative assessments of their physical bodies were complemented by skepticism about their intelligence and ability to perform in the heat of battle.

In some cities, black soldiers were celebrated and honored in majestic parades once they returned home. Perhaps none was as regal as the march of the Fifteenth Regiment of New York's National Guard down Fifth Avenue to Harlem on February 17, 1919, to the area that was emerging as the liveliest scene of African American art, literature, culture, and politics in the nation. Black soldiers typically met with a cool reception in the South and, after risking their lives to advance democracy abroad, incurred the wrath of whites deeply resentful of black men in uniform. In the worst cases, black soldiers were lynched while wearing their military regalia upon returning to the South. For those who had faced combat abroad, the threats to life and limb had become more visceral in their communities at home than they had ever been on the battlefields of Europe. In no other place in the nation did conflicts related to the convergence of race and masculinity play out with more brutality and intensity than on the black male body in the South. Black southern soldiers returning to a home where they were not appreciated or wanted were, in some respects, the most apt symbols of how bitterly the denial of citizenship and basic human rights persisted for blacks in this nation after the war.

As this chapter will illustrate, another bitter and perhaps much less obvious form of rejection experienced by some black soldiers from the South reflected anxieties about black southern identities that were escalating in the wake of the Great Migration. To discourage practices detrimental to racial uplift—such as wearing house slippers in public, using profanity, and talking loudly—the Urban League distributed pamphlets in the 1920s to African American southern migrants newly arrived in Detroit. Victoria Wolcott sees this attempt to regulate black southern behavior in a northern context as emblematic of the extent to which divisions among African Americans have been geographically constituted and, specifically, how black southerners have often been identified with a lower form of blackness and viewed as inimical to racial progress.[3] In the military, black soldiers from the South were treated as undesirables in some instances, and their experiences poignantly illustrated the role of region in constructing black masculinity. Drawing on psychoanalysis and, in the process, helping to facilitate a necessary dialogue between cultural geography and this field, David Sibley calls such "geographies of exclusion" the "social and spatial contexts of abjection," in which identities are marked as inferior, undesirable, or deviant on the basis of race, gender, sexuality, or other markers of difference.[4] Charles Fuller's drama *A Soldier's Play*, which echoes Faulkner's novel in its titling and at a thematic level, is a useful work to examine through this critical framework because the play reveals how politics of exclusion take shape in the African American context as well as ways in which they impact racial and gender formations. These thematic dimensions conform to Melvin Dixon's observation that "images of land and the conquest of identity serve as both a cultural matrix among various texts and a distinguishing feature of Afro-American literary history."[5] Condescending and ambivalent views of the U.S. South in the nation have persisted for various reasons, including the region's history of race relations, and have also shaped perceptions of black southerners. How and why the South came to be stigmatized as abject has captured the interest of contemporary scholars, who grapple with how the stigma has helped constitute categories of whites in the South as "hillbillies," "rednecks," and "white trash." But we also need to think increasingly about how African American hierarchies are constituted on a geographical basis.[6] The status of black identities within economies constituting the South as an ideological formation in the United States, along with the effects of such politics on black masculine and feminine formations, needs more critical attention.[7]

First presented by Douglas Turner Ward's Negro Ensemble Company on November 10, 1981, at Theatre Four in New York City, *A Soldier's Play* debuted just as conversations about the gap between the black middle classes and poor blacks were on the rise. Black crime in the United States was also rising at the time; the largest increase was in black male homicides at the hands of other black men. Here, Fuller fleshes out with more depth and complexity internecine struggles among blacks that he elaborated in his earlier but lesser-known play *Zooman and the Sign* (1980). The Republican right wing, under President Ronald Reagan, was inaugurating a program of political, legal, economic, social, and moral reform in the United States, prompting Amiri Baraka to complain that Fuller's play reinforced the prevailing conservatism of the time and pointed to the need for better African American access to theatrical institutions.[8] Baraka's dismissive reading obscures Fuller's assertive efforts in *A Soldier's Play* to grapple with issues ranging from the complexity of the African American relationship to white liberal politics to questions concerning how to succeed in a system in which anxieties over affirmative action were becoming more widespread and white masculinities were coming to be represented increasingly as threatened by and panicked about the prospect of displacement in the workforce by a range of minorities, including black men.[9] Still, that Baraka has been the only critic up to now to suggest Fuller's antinomies regarding black southerners in the play makes Baraka's analysis useful here. I believe that the problem of black southern representation in Fuller's play needs to be addressed more directly and elaborately, and doing so is one of my main goals in this chapter.

My critical emphasis on this play's plot necessitates a thorough and specific summary, which I want to pause and offer before proceeding any further with the discussion. Set at Fort Neal, a segregated military base in the fictional town of Tynin, Louisiana, in 1944, Fuller's two-act play draws on detection formulas and opens with the shooting death of Sergeant Vernon Waters. In a drunken stupor, Waters tells his hidden assailant: "They still hate you" (8). In the wake of his brutal and mysterious death, assumptions accrue: "Nobody colored killed the man!" (9); "the Klan did it" (10); and "colored soldiers aren't devious like that" (78).[10] Military officials bring in Captain Richard Davenport, a Howard University Law School graduate, to conduct an investigation. Poised and intelligent, he struggles to gain respect from condescending white officers at Fort Neal, including Captain Charles Taylor and Colonel Nivens, a conflict that forms a subtext in the play. We witness Captain Taylor, for example, wrestle with his feeling that "being in charge just doesn't look right on Negroes!" (20), including Davenport.

Past and present collide repeatedly within the play. Fuller illustrates this dynamic by using flashback as a narrative technique as Davenport's one-on-one interview sessions unfold with the men in Company B of the 221st Chemical Smoke Generating Company, an all-black unit. They include Corporal Bernard Cobb, PFC Melvin Peterson, Private Louis Henson, Private James Wilkie, and Private Tony Smalls. Two white officers outside the company, Lieutenant Byrd and Captain Wilcox, are also suspects. The interviews unveil an abusive Sergeant Waters who had given his men ample reason to retaliate. Several of them foreground Waters and C. J. Memphis, whom Waters had come to loathe in spite of his admiration for C. J.'s skills as a blues singer. C. J.'s extraordinary ability as a catcher kept his army teammates on a winning streak with the promise of playing the Yankees in exhibition. In the aftermath of a major team victory, the effort of the militant PFC Melvin Peterson—an Alabama native—to defend C. J. against Waters incites the sergeant's wrath and results in a brutal climactic fistfight between Waters and Peterson that the latter loses. Although Peterson is a southerner from Alabama, Waters respects him for his militaristic masculinism. Peterson, however, regards Waters as a sellout. While the tune "Don't Sit under the Apple Tree" by the Andrews Sisters can be heard overhead as acts open and yields further clues about the wartime setting, C. J.'s blues, which surface as an embedded leitmotif in the play, introduce most flashback episodes. It becomes apparent through the men's recollections that Waters had expected African Americans to be accorded civil rights upon their return to the United States after serving in the First World War. That frustrated expectation had turned into a twisted obsession with putting the best foot forward for purposes of racial uplift. Believing that African Americans from the urban North were the most acceptable exemplars of "the race" and those most likely to further the project of racial uplift, he harbored a hatred for black southerners. Through his angry outbursts and the abusive treatment of his men—especially C. J. Memphis—Waters conveys a fantasy of blackness that excludes southerners, whom he typecasts as uniformly poor, untrained, inarticulate, naïve, and embarrassing.

In act 2, Davenport's astute interviews continue and uncover more shocking details about Waters's troubled life. Davenport initially suspects Byrd and Wilcox of the murder, men who are flagrantly disrespectful and insubordinate. They admit that they encountered Waters on the road and beat him but insist they left him alive. Davenport is prepared to arrest them at the behest of an insistent Taylor, who is eager to conclude the investigation, until learning that Colonel Nivens had ballistics inspect the men's weapons on the night of Waters's murder and that the weapons had been cleared. A more probing interview with James Wilkie, who had been Waters's stooge, reveals that Wilkie deeply resented Waters for a demotion due to drunkenness on guard duty, which cost stripes that it had taken a decade to earn. Wilkie admits that Waters had eventually framed C. J. for the murder of a white soldier. From Bernard Cobb, another Mississippian, we learn that the disconsolate C. J. had been verbally tormented by Waters in jail and, bordering on insanity due to being contained, had committed suicide.

Davenport's final suspicions rest on Smalls and Peterson. Guard duty meant that they were the last men to get in the night that Waters was killed, and such an assignment would have placed weapons in their hands. Adding this insight to clues received along the way—such as the information that military-issued slugs had been removed from the body and that the Klan ordinarily removed stripes and insignia before lynching a soldier—Davenport determines that these two men are the likely assailants. This conclusion is confirmed all the more by their panicked escape in an attempt to avoid being questioned. In murdering Waters, Peterson avenges his brutal beating and also takes revenge "For C. J.! Everybody" (97). When Peterson is captured in Alabama, both men are sent to prison. When the play closes with Davenport's final soliloquy, Peterson and Smalls are on their way to prison and the remaining members of the company are deployed overseas to the war, the color line barring black men from combat having been lifted. All the men die in a surprise raid by Germans.

Like Faulkner, Fuller presents a lingering ghost figure that functions as a fetish around whom the action mainly revolves, along with an obsessive admirer who potentially wishes death on the innocent angel. While the play's echoes with *Soldiers' Pay* are fascinating (and Faulkner's novel serves as one useful context in American literary history to ponder), Fuller based *A Soldier's Play* on Herman Melville's 1891 novel *Billy Budd, Sailor*, whose title character is roughly parallel to C. J. Both characters are destroyed by military protocol enforced by the moral vision of a single high-ranking officer. But while Billy Budd is undisputedly the "sailor" referenced in Melville's title, critics have usually assumed that either Waters or Davenport is the likely "soldier" in Fuller's play's title. That Fuller provides so little room to imagine that this is a play about C. J. contributes to the elemental elision of C. J.'s subjectivity. This hierarchy has been reinforced in criticism on the play, which construes Waters or Davenport as the significant characters and implies C. J. to be more incidental to the action. Esther Harriott concludes that "Waters is Fuller's best creation thus far" and observes that his self-hatred makes him "more complex than the others."[11] Stanley Crouch points out that "a creation like Sergeant Vernon Waters is unlike what we are accustomed to seeing. He dominates *A Soldier's Play*, determining its reach and showing off Fuller's range."[12] Theater critics Edith Oliver and Joe Cunneen explicitly identify Waters as the character invoked in the title.[13] This logic has obscured the play's thematic engagement with its prominent southern figure, C. J. In Fuller's play, the angel hangs, to borrow Melvillean phrasing, in the form of the ever disembodied C. J., and the overriding question should be *why*. The elision of C. J.'s subjectivity, I shall argue, lies in the play's plot structure.

Not only has the main southern character, C. J., been ignored as a character, but the southern geography of this play has also largely been overlooked. The few critics who have written about the play acknowledge Waters's racial anxiety but not Fuller's reliance on the South as a structuring device for explaining it and for the setting. The play has been ignored in southern literature, probably because its conventional logic of canon formation would likely discount Fuller on the basis of his Philadelphia, Pennsylvania, birthplace. *A Soldier's Play* has not fared much better in African American literary studies. While Amiri Baraka was among its most vocal critics when it first appeared, the play has received cursory acknowledgment, if any at all, in the major critical and theoretical studies of African American drama.[14] Nor has the play found its way into the profusion of contemporary critical dialogues on masculinity, even with increased efforts in recent years to illustrate how race constitutes masculine formations.[15] Still, the critical analysis and representation of black men has been foremost on Fuller's literary agenda: "My concern throughout my work has been to depict African-Americans, especially African-American men, not as the stereotypes we have seen for years, but as we see ourselves."[16] That *A Soldier's Play* has been too seldom examined is perhaps most surprising in light of its Pulitzer Prize in Drama in 1982, the second dramatic work by an African American to be thus honored after Charles Gordone's *No Place to Be Somebody* (1969). In 1984 a film version of *A Soldier's Play* was produced by Norman Jewison, under the title *A Soldier's Story*. The screenplay by Fuller received an Academy Award nomination.

Recognizing the status of the South in the plot's development is crucial when considering the statement *A Soldier's Play* makes about the role of geography in helping to script versions of masculinity and blackness viewed as authentic and acceptable in the African American context. Fuller compellingly highlights anxieties among blacks over black southerners as well as disarticulations of black southerners from the category of black and from conventional notions of black masculinity. The play prompts us to move beyond generalities when it comes to thinking black men and toward an acknowledgment of geography as one of the numerous factors that make this category a highly variegated and guarded one in which not all models of black masculinity are accorded legibility or equal value. But one reason that the play has been critically neglected may be the ambiguity of its polemic. Fuller signals uncertainty, even ambivalence, about the role that black southern identities should play in constituting blackness as a concept.

This conflict is most evident in the fact that *A Soldier's Play* very purposefully offers a heroic and representative model of black manhood through strategies of embodying an urban northern man, Captain Richard Davenport, as a handsome, hotshot attorney who has the singular intelligence and muscle to go head to head with white military officers as he works to solve the mystery of Sergeant Waters's murder. At times, the play appears to critique ideologies of black southern folk romanticism that have been invoked to signify black racial authenticity within black modernist and nationalist aesthetics, as developed in the 1920s during the Harlem Renaissance and in the 1960s during the black-liberation era. But Fuller's play can also be seen as reconstituting authentic, desirable black subjectivity as male and necessarily urban—and urbane. In a play whose most fundamental conclusion, offered by Davenport, links the grim fates of its men to "the madness of race in America" (99), Fuller's attempt to dismantle the conventional scripts about race paradoxically culminates in the realignment of conventional patriarchal logic. The extent to which the categories urban northern and rural southern inform a logic of racial and gender distinction is most apparent in Fuller's masculinist construction of Davenport as the astute, confident lawyer and the containment of C. J. within "*the strange light of the past*" (26)—dead when the play begins. The resulting hierarchical formulation of black masculinity unwittingly construes black male southerners as weak, flawed, and expendable. Furthermore, the play's beginning, which commences with the dramatic death of Waters, contributes to C. J.'s displacement from the material world of the play and to his marginality within the plot. Fuller's play presents an interpretive quandary of major proportions due to its curious underlying equivocations. Through a deconstructive look at the play, however, we can recognize that C. J. is the primary catalyst for the sequence of events that makes the plot initiated by the death of Waters possible in the first place.

The racial politics of *A Soldier's Play* are enfolded, of course, in the U.S. military. If black men in the United States have come to carry the burden of overrepresentation in the military in terms of their draft and enlistment proportions since the Korean War, and if we now live in a time during which, as Richard Slotkin has observed, the nation's prevailing fantasy is one of interracial and interethnic harmony in the military, *A Soldier's Play* addresses the historical problem of segregation in the military and the subjection of black men to a rigid politics of exclusion.[17] Fuller confirms his ongoing preoccupation with history in interviews when he remarks that "I am a heavy reader of history" and "I'm concerned about history, and about human beings."[18] His fascination with military history has been most pronounced, beginning with his 1976 play entitled *The Brownsville Raid*. This work recreates the incident at Fort Lee, Texas, in 1906 entailing the dishonorable discharge of 167 men by order of President Theodore Roosevelt, including six men who held medals of honor, due to allegations that they fired shots into a civilian community. Like *A Soldier's Play*, it highlights racial tensions.[19] Fuller continues the tradition in African American literature of treating the intersection of the military, race, and the psychology of the African American soldier that such authors as Junius Edwards, John A. Williams, Gwendolyn Brooks, and John Oliver Killens have addressed in the past. William Wells Brown established the foundation for this tradition in his inaugural study of African Americans in the military, *The Negro in the American Rebellion* (1867).[20]

A Soldier's Play relates Waters's abusive treatment of C. J. and appraisal of him as an "ignorant, low-class geechy" (39) and a "fool" (73) who can "barely read and write his own name" (90) to the stringent and highly specific politics of exclusion to which black men from the South were subjected, as revealed, for instance, in Colonel E. D. Anderson's report entitled "Disposal of the Colored Drafted Men" that the War Plans Division released on May 16, 1918, on behalf of the Operations Branch. The report is perhaps one of the most useful documents that we have for understanding the hierarchical culture of the American military, which separated blacks and whites and facilitated the abuse of power that Waters embodies. The systemic distinctions in this hierarchy were based on region and focused on a "day laborer class" of soldiers roughly equivalent to the "backwoods Negro." Anderson repeatedly describes these draftees as "unfit," "ignorant," and low in intelligence and skill, several times remarking their inferiority to the "cream of the colored draft." Ruminating on their high rates of disease, he offers a percentage breakdown of their afflictions, including "hernia," "tuberculosis," "rheumatism," "extreme flat foot," and "syphilis," all of which rendered them unsuitable for deployment overseas. According to Anderson, "The enemy is constantly looking for a weak place in the line and if he can find a part of the line held by troops composed of culls of the colored race, all he has to do is to concentrate on that, break through and then he will be in rear of high class troops who will be at a terrible disadvantage" (DCDM

191–92).[21] Anderson implies that black troops from the South lack the physical wherewithal—and really the courage and intelligence—to fight against hardy "opposing German troops who consist of men of high average education and thoroughly trained" (191).

Anderson drew the information in his report from several medical reports, including one from the surgeon general revealing that approximately 50 percent of black southern draftees had venereal diseases. He concluded that "the physical condition of these negroes is very poor" and recommended that such "unfit" men be eliminated and prevented from embarking overseas for service (192–93). Anderson's suggested strategy is to assign these black draftees to reserve labor battalions to keep them out of trouble, give them useful work to do, and allow them the privilege of medical treatment for their venereal diseases: "The colored men instead of laying around camps accomplishing nothing of value, getting sicker and sicker and in trouble generally, are kept out of trouble by being kept busy at useful work and there is a chance for recommendation of the colored men as the Medical Department can be working on them in the meanwhile, curing them of venereal and other diseases and putting them in shape" (193). He assumes that white soldiers are more capable of and prepared for service overseas, arguing that his strategy will in turn release them from labor battalions for full-time combat instruction.

Anderson reasons that although the "backwoods" soldiers are inferior, they must be conscripted for the purpose of labor during "these days of conservation, when every rag, bone and tin can is saved" (195). Meanings of the term *disposal* that refer to "placement" and "distribution" are ostensibly invoked in the title of Anderson's report. However, if we consider Julia Kristeva's now classic theoretical elaboration of the abject as that which is "jettisoned" and "radically excluded," especially in light of contemporary cultural geographers' uses of her work in psychoanalysis to examine spaces that are constituted as undesirable, the report's construal of black southern soldiers as expendable and undesirable combatants also makes resonant the meanings of *disposal* as a throwing away or getting rid of waste. Indeed, Kristeva frames the Second World War, in light of its suffering and horror, as a quintessential scene of abjection and ponders the possibilities for its representation in literature, concluding that literature "represents the ultimate coding of our crises, of our most intimate and serious apocalypses."[22] Formulations of poor, usually rural whites as "white trash"—an epithet that placed this purportedly degenerate and pathological category at the bottom of the social hierarchy of whiteness—exist in a continuum with the military's pathologizing, class-based formulation of black men in the South. Both ideologies were based on geography and, in their respective ways and times, reinforced the region's platform of white supremacy that consolidated in the late nineteenth century.[23] During the war, black southern soldiers' appropriation for work in labor camps to compensate for the absence of white manpower overseas was a gross parallel in some ways, of course, to the absorption of black migrants into the northern wartime labor market due to the labor shortage and the decline in European immigration.

The plan that Anderson offers also has the flavor of a civilizing mission: "This will be the first time in their lives that 9 of 10 negroes ever had any discipline, instruction, or medical treatment, or lived under sanitary conditions and they should improve greatly" (193). Furthermore, we must remember that "Disposal of the Colored Drafted Men" held implications for the vast majority of black servicemen in the United States, for although the Great Migration in the 1920s had already begun to shift the balance of the African American population to cities in the North, most blacks still lived in the South at the time the report was issued. "The negroes mainly come from the southern states," Anderson notes.

> It would be a saving of transportation to assemble the drafted negroes in camps nearest their homes and organize them into labor battalions and put them to work. Each southern state had negroes in blue overalls working throughout the state with a pick and shovel . . . . When these colored men are drafted they are put in blue overalls (fatigue clothes) and continue to do work with a pick and shovel where they were working previously. (199)

Anderson implies that the "day laboring class" has been seasoned by the predominant labor practices in southern contexts for the type of work that he is recommending they undertake in the military. As Arthur E. Barbeau and Florette Henri have pointed out, Anderson fundamentally proposes that these southern draftees "serve in the military equivalent of chain gangs."[24] Because the men were mainly from the South, he explicitly states that the issue of race prejudice is irrelevant in their consignment to labor. Historically, the American military institutionalized the expropriation of a laboring class that was disproportionately black and male, extending into the twentieth century the egregious convict lease practices that had been pervasive in the South during the Reconstruction era and anticipating machinations decried by critics of the prison-industrial complex in the contemporary era, such as Angela Davis.[25] If many black soldiers in the South were in some ways indeed "unfit" for military service, then their detractors were slow to recognize that a social and political infrastructure that insistently denied educational opportunities to blacks in the region and sabotaged efforts to establish a viable and integrated public school system was in some measure to blame.

The military's assertive stigmatizing of black soldiers from the South and its preference for northern soldiers during World War I represented a sound reversal of logic that had existed just a few generations earlier during the Civil War, as evidenced in Colonel Thomas Wentworth Higginson's *Army Life in a Black Regiment*. Higginson charges northern troops, both black and white, with a tendency to flee from wartime service because they had much less at stake than the black southern soldier.

> The question was often asked, whether the Southern slaves or the Northern free blacks made the best soldiers. . . . I preferred those who had been slaves, for their greater docility and affectionateness, for the powerful stimulus which their new freedom gave, and for the fact that they were fighting, in a manner, for their own homes and firesides. Every one of these considerations afforded a special aid to discipline, and cemented a peculiar tie of sympathy between them and their officers. They seemed like clansmen, and had a more confiding and filial relation to us than seemed to me to exist in the Northern colored regiments.[26]

Higginson's stated preferences for black southern soldiers, which reflects a view of them as submissive and servile—and is amplified in his repeated references to them as childlike—draws on the plantation myth and obscures their agency during the war, even if it invokes with a degree of accuracy the subject positions of black southerners who, in their day-to-day material lives, had been subordinated into what is now popularly referred to among black nationalists as a "slave mentality" through systemic forms of white surveillance, patrol, and discipline in the South aimed at stifling any and all signs of rebellion. Indeed, foremost on the agenda of W. E. B. Du Bois's *Black Reconstruction in America: 1860–1880* is an attempt to clarify the pivotal role that subaltern actions of black slaves in the South played not only in catalyzing the Civil War but also in disrupting plantation economies of the

South through frequent desertions, once the war began, through a "general strike."[27] The role of black men as workers in the military, of course, further illustrates the organic and even constitutive relation of African Americans to the history of labor in the United States and has important implications for dialogues in contemporary labor studies.

Anderson's report came in the wake of the 1915 release of D. W. Griffith's *Birth of a Nation* into the national context, whose ideological representations of black men in the South as political incompetents and bestial rapists, as I acknowledge in chapter 1, were the focal point. Even more important, Anderson's report should be situated in relation to the descriptions of black soldiers and officers as inferior and insufficiently skilled that were widely generated in the aftermath of World War I by such figures as Allan Greer, Gen. W. H. Hay, and Charles Ballou as part of an agenda to achieve downsizing in the United States military.[28] As Ulysses Lee points out in his monumental study *The Employment of Negro Troops*, policies generated in the First World War, including those that explicitly invoked southern soldiers, had residual effects in the Second World War, which is, again, the larger context for the action in *A Soldier's Play*. In his words, "The army, basing its theory on World War I test scores and actual distribution of skills among Negroes, desired proportionately more Northern than Southern Negroes for technical and combat units."[29] Arguments like those offered in Anderson's report provided support and further justification for a politics of segregation that was normative in the American military and in the South more broadly and reinforced a view of black southern men as pathological, diseased, and expendable. Apparently drawing from this same ideology to justify its medical mission, the now infamous Tuskegee study clandestinely conducted by the U.S. Public Health Service for forty years (1932–72) assessed the effects of the syphilis virus on a group of 399 black men in the Tuskegee, Alabama, area by withholding standard medical treatment.[30] Anderson's report, including his recommendation that southern black soldiers be singled out for medical treatment, reveals that black men's bodies in the South were viewed as pathological and abject by the military and suggests that the climate was being primed in the region for such a perverse medical experiment at least a decade before it actually began. It seems clear that taxonomies generated within the American military for classifying black men, implicitly and explicitly schematizing them thorough a North-South dichotomy, in effect enabled a scripting of the black southern male body as inferior and revealed ways in which differences based on class, along with invocations of region, worked in constituting the nation's discourses on race.

These historical military ideologies are re-created in *A Soldier's Play* and have special implications for a black rural southern character like C. J. Memphis. They become all the more plausible when recalling that even nowadays the American military, notwithstanding higher interracial marriage rates than the mainstream, remains one of the most inhospitable contexts for negotiating nonnormative racial, gender, and sexual identities—as indicated by issues that have been highlighted in the national media over the past decade like the sexual harassment of women by high-ranking officials, hate crimes based on racial and ethnic background, and the notorious "Don't Ask, Don't Tell" policy. Moreover, even the military's efforts in the contemporary era to enlist recruits with more education to handle the increasingly sophisticated new defense technologies designed to maintain American dominance within the global arena may affect the promotion potential of volunteers who have been predominately minority and working class and demonstrates this institution's condescending historical logic. Fuller, a veteran of black theater who most notably co-founded and directed the Afro-American Arts Theater in Philadelphia, has written short stories, poetry, and essays and spent four years in the United States Army in both Japan and Korea. The latter experience perhaps also shapes the play and points to other regional and ethnic contexts for which the history of the American military has implications in constituting discourses of race.

One of the ways in which Fuller has become known in his career has been his close friendship with Black Arts proponent Larry Neal. *A Soldier's Play* asserted Fuller's role in redefining the possibilities for black theater in the postmodern era, which included radically rethinking the philosophy of the Black Aesthetic and challenging conventional ways of thinking about black identity that were based on a monolithic view of black community. In grappling with the complex African American geographical landscape of the early twentieth century, Fuller affirms the salience of black folk identities such as C. J.'s to the definition of blackness and attempts to move beyond the romantic folk fetishes of the Black Aesthetic. This move had a parallel when the play was released in the early 1980s among black literary theorists and critics in the academy who were helping to reshape the contours of African American literary studies by drawing on poststructuralist theory to examine black texts through the lens of the vernacular and, in the process, were challenging essentialist formulations of black identity.[31] Although Fuller succeeds in illustrating the complexity of African American identity by highlighting internal racial conflict and debunking stereotypes, he ultimately falls short of offering an inclusive model of black identity in terms of geography and gender and links the most desirable blackness to an economically privileged and educated urban elite.

In her essay entitled "Writing the Absent Potential: Drama, Performance, and the Canon of African-American Literature," Sandra Richards argues that drama has been marginal and excluded in critical studies of African American literature. She relates this problem to a range of factors, including the peripheral status of drama within Western literature and the volatile position of theater and drama departments within academic institutions. Yet Richards suggests that drama is indispensable for studying the category of the folk so frequently highlighted in African American literary criticism. In her words, "The critical tradition within African American literature locates 'authentic' cultural expression on the terrain of the folk, but the folk have articulated their presence most brilliantly in those realms with which literature is uncomfortable, namely in areas centered in performance."[32] As a remedy, Richards stresses the importance of recognizing drama as an "absent potential" within African American literary criticism whose "latent intertexts," which emerge in performance, must be acknowledged to complement the obsession with the written word among the field's critics. By Richards's logic, a drama like Fuller's is an ideal and appropriate medium in which to represent black folk identities while at the same time critiquing African American folk romanticism. But *A Soldier's Play* illustrates that even drama will not necessarily ensure a subjective presence and clarity for black folk characters. Instead, a range of factors, including plot and characterization, makes all the difference.

If nothing else, however, it seems true that because of its reliance on dialogue, methodical descriptions of action, and attention to setting, drama is a fitting genre in which to bring into bold relief historical intramural conflicts among blacks related to geography as well as interracial tensions. The embrace of this medium even seems symbolic if we consider that, temporally, the play spans the interwar years, a period when drama began to gain mainstream popularity in the United States. While Fuller emerged as a playwright working largely out of the mainstream, his play extends and finesses the emphasis on social commentary—giving it specificity for

African American life and culture—that had become dominant in American drama by the mid-twentieth century. And that Fuller was born in Philadelphia, one of the earliest and most successful venues for drama in the United States, made the scripting of such a powerful play a fitting destiny for him indeed. By examining *A Soldier's Play*, we can see how the ideological portrait of the sexually neutralized and docile "Uncle Tom" and related types that emerged in the antebellum era and the black rapist that surfaced in the late nineteenth century were merely foundational in the establishment of a much broader and persistent spectrum for representing the black male body in the South as abject and pathological. While southern-based stereotypes of black men have not been as saliently enunciated or signaled as graphically as the specter of lynching ideologically manifested the myth of the black rapist beginning in the late nineteenth century, and the world of theater and advertising materialized the docile "Uncle Tom," Fuller's play helps illustrate how raced and gendered ideologies of black masculinity with geographical specificity persisted in the twentieth century.

Geography and Black Identity

The potential of geography to shape essentialist and exclusionary notions of black subjectivity, and the role of region in constituting discourses of race, are important concerns in *A Soldier's Play*. It is in part through the strategy of invoking the role of geography in African American identity formations that Fuller achieves the array of intricate and innovative characterizations for which the play has been critically acclaimed. The stage directions that stipulate the positioning of platforms at varying levels materialize the hierarchy of the military and the disparate ranks among the play's characters. Still, making all areas easily accessible to all characters suggests the importance of a community's inclusiveness. The precise number of characters, twelve, which is the requisite number for a jury, seems purposeful in light of Fuller's intention to evoke the look and feel of a courtroom. The setting on the imaginary southern base in Louisiana works to intensify racial conflicts, for in addition to the subordinate treatment black soldiers experience there, they are also frequent victims of lynching by the Klan in the local community of Tynin. The situation is so extreme that some of the men in the unit presume that Waters was the victim of a lynching, and Henson believes that facing the battlefields of Europe would be better than remaining in the South. Lighting not only is the main device for differentiating the two primary spaces in the play—the barracks and the office that Davenport uses—but also marks the distinction between past and present. That the barracks feature a poster of the boxer Joe Louis dressed as a soldier and the office features a picture of President Franklin D. Roosevelt on the wall signals the racial differences among white and black soldiers.

A Soldier's Play suggests a connection between the institutionalized abuse that Waters has experienced within a range of white-supremacist military contexts and his daily interactions with African American enlisted men from the South, to which higher-ranking white officers on the base are entirely oblivious. Fuller illustrates this connection most revealingly by tracing Waters's contempt for black southerners back to an episode in a nightclub in France during World War I. Resenting that African American soldiers had been awarded medals, which might make them attractive to "French gals" and threaten the American taboo against interracial sex, the white soldiers orchestrated an impromptu performance, in minstrel-show fashion, that featured a compliant "ignorant colored soldier" enacting the racist stereotype of black men as animals: "They sat him on a big, round table in the Café Napoleon, put a reed in his hand, a crown on his head, a blanket on his shoulders, and made him eat bananas in front of them Frenchies. And ohhh, the white boys danced that night—passed out leaflets with that boy's picture on them—called him Moonshine, King of the Monkeys" (90). Pinning a tail to the actor, they encourage him to "parade around naked making monkey sounds" (90). The dehumanizing and pathological view of the black male body and sexuality that Waters describes accords with scripts of black men in the late nineteenth century as bestial rapists who posed a danger to white women in the South. Phillipa Levine has pointed out that during World War I, mechanisms of social control were mutually leveled at white women and black soldiers, whose sexual proclivities were viewed as analogously excessive and pathological within the project of imperial racism.[33] By recuperating and upholding within a European context the conventional taboos and sanctions against interracial sex and humiliating their African American comrades who have just been awarded medals, the white soldiers underscore the abject status of black soldiers in the American military. In real life, this problem was, of course, most patently evident in the widespread lynching of black soldiers in the South after the war ended.

During World War I the military expressly propagated a pathological view of the black male body and sexuality at an institutional level. In response to the concern among American military officials that blacks were being treated as social equals in France and were fraternizing too frequently with white women, the French colonel Linard issued a document entitled "Secret Information Concerning Black American Troops" to some French officers and civilian officials. The document explained the importance of maintaining black and white social separation to discourage "race mongrelization" in the United States and curtailing excessive praise of black accomplishments in the military, particularly in front of white Americans. Furthermore, it urged white officers to limit their contact with black officers. It incited outcry when read by M. René Boisneuf before the French National Assembly in July 1919, who also cited instances of abuse of black soldiers by white American MP's, including "cases where blacks whom the French had decorated for bravery had subsequently been abused, beaten, and even murdered."[34] This document was among those that revealed widespread panic among white army officers about sexual contact between black men and white women and indicated how the military was instrumental in propagating the myth of black men as rapists. Like Anderson's report, which highlighted health issues, it reveals ways in which the black male body was viewed as pathological and perverse in the military and illustrates how sexual ideologies that originated in the South were the germ for stereotyping all black men in the nation.

Paradoxically, as Petrine Archer-Straw has pointed out, the perception of blackness in France, and in Paris in particular, was complex enough that blackness also served as a primary signifier of the modern.[35] During the decade following World War I, Paris emerged as a premier scene of African American artistic development in tandem with Harlem. Black American soldiers played an important role in helping to establish this connection. According to Michel Fabre,

Until the Great War the myth of French culture and hospitality prevailed mainly among the black elite. In America the popular black press more often vaunted French racial liberalism—so much so that when the First World War broke out great numbers of blacks volunteered to defend the 'land of democracy.' In 1917 hundreds of thousands of them landed in France. Despite American military regulations that forbade fraternizing, these soldiers established relationships with French fighters and with local people. This was their first taste of true equality. . . . The soldiers brought over jazz. . . . They took back home an image of the tolerance and generosity shown to blacks in France.[36]

More recently, Brent Hayes Edwards has pointed out that Paris served as the epicenter for the production of a modernist and transnational model of blackness in the interwar years.[37] In the United States, where Harlem was mecca for black artistic development, the South was a key site with which many blacks grappled in attempting to forge an artistic sensibility, to define notions of blackness during the modernist era, and to develop agendas for black uplift. The flashback scenes to France in Fuller's play well suggest the utility of examining the South in relation to global and transnational contexts, a strategy that has increasingly informed critical and theoretical approaches in southern studies in recent years.

In reflecting on his father's experiences in the army, Henry Louis Gates Jr. speaks to the military's diverse black regional demographics:

> Daddy's major contact with Negro cultures from Elsewhere had been in the army, at Camp Lee, Virginia. He used to tell us all kinds of stories about the colored troops at Camp Lee, especially blacks from the rural South. It was clear that the army . . . had been a great cauldron, mixing the New Negro culture, which had developed in the cities since the great migration of the twenties and thirties, and the Old Negro culture, the remnants of the traditional rural black culture in the South.[38]

Gates's observations, and particularly his capitalization of "Elsewhere," signal geography as a distinct marker within the category of blackness and as instrumental in fashioning notions of black racial selfhood. That the military's mixing of blacks from the rural South and the urban North could also prove to be volatile is illustrated in Fuller's creation of the nightclub spectacle in France, which ends with the murder of the black soldier from the South by Waters and other outraged African American soldiers from the North: "And when we slit his throat, you know that fool asked us what he had done wrong?" (90). Furthermore, Fuller's scene also acknowledges racial conflicts related to heightened levels of interracial interaction between black and white men in the military.

That Waters sees in C. J. the "ignorant colored soldier" in the nightclub of the past is clear when he visits C. J. in the stockade after framing him for murder.

There use ta be a time when we'd see somebody like you, singin', clownin',—yas-sah-bossin'—and we wouldn't do anything. . . . Folks liked that—you were good—homey kinda' niggah—they paraded you, reminded them of the old days—corn-bread bakin', greens and ham cookin',—Daddy out pickin' cotton, Grandmammy sit on the front porch smokin' a pipe. . . . Not no more. The day of the geechy is gone, boy—the only thing that can move the race is power. It's all the white respects—and people like you just make us seem like fools. And we can't let nobody go on believin' we all like you! You bring us down—make people think the whole race is unfit! (72–73)

C. J. epitomizes a blackness that Waters perceives as bygone and necessary to disown for integration into a modernizing nation. Waters begrudges black southerners a role in defining African American identity in the United States and implies African Americans from the urban North to be the most acceptable exemplars of "the race" and those most likely to further the project of black uplift. His fantasy of black racial selfhood is elitist and premised on a view of blacks from the rural South as uniformly poor, untrained, inarticulate, and illiterate. As historian Kevin K. Gaines points out in *Uplifting the Race: Black Leadership, Politics and Culture in the Twentieth Century*, "An elite self-image that might overcome powerlessness and racial stigmas perhaps required the displacement of feelings of anger and shame onto other powerless blacks, or perhaps rival elites, even in the name of racial uplift."[39]

Notwithstanding the Croix de Guerre that he earned, we learn that Waters is deeply disappointed over the lack of change after the First World War, a history that profoundly shapes his hopes for improving the possibilities for black upward mobility. Waters believes that emulating the speech and thinking of "white folks" will bring their approval and open the way to social advancement. This philosophy of black racial uplift is also shaped by Waters's conditioning within a hierarchical military and by his embrace of notions of meritocracy. He runs the 221st Chemical Smoke Generating Company "like it was a chain gang" (33), demotes Wilkie, and plans to promote Peterson. However, Fuller points to the idealism and hopelessness of this outlook by stressing this character's obliviousness to the persisting politics of American racism and segregation that relegate the company to menial tasks on the base and exclude black soldiers from combat abroad. Furthermore, Fuller uses Waters's racial delusions and blind spots to highlight the irony in this character's scripting of C. J. as naïve. C. J., for instance, seems to understand Waters's racial dilemma with more depth and clarity than other men in the unit. He brushes off the harsh diatribes and admits to Peterson that he feels sorry for Waters because "Any man ain't sure where he belongs must be in a whole lotta pain" (45). Waters is the character in the play who undergoes the most radical transformation by concluding that his accommodations to white supremacy will not gain him acceptance or approval and vowing not to obey white authority anymore. Peterson fails to recognize this breakthrough and brashly takes Waters's life before the lessons can be put into practice. Indeed, the play suggests that Peterson was naïve and impulsive when it came to Waters and that the fight was ill conceived. For although time might be easily overlooked as a factor in organizing action in the play, it is significant that Peterson was the man with the least knowledge of Waters in the company and confronted him a month after first arriving. Peterson's flashback scene is the longest and most detailed in the play, however, and marks the climax by representing the turning point at which the character Waters sinks into unremitting ruthlessness and cruelty. In general, the play incorporates a range of temporal gaps that we are forced to imagine or fill in as a supplement to witnessing the flashbacks that come in interviews with Davenport.

In thinking about possibilities for reformulating the definition of blackness, Waters chooses a particular region—the urban North—as the dominant site of black identification. He links this region to black survival and perseverance, a north-south binary schema that parallels his hierarchical valuation of black and white identities. In *Displacement, Diaspora and Geographies of Identity*, Smadar Lavie and Ted Swedenberg discuss the need to move beyond conventional geographical models that perpetuate "the notion that there is an immutable link between cultures, peoples, or identities and specific places." Lavie and Swedenberg go on to comment that

> The confidence in [a] permanent join between a particular culture and a stable terrain has served to ground our modern governing concepts of nations and cultures. In these still powerful conceptual frameworks, there is a homology between a culture, a people, or a nation and its particular terrain, and both the culture and its associated place are regarded as homogeneous in relation to other cultures/places (even if those are characterized by internal differentiation). A series of related spatially conceived hierarchical

dualities have flowed from and depended upon this mode of conceiving culture and nation.[40]

The critique of static alignments of cultural categories and geographies has implications for pondering ideologies that constitute the urban North as the preferential site of black identification in the play. As a counterpoint to the recognition of the South as a historical scene of trauma and terror, many African Americans have romantically imagined the South as an ancestral home.[41] However, Fuller reveals how perceptions of black rural southerners as the quintessence of blackness and racial historicity in the United States were counterbalanced by displacements and disavowals of such identities within black-uplift ideology of the early twentieth century.

Fuller relates Waters's geographically exclusionary definition of blackness and his project of racial uplift to the irony in his words and actions, an approach that further develops the theme of internal conflict among African Americans. In spite of his own humiliation when white soldiers in France mocked the decorations he and his compatriots had earned, Waters reacts to his men's hard-earned victory in baseball over a white team that had cheated by barking orders at them to paint the lobby of the segregated Officers Club, in effect reinforcing and perpetuating the politics of Jim Crow. Waters's actions become all the more ironic when we recognize that, although he has taken ten years' worth of stripes from Wilkie because of drunkenness on guard duty, critiques the "bowin' and scrapin'" of "Southern niggahs" (40), and assesses C. J. as "a clown in blackface" (97), it is Waters who appears "stinking drunk" and "on his knees, wallowing in self-pity" before Byrd and Wilcox (8, 79), who smiles a coon smile and dances a juba for them, and who attempts to tell them a story that they don't want to hear. The racial epithets that he hurls at his men such as "niggah" and "boy" reveal an interest in appropriating the trappings of white patriarchal power. He uses this language with even more force to malign black soldiers from the South, reinforcing the perception of C. J. as infantile and boylike and black soldiers from the South as undesirable and inferior solely on the basis of geography. He complements this linguistic violence by brutally beating Peterson ("to put a wise-ass Alabama boy" in his place [40]). The militant Peterson had come to the defense of C. J. after Waters insulted him following their victory over the white baseball team. Eventually, Waters arrests C. J. on false charges in an effort to "git rid of you [black Southerners] wherever I go" (73).

One of the things that Waters most resents is C. J.'s "country" style of speaking, yet his own language is not highly superior to it. The play's dialogue itself, if read or heard carefully, repeatedly emphasizes Waters's imperfect diction and, in particular, his tendency to drop word endings. A fifth-grade education limits his expression, despite his father's insistence on enunciating. Waters's language drives the violence, the most intense action in the play. His use of racial epithets, coupled with false murder charges, leads C. J. to hit him reflexively in the barracks, the same verbal violence that led to the fight with Peterson. Waters's cutting words, more than anything, incite the attack on him in the encounter with Byrd and Wilcox, a scene in which his language ostensibly incorporates black dialect: "My daddy said, 'Don't talk like dis'—talk like that!' 'Don't live hea'—live there!'" (53). Most significantly, we should recognize that if Peterson's gunfire reflects rage against Waters that has been building for months, it most directly attempts to silence Waters's taunting phrase, "They'll still hate you" (8), which is only fully explained at play's end when this scene is repeated. Furthermore, language is a primary feature that the play uses to draw distinctions among its range of characters. Waters uses a colloquial style of speaking with his African American unit that has the effect of reiterating their subjection, degradation, and isolation by him on the base. On the other hand, Davenport, as Taylor points out, "sounds white," and in the play's dialogue his English is almost unfailingly standard, like that of the white characters Taylor, Byrd, and Wilcox.

When we further dissect the play, however, we recognize that C. J. alone utters a word that plants the wrenching seed for Fuller's plot: Crow. On the surface, it is C. J.'s response to Taylor's question, "How the hell'd you get up so high?" to make the catch during the baseball game. C. J. frames this word with traces of black dialect in the sentence, "They say I got 'Bird' in mah blood, sir" (43). That he shamelessly makes this claim in a segregated army to a white male, begins to tell a story about it—"Man tol' my daddy the day I was born, the shadow of a crow's wings" (43)—before Taylor cuts him off, and rejects the American eagle that Taylor had hoped he would mention, according to the stage directions, makes Waters move to stop him and several men uncomfortable. When Taylor leaves, their focus is fully on C. J. However, Waters's reaction is most visceral. This scene describes him as "standing on 'eggs'" while C. J. talks to Taylor. That Waters witnesses this scene is the final nail in C. J.'s coffin and in his own. I want to suggest—

particularly in light of the drama contexts under study in this discussion and contemporary critical efforts to link language theory on performativity and the realm of theater—that C. J.'s word has a performative effect by calling up for Waters the scene in Café Napoleon and catalyzes the chain of action that consumes the both of them, including his plot to frame C. J. Its utterance takes Waters back to the degrading night in France. The very word *crow* recalls the song "Jump Jim Crow," performed by Thomas "Daddy" Rice, the father of American minstrelsy. Rice, inspired by a slave, blackened his face and inaugurated the minstrel tradition in 1828. Waters explicitly makes reference to this practice several times when he refers to C. J. as a "clown in blackface." Furthermore, the term *crow* evokes the colloquial name for the systemic segregation of public facilities—"Jim Crow"—that was adopted in the wake of the Supreme Court ruling in *Plessy v. Ferguson* in 1896. The crow, like the monkey, has been an animal associated with some of the most degrading and dehumanizing images of African Americans in the white racist mind. C. J.'s embrace of the crow registers in much the same way that the complicit southerner's embrace of the monkey in France had for Waters, and the two stereotypes are intricately connected. The word *shadow* adds another layer of meaning here if we consider the history of this word as a derogatory reference for blacks. Both *shadow* and *crow* are historical color slurs. The sense of the verb form of *crow* that refers to a "shrill cry" also speaks to C. J.'s seemingly innate ability to sing and play the blues. Just as this scene describes C. J.'s catch from a position in "center field," "Crow" maps the center in the world of the play. Its trace, and by extension, C. J.'s, secures the plot that ostensibly revolves around Waters's death and Davenport's investigation. C. J. thus functions in a way akin to Toni Morrison's Beloved, who, as Mae Henderson puts it, is "the trace (the mark left behind) that initiates the novel's plot." The texture of its language in these moments energizes and intensifies *A Soldier's Play* as a drama.

It is telling that Waters mocks the front porch along with the work and diet that he stereotypically associates with black southerners. For when he was stationed in Mississippi, he relished the "dancin'," "sweatin'," and "shoutin'" at a juke joint called the Bandana Club, perhaps precisely because its sights and sounds evoked city space in some ways. The emphasis on domestic space and a model of family in his diatribe well suggest the genocidal character of his project, for he views them as threatening in light of their potential to signify the South as a symbolic home in the African

American context and disrupt his ideal of the urban North. Waters's genocidal project of racial purification through eliminating blacks from the South is an example of a project of racial uplift gone horribly wrong. While Waters provides a basis for examining class distinctions embedded in African American racial-uplift ideologies, Fuller explicitly links Waters's rationale for eradicating black southerners to the Nazi elimination of Jews during World War II. In formulating a "psychoanalysis of space," cultural geographer Steve Pile invokes the trauma of the Holocaust to illustrate how abjection as a phenomenon aligns the human subject simultaneously with the spatial, the bodily, and the social.[42] These insights are useful for approaching the salience of geography for Waters's constitution of a category of the inferior and alien and for understanding why Waters inflicts abuse on bodies that are already subjected to cruel forms of discipline and containment. In a larger sense, the play also connects these attacks on black southerners to the ritual of lynching and other systemic violence at the hands of those invested in upholding the South's ethos of white supremacy during and after Reconstruction.

After Waters succeeds in eliminating C. J., he is haunted by memories of him, and, out of guilt, he begins to drink heavily. The levels on which the play intimately connects Waters and C. J.—and reinforces this link through the simultaneity of their presentation in several flashback scenes—line up with Kristeva's formulation of the abject as that which confuses the border between the "I" and the "Other" and poses a challenge from a site of banishment: "The abject has only one quality of the object—that of being opposed to I. If the object, however, through its opposition, settles me within the fragile texture of a desire for meaning, which, as a matter of fact, makes me ceaselessly and infinitely homologous to it, what is abject, on the contrary, the jettisoned object, is radically excluded and draws me toward the place where meaning collapses."[43] In pondering the value of Kristeva's theory for cultural geography, David Sibley underscores the importance of locating the individual in a social and material world to understand how a generalized other can be created whose exclusion in a space becomes part of the definition of a "self." According to Sibley, Kristeva's view of the abject as a presence that continually looms and lingers even after its presumed annihilation "points to the importance of anxiety, a desire to expel or to distance from the abject other as a condition of existence. This hovering presence of the abject gives it significance in defining relationships to others."[44] Waters believes that black racial uplift and survival are contingent on the elimination of C. J., who is seen not only as an individual "you" but also as a "you" in the abstract (i.e., synonymous with the man branded "Moonshine, King of the Monkeys") who represents the larger and much derided category of black southerners whom "I try to git rid of . . . wherever I go" (73). For precisely these reasons, even after his death C. J. is a character with whom Waters wages an ongoing and inescapable metaphysical battle.

Along with an intimate association with the land, the Farmer's Dust that C. J. wears around his neck and offers Peterson as a folk mechanism for ensuring victory in the fight with Waters after the baseball game is the most salient symbol of C. J.'s abjection. As Sibley notes, "Exclusionary discourse draws particularly on color, disease, animals, sexuality and nature, but they all come back to the idea of dirt as a signifier of imperfection and inferiority, the reference point being the white, often male, physically and mentally able person."[45] If we recall Anderson's thinking regarding the appropriate work for black soldiers from the rural South, C. J.'s association with a team charged to do "the dirty work on the post-garbage-clean-up" (24)—a team whose members joke that mops, dishrags, and paint brushes are the closest things they have to weapons—is no less telling.[46] As the sarcastic motto of the company proclaims, "Anything you don't want to do, the colored troops will do for you" (38); in the aftermath of Waters's death, Wilkie informs the men that they have been assigned to "shovelin' horseshit" (12) in the colonel's stables.

Several times, men describe Waters as a "crazy" man who talks to himself and, in keeping with classic symptoms of schizophrenia, who seems to be two people at once. While Waters's psychological turmoil arouses sympathy, Fuller aims to critique his obsession with gaining more recognition and status in the nation once the war ends and to scrutinize his attendant efforts to eliminate black southerners to ensure that these achievements not be compromised. Fuller makes Waters a villain and, by extension, raises an assertive critique of the stereotyping of black southerners. It is in treating these issues that Fuller's play is most critically revelatory and trenchant. It demonstrates that forms of internal exclusion that are constituted on the basis of gender and race and inflected by geography have the potential to be as inimical and corrosive to the black body and mind as those enacted by white supremacists.

That Waters, however, brings the hope for racial equality of the interwar years into his tenure at Fort Neal, and that he survives the ravages of the First World War only to be killed violently before he can fulfill his desire to participate in the second, recalls for the play's audiences the hope that black leaders had for equality in the wake of the Second World War who had witnessed the foreclosure of American democracy for African Americans in the first. Leaders from A. Philip Randolph to W. E. B. Du Bois examined the status of the soldier carefully during World War II, for the potential desegregation of the military implied possibilities for more African American civil rights stateside. The soldier, in fact, came to function as a metaphor for the African American and was instrumental in further consolidating a male-centered notion of blackness. As You-me Park and Gayle Wald point out, "The modern civil rights movement was . . . initiated in the collective imagination, at least in part, through a discourse of the citizen-soldier that conflated issues of race, masculinity, and publicity, while using these issues to foreground the denial of full citizenship to black men."[47] Released at the beginning of a decade marked by a right-wing onslaught against many of the gains made as a result of 1960s civil rights activism, *A Soldier's Play* recollects how ideological contestations grounded in race, class, and gender helped establish foundations in the 1940s for the Civil Rights movement.

By highlighting the mechanisms through which masculinities are differentially constituted within the African American context and the subjection of black men within a system based on white masculine supremacy and normativity, Fuller also brings into relief what Robyn Wiegman describes as "hierarchies within the masculine."[48] Waters ejects black southerners from conventional masculinity as much as he disposes of them in his geography of blackness, describing C. J., for example, when discussing the café incident with Wilkie as neither a "man" nor a "soldier." In affirming himself as a man born and raised in Detroit, Wilkie, in turn, presents himself in the interview with Davenport as a man born and raised in Detroit, reinforcing the incongruity between southern identity and conventional notions of masculinity. In a formal dramatic sense, Wilkie functions as a confidant who enables Waters to articulate his inner thoughts and values. He speaks of Waters as a "good soldier" in the same breath that he makes reference to Waters's "Northern" origins. C. J.'s strength and extraordinary talents in baseball, while admirable, do nothing to offset Wilkie's view of the North as a superior site of black masculine formation; he refers to C. J. as a "Big

Mississippi boy" (26), a view echoed by Taylor's remark that C. J. is "more a boy than a man" (77). Even Peterson, a fellow southerner, views C. J. as not manly enough, as cowardly and incapable of "defending himself." Gloria Naylor explores the imaging of black men from the South as infantile in her novel *Bailey's Cafe* (1992) in scenes set in the Louisiana Delta that feature a character named Billy Boy, who is encouraged to stomp in the dust for a woman's sexual arousal, "his hulking figure coming through the twilight. Man-size feet carrying that infant's brain," "a crazy man-boy smelling like a goat, kicking up dust, and howling into the twilight."[49] As a black southerner, the character Lightning Rod in the novel *The Klansman* embodies this man-boy contradiction, which helps to fuel perceptions of him as a brute and sexual predator. "The Mississippian" discussed in this book's introduction also accords with this type.

For added perspective, we might recall that this play premiered just months prior to the publication of Alice Walker's novel *The Color Purple* (1982), which also won a Pulitzer Prize and, like *A Soldier's Play*, also grappled with internal tensions among African Americans, specifically by addressing issues that had not been acknowledged widely in public discussions, such as domestic violence and incest. The controversy around what some of Walker's critics perceived to be negative representations of African American men intensified with the release of Steven Spielberg's film adaptation of the novel in 1985. The novel's enthusiastic critical engagement by academic feminists and African American literary scholars, the heated gender debates that it ignited in the 1980s, the film's critical acclaim, and the relative currency of African American male writers in the literary marketplace during the decade are all factors that may help explain why Walker's novel is better known and remembered now than *A Soldier's Play*. However, in providing such a focused and multilayered treatment of African American male subjectivity, *A Soldier's Play*, like *The Color Purple*, held important implications for the public dialogues on African American masculinity and African American gender relations that were unfolding during the 1980s. Taken together, *A Soldier's Play* and *A Soldier's Story* (the play and the film) seem distinct, too, in having served as a virtual finishing school for many African American male actors who went on to rank among those most celebrated and critically acclaimed in Hollywood, including Adolph Caesar, Howard Rollins, Larry Riley, Denzel Washington, Samuel L. Jackson, and Robert Townsend.

C. J.

In recent years, geography has been elemental in discussing representations of empire in works of fiction; however, as cultural geographers have recognized, space has been conventionally subordinate to the interest in temporality. The history of geography has thus remained invisible and neglected.[50] Numerous postmodern geographers, including Edward Soja, have prioritized Los Angeles in their critical work as they attempt to reassert the importance of space. Primarily urban-centered in focus, the field of cultural geography has failed to incorporate U.S. regional dynamics and would benefit from more focus on the U.S. South. In a move paralleling the contemporary turn toward the transnational in American studies, scholars in southern studies are increasingly considering the South in relation to postcolonial, New World, transnational, and African diasporan contexts.[51] Such critical work can serve as a valuable resource in contemporary dialogues on space, particularly as it relates to questions of identity.

In the introduction to her edited collection *The Geography of Identity*, Patricia Yaeger points out that "even though literature may not be valuable for its straightforward geography, it is extraordinarily useful in its constant, uncanny rendering of laborious space."[52] Drawing on Virginia Woolf's mediations on Shakespeare's hypothetical sister Judith, identifying her as "the feminist equivalent of the Tomb of the Unknown Soldier," Yaeger argues that recognizing ways in which the labor of phantoms—who often do not crystallize as characters—nevertheless shapes the material world represented in a text can help us discern the imprint of geography in literary works. Yaeger eschews Henri Lefebvre's skepticism regarding the utility of literature for conversations about space. Her elaboration of the labor of the phantom in the text is useful for examining C. J.'s status in *A Soldier's Play* as a character ever trapped in "*limbo*" (26). Although he remains excluded, the geography of the play becomes traceable through him. First, there is the utterance of his pivotal word "crow," which gives scenic clarity to France as an international context. Although C. J. is a ghost in the play, we come to understand that his baseball-playing talents enabled the success and spirit of the team as much as his jailing and death placed the team on the path to dissolution, which led to their consolidation as the 221st Chemical Smoke Generating Company. These abstract manifestations of labor are useful, of course, to juxtapose with the literal work that the play links to the company. Fuller thus uses C. J. to challenge many of the military's historical stereotypes about black men from the South. Unlike Cobb, who is wracked by venereal diseases, C. J. is conscientious about protecting himself from infection. He has wisdom and intelligence that belie the simplicity perceived by others. Even Davenport concludes that the real drama seems to lie between Waters and C. J.

C. J. is the only character, however, who is forever absent and lacks a voice. His story is entirely encapsulated in flashbacks and narrated from the point of view of other characters. We must rely solely on the memories of Wilkie, Cobb, Smalls, Henson, and Peterson to apprehend him. Through these characters' detailed recollections, we encounter C. J.'s words and actions.[53] In Jacques Derrida's words, "What seems impossible is to speak always *of the* specter, to speak to the specter, to speak with it, therefore especially *to make* or let a spirit speak."[54] Even C. J.'s explanations for the bird in his blood and how it got there reveal him as a person who is merely talked about and defined by others in his community. The unrepresentability of his suicide, particularly if we contrast its quietude with the spectacle of Waters's violent death that confronts us at both the beginning and end of the play, further underscores the problem of C. J.'s marginality. As Cobb reports, "The next day—afta' the day I saw him? C. J., he hung hisself, sir! Suicide—jes' couldn't stand it. M.P.'s found him hung from the bars" (74). According to Esther Harriot, "The effect of C. J.'s suicide . . . is dulled by reducing it to a few expository lines" (108).[55] Ironically, C. J.'s displacement to the interstices of the plot in effect reconstitutes the forms of spatial encapsulation that Fuller reveals as so destructive through the stockade scenes and, more broadly, through his critique of the politics of exclusion on the basis of geography in the African American context. Cobb recalls C. J.'s exclamations of misery when confined in the stockade: "It's hard to breathe in these little spaces, Cobb—man wasn' made for this hea'—nothin' was! I don't think I'll eva' see a' animal in a cage agin' and not feel sorry for it. . . . I'd rather be on the chain gang" (71); "I don't think I'm comin' outta here, Cobb—feel like I'm goin' crazy. Can't walk in hea'—can't see the Sun! I tried singin', Cobb, but nothin' won't come out. I sure don't wanna die in this jail!" (71).[56] Here we see the levels on which the character C. J. perceives his enclosure in the stockade as dehumanizing and emasculating. The stockade leaves C. J. with a feeling of unrelenting suffocation and marks him for death. His loss of senses like his sight redoubles his fear that he is also losing his mind. Fuller links C. J.'s madness and bodily deterioration (i.e., "He looked pale and ashy—like something dead" [70]) to this spatial entombment. It is clear that he undergoes a symbolic death in the stockade even before his suicide. This scene, along with C. J.'s fixedness as a ghost, strikingly marks his abjection.

The elapsed time within the play's plot schema is also useful to recognize at this juncture. That C. J. spends two days in the stockade before taking his own life bespeaks the intensity of his anguish in this small, suffocating space. Significantly, as Waters speaks in these scenes, the stage directions reveal that C. J. hums. The stage directions' call for the isolation of Waters and C. J., as well as the use of such technical effects as lighting to bring them into focus individually as characters as they speak, help make C. J.'s alienation visceral. Cobb's suspicion that the account of Waters's visit to the stockade is untrue because C. J. has become unglued mentally points to the unreliability of the narratives that we receive from this character and of the stories about him that others recollect. Fuller's ephemeral and disembodied representation of C. J. figuratively recasts the ideological and institutional economies that have historically pathologized or annihilated the black southern male body, marking it as fundamentally different and other.

In spite of an agenda that entails an effort to unsettle sexed, raced, and gendered hierarchies of masculinity and to represent a diverse and complex range of black masculine formations, Fuller's play is highly conventional in defining black masculinity. The result is a reinforcement of the ideologies of masculinity and geography that the play ostensibly critiques. C. J.'s lack of subjectivity and his disembodiment can be clarified further if we contrast his delineation with that of the eponymous Davenport, who is first introduced to us in a long monologue in act 1 beginning with the subjectifying command, "Call me Davenport," à la Herman Melville's Ishmael. Davenport comes across as the portrait of the ideal and authentic black man, and he is the character in which most of the play's energies are invested. The stage directions describe him as *"dressed sharply in an M.P. uniform, his hat cocked to the side and strapped down, the way airmen wear theirs. He is carrying a briefcase, and we are aware of a man who is very confident and self-assured. He is smiling as he faces the audience, cleaning his glasses as he begins to speak"* (16). Davenport epitomizes the spit-and-polish military style so much admired by Waters. His sunglasses, which he has deliberately chosen to evoke MacArthur, enhance his calm, cool posture. Similarly, act 2 begins with a focus on Davenport *"putting on his shirt, tie, bars, etc."* (59), which emphasizes the body and aligns him with an assertive, no-nonsense masculinity. In highlighting a military context with rigid hierarchies that are marked by uniforms and to develop the characters in more depth, the play relies on decorum as a dramatic convention. Clothing functions as a vital tool in Davenport's characterization in the play and alone testifies to his strength. In the film *A Soldier's Story*, actor Howard Rollins, who was known then primarily for his portrayal of the stalwart urban revolutionary Coalhouse Walker Jr. in *Ragtime* (1981), fully actualizes these aesthetics in the charismatic portrayal of Davenport. As Pauline Kael remarks, Rollins, "photographed so that he has a heroic, sculptural presence," is the "visual star of movie."[57]

To complement these aesthetics, the play highlights Davenport's ongoing struggle to get at the truth about the murder as Captain Taylor, who not only resents Davenport's methodical approach but also his assignment to the case in the first place, continually attempts to hinder the investigation. Notwithstanding constant reminders that the investigation is just for show and that no black officer will ever be allowed to charge whites with a crime, a determined Davenport persists, threatening to accuse the self-righteously liberal Taylor of racism in the black press rather than consent to being taken off the case. Fuller makes a metaphorical association between Davenport's and Taylor's battle and the larger race problem in the United States; furthermore, their conflict is a masculinist battle of wills. Taylor is shocked, confused, and outraged that Davenport releases Byrd and Wilcox but humbled when Davenport uncovers Peterson and Smalls as the true assailants. In the end, Taylor admits that he was "wrong" (100), and Davenport comes across as the better and stronger man.

In the play, the structure of the dialogue signals this conflict most saliently. At several points, Davenport and Taylor argue back and forth in phrases that are punctuated by short and exclamatory lines, which give intensity to their language and signal the weightiness and passion of their confrontation. This structure in the dialogue also marks their binary racial categories as black and white men. Both acts end by highlighting an exchange between these characters, with Davenport having the last word. The first act ends with Taylor condescendingly challenging Davenport to complete the investigation:

Taylor:	Prove it, hotshot—I told you all I know, now you go out and prove it!
Davenport:	I will, Captain! You can bet your sweet ass on that! I will! (55)

Similarly, the play ends with Taylor's concession that somehow he will have to get used to blacks having positions of authority:

Davenport:	Oh, you'll get used to it—you can bet your ass on that. Captain—you will get used to it. (100)

In the schema of the play, the organization of this dialogue with Taylor points to its further significance. For it comes after Davenport's long monologue that overviews the fates of all the men, which might have just as easily ended the play. The recurring phrase, "You can bet your ass on that," establishes continuity between these scenes, and their parallel structural positioning in the play reveals how racial conflicts between blacks and whites enfold and frame internecine conflicts among blacks. Davenport's calm expression in the latter scene and his modulated tone are significant factors, for they suggest that he is finally at peace with Taylor. Moreover, Davenport's use of profanity in these exchanges contrasts strikingly with his usual verbal reserve, assert the primacy of his voice, and, ultimately, signal his victory. In the play's dialogue, beyond Waters's biting harangues, the most intense and hostile verbal exchanges occur between Davenport and the white male characters. But Waters backs down to Taylor. Davenport doesn't. Because Davenport solves the murder mystery through methods that prove to be more savvy and revealing than those of high-ranking white military officers and humbles arrogant young, white officers such as Byrd and Wilcox, he strikes a blow against the military's beliefs in black soldiers' inferiority and incompetence and reveals segregation as a baseless and counterproductive social practice.

Faulkner's *Soldiers' Pay* can be used further as a point of comparison—and to help us understand the unique challenges that Fuller relates to black men in the U.S. military because of their racial category—if we recognize that Davenport's captain's bars do not inspire the kind of envy among men in the company that Mahon's eagle's wings evoke in Gilligan and Lowe. Instead, the company beams with pride given Davenport's hard-won accomplishments as a black man in a racist military and admire the authority that he wields. Equally provocative, in light of this novel, is the resentment that southern white male soldiers like Byrd and Wilcox implicitly hold toward Taylor because of his attempt to force them to recognize the authority of a black man while their preference is to adhere to the protocols of segregation. While Faulkner relates the physical and emotional impact of war to Mahon's transformation into a ghost in the novel, Fuller illustrates how the politics of race in the military and in the nation make ghosts of black men like Waters and C. J. before they even reach the battlefield.

It is necessary to recall Davenport's characterization as Fuller's effort to honor and mourn Larry Neal, the man to whom the play is dedicated, for whom the base is named, and from whom the character Davenport is drawn. However, the gender politics of the play that surface when we read it on its own terms are troublesome. While C. J.'s othering seems to undermine the critical commentary that the play makes about the devaluation of black southern identities within discourses of blackness, *A Soldier's Play* also profoundly compromises its critique of hierarchical and geographically essentialist formulations of black masculinity in Fuller's depiction of the urban North as a superior site of African American masculine formation. Ironically, the logic of Waters's project of racial uplift and self-definition, which alienates and excludes black southerners, is played out in the formulation of Davenport. In this sense, the play replicates the very problem that it critiques. The message of *A Soldier's Play* is that only a man with Davenport's education, urban roots, polish, intelligence, sophistication, command, and stamina is fit to get to the bottom of the murder mystery and to go head to head with the white male power structure of the military. Where it so self-consciously attaches this range of attributes to Davenport, the play even recalls Anderson's logic in "Disposal of the Colored Drafted Men." The play's representation of Davenport also reinforces the masculinist logic within black antiracist discourse that scripts the category of African American as essentially male and conforms to highly conventional national mythologies of masculinity and heroism.

We see Davenport at his most assertive at the end of the play, when he stands as the lone survivor reporting that all officers and enlisted men in the 221st Chemical Smoke Generating Company were killed in the Ruhr Valley during a German advance. Taylor was presumably among them. Davenport is the play's most omniscient character, the one who lives to pass on the stories after the others are gone. Davenport's vitality at the end, which is enhanced by the victory against Taylor, comes into bold relief when contrasted with C. J., who is, again, a trace when Fuller's plot begins and remains a trace once the plot has been resolved. Baraka notes this distinction by arguing that the play limits by death "a young blood from . . . the deep South who represents the oldest, blackest folk ties of the African American . . . Southern blackness that connects, through slavery, directly back to Africa" and leaves Davenport, Fuller's "real hero," as the "lone surviving Negro."[58] Baraka reads the play's acclaim in the early 1980s, a time when African American theater was increasingly losing financial support, as an extension of the problem of tokenism that the play also represents in Davenport's victory within the system at Fort Neal and in contrast with the loss of the rest of the company's men. While his analysis is insightful where it points to the expendability and devaluation of southern subjectivity and to the body's articulations as geography in the play, Baraka's configuration of C. J. as the epitome of African American ancestry and historicity in the United States is romanticizing and serves to entomb this character in the past, robbing him of dynamism in much the same way that Fuller consigns him to death.

The binary construction of C. J. and Davenport and the gendered and geographical hierarchy in the play highlight what Steve Pile describes from the standpoint of cultural geography as dualistic formulas for constituting masculinities that obscure the range of conceivable masculine formations. As Pile points out, "Dualistic epistemologies—whether they distinguish between Reason and Emotion, man and boy, strong and weak, and so on— help to distinguish between what is valued and what is not and also to maintain that distinction." Furthermore, Pile argues that "forms of masculinity are located in socially (historically and geographically) specific forms of power."[59] Hierarchical constructions of masculinity are thus inflected by geography and shed light on the North-South schema that grounds the relative value of black masculine formations in *A Soldier's Play* and serves as a framework in which Fuller reproduces the ideology of black southern maleness as undesirable and inferior. Such formulations are also reminiscent of the "spatially conceived hierarchical dualities" that Lavie and Swedenberg discuss.

Notwithstanding the trajectory of analysis that I have pursued, it is important to acknowledge alternative interpretive possibilities for Fuller's play. Of course, the detection genre, the play's major organizing terrain, might also conceivably account for C. J.'s invisibility, silence, and death as a character. We could also draw on it to explain and rationalize a range of other effects, such as Davenport's singular voice, his intellect, and his urban identity, for many heroes in works of African American detection tend to fit this profile. However, while I do not view detection as incidental to this work, I believe that it would explain Fuller's strategies much too prescriptively to be taken at face value. Similarly, we might interpret C. J.'s voicelessness as part of Fuller's effort to establish continuities with Melville's inarticulate character Billy Budd.

The absence of women parallels the alienation of southern subjectivity in *A Soldier's Play*. One notable difference between the play and the Jewison film is that the latter incorporates a character named Mary and the setting of Mary's Ribs and Catfish as the place in Tynin where black men on the base seek recreation and where C. J. frequently performs. The film opens with Mary singing "Pouring Whiskey Blues." As Waters staggers out of her place and down the road to his death, the camera cuts back and forth from her face to his, and we hear her song for a while faintly as the road begins to look increasingly dark and threatening. Yet like the various women we hear about in the play though never see, Mary, who sings seductively, is reductively represented as sexual.[60]

Before the production of the film began, Fuller remarked that a cinematic Davenport should be "much more real than when we watched him on the stage" and that Davenport is "the person they're going to put all the money in."[61] In his view, film had even more potential to portray the charisma of Davenport than drama. The shift from the lighter-skinned Charles Brown, who played Davenport onstage, to the casting of the totally opposite tall, dark, angular actor Howard Rollins in the film, is provocative to ponder. Rollins may have been perceived as more ideal for representing the black masculinist persona that Fuller hoped the character Davenport would embody. For while classic Western aesthetics have construed darkness as an ideal of masculinity while at the same time devaluing blackness, the tall, dark-skinned, handsome masculine model that Davenport represents has found more favor and acceptance as these dominant beauty ideals have continued to evolve and become more inclusive.

Fuller has indicated that one of his main purposes in the play is to examine how racism affects relations among blacks and shapes their psychology.[62] The deleterious effects on internecine relations among blacks situated within the context of a racially oppressive national culture (i.e., as a result of "the madness of race in America") are most explicitly addressed when Davenport comments on the fates of C. J., Waters, Smalls, and Peterson toward the conclusion of the play. The emphasis on the psychology of the black subject makes it curious that the discourse of psychoanalysis has not been invoked previously in criticism on the play. Though I have highlighted theories of abjection within psychoanalysis thus far in my analysis in this chapter, the lens of conventional Freudian ego psychology illustrates that sessions with Davenport have a psychotherapeutic effect on the men, helping them extract deeply repressed and traumatizing memories. Dialogue with Davenport is key, for instance, to Wilkie's psychic release in the play; Wilkie is broken down in the second session to the point that he faces all the facts that he had reflexively denied in the first—that Waters was not a nice guy or a genuine friend, that Waters despised C. J., and that he harbored lingering anger over how Waters had taken his stripes.[63]

Passing and Southern Identity

In a 1984 article in *People* magazine, provocatively entitled "Larry Riley's Smartest Move Was Deciding to Play Dumb," Riley, the actor who portrayed the character C. J. Memphis on both stage and screen, is quoted as having said, "I thought C. J. was stupid . . . just dumb and ignorant. I grew up with [the same kind of] people and hated them because they didn't pronounce their words right. I wouldn't let anyone know I was from a rural southern background. I was headed for bigger and better things."[64] The irony here is that the opportunity to embody, as an actor, what he was pretending not to be in his own life facilitates the major breakthrough in his acting career. This façade may have even provided early acting experience— unconscious, practical preparation for Riley's profession. It is interesting, too, that Riley made this confession about a rural southern background at a point when more professional security and wider public acceptance had made it relatively safe and even prudent for him to claim such a heritage.

In this interview, Riley confesses the kind of shame about southern identity and embraces the same strategies of geographical disavowal that Fuller addresses in the portrayal of the character Melvin Peterson in *A Soldier's Play*. As in the case of Davenport, Fuller relies on clothing to portray Peterson as a "model soldier" (31). The stage directions indicate that he is the most conservatively and neatly dressed of all the men in his company and that he "looks angelic" (9). Prominently displayed stripes reveal this character's hopes to rise up in the ranks of the army, but an Alabama background is forever his bane. His behavior thoroughly belies his description and reveals the play's investment in illustrating how appearances can be deceiving.

Passing has conventionally been referred to as the phenomenon of crossing over surreptitiously from black to white and as a practice that unsettles the discourses of race as they have been legally, socially, and scientifically developed in U.S. history. We have come to understand passing in terms of how it disturbs inscriptions of race on the body and its potential to reconfigure identity on the basis of gender, nation, and sexual orientation, but it is useful to ponder Peterson's geographical realignments that are based on shame about southernness in light of this phenomenon. As Elaine Ginsberg has pointed out, passing and geographical migration have been necessarily interwoven to avoid the discovery of the passing subject's "true identity."[65] While the main concern of passing has ordinarily been the disavowal of one's race as opposed to region, these insights make the relation of passing to a black southern migrant like Peterson fascinating to consider. In Fuller's play, the view of the South as an undesirable geography of identification is shaped by an awareness of such stereotypes of black southerners as the lack of education, inarticulateness, docility, and being superstitious. As the play reveals, the character Peterson fashions himself through voice, dress, and a militant posture to ensure that he will have no such legibility, to the point of impressing Waters as an ideal soldier. Having been removed from the South through migration to Hollywood, when Davenport asks where he is from, Peterson dillydallies around his southern origins with the response "Hollywood, California—by way of Alabama" (32).

William Demastes argues that Peterson is "a Southerner who has been introduced to a more sophisticated world and has developed the tools to defend himself, to stand up for himself," and who "maintains his attachment to his black heritage."[66] However, I believe that this reading obscures this character's conflicted relationship to the South as well as the potential for resistance and self-defense among blacks who choose to remain in the South, an issue I discussed in the previous chapter. Tellingly, Peterson spurns the urge to invest his faith in conjuring, rejecting with hostility the Farmer's Dust that C. J. offers for the fight with Waters. Peterson makes it clear that he wants nothing to do with "that backwater crap" (45).[67] Not only does this scene reveal this character's disgust for black folk practices and further suggest his anxieties over the semiotics stereotypically associated with black southern identities, but contempt for the rural South is also evident. Through Peterson, Fuller illustrates that, even among black southerners, hierarchies of identity exist and are based on distinctions between rural and urban. Peterson's character reveals how much some black southerners even feel uneasy and embarrassed by their background and brings their internal conflicts and anxieties into relief. Still, by invoking the "rednecks" of the Louisiana town where Fort Neal is located and instances of black soldiers' lynching by the Ku Klux Klan, *A Soldier's Play* also links the South's negotiation as a site of disavowal to the region's looming status in the cultural imagination as a historical scene of racist violence and disenfranchisement for African Americans.

If he resists its tangible symbols, Peterson ultimately fails to escape abjection as a black southerner.[68] Significantly, his most intense moment of identification with the South occurs when he hits bottom and flees to Alabama to escape the charge for Waters's murder. The effect of his capture is twofold. His "true" regional identity is uncovered inasmuch as his status as a criminal is exposed. "Southern" and "criminal" are voiced almost synonymously as markers of his identity. Presumably, Peterson hides out in Alabama in the first place because it is the last place on earth where anyone would expect to find him. Drawing on passing as a critical lens reveals how southernness functions as an undesirable and expendable marker of identification for this character and helps us understand this character's performance of southern disavowal as another dramatic layer in *A Soldier's Play*.

Waters's and C. J.'s intertwining deaths, and the dénouement that chronicles the fates of the company men, categorize the play as a veritable work of tragedy with a universal message about the consequences of racial ideology in the nation. In recollecting and reconstructing the history of African American soldiers in the First and Second World Wars, Fuller expands and unsettles the tapestries of American literary narration that have frequently obscured or excluded them. He takes us on a journey between past and present and features subjects that are black and white to illustrate the deeper psychic scars of war experience. War emerges, in the end, as a metaphor for the battleground of American race relations. His play functions as a magnifying glass that gives visual clarity and focus to deep and sometimes bitter and painful conflicts based on geography that have remained unacknowledged in African American life but have intricately and in some instances tragically shaped how people live—and even how they die. It forces us to grapple with geography as a viable and salient feature in formulating race and masculinity. In the end, however, it does not go far enough. Urbanity dominates Fuller's formulation of a black masculine ideal, defining what is strong and capable.

The play's southern geography, while typically unappreciated, opens up a range of interpretive possibilities when we recognize it as central, rather than incidental, to all that is going on. His play is the kind that ultimately poses a challenge to southern literature itself. It shows how much southern literature might be enriched by breaking its own more traditional rules and expanding its textual repertoires to become more inclusive of works written by authors who were not born in the South and who don't live there but who have things to say about it. Such works, as Fuller's play illustrates, can produce valuable epistemologies on the region that are forces to be reckoned with. They also reveal how much the South continues to function as a highly imaginative construct in the nation.

That *A Soldier's Play* has remained largely neglected is especially regrettable when considering its focused—if flawed—treatment of the impact of geography on discourses of race and masculinity in the United States. The elision of the character C. J. demonstrates the vulnerability of the South as a region to erasure and invisibility in African American literary and cultural discourses. Nevertheless, it is also provocative, in a sense, to read C. J. as an emblem of African American invisibility: ultimately, he is not the play's only specter. *A Soldier's Play* is concerned about the pain and anguish among African Americans that people never see or that they refuse to see. In the Waters murder mystery, the major revelation beyond Peterson as the triggerman is that the case was never open and shut or black and white. Though Davenport circumvents a racist military bureaucracy that failed to discover who committed the crime, military officials at Fort Neal who failed to recognize the possibility of internecine conflict among black soldiers during the investigation are paradoxically eager to sum up the death as "just another black mess of cuttin', slashin', and shootin'! . . . the usual common violence any commander faces in Negro military units" (99). This perception itself reflects their view of black men in the military as criminal and pathological. They empty the incident of its deeper implications. This nonchalance on the part of the military is decisively punctuated through the mistake that makes way for Waters to be falsely proclaimed a hero. Fuller reveals the invisibility of internal conflict among African Americans at Fort Neal to be as pronounced at the end of the play as it is at the beginning, and he relates this problem to the historically racist politics of the military. More broadly, Fuller's play recalls the vulnerability of black soldiers under the law in the military during the war and their frequent denial of justice and fair treatment.[69]

Waters's genocidal scheme to eliminate black southerners reflects the blame he displaces onto black southerners like "Moonshine King of the Monkeys" and C. J., rather than onto the military where it belongs, for the military's failure to award sufficient honors to African American soldiers in World War I. In our own time, that the prestigious Medal of Honor was withheld until recently from Vernon Baker and six other African American men who had performed valiantly in World War II further underscores the warped perspective that Fuller dramatizes through Waters. A cover story in *U.S. News & World Report* in 1996 reports that "the last act of a grateful nation's half-century commemoration of the Allied victory in World War II may be a simple and long-delayed act of justice: Seven black American soldiers, all but one now dead, will be awarded the Medal of Honor for their valor and self-sacrifice while fighting for a segregated country in a segregated Army."[70] That black men in the South were highly accessible to bearing the violence of American racialist ideologies on their bodies made them some of the most vulnerable men in the nation. Their subjection to forms of violence and abuse that disproportionately victimized black males makes their devaluation within formulations of "authentic" masculinity and blackness all the more unsettling.

A final lesson offered by *A Soldier's Play* may be that art can imitate life in sobering ways, for the tragic dimensions spill out and echo profoundly in the lives of the real men who were closest to it. There can be no encore performances of this play with the original cast. Adolph Caesar, who played Sgt. Waters on stage over six hundred times, and who finally portrayed him in the film, died of a heart attack in 1986 at age forty-eight.[71] Larry Riley, "C. J." on both stage and screen, died of AIDS-related kidney failure in 1992 at age thirty-nine. Howard Rollins, the straitlaced Davenport in the film, struggled with drug addiction and had numerous drug-related run-ins with the law before he succumbed to lymphoma in 1996 at age forty-six. These losses move one to lament the seemingly inescapable grip of the lone-survivor narrative. For of all of Fuller's extremely talented and promising young main actors, only Denzel Washington, who portrayed Peterson onstage and on the screen and who in his remarkable acting career has garnered honors ranging from two Academy Awards to selection as the "Sexiest Man Alive" by *People* magazine in 1996, remains.[72]

CHAPTER 3

Ralph Ellison's Rural Geography

Geography is the most prominent structuring device in Nella Larsen's 1928 novella *Quicksand*, in which experiences on a journey across a range of settings, including two sojourns in the South, are all pivotal and fateful in the development of the tragic mulatta protagonist, Helga Crane. Larsen's emphasis on the rural South as a context for Helga's decline evokes the region's history of antipathy for racial intermixture and reveals geography's organic impact in developing the trope of the tragic mulatto in African American literary history. Helga's impulsive marriage to the bombastic Reverend Mr. Pleasant Green takes her to a figurative hell in Alabama, where she descends into misery, disillusionment, and, as the novel's title implies, death. The minister, as Helga sees him, is a "fattish" and "rattish yellow man," curious animal imagery that implies her view of him as pestilential and beneath what is human; furthermore, he disgusts her because he smacks his food while eating, has fingernails that are always rimmed with black, reeks of sweat, and never washes or changes his clothes.[1] The minister's long title and very name illustrate his verbiage and mark him as an emblem of the rural geography to which they retreat to work: ministering his flock. Like his name, which invokes the bitter irony Helga encounters in a landscape where she is unhappy, this language recalls pastoral imagery. The awkward name also signals his remove from Helga and their lack of intimacy. By the novella's end, she is pregnant with her fifth child almost immediately after birthing her fourth, which implies his unrelenting demand for sex. There is nothing good or pure about him, in the sense of what we might expect from a minister, and even his church, because it was formerly a stable, smells of manure. Their home and children become dirty and unkempt as a result of her frustrations, mirroring the filth of his body. While none of Helga's relationships is satisfying, including encounters with James Vayle, Robert Anderson, and Axel Olsen, Green is a gross and vulgar contradiction to the previous men in her life and proves to be most inimical and injurious to her physical and psychological well-being.[2]

In *Quicksand*, one of the main thematic concerns is how Helga's interracial body and style constitute her otherness in various geographies. Her body becomes flamboyantly excessive in Denmark, where her doting relatives pressure her to wear garish fashions and the artist Axel Olsen, who remarks that she has the soul of a prostitute, captures her image in an unflattering painting. These dimensions of the novella recall the historical constitution of black female bodies—from Sara Baartman ("The Hottentot Venus") to Josephine Baker—as excessively sexual in Europe. We need to recognize, however, that *Quicksand* also intricately relates geography to the construction of the black masculine body. Larsen's *Quicksand* constructs a hierarchy of masculinity based on geography and associates an abject and undesirable form of black masculinity with the rural South. Its logic attests to the historical association of the black male body in the South with ideologies of a perverse and excessive sexuality, and to the even deeper and more complex racial and sexual pathologies that have frequently been attached to black male bodies in rural contexts.

The Tuskegee Syphilis Study, which I briefly mentioned in the previous chapter, reigns as one of the most notorious examples in U.S. history of the unethical use of medicine in the systematic and arguably genocidal annihilation of black male bodies in the rural South. Syphilis is a disease, primarily transmitted through close sexual contact, whose symptoms emerge in several stages, are highly variable, and, in the final stages, after a latent period, can severely affect the neurological and cardiovascular systems. The Tuskegee Study, which was governmentally sponsored under the auspices of the U.S. Public Health Service, involved researchers' observation of the effects of syphilis by monitoring a group of poor and largely illiterate black men in the Macon County, Alabama, vicinity who were mainly sharecroppers. Participants reported annually for physical examinations and blood tests in exchange for small forms of compensation, such as free lunches and transportation, and were unaware of the nature of the experiment. Most unsettling perhaps is that even after penicillin therapy was identified in 1943 as a cure for the disease, it was not administered to men in this study as a form of treatment. The study was finally exposed in 1972 by the Associated Press in the wake of ethical concerns raised by Public Health Service worker Peter Buxtun. Many of its subjects first became aware that they had been part of a vast medical experiment through the wide press coverage of the story. In 1973 several participants in the study gave testimony about their experiences in U.S. Senate hearings on human experimentation headed by Senator Edward Kennedy. Fred D. Gray, the civil rights attorney who filed a lawsuit on behalf of the group of men, won a settlement for the survivors and went on to press for an apology from the government for this perverse project, which President Bill Clinton formally granted in 1997.

This experiment would not have been conceivable without an established view of the black male body in the rural South as expendable, degenerate, and biologically inferior. Race, gender, and geography were crucial factors in establishing the conditions for it and helped to demarcate its group of participants. In other words, it is important to recognize that, in the end, it happened not only as a result of *who* these men were but also because of *where* they were. Gray has stressed the need to understand the existing social conditions in Macon County at the time that the study began during the Depression era in a racially segregated southern area and observes that "only those who were poor, uneducated, rural, and African American were recruited."[3] In *The Racial Economy of Science*, Sandra Harding points out that greater possibilities for the intersection of science and race exist in places structured by such rigid, polarized systems of racial classification as the post-Emancipation U.S. South.⁴ It is astounding, really, that the experiment, whose results were periodically shared in medical journals, did not become an ethical concern in the national public sphere earlier and that it was kept underground and shrouded in secrecy for so many years. It is odd, too, that such a perverse experiment unfolded for decades in the shadow of the famed Tuskegee Normal and Industrial Institute, the college founded by Booker T. Washington in 1881 to educate African Americans and that, through the career of the acclaimed inventor George Washington Carver, emerged as a bastion of scientific innovation and discovery. The Tuskegee Study is the kind of tragedy that could easily be forgotten in our time, when memory is increasingly short and there has been a persistent failure in the national context to engage in honest and open dialogue on race. That denial and silence continue to shape perceptions of this study—and to distort its race and class politics—is also evident in its popular representation in the 1997 film *Miss Evers' Boys*. This film, as critics like Gray have pointed out, portrays a black physician as the study's primary supervisor and advocate, in effect obscuring the historical role of federal and state officials in facilitating the study and the reality that all the doctors involved were white. Moreover, by focusing its plot on four participants and portraying them as dancers and musicians, *Miss Evers' Boys* downplays the lot of most men as poor, rural sharecroppers.

Sander Gilman acknowledges that by the end of the nineteenth century, syphilis was a topic of heightened interest in the work of psychiatrists like Freud, who linked it to sexual pathology, even as Freud, in critiquing the medical and scientific concept of degeneracy, believed civilization's obsession and panic regarding syphilis epitomized its own sexual degeneracy. The potential of the disease to destroy the body internally from one generation to another, coupled with its mythic connection to sexuality, "made it one of the late nineteenth century paradigms for degenerative sexuality." During this period, Gilman notes that the prostitute epitomized the syphilitic and served as a basis for constituting difference and otherness as notions of sexual pathology were transferred from the private, individual realm to the public realm through pervasive concern surrounding syphilis as a venereal disease.⁵ If the prostitute was typically isolated and stereotyped as syphilitic in late-nineteenth-century Europe, the face of syphilis that emerged in the U.S. South in the 1930s as an object of fascination in science and medicine was black and male. In this region, blackness embodied what was fundamentally different and other, perceived as pathological, and linked to sexual perversion. The discourse on venereal disease in the South in the early twentieth century, which was prominently shaped by military medicine, reinforced notions of racial difference, particularly the idea of a diseased and infected black body. The post-Emancipation mythology that associated blackness with a rapacious and sexually insatiable masculinity and perceived it as a threat to an ideology of pure and normative whiteness should be understood as the context in which this group of black men were implicitly classified as degenerates. The Tuskegee Syphilis Study was fueled by a stereotype of inherent black racial difference and sexual deviance and rationalized the state of its black male subjects as chronically diseased. The study regarded the participants as socially expendable men whose basic human rights were worthy of no regard or protection. By allowing its subjects' bodies to fester with disease, deteriorate, and in some cases die gradually, the study serves as a shocking and sobering illustration of how black men in the South were systemically subjected to state-sanctioned forms of violence annihilative and mutilating of the body and were marked as inherently pathological in the twentieth century.

If this experiment is emblematic of an overdetermined and misguided use of African Americans as subjects in medical experiments, one problem in the contemporary era is perhaps the reverse, in light of the conventional prioritization of white males as representative subjects in medical research and the persisting lack of national concern about health issues and diseases that disproportionately affect African Americans. Cathy Cohen, for instance, has discussed the "invisibility" of African Americans at the Centers for Disease Control, the nation's primary public health institution, given its early years of research on AIDS/HIV that emphasized the impact of the disease on gay white males and excluded minority communities. This feeling of benign neglect has even fed conspiracy theories that the government has willfully ignored the ravages of this epidemic in the African American context.[6]

Through the character Jim Trueblood, an Alabama sharecropper whose incestuous encounter with his daughter, Matty Lou, arouses scholarly curiosity and makes him a spectacle among whites in the surrounding region eager to hear about his transgression, Ralph Ellison's monumental 1952 novel *Invisible Man* offers a provocative thematic treatment of race and sexuality in shaping notions of a pathological black masculinity in the rural South. As Trueblood reports to the wealthy white philanthropist and the novel's young, unnamed, black male protagonist, "The white folks took up for me. And the white folks took to coming out here to see us and talk with us. Some of 'em was big white folks, too, from the big school way cross the State. Asked me lots 'bout what I thought 'bout things, and 'bout my folks and the kids, and wrote it all down in a book" (53).[7] *Invisible Man* suggests that this fascination with Trueblood is steeped in lingering stereotypes of a hypersexed, rapacious black masculine body in the southern mind and highlights white-supremacist ideologies of black sexuality. As a novelist, Ellison pushed the envelope in crafting a character like Trueblood, ascribing him such a salient narrative voice through the technique of an extended embedded monologue with a heightened level of theatricality, and in representing a topic such as incest so graphically. *Invisible Man* further registers a visceral awareness of how race, sexuality, and masculinity work together to shape forms of subjection for the black body within medicine and science through the experience of the protagonist in a hospital after an explosion at the Long Island plant where he has just started working. The protagonist's race and gender inform the view of the doctors treating him as they consider the opportunity that his presence provides them to conduct several experiments, such as a prefrontal lobotomy and castration, even though they eventually decide to administer a series of painful electric shocks: "The pulse came swift and staccato, increasing gradually until I fairly danced between the nodes. My teeth chattered. I closed my eyes and bit my lips to smother my screams. Warm blood filled my mouth. Between my lids I saw a circle of hands and faces, dazzling with light. Some were scribbling upon charts" (237). The doctors' consideration of a form of bodily mutilation typically associated with lynching allows Ellison to link the ravages against the black masculine body in the South to the terrain of the urban North. Jim Trueblood's emergence as an academic curiosity, along with the undue liberties that doctors take while examining the protagonist in the hospital, eerily attest to the conceivability of an unethical medical experiment such as the Tuskegee Study decades before it was uncovered. Ellison illustrates the vulnerability and accessibility of rural black men to scientific and medical exploitation.

Invisible Man is a useful work to draw on for my purposes not only in light of these themes but also because of how it illustrates the marginality of rural identities in the African American context and the devaluation of the rural in the construction of black masculinity. The elite black college that Ellison's protagonist attends, which recalls the historic Tuskegee Institute, views rural blacks in the country as a subordinate and undesirable class of African Americans and helps keep them on the margins in the county. Thus far in this book, I have touched on ideological perceptions of rural people, including rural people in the South and black rural southerners in particular. At this point, I want to turn to a more direct and focused discussion of this problem. For it is important to acknowledge instances in which the rural adds complexity to black southern identities, compounds ideological perceptions of their difference and otherness, and heightens politics of marginality and exclusion in the African American context. If the South has historically been an abject and "other" geography in the United States, rural contexts in and beyond the South have been even more subject to such politics of exclusion. However, as is the case with the more general problem of southern abjection in the nation, the problem of rural otherness has typically been discussed in critical dialogues primarily in relation to white identities in an effort to ponder the meanings of such categories as "rednecks," "hillbillies," "mountain people," and "white trash."[8] Fields like whiteness studies have substantially expanded the scholarship on these topics over the past decade. Rarely have their methodologies been comparative, in ways that might allow for consideration of how such politics of difference produce very particular raced, sexed, and gendered ideological scripts of black rural subjects in the South. Approaches that fail to acknowledge the impact of the South's history as a pariah region in the United States and attendant ideologies of southern identity on a range of race and gender categories, including black rural southerners, reinforce the myth of the South as a racially monolithic (i.e., white) region. Such thinking also obscures the historical racial subjection of blacks in helping to constitute perceptions of the South as abject in the nation. Indeed, the history of the Civil War, Reconstruction, Jim Crow, and civil rights reveals that black people in the South have stood at the center, rather than at the margin, of the southern problem. The sheer intellectual genius of W. E. B. Du Bois was quite evident at the level at which he not only revealed the mutuality in the articulation of the southern problem with the Negro problem in the nation but also pursued a comparative study of the disenfranchised poor white laboring class alongside blacks who chiefly made up the slave class in the U.S. South during the nineteenth century.[9]

It is particularly significant that poor whites have most often been associated with stereotypes in the South, a phenomenon that reflects their subordination and abjection within a category whose most valued members have been wealthy, propertied elites. But the history of poor whites in the South is incomprehensible without some awareness of the evolution of the history of poor, rural blacks, a population that in some cases has roots extending back to the era of slavery. Within the system of racial distinction that emerged in the antebellum South based on a pure notion of whiteness—no matter how economically disenfranchised poor whites were—posing the most radical challenge to the system in which they were subordinated would have meant aligning themselves with blacks. Such a strategy was unthinkable for those who found their human dignity in being classed apart from and superior to blacks who were in a similar (and in some instances even better) economic condition. As David B. Danbom observes in *Born in the Country: A History of Rural America*, "Slavery potentially divided rich and poor, because wealth and social status were closely related to the ownership of slaves. . . . But slavery probably served to unify whites to a greater extent than it divided them. The presence of blacks gave all whites a degree of equality. No matter how low on the social scale a southerner might be, he was equal to the highest planter in the sense that he enjoyed freedom, and his race made him the superior of every black." Danbom links the very possibilities for historiography of the rural to the development of scholarship in rural social history since the 1960s on such topics as ethnicity, gender, kinship, and slavery. [10]

In *Sex, Race, and Science: Eugenics in the Deep South*, Edward J. Larson points out that the theory and practice of eugenics in the region up to World War II, a byproduct of the theories of human heredity that had developed in the United States and western Europe from the late nineteenth century, were chiefly concerned with regulating the sexual reproduction of people categorized as "poor white trash" to uphold notions of white racial purity. [11] While no racialist epithets malign poor blacks in the South as ubiquitously as the term "white trash" has signaled the view of poor white southerners as pathological, black rural southerners have sometimes been subjected to vehement stereotyping in and beyond the African American category. Indeed, it may be true that the romanticizing of black rural southerners to authenticate and historicize the category of black in the United States obscures the more hostile and pejorative ideologies that script these identities as undesirable and alien in the African American context. The prioritization of the "folk" in the signification of African American subjectivity is, of course, a long-standing convention in the African American literary and cultural context. Hazel Carby has discussed Larsen's depiction of Helga Crane's misery in the rural South to critique the fascination with the "folk" among contemporary African American literary critics and has done sustained critical work on the phenomenon of prioritizing this category in fashioning the concept of the African American. She interprets the emphasis on the "folk" in the African American literary enterprise as cultural critics' displacement of late-twentieth-century social crises of major proportions, including the plight of the inner city, the high rates of black male incarceration, and the inadequacy or nonexistence of health care for black children. [12] In her words, "to establish the black 'folk' as representative of the black community at large was and still is a convenient method for ignoring the specific contradictions of an urban existence in which most of us live." [13]

In spite of its utility, Carby's critique begs much debated and long-standing questions related to the responsibility of black intellectual and middle classes to the project of black community uplift and, in the process, recasts the critically vexed fusion of the African American literary text and the sociological. Her formulation in effect replaces an essentialist black rural context with an essentialist notion of black urbanites in the signification of African American subjectivity. The further irony is that in highlighting the inordinate degree of emphasis in the academy on black rural folk that obscures the "urban" lived reality of the vast majority of black Americans in the United States, this analysis renders invisible and insignificant blacks who *do* continue to live in the rural South, such as those discussed in the work of the anthropologist Carol Stack. [14] We are almost led to infer, even, that the bulk of available resources in the African American community in terms of time and money, wherever and to whatever extent they exist, is being channeled into an all but evaporated black rural South to the detriment of disadvantaged black populations concentrated in inner cities. To be sure, whatever fascination with black rural southerners there has been in academia has in no way translated into an interest in and preoccupation with them as objects of social concern to address, for instance, the deplorable material conditions that many blacks living in rural southern contexts have continued to face, such as the lack of access to public utilities, decent housing, jobs, health care, schools, etc. Indeed, while Carby valuably instructs us about the costs of a hegemonic black rural folk ideology for blacks in urban contexts, we also need to think about how the evocation of black rural identities to signify a romanticized African American past in the United States (i.e., ancestral, historical, spiritual) obscures and displaces the material circumstances, and perhaps even the very existence, of blacks who live, breathe, work, and hopefully play in the rural South in the contemporary era. If we dismiss black rural southerners, of course, we risk recasting the very ideologies that have typically constituted them as invisible, expendable, and excluded in the African American context. Indeed, it is important to recognize the historical origins of many urban problems among populations in the rural South.

Such urban-centered epistemologies of blackness belie the continuing significance of the U.S. South and its rural contexts as factors in shaping black identity. Furthermore, they obscure the ways in which this impact even goes beyond and at times unsettles the romance that has so often shaped relationships to the region among blacks. They do not take us far beyond binary and exclusionary models of black identity that rely on raced and gendered discourses of authenticity that effectively co-opt and particularize discourses of blackness to the United States. In failing to recognize the urban as yet another hegemonic script of blackness, they risk negating diaspora scripts of black identity. In the contemporary era, "urban" as a trope of authentic blackness typically goes uninterrogated and sometimes functions in ways akin to how whiteness operates as the invisible and normative sign of American subjectivity. It is necessary to move beyond the binary logic that alternatively scripts "urban" and "rural" subjects as "real" or "authentic" blacks, a critical move that to some extent seems contingent on refashioning and expanding discourses on gender and blackness within diaspora and global contexts. Within such a framework, and perhaps beyond the pitfalls of black southern romance, we will be able to consider a range of scripts of blackness that have southern specificity in the global arena, recognize the U.S. South's role in constituting scripts of blackness that have national and global proportions, and expand the frameworks for interpreting black and southern historical roles in the making of modernity, in light of historically southern-based economies of plantation slavery. In a global context with heightened flows of material goods and cultural exchanges, the concept of blackness has sometimes been highly visible and usable in mediating a range of racial and ethnic identity formations, even as bodies categorized as black have remained abject and undesirable. A similar dynamic is discernible in ideological uses of the concept of the rural in the African American context, which frequently function to stabilize essentialist notions of blackness even as rural people are treated as dispensable in real life.

Although she has developed her critique primarily through close analysis of novels by black women writers—most notably by taking up Nella Larsen's counternarrative to the view of black rural folk as romantic in *Quicksand*—Carby counts Ellison among black male fiction writers who "refused a romantic evocation of the folk."[15] She points out that many critics have attempted to make his signature work reducible to its folk aesthetics, remarking that "a large portion of the criticism written about Ralph Ellison's *Invisible Man* (1952) focuses on a minor section of the text, the 'Trueblood' episode, a representation of a 'folk' figure that covers twenty pages out of a novel of 568 pages, most of which is set in an urban context."[16] Houston A. Baker Jr. has offered the classic critical reading of this scene in the novel.[17] However, it is important to recognize the assertion with which a range of folk forms suffuses the novel. As Robert O'Meally has reminded us, "Folklore is not considered [in Ellison's work] as a body of quaint, 'folksy' items for a catalogue of oddments. Nor is folklore associated with a particular level of society or with a particular historical era. Folklore is a dynamic, current process of speaking and singing in certain circumstances. Afro-American folklore—sermons, tales, games, jokes, boasts, toasts, blues, and spirituals—is a rich source for the writer."[18] In a larger sense, this diffusiveness of folk idioms in the novel reflects Ellison's belief in the permeability of such racial categories as black and white in light of their inevitable syncretisms and in the elemental role that African Americans have played in shaping the national culture through language and music. This pluralism is also manifest in Ellison's critique of geographically narrow and essentialist formulations of African American selfhood that alienate rural identities, even as he remains invested in a critique of rural romanticism.

Ellison remarked that "Every serious novel is, beyond its immediate thematic preoccupations, a discussion of the craft, a conquest of the form, and a conflict with its difficulties; a pursuit of its felicities and beauty."[19] Ellison produced a masterful and epic model of the novel as a genre in American literature in part by using geography as an organizing device and by examining its role in constructing identity. As we move past the half-century mark since its original publication date, Ellison's novel's attempts to capture the complex political and cultural life and spirit of Harlem after the Great Depression began should be of no more concern than his exploration of African American agrarian life in the South. Though Carby's fundamental cautions against folk romance are right and should be heeded, it is also true that every critical treatment of a memoir, novel, film, or dramatic production representing black rural or southern identities will not necessarily perpetuate this problem. Indeed, in recent years, black popular culture has been far more instrumental in disseminating and popularizing a black "folk" ideology than African American literary criticism, which has largely been contained within academia.

We might further interpret Carby's frustration over black folk fetishes in African American literary scholarship in relation to the discourse in intellectual history that has viewed a preoccupation with the South as regressive and inimical to national interests. This view is understandable, and even admirable in a sense, but, as the recent work of Kenneth Warren reveals, it was not necessarily a view shared by Ellison. In his recent critical study on the author, Warren points out that whereas "northern intellectuals viewed the south as a monolith of backwardness and embarrassment" and had little interest in nuances of the South, Ellison remained deeply committed to reckoning with its past, sought alternatives to the vision of a post-southern America, and critiqued its manifestations in work ranging from George Washington Cable's to Howard Zinn's. "From the point of view of Cable and Zinn," Warren remarks, "the rise of the twentieth-century southern writer as a southerner was a step backward rather than forward. A vibrant southern literature necessarily subtended a politics and culture devoted more to the past than the future." Furthermore, Warren notes, "Ellison argued that the road to an egalitarian future required a confrontation with the past—a past that when looked at properly was an amalgam of southern, Negro, and American identities."[20] In this essay's titular allusion to the notorious "southern strategy" that was designed to undermine the gains of the Civil Rights era, Warren implies that Ellison's approach to the South as a novelist and critic was methodically subversive. Significantly, Ellison's outlook also affirmed the utility of an enduring southern literary heritage and the value in the creative vision of the southern artist and writer.

Of course, symbolic deaths have often been the path to renewal in southern life and history. This has sometimes been the case, too, in southern letters. Death wishes have been directed periodically at such fields as southern literature and southern studies not so much to dismiss southern scholarship or to see it "disappear" as to renew or expand it in some ways. As some of his critics have noted, Ellison's origins in Oklahoma and his experiences in the South shaped his sensibility as a writer and helped him disrupt and complicate the binary south-to-north migratory narrative so dominant in African American cultural consciousness and so central in the development of its liberation discourse. *Invisible Man* needs to be recognized as a regional masterpiece as much as it has been celebrated as a national one. Even so, acknowledging Ellison is still not a matter of course in some contemporary southern literary anthologies, perhaps in part because of the same birth-origin litmus test for authenticating southern literature that has excluded potentially relevant works by authors like Charles Fuller.

Invisible Man provides a meditation on the psychic and social repercussions of slavery in the United States. It probes the South's deep-seated historical mythology of the black male body as sexually pathological, along with the racial voyeurism that it excites, which has been most evident in the graphic and brutal castration rituals associated with lynching. The mythic script of black masculinity as rapacious helped sustain the narrative of white masculine gentility linked to the Old South. The electrified rug on which the protagonist and other black teenage boys scuffle around for coins seems to serve as a symbol, at one level, of how charged and potentially deadly sexual encounters were between white women and black men in the region during the Reconstruction and Jim Crow eras because of such perceptions. That is to say, it does not seem accidental that Ellison positions this scuffle immediately after the boys are tantalized and threatened by the unveiling of a "Magnificent Blond—stark naked" (19). These boys are let loose to fight among themselves like animals before a group of the town's distinguished men, who have as little regard for them as spectators at the Colosseum of ancient Rome had who were eager to see early Christians attacked by wild beasts. The fight demonstrates the subjection of black men in the South under white-supremacist domination and their alienation from all the rights and privileges of citizenship. Its inhumanity inevitably indicts the white male spectators as perverse and far removed from the cherished ideal of gentility. Furthermore, Ellison recognizes that white feminine subjection and subordination were a necessity within white supremacy and points to this ideology's inherent masculinism.

Drawing primarily on rural studies, and particularly on theoretical perspectives in this field that have been developed within cultural geography, this chapter examines the specific narrative strategies that Ellison deploys to illustrate how such ideologies of black masculine difference intensify in relation to the rural South. Psychoanalysis, whose combination with cultural geography is valuable for examining forms of regional stratification in the African American context, also informs my reading of the novel. Indeed, some of the most significant scholarship on Ellison's novel, which feeds my dialogue, has been grounded in psychoanalysis.[21] Trueblood exemplifies a deviant model of black masculinity primarily because of the perversion of incest. His otherness is inscribed on his body through the gaping ax wound that lures flies and leaves him disfigured, a wound that his wife, Kate, inflicts upon discovering his violation. In addition to considering how ideologies of the rural are inscribed on the body and signaled in processes of narration, this chapter examines Ellison's use of geography to plot Trueblood's exclusion. I argue that the portions of the novel set in the rural South are central in shaping the development of the protagonist as a character and in establishing his patterns of narration.

Invisible Man testifies to the undesirability of the rural in constituting notions of masculinity and blackness, the topics that figure most dominantly in the novel. I believe that a continued close examination of the novel's rural geography is necessary for a more textured understanding of the novel's complicated discourse on race and gender and, in particular, to grasp the critique that the novel raises of exclusionary approaches to defining African American identity. *Invisible Man* is a valuable literary work to draw on for examining the role of geography in shaping such concepts as the African American and the American, and especially for pondering the complex and sometimes ambivalent tropes of the rural in the formulation of definitions of blackness. It is important to examine ways in which black rural southerners have been invoked as authentic blacks in relation to ideologies that paradoxically construe them as incompatible with notions of black selfhood. *Invisible Man* makes these differences very clear, to the point that we might say that the novel, inasmuch as it critiques exclusionary notions of American citizenship, invests itself, at least partially, in a project of rigorous deconstructive work on the very idea of the African American. Ellison advances a dialogue in his novel that had been established in the repertoires of African American literary history by such writers as Nella Larsen, Claude McKay, Langston Hughes, Jean Toomer, Zora Neale Hurston, George Schuyler,

Richard Wright, and W. E. B. Du Bois, who were all grappling with questions concerning the status of the "folk" in defining African American subjectivity.

Invisible Man offers one of the most salient examples in African American literary history of a novel in which a rural geography centrally influences the development of the plot and shapes the protagonist's characterization. Ellison's recognition of geography as organic in shaping African American identity in several other instances only further affirms my sense that it is useful to give the rural dimensions of the novel more focused consideration. He makes one of his most profound and forthright comments on this subject in his essay "Going to the Territory," which was delivered at Brown University's Ralph Ellison Festival in 1979. Since slavery, he notes, a sense that "geography is fate" has existed in African American consciousness:

> Not only had [slaves] observed the transformation of individual fortune
> made possible by the westward movement along the frontier, but the
> Mason-Dixon Line had taught them the relationship between geography
> and freedom. They knew that to be sold down the Mississippi River usually
> meant that they would suffer a harsher form of slavery. And they knew
> that to escape across the Mason-Dixon Line northward was to move in
> the direction of a greater freedom. But freedom was also to be found in the
> West of the old Indian Territory.[22]

Ellison intimately links geography to a sense of selfhood in African Americans and relates it existentially to their experience in the nation's history. In doing so, he reveals geography's potential to contain or even destroy the body. Even more specifically, Ellison suggests that containment in or freedom from the South had everything to do with the quality of life that African Americans achieved during the era of slavery. Indeed, his formulation implies the South to be inescapable and indispensable in dialogues on African American subjectivity.

Rural Others

Over the past decade, the most significant innovations in the theoretical project of rural studies have been a turn toward poststructuralist and postmodern approaches and an emphasis on the rural as a sociocultural construct. In some cases, these paradigm shifts have been situated within cultural geography, which seems to be an appropriate framework for thinking about the rural in light of how this area examines the impact of geography on identity and notions of otherness. The main advantage of new theoretical approaches in rural studies is that they facilitate the formulation of research questions related to social and cultural aspects of rural identity that have not been of concern in conventional fields such as rural development. In the United States, there has been no parallel to the sustained and systematic critical inquiry about rural identities that has existed in relation to Britain. Much of the theoretical work on the rural that we have to draw on focuses on the "countryside" within the British context and notions of national belonging that recuperate the rural in an effort to formulate a racially exclusive (i.e., white-centered) Englishness.

Of the works on the British countryside, it is useful to highlight two studies, in particular, that have been instrumental in promoting new theoretical methods in rural studies. The first, *Writing the Rural: Five Cultural Geographies*, was produced by a collective of writers that included Paul Cloke, Marcus Doel, David Matless, Martin Phillips, and Nigel Thrift. Significantly, Cloke and Thrift trace the resurgence of interest in the rural in the contemporary era back to the publication of Raymond Williams's *The Country and the City* in 1973. As they point out, "The rural is now routinely linked to gender, sexuality and ethnicity in ways which would have been considered remarkable only a few years ago. In turn, as the differences have multiplied so the idea of the rural as a fixed location has faded. It is now an infinitely more mobile and malleable term."[23] Paul Cloke and Jo Little's edited collection, *Contested Countryside Cultures: Otherness, Marginalisation, and Rurality*, represents another signal contribution to this field. The editors observe that "rural areas have proved to be a magnetic attraction for those seeking to practice cultural geography's theorisations of difference and otherness."[24]

These theoretical approaches in rural studies build upon the long history of examining issues related to the rural in British literature, art, and politics. However, the evocation of the rural in constituting notions of national belonging has worked differently in the United States, and such theories are not always translatable to this national context. These critical approaches are useful for my study of the interplay of race and the rural in the U.S. South, and particularly for my reading of Ellison's novel, where they recognize the rich contributions of black British studies in developing theories related to race and otherness and acknowledge the implications of the work in this field for rural cultural geography.[25] It is not surprising that some of the critics who have been most preoccupied with the status of rural identity in formulating exclusionary definitions of African Americans have been intellectuals in black British studies such as Hazel Carby and Paul Gilroy. Gilroy's work on racial dynamics in the British context and on the dominance of the term *African American* in defining blackness in the African diaspora has tremendously expanded the critical possibilities for examining how the concept of the African American helps constitute distinctions on the basis of geography among blacks in this nation. For instance, he critiques the exclusion of black rural southerners in urban-oriented Afrocentric and black neonationalist movements, which peaked in the early 1990s:

> The other thing that [an emphasis on Afrocentricity] makes me think is
> that if you come from the south, [you come] from a rural background.
> What about the regional basis of these Afrocentric discourses and their
> concentration in particular locations? What would it mean to offer someone
> African identity and clothing and a new name in those parts of black
> America which are not urban and which are still part of an older "peasant"
> experience that is much closer to slavery in its ways of organizing labor and
> relating to nature? What about the psycho-history of the people who didn't
> migrate northwards or drift into urban spaces? How different are they from
> those who did leave? Is Afrocentrism a form of nostalgia that thrives where
> that separation from the land and the scale of life associated with rural
> living are greatest?[26]

Gilroy's analysis speaks well to how geography implicitly and explicitly shapes formulations of identity among African Americans. The politics that he describes also suggest the importance of making black rural identities in the U.S. South and throughout the African diaspora more legible within contemporary critical studies of the rural.

British-oriented rural studies also seem useful for an increasingly comparative field such as southern studies, not only in light of the body of scholarship that has examined the South's historical European influences but also in light of the contemporary move of southern studies toward a consideration of the South in the United States in relation to global contexts and away from insular national frameworks.[27] In general, an examination of the rural should be elemental in southern studies, for in spite of the geographical diversity of the U.S. South, the region is routinely imagined *as* rural. That is to say, though rural areas are located throughout the nation and though many urban areas are located in the South, it is nevertheless true that when some people think "South," they think rural.

Barbara Ching and Gerald W. Creed are among scholars in the United States who have begun to address the rural and to advance this dialogue within a transnational framework. They emphasize the study of the rural as a grounded metaphor and recognize the urban bias in a range of fields, including postmodern social theory.[28] Their interventions are especially valuable when considering that concern about the interplay of the global and local within postmodern social theory has not necessarily led to a serious critical regard for questions related to the rural. Ching and Creed's belief that any space can be experienced as either urban or rural is aligned with the most recent developments in rural studies that eschew singular or geographically fixed definitions of the rural. Such work has helped uproot concepts of the rural and the urban from the binary south-north schema in the United States to which they have frequently been attached in the cultural imagination, to clarify dispersals of these geographies throughout the nation, and to illustrate various kinds of spaces that exist in between.

This range of critical work is a resource that might provide some of the building blocks necessary for developing a theoretical discourse on the relation of race and the rural and the status of the rural in shaping identity in the African American context. We must increasingly acknowledge ways in which identities are relatively positioned as rural based on distinctions across racial categories. In the United States, references to an abstracted "rural" subjectivity have typically elided the rigid, polarizing, historical racial hierarchies in the South.

A House Set off from the Rest

Among African Americans, the sentimental, nostalgic, and romantic responses to black rural southerners are more familiar than such responses as shame and disgust. Ellison's *Invisible Man* demonstrates how geography shapes politics of exclusion by creating hierarchies and distinctions within the category of black and also highlights the construal of rural black southerners as an inferior and abject caste. Events in the novel are intricately tied to particular geographies and unfold in an extended analepsis sandwiched between a prologue and epilogue that also incorporate temporal lapses back in time. Through painstaking strategies of characterization, Trueblood functions as Ellison's primary instrument for shifting the geography of the novel to a rural setting. That this rural geography is classed as subordinate to other southern geographies in the novel is a distinction that Ellison emphasizes by setting most of the action in town, where the college is located. The hierarchy of places thus parallels the novel's hierarchy of identities. The isolation of the rural characters in their cabin, itself a small space, heightens the interactions among them. The peripheral rural geography, as is frequently the case with marginal spaces in novels, is linked directly to social transgression. In *Invisible Man*, this transgression takes the form of incest. The alienation of Trueblood because of his violation of the incest taboo only further consolidates lines of exclusion that are already deeply entrenched and staunchly upheld against him and others in the rural outposts by blacks at the college. In one of her typically brilliant essays, Hortense Spillers provides a revealing psychoanalytic treatment of the incest theme in the novel in relation to the alien geography where Trueblood lives, pointing out that this act is anticipated by the narrator's "fall into an alternative topographical center," "out on a radically different plain of human and symbolic activity."[29] Furthermore, her analysis registers the status of the rural territory as abject in the novel. Mr. Norton's urgent and emphatic request to the protagonist to "Drive me away from here," "Away!" (69) also implies the moral, spiritual, and physical depravity that is associated with this landscape in the novel. Beyond signaling the perversion of incest, that the narrator "blundered" down a road that "seemed unfamiliar," which lies "beyond the farthest extension of the school-owned lands" and "off the highway" (46, 40), also anticipates the dissolution of his college career due to the machinations of Dr. Bledsoe. While the novel's map moves to the urban North, this rural byway functions as a primary catalyst for the narrator's journey and psychic evolution.

The narrator describes this rural area as a wasteland. The desolation of the landscape is also imprinted on its architectures. As the narrator recalls, "We were passing a collection of shacks and log cabins now, bleached white and warped by the weather. Sun-tortured shingles lay on the roofs like decks of water-soaked cards spread out to dry. The houses consisted of two square rooms joined together by a common floor with a porch in between. As we passed we could look through to the fields beyond. I stopped the car at [Mr. Norton's] excited command in front of a house set off from the rest" (46). This dilapidated house, which belongs to Jim Trueblood, is a visible sign of the moral depravity and physical degeneracy that bespeak his impoverished condition. In these passages, Ellison revises gothic conventions that were established in the fiction of such American authors as Nathaniel Hawthorne and Edgar Allan Poe to depict architectural decay, crumbling lineage, and sexual aberrance, conventions that also recur in southern literature. Furthermore, Ellison stresses the difference of this character from other rural folk. By highlighting Trueblood's cabin as peripheral within this schema of houses and shacks that is otherwise architecturally uniform, the novel offers a further spatial mapping of his alienation within the rural community. It demonstrates how varying kinds of spaces, from geography to architecture, are mutually constitutive in reflecting forms of difference and otherness also inscribed on the body.

Even before the incest, Trueblood's contact with the college was limited. In the narrator's words, "All of us at the college hated the black-belt people, the 'peasants,' during those days! We were trying to lift them up and they, like Trueblood, did everything it seemed to pull us down" (47). Ellison relates the quartet performances to Trueblood's status as a sexually perverse exhibition at which a consuming white gaze is directed, and thus relates the objectification of the Black Belt blacks in the novel to a complex schema of black-white social relations within the nation. Black Belt blacks are despised and viewed as detrimental to the uplift ideology that governs the college and are subordinated within its class-exclusive definition of black racial identity, a problem heralded within the "Blackness of Blackness" sermon of the prologue. Their toleration by other blacks is purely provisional and opportunistic. These dynamics reveal the role of geography in helping constitute hierarchical notions of black racial identity. Trueblood stands apart from the other rural men as he leads the quartet and is distinct from them in making "high, plaintively animal sounds" (47). These passages acknowledge a perception of him as dehumanized and as a kind of untouchable in the community who is better avoided and left alone. It is a dehumanization evident in the mechanistic, routine way in which he is paraded out and compelled to sing before the school's white audiences. The scientific curiosity that he becomes, along with the view of his body as degenerate on the basis of race, sexuality, and gender, only hyperbolize the scripts of him as different and other that are already evident.

The scar is a deformation of the body that will potentially extend to Matty Lou's child due to its incestuous paternity. The difference inscribed on Trueblood's body through its gaping scar mirrors the alienation of his house on the rural landscape. The incest ultimately compounds a difference and undesirability that had already mapped this character as other within and beyond his rural world. It thoroughly alienates him and makes him unspeakable, to the point that "his name was never mentioned above a whisper" by those at the college (46). In its wake, white voyeurs in this instance prevent officials at the college from actualizing the plan to ship him and his family out of the county. Ultimately, Trueblood comes to epitomize the most objectionable qualities imaginable among the intensely derided black peasant class that has proved itself unwieldy to attempts at racial uplift, and he is regarded as a disgrace (52). Furthermore, his incest has made him a virtually invisible outcast to whom his wife and daughter are "barely speaking" and at whom they are "hardly looking" (50). The narrator feels instinctive revulsion for Trueblood and shrugs off the hand that the farmer places on his shoulder. Indeed, terms such as *off*, *out*, and *away* saturate this section of the novel and reinforce the detachment with which Trueblood is dealt by everyone; the character is shunned and quarantined as if he had an infectious disease. Words such as *beyond* and *blundered* evoke the transgression, boundary crossing, and aberrance inherent in the incest. Recurrent images of blackness and darkness in this section, including the "soot-black" pot in which Matty Lou and Kate are washing and the "black dark" room in which the incest occurred (54), play on Western ideological associations of this color with impurity, disease, and depravity, particularly of a sexual nature, and further signal this character's pathology. The Black Belt geographical region in which Trueblood is located extends these figurative meanings. Such imagery functions as the obverse of a pure and innocent whiteness linked to such feminine models as the nude blonde and Norton's daughter and mediates and masks forms of white masculine sexual transgression. The reliance on this imagery, indeed, might be recognized as another level on which Ellison throws into relief the multifaceted quality of blackness within the novel's visual economy.

Several comparisons to animals in his dream, such as boar pigs and boss quails, like his "plaintive cries," extend this character's linguistic linkages to notions of the primitive and reflect his internalization of his debasement. The flies and gnats that buzz around his scar, pests that typically plague animals rather than human beings, reinforce these associations. Like his wound that is open to these bugs, he is open and accessible as white spectators come to consume the dirty details of his story. Furthermore, the insects evoke the breeding of pestilential disease, link his body to decay, and suggest its openness to further contamination.

Invisible Man critiques Mr. Norton's hierarchical view of race through his remarks on "degenerate" human stock. Significantly, he relates pathology to rural identities even before he learns of the incest, viewing Matty Lou's pregnancy without a husband as a typical phenomenon in such environments. The pregnancies, along with identical dresses, throw the bodies of Kate and Matty Lou into relief against the rural landscape. Their rounded bellies that mirror each other allude to the shared paternity of their babies. It is a sameness that paradoxically links them to perversion and difference. Trueblood's other children, with their little potbellies, show signs of malnutrition and thus have visible indicators of difference inscribed on their bodies also. The potential of rural geographies to imprint the body is further evident in Mr. Norton's fall at the Golden Day bar and in the raw place on his forehead afterward. The bruise iterates Trueblood's scar and suggests Mr. Norton's deep-seated and perverse desires for incest. Through the vet who insults Mr. Norton, a talented physician trained in France, Ellison acknowledges the lack of democracy for black military men in the South after World War I. Crassly, Ellison relates the vet's institutionalization to having been driven out of town by a mob of masked men (Klansmen?) for saving a human life.

If cultural geography is a useful framework for pondering the othering of southerners in the nation, then this field is perhaps especially appropriate for examining the rural when we consider the redoubled intensity with which contexts that are both southern *and* rural are sometimes vilified. Drawing on David Sibley's theoretical work on "geographies of exclusion," which is informed by perspectives in psychoanalysis such as Julia Kristeva's theories of abjection, Paul Cloke and Jo Little point out that "representations of rurality and rural life are replete with . . . devices of exclusion and marginalisation by which mainstream 'self' serves to 'other' the positioning of all kinds of people in the socio-spatial relations of different countrysides." They mention Sibley's references to ways in which red-coated huntsmen and idyllic villages are mobilized in the constitution of a conservative and nostalgic scripting of Englishness to remind us that hierarchies within rural contexts mitigate against the notion of a "generalised rural other."[30] The differential positioning of rural identities that Cloke and Little describe is useful for pondering *Invisible Man*'s multilayered schematization of Trueblood's alienation within a southern rural context.

The violation of the incest taboo and the scar signal Trueblood's abjection, and racial and spatial abjection are closely related in the novel. Moreover, we must remember that part of what makes the protagonist so irredeemable and unforgivable in Dr. Bledsoe's eyes is having ventured with Mr. Norton across spatial boundaries into such derided areas as the countryside and the Golden Day bar frequented by mentally ill veterans, a place whose very veneer marks it as a degenerate environment. The narrator contrasts architectures such as Trueblood's cabin and the Golden Day with those of the school in a passage that merits quoting at length:

> And in my mind I could see the brightly trimmed and freshly decorated campus buildings as they appeared on spring mornings—after the fall painting and the light winter snows, with a cloud riding over and a darting bird above—framed by the trees and encircling vines. The buildings had always seemed more impressive because they were the only buildings to receive regular painting; usually, the nearby houses and cabins were left untouched to become the dull grained gray of weathered wood. And I remembered how the splinters in some of the boards were raised from the grain by the wind, the sun and the rain until the clapboards shone with a satiny, silvery, silver-fish sheen: like Trueblood's cabin, or the Golden Day. . . . The Golden Day had once been painted white; now its paint was flaking away with the years, the scratch of a finger being enough to send it showering down. Damn the Golden Day! But it was strange how life connected up; because I had carried Mr. Norton to the old rundown building with rotting paint, I was here. (201)

The buildings of the campus and the picturesque natural environment that serves as their backdrop markedly contrast with the arid conditions in the countryside. The neglected houses and cabins on the campus mirror the dilapidated cabins in the countryside to some extent, a juxtaposition that reveals hierarchies of spatial difference even within the campus context. These reflections occur as the narrator learns the ropes on his job at the Liberty paints company in Long Island, which manufactures the brilliant color Optic White that emblematizes the purest and most resplendent whiteness. He ponders the error that he made in exposing Mr. Norton to people who are the equivalent of dirty linen in the race and realizes that part of this offense had to do with having shown Mr. Norton spaces that are considered to be inferior. Dr. Bledsoe affirms the link between space and invisibility, a larger theme of the novel, when he points out that whites are ordinarily only taken to places that the administration want them to see.

The cottage, as David Simpson observes, "came to stand for everything that seemed most admirably and solidly British (and in another historical sleight of hand, most *English*)."[31] Simpson suggests the extent to which this architecture was inscribed by race and class. Studies by R. W. Brunskill and Lawrence Grow have acknowledged British influences on the construction of the cottage as a form of vernacular architecture in the United States.[32] As Grow observes, "Wealthy merchants of colonial New York retired on weekends to rustic cottages up the Hudson far from business and formal social life. A pretty, quaint cottage was considered a fitting and fashionable form of building for informal living in the late eighteenth and early nineteenth centuries. This romantic view of cottage life was expressed in poetry, music, art, and fiction, as well as architecture."[33] This romantic perception and experience of the cottage has been less accessible in the African American context. Contrarily, from the era of slavery in the United States, the cabin and related spaces were most closely identified with African American identities and symbolically marked their subjection on the basis of race and class. These linkages are evident in the cruel fate of Frederick Douglass's grandmother, whose owners "took her out to the woods, built her a little hut, put up a little mud chimney, and then made her welcome to the privilege of supporting herself there in perfect loneliness; thus virtually turning her out to die!"[34] Notwithstanding its romances as seen in the 1943 film *Cabin in the Sky*, the cabin has typically signified African American economic and social exclusion in the nation.

In Jean Toomer's *Cane* (1923), a reworking of the pastoral, the narrator views the cabin home as a spatial catalyst for budding feminine sexuality in "Karintha," the first sketch:

> Homes in Georgia are most often built on the two-room plan. In one, you cook and eat, in the other you sleep, and there the love goes on. Karintha had seen or heard, perhaps she had felt her parents loving. One could but imitate one's parents, for to follow them was the way of God. She played "home" with a small boy who was not afraid to do her bidding.[35]

For the narrator, the cabin facilitates Karintha's alluring feminine sexuality "ripened too soon" and leads to a sexual transgression. Similarly, in *Invisible Man*, Ellison relates black cabin spatiality to the incest between Trueblood and Matty Lou, who is sleeping on a pallet between him and his wife. More broadly, southern geography shapes the incest narrative in the novel. Memories of taboos against interracial sex in the South and the concomitant myth in the region of black men as rapists, coupled with Trueblood's awareness of the racist linkage of sexual perversion with blackness ("They just nigguhs, leave 'em do it" [58]), catalyze his transgression of the incest taboo. In his dream, Trueblood crosses social boundaries separating black and white by going through the front door at Mr. Broadnax's place in the allegorical dream sequence that entails a search for fat meat, and subsequently enters another door that takes him into the bedroom of a white woman. This scenario reinforces levels on which the novel signals Trueblood as spatially othered as much as it affirms the impact of the past on his present actions.

It is significant that the incest occurs immediately after this portion of his dream sequence concludes, which demonstrates that Ellison's use of time is as methodical as his use of space. The representation of the alien status of Trueblood is also temporal. The clock itself might be interpreted as a symbol of the confluence of time and space in Ellison's novel. Trueblood is invoked in relation to the "Old stories" and "old families" (46, 47). That he is linked to a house that "appears quite old" (47), "an old cabin with its chinks filled with chalk-white clay, with bright new shingles patching its roof" (46), underscores the simultaneity with which the novel maps an identity for him that is temporal and spatial. However, the association of the Black Belt with the distant past is most evident in the perception of the performances of Trueblood's quartet on campus. These Sunday evenings in effect dramatize the difference and the distance between those located in the countryside and those affiliated with the school. Furthermore, in these scenes, perceptions of rural blacks as quaint, charming, and alluring coexist with the view of them as revolting and shameful even among black southerners, micropolitics that can be obscured as easily within such binary frameworks as north-south and rural-urban as by the concept of the generalized rural other that Cloke and Little describe.[36]

In the Trueblood scene, Ellison explores stereotypes of rural contexts as incestuous. Indeed, we can recognize the incest as a further level on which the novel maps the rural and thus a further indication of the novel's preoccupation with geography. However, the novel unsettles such geographical essentialisms concerning the rural by prefacing the encounter with Trueblood with hints at the white northern philanthropist's sexual attraction to his own daughter and by making reference to Mr. Norton's "blue eyes blazing into the black face with something like envy and indignation" upon hearing that Trueblood "looked upon chaos" without being destroyed and failed "to cast out the offending eye" (51). That Mr. Norton immediately requests to "go where there is shade" further implies the proverbial plank in his own eye (51). There is also an allusion here to the crystallization of Lot's wife Sarah, a phenomenon that in biblical narrative preceded Lot's incestuous encounters with his two daughters.[37] In addition to acknowledging the spectacled black body as a site of white voyeuristic sexual fascination, Ellison's novel well suggests ways in which rural bodies in the South have been made serviceable for the purpose of playing out fantasies of sexual transgression and perversion in this nation. That the Black Belt is figured saliently in Ellison's novel seems logical, too, because rural identities are ideal ones in relation to which we might examine questions of invisibility, an issue to which the recurrent references to sight in this scene also seem to point. As Barbara Ching and Gerald W. Creed point out, "the rural-identified may experience their marginalization as both invisibility and as spectacularly exaggerated denigration."[38]

In the nineteenth century sociological studies emphasized the lack of stability in black families and the need for white paternal mastery. By the turn of the twentieth century, W. E. B. Du Bois had begun to develop an academic counternarrative to ideologies of cultural and racial difference in social science while linking the persisting social problems of blacks in the South to a study of the emergent ghetto in the city of Philadelphia.[39] Joblessness, crime, and out-of-wedlock births expanded exponentially with African American migrations to the urban North in the first decades of the twentieth century. By the mid-1900s these issues had registered as a concern in the work of such sociologists as Gunnar Myrdal, who associated black families with pathology. Ralph Ellison was famously skeptical of sociology's seemingly insistent pathological view of blacks. This perspective perhaps informs his more complex and multilayered treatment of these problems through characters like Trueblood in fiction. The geographical dialectics of *Invisible Man* illustrate the rural southern origins of the "underclass" in the urban North. It is telling that Ellison acknowledges the status of the rural space as other and as one that is shunned, in part because of its perception as pathological, a perception that he relates to its poverty. Ultimately, sexuality emerges as the basis of these perceptions of pathology among the rural, which are manifest among blacks and whites alike. The novel dramatizes how perceptions of the rural as pathological are displaced onto a black masculine body and sexuality in this southern community.

Ellison's narrator's reluctance and embarrassment as he buys a yam suggests that deeply entrenched internecine stereotypes and prejudices against black rural southerners were equally—if not more—intense in the urban North. *Invisible Man* further acknowledges pronouncements of the ideological view of black rural southerners in the novel's Harlem section when a woman harshly berates the narrator after he drops a parcel into her curbside trash can. As she exclaims, "We keep our place clean and respectable and we don't want you field niggers coming up from the South and ruining things," and "I'm sick and tired of having you southern Negroes mess up things for the rest of us!" (328). Evidence of this impression is apparent, too, where the protagonist sees a new life in the North as an opportunity to shed his southern accent: "But here in the North I would slough off my southern ways of speech. Indeed, I would have one way of speaking in the North and another in the South" (164). Like the character Melvin Peterson in Charles Fuller's *A Soldier's Play*, Ellison's narrator feels shame over his southern background and plots to pass as a native northerner.

Invisible Man, like Toni Morrison's 1970 novel *The Bluest Eye*, highlights the status of black rural migrants in the urban North as inferior, marginal, and expendable in the African American context. Morrison chronicles the longing of a black girl named Pecola Breedlove for blue eyes, her rape by her father, and her decline into madness. *The Bluest Eye* links a decaying space to the social marginality and disavowal of an African American family but places the emphasis on an urban setting. A decrepit storefront home and its dilapidated furnishings feeds the Breedloves' consuming feeling of aesthetic inferiority and ugliness and constitutes their status as social outcasts. It is an alienation that intensifies once the father, Cholly, sets this home on fire, leading to the family's homelessness and brief separation: "Cholly Breedlove . . . a renting black, having put his family outdoors, had catapulted himself beyond the reaches of human consideration. He had joined the animals; was, indeed, an old dog, a snake, a ratty nigger."[40] By novel's end, Cholly's rape of Pecola deepens and intensifies perceptions of him as abject and inhuman. *The Bluest Eye* reveals that spatialized forms of black masculine abjection are not necessarily reducible to the rural South. Contrarily, Morrison offers a narrative of black masculine abjection in the urban North literalized in Cholly's abandonment by his mother on a trash heap when he was four days old.

Many critics have noted the impact of Trueblood and other folk elements on the narrator's development in the novel and have recognized these dimensions as part of the sum total of experiences that bring the narrator to a retreat in the basement. While much has been made of the south-to-north migration in the novel, what becomes clear with a microcosmic exploration of geography to examine the contours of the rural is that the invisibility which the novel enunciates in relation to the narrator is also refracted across a range of subject positions. That is to say, the invisibility and sense of otherness that the novel relates to the narrator—and his positioning within a border area outside Harlem where he plays Louis Armstrong—can be read as a further iteration of the geographical schema of the novel's Trueblood section. If we can identify the examination of the status of black and male identity in relation to the concept of the American as the larger problem with which *Invisible Man* concerns itself, the novel frames this investigation with a concomitant examination of the status of black southern rural identities in constituting the African American and black rural masculine identities in particular. Indeed, the novel recasts this invisibility and outsider status in Black Belt blacks. In this sense, the entirety of the novel, I suggest, can be thought of as a diffusion of this part, which is one reason that we cannot afford to ignore or dismiss these rural scenes.

Ellison's novel primarily relates space to processes of black masculine formation through the protagonist's sequestration in the basement to mark this character's invisibility. Space performs a very similar function for Ellison in scripting rural identities. The novel highlights architecture to emphasize Trueblood's exclusion and marginality as a rural man in the African American context. Furthermore, I want to suggest that the dilapidated cabin functions as an emblem of Trueblood's wounded and perverse masculine body. In this instance, it is useful to recall cultural geography's acknowledgment of articulations of the body as geography and the spatiality of masculine hierarchies. At the same time, it is intriguing to ponder levels on which the cabin emblematizes Trueblood's wounded psyche and sense of masculine selfhood. In a critical effort to clarify the historical impact of architectures on black male identity, Maurice O. Wallace has argued that "the black masculinist fondness for the home, the shanty, the underground room, the crypt, and the closet . . . speaks for a longing to abscond from the neurotically uncanny experience of social spectragraphia by a retreat away from the public sphere where the gaze tyrannizes into the remote interiority of that other construction of space: consciousness."[41] Drawing on Wallace's analysis, we can interpret Ellison's geographical grid, and the isolated cabin in which Trueblood is situated, as a marker of the race and gender of this character. The cabin materializes the trauma of Trueblood's subjection to an intrusive white gaze. It functions as a shield and cover for his nakedness before it, protecting him in the wake of his emergence as a public spectacle. This hyperembodiment is evident in Trueblood's performances at the university. It is a hyperembodiment that is abstracted and iterated with more intensity in the wake of the incest. Ellison links Trueblood's invisibility and abjection as a man who is black and rural to this background and, later, to the currency of the raced and sexed incest narrative. In the case of Mr. Norton, race and class privilege mask sexual perversion, which Ellison implies to be not only steeped in incestuous desires but also necrophilic. Hence, the novel illustrates how the politics of invisibility that delimit black male subjectivity in the national arena are channeled in relation to the rural.

If the rural more generally has sometimes been viewed as inimical within the project of black uplift and self-definition, then the signification of the rural as undesirable in shaping definitions of black masculinity is also important to recognize. *Invisible Man* clarifies the levels on which ideologies of inferiority and otherness that are grounded in geography, and particularly ones that alienate and exclude southern identities, become even more intense and complex in relation to the rural. The novel also demonstrates how the rural serves as a basis on which differences and distinctions are demarcated within the category of black men, even among men in the South. Whereas black male characters in the South from the narrator to Dr. Bledsoe are viewed as palatable within the project of African American uplift, for instance, Trueblood is not. Even before the incest, he and rural blacks are regarded as a lost and hopeless cause. Like Larsen, Ellison links the rural to an intensified form of black masculine abjection in the South. To be sure, black men perceived as "country" on the basis of such qualities as speech, dress, and mannerisms, even if celebrated and admired for voicing old-fashioned, down-home folk wisdom, have rarely been regarded as ideal models of black masculinity or desired as leaders in the African American context. It may be, even, that black men in the rural South are among those most vulnerable to politics of exclusion on the basis of geography in the African American context. Still, such politics are rarely acknowledged or discussed. Furthermore, such identities have largely remained invisible in contemporary critical and theoretical work on black masculinity, in part because of the prioritization of urban contexts in these dialogues.

Invisible Man suggests that the contours of the rural landscape are capable of unsettling inscriptions of gender, and perhaps also of race, on the body: "There were no trees and the air was brilliant. Far down the road the sun glared cruelly against a tin sign nailed to a barn. A lone figure bending over a hoe on the hillside raised up wearily and waved, more a shadow against the skyline than a man" (40). Contestations over definitions of masculinity in the Trueblood scene shape the broader thematic contours of the novel, which address existential questions related to identity, visibility, race, and masculinity. However, the struggle over Trueblood's masculine self-definition is most evident in the exchange with Kate following his sexual encounter with Matty Lou:

> "How come you don't go on 'way and leave us?" is the first words Kate says to me. "Ain't you done enough to me and this chile?"
> "I cain't leave you," I says. "I'm a man and man don't leave his family."
> She says, "Naw, you ain't no man. No man'd do what you did."
> "I'm still a man," I says. (66)

Kate's question in this exchange, by voicing a preference for distance from him, further relates space to the cumulative script of Trueblood as undesirable and alien that the section reveals.

As Houston A. Baker Jr. has observed, the anxiety over the status of African American manhood and its vulnerability to usurpation centrally shapes the dynamics in the Trueblood scene:

> While a number of episodes in *Invisible Man* (including Trueblood's dream) suggest the illusory freedoms and taboo-induced fears accompanying interaction between the black phallus and white women, only the Trueblood encounter reveals the phallus as producing Afro-American generations rather than wasting its seed upon the water. The cosmic force of the phallus

thus becomes, in the ritual action of the Trueblood episode, symbolic of a type of royal paternity, an aristocratic procreativity turned inward to ensure the royalty (the "truth," "legitimacy," or "authenticity") of an enduring black line of descent. In his outgoing phallic energy, therefore, the sharecropper is (as we learn on his first appearance in *Invisible Man*) a "hard worker" who takes care of "his family's needs." His family may, in a very real sense, be construed as the entire clan, or tribe, of Afro-America.[42]

Sharecropping families tended to have many children for the very practical reason of working the land for survival in the agrarian South, and thus the practice in a very material sense may have been related, even, to the possibilities for the perpetuity of African Americans in the United States in earlier historical moments—even as the precarious conditions that this population encountered in the South, such as poverty, disease, and racial terror, yielded high mortality rates. Furthermore, as bell hooks has observed, black men in the rural South had more autonomy to actualize patriarchal definitions of black masculinity once mass migrations to the urban North began, which were more difficult for black men living in urban contexts to approximate due to persisting joblessness.[43] Baker's idea that *Invisible Man* symbolically rests African American racial futurity and livelihood on Trueblood's assertion of patrimony is also compelling in light of its psychoanalytic moorings. Through his analysis, we can recognize how the novel frustrates systems of paternal inheritance from the beginning by foregrounding the narrator's grandfather, who encourages subversion through obsequious postures conventionally associated with the Uncle Tom. This aspect of the narrator's history is rendered ironic through the grotesque minstrel images on the bank that he discovers and keeps despite several efforts to dispose of it. The grandfather admits to having lost dignity by giving up the gun during Reconstruction. His comment attests to historical models of black southern masculine insurgency and resistance. He appears to the narrator in a dream suggesting how important it is to "keep this nigger boy running," which, in effect, foreordained the narrator's preoccupation with flight and escape across several geographies, signaling the novel's crisis of paternal inheritance. Yet I am also intrigued by ways in which perceptions of the rural as undesirable and "other" limit Trueblood's potential to stand in as a representative embodiment of black manhood as well as the possibilities for construing his family as an exemplar of the category of African American. The temporal and spatial disavowals of this character imply black rural identity to be expendable within definitions of blackness and masculinity. Through a closer analysis of Trueblood's story's content in the section that follows, we can uncover deeper layers of the novel's geography and examine more specific ways in which the novel's larger narrative patterns reflect this rural section.

Space and the Story

As is often the case with novels as a genre, *Invisible Man* presents a hierarchy of narratives. The protagonist's long embedded narrative that incorporates stories, sermons, and speeches from a range of characters takes readers on a journey back to his past. The time of telling Trueblood's tale sets it apart and establishes its authority within the stream of the narrator's story. On some levels, and in a formal sense, it also recalls the digressions that sometimes interrupted and supplemented first-person narratives in Spanish and English novels in earlier centuries.[44] Trueblood's strategies of narration and the shape of his story are constituted by the rural geography in which he is situated. In this sense, the rural scenes are an indispensable interpretive framework for the long narrative that the protagonist surrenders and organically shape it. Trueblood's story itself also enacts a further spatial mapping of his otherness in the novel.

Kathleen Stewart has related the otherness of rural identities to the production of local narratives in rural settings that run counter to the dominant mythic American narratives, which are steeped in cultural signifiers devoid of historical and social specificity. She relates these alternative narratives to "the space on the side of the road," which "enacts the density, texture and force of a lived cultural experience somewhere in the hinterlands of 'America.'" Such narratives give priority to the storyteller. This framework is useful for pondering how Trueblood's tale of incest shapes the rural geography in *Invisible Man*.[45] His story, which describes the why and how of the incestuous encounter with Matty Lou, mediates his encounter with the narrator and Mr. Norton. Where they are in the mnemonic space on the side of the road in every way enables the telling of the story and reinforces its meaning. Trueblood's cabin is literally located on the side of a desolate country road whose white dividing line signals the narrator's momentary suspension there. Just as Mr. Norton and the protagonist literally wind up in this alien space where they meet Trueblood, so the plot of the story that Trueblood tells them incorporates an embedded narrative of this space, "where meanings or messages lie immanent in things and the narrator or protagonist ends up in an 'Other' world."[46] Trueblood recollects several spaces, both real and imagined. His narrative of entrapment in the clock, which epitomizes his experience of otherworldliness in the novel, bears quoting at length:

> And I caint stop—although I got a feelin' somethin' is wrong. I git aloose from the woman now and I'm runnin' for the clock. At first I couldn't git the door open, it had some kinda crinkly stuff like steel wool on the facing. But I gits it open and gits inside and it's hot and dark in there. I goes up a dark tunnel, up near where the machinery is making all that noise and heat. It's like the power plant they got up to the school. It's burning hot as iffen the house was caught on fire, and I starts to runnin', tryin' to git out. I runs and runs till I should be tired but ain't tired but feelin' more rested as I runs, and runnin' right up over the town. Only I'm still in the *tunnel*. Then way up ahead I sees a bright light like a jack-o-lantern over a graveyard. It gits brighter and brighter and I know I got to catch up with it or else. Then all at once I was right up with it and it burst like a great big electric light in my eyes and scalded me all over. Only it wasn't a scald, but like I was drownin' in a lake where the water was hot on the top and had cold numbin' currents down under it. Then all at once I'm through it and I'm relieved to be out and in the cool daylight again. (59)

In this space, images of darkness, as contrasted with images of brightness and lightness, recast the juxtaposition of black and white bodies. We can say that it is story that primarily enables the literal incestuous encounter with Matty Lou. These dynamics conform to Stewart's description of "a world . . . in which events are always mediated by story and in which the story of finding oneself on the side of the road is a conventional opening that posits, among other things, that things happen, that *places* mark the space of lingering impacts and unseen forces, that the world speaks to people who find themselves caught in it."[47] The curious story of ending up in the house and the clock licenses his process of narration. These spaces have left a psychic impact, shape his actions, and also mark the transgression of incest. In keeping with Stewart's idea that the space of story becomes so encompassing that "action follows fabulation," Trueblood becomes caught up in his dream to the point that the culmination is the commission of a sexual act with his daughter.[48] Furthermore, the "real" of this incestuous encounter is only retrievable and imaginable for him through the mediation of story. As the language of the novel reveals, the narrator, by making a fateful turn off the highway, ends up in a place where he does not belong, a forbidden place, in effect mirroring Trueblood's transgression of incest. Through the narrator, Ellison's novel reinforces its linkages between traversal into forbidden space and forbidden sex. The protagonist's first-person story that makes up the novel, like Trueblood's, is profoundly marked by an encounter with a space on the side of the road.

Again, the raw wound on Trueblood's face, the trace of his wife's ax attack that occurred in the aftermath of his intercourse with Matty Lou, signals his bodily abjection in the psychoanalytic sense. If, as Kathleen Stewart observes, the body or mind marked by events is what authorizes narration in the space on the side of the road and inscribes the listener into the space of the story, then we can further read this wound as the sign that bequeaths him authority to speak.[49] In keeping with the characteristics that Stewart outlines, Mr. Norton and the narrator are suspended in time and space in the scene of the story. As the narrator reports, "I looked at Mr. Norton and stood up, listening to Trueblood so intensely he didn't see me, and I sat down again, cursing the farmer silently. To hell with his dream!" (57). Similarly, the narrator acknowledges his own absorption in Trueblood's narrative: "As I listened I had been so torn between humiliation and fascination that I had to lessen my sense of shame. I kept my attention riveted upon his intense face" (68). Indeed, in the case of Mr. Norton, an implied covetousness of his daughter is the key factor that makes him both subject and object and places him inside and outside of Trueblood's story as a listener. The material conditions under which Trueblood lives, especially prior to the incest that brings an economic windfall for his family, along with the hierarchical dynamic between the countryside and the college, are factors that further align his narrative with the space on the side of the road elaborated by Stewart, a space frequently occupied by industry and other exploitative forces.

Before I conclude this chapter, I want to acknowledge interpretive frameworks beyond the theories of abjection in psychoanalysis that are useful for pondering the rural geography in *Invisible Man* and, in particular, the cabin space. In *The Poetics of Space: The Classic Look at How We Experience Intimate Places*, Gaston Bachelard acknowledges linkages between the house and memory and the importance of considering the spatiality of memories within the realm of psychoanalysis. In his words, "Of course, thanks to the house, a great many of our memories are housed, and if the house is a bit elaborate, if it has a cellar and garret nooks and corridors, our memories have refuges that are all the more clearly delineated. All our lives we come back to them in our daydreams. A psychoanalyst should, therefore, turn his attention to the simple localization of our memories."[50] In *Invisible Man*, the narrator observes that Trueblood knows the land well enough to get around in utter darkness. This information therefore makes a little suspect Trueblood's assertion that the incest occurs in part because the room was "as black as the middle of a bucket of tar" (54), and because positioning in the dark room next to Matty Lou evoked memories of a former lover. In general, this scene raises moral and ethical concerns of the highest order. As many of its critics have pointed out, there is really no interpretive sleight of hand that can move us beyond its horror or reprehensibility. The explanation that Trueblood provides is fascinating to analyze in light of Gaston Bachelard's observation that "the house is not experienced from day to day only, on the thread of a narrative, or in the telling of our own story. Through dreams, the various dwelling-places in our lives co-penetrate and retain the treasures of former days." Bachelard outlines the concept of topoanalysis, which he defines as "the systematic psychological study of the intimate sites of our lives," to attempt to remedy the benign neglect of the daydream within the discourse of psychoanalysis, along with the prioritization of time over space.[51] Though Bachelard suggests that dreams return us to the most primal and influential houses in our lives, which he locates in childhood, it is important to acknowledge that his analysis is implicitly shaped by and oriented toward a white, European, middle-class subjectivity. This emphasis emblematizes the historical indifference of psychoanalysis to questions of race, a critical indifference that Hortense Spillers, Christopher Lane, Anne Cheng, and Claudia Tate have addressed. Furthermore, it suggests the limitations inherent in any attempt to apply the discourses of psychoanalysis to black identity.[52] Nevertheless, we can draw effectively on Bachelard to ponder the cumulative and looming impact of the several home spaces that Trueblood experiences in his adulthood. Bachelard's theoretical model seems all the more appropriate for pondering this character because daydream (albeit at night and under the covers) *is* precisely where the fateful dream sequence begins.

Bachelard's model is one that we might apply productively to Ellison's narrator. As Bachelard points out, "We should have to undertake a topo-analysis of all the space that has invited us to come out of ourselves." He goes on to suggest that "each of us . . . should speak of his roads, his crossroads, his roadside benches; each one of us should make a surveyor's map of his lost fields and meadows."[53] The event of the novel, as rendered through an uninterrupted stream of flashbacks set in both northern and southern contexts, rehearses all the encounters that illustrate the narrator's frustrated and misguided attempts to find himself. The novel is inherently spatial in attempting to revisit these roads and to recuperate memories that are implied to be necessary, both to reconcile the narrator with his past and to establish the possibilities for his reemergence from the basement. The narrator's home, which is a "hole" at the time we are hearing the story, is the space through which the narrator reflects on his past homes and surrenders the novel as a meditation on the philosophical question, What did *I do* to be so black and blue? For the narrator, an engagement with the South is psychologically recursive and inextricable to his identity, even as he has opted to remain physically removed from the region, "for all of it is a part of me" (579). To the extent that they evoke the roadside, memory, and processes of storytelling, the theories of Bachelard and Stewart are strikingly resonant and therefore all the more useful to juxtapose here.

An August 2003 *Essence* magazine article entitled "Back to the Land" featured an African American family that moved from a Detroit home, an "urban prison" with metal bars where sirens were heard frequently, to a 4,400-square-foot house on "acres of land" in Cairo, Georgia, with "a swimming pool, a pond, three pastures and an old red barn," and sounds of "frogs" and "chirping birds." According to the article, "More families are moving to rural areas, especially in the South, for more spacious housing—and for peace of mind."[54] This romantic myth of abundant, pastoral living in the rural South has been concomitant with the phenomenon of return migrations to the region among African Americans in recent years. It illustrates how the rural South is often still invoked to signify quintessentially what blackness is, where blacks in the United States have come from historically, and where some of them are interested in going. Still, these idealized representations of the rural should never obscure the politics of ridiculing, mocking, and scorning black rural southerners that continue to be evident even nowadays, for instance, on African American comedy circuits. Moreover, they easily veil such social factors as escalating rates of drug abuse and the HIV/AIDS crisis in such contexts.

In a nation that was increasingly modernizing and undergoing processes of social change that had begun to unsettle and reorganize the race relations that had marked the long Jim Crow era, Ellison captures the layers and complex contours of the rural South through his landscape in *Invisible Man*. His novel confronts class politics underlying meanings of blackness. It unsettles socially exclusive definitions of the African American that constitute black, rural, and southern identities as anterior and elemental because they lie beyond the pale of middle-class notions of racial selfhood. Through its narrative strategies, the novel boldly puts the rural "out there." At this level, it tropes the rural specularity that it critiques thematically, while contravening and resisting the typical representations of the rural as other within the African American category. The visual framing of the rural in this novel thus extends the salient hermeneutics on invisibility, race, and masculinity. *Invisible Man* suggests that if manhood is difficult to actualize and assert against the hegemony of American racism, which prevents black men from being seen and from procuring the rights and privileges of citizenship, then the stakes for actualizing this ideal are further complicated on the rural terrain. It demonstrates that rural identity in the South in a time of Jim Crow meant being open and accessible to hyperembodiment, scrutiny, and spectatorship, and, potentially, forms of abuse and exploitation in science and medicine. The novel presents an epic counternarrative to the regional and ultimately national myth of an abject and sexually perverse black masculinity that, emerging in the nineteenth century, was designed to confine and rationalize the conservation of citizenship and democracy for white men, which was steeped in the fantasy of a pathological black masculine body. Furthermore, the novel shows how the rural variably defined what blackness was within a racist imagination and demarcated what it was not or should not be within ideologies of uplift. Therein, among blacks and whites alike, it emerges as a sign of quintessential otherness and pronounced difference.

The view of black "folk" identity as retrograde and temporally displaced is one that Leigh Anne Duck has recently related to early-twentieth-century writers ranging from Jean Toomer to George S. Schuyler, linking the migrant pathology generated within the urban northern black middle classes to this perceived temporal disjunction.[55] Through his emphasis on masculine bodies, Ellison reveals how pathologies of black rural southerners had roots in the rural South and continuities and parallels in the urban North. In the process, he reveals the limitations in notions of black folk and rural romance.

Like scripts of blackness, the scripts of whiteness that have emerged from the South have by no means been monolithic. The South has served as a central ideological wellspring in the nation for socially inferior and undesirable notions of white identity that have been complemented by elitist and purist models of whiteness. Hence, in some cases, ideologies of authentic whiteness have been as charged and weighted as those related to authentic blackness. These ideologies have been mutually constitutive. As Ellison shows, both have worked dialectically in shaping the nation's dominant notions of racial identity and belonging. In juxtaposing (1) the processes of African American subjection in constituting an exclusive notion of American subjectivity on the basis of race and class with (2) the subjection of black rural identities in producing elite notions of African American identity, Ellison reveals the instrumentality of black rural southerners in unsettling such categories as "African American" and "American." His novel confirms the indispensability of the South for thinking about questions and processes related to identity formation in the nation. It shows us that we can no more afford for the rural to be a marginal term in studying the South than we can afford to "other" blackness in studying the rural. It reminds us that if the problem of race in the United States from the antebellum period and the Civil War to the Civil Rights era and into the current millennial age has been national in scope, the national problem is also southern at heart. Furthermore, the spectral memory of the South for the narrator points to how much the region figures as a central historical example in constituting the discourses of race in the United States.

Nevertheless, there are clear limits in Ellison's vision of the rural and the level of cultural authority that its subjects can claim. Ellison's relation of the development of the narrator's philosophy of hibernation and withdrawal to the encounter with the Black Belt easily implies the South to be a passive and dormant site of black political resistance. Furthermore, *Invisible Man* makes urban geography indispensable to the formation of black leadership. Notwithstanding his foundations in the South, the journey north is a prelude to the narrator's assumption of a role of African American cultural authority. Similarly, the novel advances the logic of the urban as authentic in definitions of black masculinity. It expands the groundwork for a mythology of black urban masculine strength and black southern masculine weakness that, as the next chapter will reveal, became pervasive during the black-liberation era. Indeed, *Invisible Man* may have been prophetic in anticipating the political manipulations and betrayals that Malcolm X encountered as a young minister in the Nation of Islam and in staging the self-conscious and highly stylized transformation of a "country boy" into a radical urban political leader.[56] It might be said, however, that this logic of black masculine authenticity, with its regional inflections, would drastically circumscribe the view of Ellison himself as a novelist. That is to say, while Ellison's novel reached heights of critical acclaim that made the author worthy of a National Book Award in 1953, he suffered castigation just as extreme during the 1960s when he was labeled an "Uncle Tom" whose repertoire lacked political relevance to the black-liberation struggle. These accusations reflected the politics of invoking the "Uncle Tom" epithet in the African American context to signal a lack of authenticity in terms of race and masculinity. The following chapter ponders the seldom acknowledged regional contours of these politics.

CHAPTER 4

Spike Lee's Uncle Toms and Urban Revolutionaries

Bruce Perry's 1992 biography of Malcolm X was controversial due to a variety of claims, with the most provocative of them being that the young Malcolm engaged in same-sex relations with a white boy as a teenager—and later on as an unemployed young adult in New York—to earn income and to decrease his dependence on women for money.[1] In a sense, Perry's biography recasts the sensationalism of Malcolm X's autobiography with little difference. That is to say, Perry's portrait in the biography lies on a continuum with the descriptors of Malcolm X as a former "hoodlum," "thief," "dope peddler," and "pimp" that were explicitly invoked in the marketing of the autobiography when it was published in 1965.[2] One only need stir "homosexual" into the mix. In this sense, that such experiences may have occurred registers as yet another potential layer of pathological behavior in Malcolm X's past.

Regardless of the truth content in Perry's claims, a discussion of sexuality is perhaps one of the last frontiers that remain to be explored where Malcolm X is concerned. Such a conversation seems both necessary for and indispensable to a more complex and in-depth understanding of who Malcolm X was. His lived experiences as a heterosexual man have often been treated far too evasively. As Arnold Rampersad has pointed out, there has been little insight into the impact of factors such as twelve years of celibacy, sexed and gendered fashioning in the Nation of Islam, and outrage over Elijah Muhammad's extramarital affairs on Malcolm X's political formation.[3] Those who have regarded Malcolm X as an ideal exemplar of black masculinity in the decades after his death have rarely embraced, recuperated, or recognized the conservative aspect of his political philosophy related to sex, and they even seem to overlook it insistently. In some black-nationalist circles, for instance, if aspects of his philosophy perceived to be in keeping with the tenets of the Nation of Islam—such as those related to food, smoking, drinking, and dating endogamy—have been embraced, the embrace typically stops short on the matter of sex.

Silence about sexuality has also been evident in popular representations of Malcolm X. For instance, while acknowledging that Malcolm X and his friend Shorty's harsh jail sentences had less to do with their charges for petty theft and were more related to the judge's rage over their "crime" of "sleeping with white women," Spike Lee's 1992 epic film *Malcolm X* only goes so far as to depict its Malcolm X, whose portrayal earned the actor Denzel Washington an Academy Award nomination, kissing the white "Sophia" in a convertible under moonlight and in a postcoital phase with her when they have become lovers.[4]

As Laura Kipnis points out, "the national sex scandal" has become a weapon of choice in the contemporary public sphere for purposes of disciplining and shaming prominent male leaders.[5] Although, in more recent years, the increasingly invasive media have also expressed much intrigue toward the sexual indiscretions of prominent leaders, sex controversies have not been linked to Malcolm X in the way that they have emerged in relation to several other major leaders of his time. No evidence has ever turned up to suggest that Malcolm X engaged in extramarital affairs. While the sexual excesses of his youth are well known, he was by every indication faithful to his wife, Betty Shabazz, with whom he fathered six daughters, including twins born after his death.

Still, Malcolm X's personal sexual history is not necessarily the most fecund basis for dialogues about the topic of Malcolm X and sex. Furthermore, I want to suggest that the possible past homosexual encounters that Perry describes are not even the *only* conceivable point from which we might begin to move productively toward a queer epistemology on Malcolm X. As Marlon Ross has pointed out, "Beyond the necessary task of exposing homophobia, beyond the attempt to read the fixed sexual identity of writers, readers, and situations in African American literature and history, beyond attempting to articulate a unique position from which black queerness can be recognized, we need to examine the formal and material practices that mark sexual identity as a resource for racial identification and racial identity as a resource for sexual identification within and across historical moments within and across cultural traditions." Furthermore, Ross has observed that "the preference for sexualized invective—and more specifically the gesture of queerbaiting" was "a common feature of black cultural nationalism from the 1960s to the present," and that the dozens are "a mode of street-smart verbal jousting affiliated with urban, working-class supermasculine (i.e., avowedly heterosexual) African-American culture since at least the early twentieth century."[6] I want to suggest that Malcolm X's speech repertoires offer useful insights for thinking toward a more extensive discourse on sexuality, including the topic of queerness.

Malcolm X has served as a prominent symbol of black masculinity since the era of black liberation. However, beyond the sheer power of his heroic masculine iconicity, there has been little interest in looking at how he constituted a discourse on authentic blackness and maleness that was strongly inflected by ideologies of sexuality in his speeches.[7] Some of his speeches construct a hierarchical black masculinity through a north-south binary and also produce tropes of Martin Luther King Jr.—and, by extension, black men in the South more generally—as homosexual, constituting them as alien, inferior, and ineffective within the black-liberation movement. The critique directed at King's platforms on integration and nonviolence in the southern-based Civil Rights movement cast him as an inadequate and inferior revolutionary, frequently invoking him as an "Uncle Tom" and "house

Negro." With its homophobic innuendoes of homosexuality, it construed black southern male bodies as pathological. In doing so, it ironically re-cast the historical economy of ideologies of black masculinity in the South that reflected white raced and sexed stereotypes, including the Uncle Tom that was steeped in ideological scripts of the body and sexuality, along with representations of black Reconstruction politicians as incompetent. (It is ar-guable, even, that he invoked the Uncle Tom alongside black rapist mythol-ogy in certain instances.) These aspects of Malcolm X's speech discourse suggest the necessity for a more expansive understanding of geography in constituting black masculinity. As we shall see in this chapter, some of its traces were evident in later black-liberation thought and such popular-culture media as Spike Lee's films.

That there has not been enough open discussion about Malcolm X and issues related to sex and sexuality is certainly a factor that also makes the paucity of conversations on the sexual and gender politics of his speeches understandable. While Malcolm X's autobiography remains the most fa-miliar literary legacy of the leader, it is important to remember that Mal-colm X's speeches were what primarily made him captivating as a leader during his lifetime, to the point that he received constant coverage in the national press. Indeed, a good bit of his schedule during his final years was devoted to speaking to students at many institutions of higher education in and beyond the United States, including Harvard on multiple occasions. He, like King, helped originate the modern black public intellectual in the sense that has frequently been defined by such scholars as Cornel West, Michael Eric Dyson, and bell hooks. Mike Wallace's five-part report enti-tled "The Hate That Hate Produced" in 1959 began to give Malcolm X— who was at the time the national spokesperson for Elijah Muhammad and minister of Nation of Islam Temple No. 7 in New York—a level of visibility in the mainstream national media that would remain high. His legacy has had a continuing influence on black political and intellectual thought over four decades after his assassination. The rebirth of the Nation of Islam un-der Louis Farrakhan in the wake of Elijah Muhammad's death also helped sustain the interest in Malcolm X's life and work. Malcolm X's circulation as a commodity in black popular culture, which culminated in Spike Lee's circulation of paraphernalia with the lone symbol "X" as a way of marketing the film *Malcolm X*, helped make Malcolm X more familiar and accessible to younger generations born after the black-liberation era. Law professor

Patricia J. Williams has discussed this film's presentation of a less fiery Malcolm X that even white Americans could embrace and that someone like the controversial conservative Supreme Court justice Clarence Thomas could regard as a role model. Perhaps it even helped set the stage for Malcolm X's ironic (and co-opting) absorption into the pantheon of American national heroes during the 1990s.[8] Being enshrined on a U.S. Postal Service stamp in 1999 is an honor that Malcolm X surely would not have ever imagined he would receive in the United States.

On one level, we can ponder how geography helps shape constructions of black masculinity by examining his personal transition from rural to urban as well as the central role the urban has played in his aestheticization in black popular contexts. In his typical representations in films, art, photography, and music, the articulate, suited, bespectacled, and hat-wearing man that Malcolm X fashioned himself into under the tutelage of Elijah Muhammad and the Nation of Islam has been prioritized and circulated. There has been comparatively little popular interest in exploring phases of Malcolm X's life *before* he became a member of this organization, including his childhood in Omaha, Nebraska, and his youth in Lansing, Michigan. The image of Malcolm X embraced in the black popular arena of the 1990s, for instance, was a far cry from the one of the youth Malcolm Little who, in his sister Ella's estimation, came close to looking like "countrified members of the Little family come up from Georgia" (47).[9] In *The Autobiography of Malcolm X*, he describes his appearance when he first moved to Boston to live with her:

> I looked like Li'l Abner. Mason, Michigan, was written all over me. My kinky reddish hair was cut hick style, and I didn't even use grease in it. My green suit's coat sleeves stopped above my wrists, the pants legs showed three inches of socks. Just a shade lighter green than the suit was my narrow-collared, three-quarter length Lansing department store topcoat. (47)

This image would be drastically modified almost immediately, with Malcolm making himself over to fit into his new environment by adopting the zoot suit, conking his hair, using the popular slang of the time, moving around on the nightclub circuit in the city, and participating in economies of gambling and petty theft. A native of Omaha, Nebraska, and a transplant to Boston by way of Lansing, Michigan, Malcolm's plight suggests that it was not only rural black migrants from the South who faced the challenge of fitting in and surviving in the urban North and who felt the pressure to alter or mask their "country" ways in an effort to conform linguistically, stylistically, and behaviorally to the tenor of life in the city (à la Ellison's Invisible Man as described in the previous chapter). Rural blacks migrating from almost anywhere to a city like Boston would have been in the same boat as the black migrants from the deep South who made up the vast majority of the population entering urban cities in the early decades of the twentieth century. As Robin D. G. Kelley has noted, the stylistic transformation was the key symbol of the young Malcolm's urbanization.[10] The Li'l Abner–like appearance described by Malcolm X has been conventionally incompatible with the hipster aesthetics of the city, which were the early foundations of what Richard Majors and Janet Mancini Billson have outlined as the "cool pose" so central to the fashioning of style, voice, and behavior among some black men in contemporary urban contexts.[11] That urban aesthetics would be prioritized in contemporary black popular culture is also understandable in light of John Jeffries's observation that "in black popular culture, the city is hip. It's the locale of cool. In order to be 'with it,' you must be in the city, or at a minimum, urban culture must be transplanted, simulated, or replicated outside the city whenever possible."[12]

As Shane White and Graham White point out, clothing has been a salient element in defining African American cultural specificity in the public sphere.[13] The later radical stylistic transformations that Malcolm X would undergo upon entering the Nation of Islam, such as getting rid of his conk while still in prison and wearing business attire upon his release, along with renouncing drinking, cursing, and all other perceived vices, reflected the discipline that the organization expected and required of all its members. This metamorphosis into "Minister Malcolm" paralleled the makeover as a "hipster" that he underwent years earlier upon first arriving in the city, for clothing—including the conservative Euro-American style of suit that was adopted among members of the Nation to evoke the manner and respectability conventionally associated with white men of the white-collar class—was perceived as part and parcel of what made the man in the organization. This conservative fashion was fundamental to shaping Malcolm X into the authoritative, charismatic leader that he became first in Harlem and, eventually, in the national context. For instance, Imam Benjamin Karim, who was to become the assistant to Malcolm X at Temple No. 7 in Harlem, chronicles his first impressions of the dress and attitude of members of the organization, which he joined soon after witnessing Malcolm X's charismatic confrontation of police in Harlem on behalf of a police brutality victim: "Inside, what struck me immediately was the 'uprightness,' the sobriety of the brothers walking around. I am not sure whether the first impression was favorable or unfavorable, but I am sure that with my conked hair in contrast to their close-cut haircuts and my dress and demeanor quite different from their sober, dignified air, I was not fully at ease." Upon becoming Benjamin 2X, Karim underwent a transformation similar to the one that Malcolm X had experienced: "By the time this happened I was a changed person, inside and out. I cut my hair and began to look like those other brothers I had noted with a mixture of curiosity and concern that first day at the mosque. I was never much of a drinker, but now I drank not at all. I had been a fairly flamboyant dresser, but now I dressed soberly. I had been a great curser, but now I stopped completely. I had been a pork eater, and now I stopped completely. . . . It was as though I had been reborn, a new person."[14] Already seasoned by the perils and threats with which he had to contend in the black male–dominated urban underworld as a hustler and petty thief, as well as by his experiences as a worker of low-wage jobs in the city as a shoeshine and busboy, it is perhaps safe to say that for Malcolm X, the adoption of this style took him into yet another phase of his urbanization, so that he would come to see himself as organ and voice for blacks in the urban North and as the epitome of the type of northern black man whose disenfranchisement, invisibility, and poverty might well someday erupt into violent revolutionary action against the dominant social order.

The popular representation of Malcolm X as the epitome of revolutionary black masculinity in the United States and the highlighting of his urban identity has also obscured other geographical details of his life such as his West Indian background. Chapters 2 and 3 of this study acknowledge that such terms as *southern*, *country*, and *rural* are frequently perceived to be incompatible with perceptions of authentic black masculinity. Portrayals of Malcolm X in the black popular context distance him from his rural roots because rurality would not mesh with images of him as masculine and militant, the qualities for which he has been most cherished, admired, and nostalgically remembered. Reducing Malcolm X to his urban identity has been very crucial to his authentication as a model of conventional black masculinity. As Barbara Ching and Gerald W. Creed have observed, "Rural and urban distinctions . . . are important dimensions of identity and hierarchy."[15]

This logic is quite apparent, for instance, in Spike Lee's *Malcolm X*, by far the most ubiquitous popular representation of Malcolm X in recent years. The film embeds the rural background of Malcolm X in several flashback sequences to his childhood in Omaha, such as the Ku Klux Klan breaking windows in the Little family's home because of his father's work as a Garveyite. However, immediate action in the film begins with an emphasis on the young-adult Malcolm's transformation into a conked, zoot-suited, urban hipster. It is very telling that we see little of what Malcolm X calls attention to in his autobiography as the "country" aspects of his identity, of which he had been admittedly ashamed: "Like hundreds of thousands of country-bred Negroes who had come to the Northern black ghetto before me, and have come since, I'd acquired all the other fashionable ghetto adornments—the zoot suits and conk . . . liquor, cigarettes, then reefers—all to erase my embarrassing background" (66). Here, the autobiography is especially revealing where it suggests the contrived and performative character of urban-centered models of black masculinity. Showing "country" aspects of Malcolm X may have had the effect of mitigating the iconic force of the ideal black masculine revolutionary model that the film seems invested in construing the leader to have been. Lee's film, I suggest, affirms the primacy of the urban in aestheticizing and authenticating black masculinity as much as it reconstitutes the conventional linkages between the black-nationalist revolutionary activist and the urban at later junctures once Malcolm metamorphoses into a Nation of Islam disciple. The film's commitment to associating Malcolm X with an urban context is apparent in the scenes presented at the beginning that feature Malcolm X as his scalp burns while his hair is conked with a homemade preparation and the spectacle of a walk with his friend Shorty in new zoot suits. They are clearly designed for comic relief. To have introduced the character upon his arrival at Ella's in Boston looking like "Li'l Abner," however, would have no doubt had similar if not more pronounced comedic effects.[16] Disavowals of the rural aspects of Malcolm X's identity seem to occur even as the film paradoxically suggests through the flashbacks that the traumatic memories of his life and experiences in rural contexts were fundamental to the eventual development of his consciousness as a revolutionary. Malcolm X's appearance in the months before his death wearing a beard and traditional Muslim garb while on trips to Mecca marked the final major stylistic transition in his life while signifying his separation from Nation of Islam ideology. What we lose when there is an exclusive focus on the urban in constructing and marketing Malcolm X as a popular icon is a more comprehensive look at the various details of his life that formed the radical political outlook for which he became best known, from his early life as one of few blacks in a predominately white environment in rural America to his status as the child of West Indian immigrants. For instance, Malcolm X acknowledged during his final speech at Harvard on December 16, 1964, that his "Chickens Coming Home to Roost" statement—which is one of the most radical ones that he ever made—had been informed by his status as "an old farm boy myself."[17]

Malcolm X's constitution of the ideal black revolutionaries as urban northern and the most inferior ones as southern points to the salience of geography in shaping discourses of race and masculinity in the African American context. In his autobiography, Malcolm X most directly refers to black men in the South within a critique of northern liberalism. It is important to acknowledge that he is ostensibly quite respectful of their leadership on what he implies to be their particular battlefield of black liberation. Nevertheless, his ultimate message is that they have a less challenging role in racial struggle given that the overt character of racism in the South makes the enemy easier to recognize than in the urban North. By highlighting his lack of familiarity with the South, he implies that the North alone taught him the depths of American racism. The vitriol of racism in the North, by his account, has made black northern men the most dangerous ones in the nation.

The rhetoric that helped shape what I am suggesting to have been a geographically inflected and hierarchical formulation of black masculinity is most apparent and straightforward in several speeches. "Twenty Million Black People in a Political, Economic, and Mental Prison," which was delivered January 23, 1963, at Michigan State University, and his famous "Message to the Grassroots," which was delivered November 10, 1963, at the Northern Negro Grass Roots Leadership Conference in Detroit, Michigan, a few weeks prior to his silencing by the Nation, are both prime examples. In these speeches, he invokes the division of labor of the plantation during slavery to assert that proximity to two key personality types—the "house

Negro" and the "field Negro"—will determine whether black leaders perceive black nationalism to be a viable option:

> There were two kinds of slaves, the house Negro and the field Negro. The house Negroes—they lived in the house with master, they dressed pretty good, they ate good because they ate his food—what he left. They lived in the attic or the basement, but still they lived near the master; and they loved the master more than the master loved himself. They would give their life to save the master's house—quicker than the master would. If the master said, "We got a good house here," the house Negro would say, "Yeah, we got a good house here." Whenever the master said "we," he said "we." That's how you can tell a house Negro.
>
> On that same plantation, there was the field Negro. The field Negroes—those were the masses. There were always more field Negroes than there were Negroes in the house. The Negro in the field caught hell. He ate leftovers. In the same house they ate high up on the hog. The Negro in the field didn't get anything but what was left of the insides of the hog. They call it "chitt'lings" nowadays. . . .
>
> Just as the slavemaster of that day used Tom, the house Negro, to keep the field Negroes in check, the same old slavemaster today has Negroes who are nothing but modern Uncle Toms, twentieth-century Uncle Toms, to keep you and me in check, to keep us under control, keep us passive and peaceful and nonviolent. That's Tom making you nonviolent.[18]

For Malcolm X, the "house Negro" is of course a synonym for the Uncle Tom. He attaches these terms to the prevailing black civil rights leadership in the United States that, in his view, is endorsed by the white political establishment. He implies Martin Luther King Jr. to be the Uncle Tom par excellence. Malcolm X makes a more explicit linkage between Martin Luther King and the Uncle Tom in commenting at Michigan State that "there are a large number of black people in this country who don't endorse any phase of what Dr. Martin Luther King and these other twentieth-century religious Uncle Toms are putting in front of the public eye."[19] On the other hand, Malcolm X suggests himself, along with the masses of black people, to be representative of the "field Negro" type. In such passages, we have some of the most memorable contributions of Malcolm X's career to a discourse on "authentic blackness," an issue that has been acknowledged and discussed widely. Seldom discussed, however, are the levels on which his remarks in these speeches have significance insofar as they construct a discourse of authenticity regarding black masculinity and set forth a hierarchy among black men with geographical inflections. In Malcolm X's itinerary, the house Negro, or Uncle Tom, embodied the most abject form of black masculinity. Here and elsewhere in his rhetoric, he associates "real" blackness with the embrace of black nationalism and a will toward black revolution. He marks the house Negro as counterrevolutionary and inimical to black nation-building for failing to understand such concepts as "black nationalism" and "black revolution."[20] Furthermore, Malcolm X underscores the abjection of this type and its racial unbelonging by rhetorically indicating a preference for the term *field nigger* as opposed to *field Negro*.[21]

Given his fair complexion, which within this binary would have been more consistent with the house Negro, Malcolm X's insistent identification with the field Negro as a type may well have reflected some of his own anxieties about class, color, and black authenticity.[22] However, in addition to addressing class differences among blacks, the house Negro–field Negro dichotomy was just as much—if not more—about positing cleavages among blacks, and black men specifically, on the basis of gender, geography, and sexuality. For in addition to its mobilization as a categorical signifier of the black middle class, we need to recognize the levels on which the "Uncle Tom"/"house Negro" metaphor invoked in Malcolm X's speeches worked ideologically to construe a geographical hierarchy of black masculinity in the United States. It becomes clear that the rhetorical marking in Malcolm X's speeches of Martin Luther King as a "house Negro"/"Uncle Tom"—in effect, as cowardly, counterrevolutionary, and docile—held implications for black southern men as a category more generally when we consider King's southern status. For Malcolm X scripted black northern men as insurgent types, and the geographical dichotomy of South and North was the primary framework within which he schematized black political divisions. One might infer from this binary formulation that, contrary to the urban northern black men who were veritable bombs waiting to explode, black southern men were not assertive and therefore lacked what it took to be true revolutionaries. Explicitly and implicitly, his platform anointed black northern men as the most insurgent and potentially revolutionary types of black men.[23] Because Malcolm X linked black-revolutionary thinking to authentic blackness, he suggested that black men in the South lacked black racial authenticity. By implying them to be less insurgent, he also suggested that they were not real men.

Furthermore, Malcolm X's references to the Uncle Tom were just as much about questioning the sexual authenticity (i.e., the heterosexuality) of their targets as they were about questioning authenticity in terms of race and gender. The house Negro/Uncle Tom allegory suggests that this type was obsessive with his master to the point of conceivably having a sexual interest in him, as remarks in "Twenty Million Black People in a Political, Economic, and Mental Prison" reveal: "This type of so-called Negro, by being intoxicated over the white man, . . . never sees beyond the white man."[24] In similar fashion, Malcolm X's remarks in "Homecoming Rally of the OAAU" (November 29, 1964) about Moise Tshombe, who was implicated in the plot to assassinate Patrice Lumumba, and whom Malcolm X intimately related to the Uncle Tom in other speeches, are revealing where they proclaim Tshombe as "a bed partner for Lyndon B. Johnson."[25] Though he makes it clear that he does not mean to imply a literal bed partnership, his evocation of this metaphor is provocative nevertheless and, I want to stress, reflected his strategy of casting the Uncle Tom as homosexual.

This strategy is explicit where Malcolm X's speeches cite the handkerchief-head to describe Martin Luther King and the broader civil rights leadership. The handkerchief-head is a type that rendered Uncle Tom as feminized and cross-dressed with a bandana, evoking the mammy as emblematized, for instance, in the Aunt Jemima advertising trademark. Inflected by the homophobia and misogyny that were characteristic of Nation of Islam politics, the invocation of the handkerchief-head in Malcolm X's speeches at bottom coded Martin Luther King as feminine and gay. These references to King and his larger civil rights cohort are evident in a number of instances, including Malcolm X's "The Ballot or the Bullet" speech in which he refers to "these handkerchief-heads who have been dillydallying and pussyfooting and compromising—we don't intend to let them pussyfoot and dillydally and compromise any longer."[26]

The consistent citations of the Uncle Tom within the oral rhetoric of Malcolm X—which implicitly and explicitly labeled King as emasculated and therefore divergent from patriarchal black masculinity—were animated by a staunch homosexual panic. I want to suggest that this is one of the most productive spaces from which we might expand the dialogue on the status of sexuality in shaping a subject as complex as Malcolm X, above and beyond his biographical background. The use of such references served as a strategy for questioning and attacking the manhood and masculinity of the prevailing civil rights leadership in the United States, was misogynistic in casting their agendas as lacking the proper level of assertiveness by investing in strategies of nonviolent resistance and therefore as feminine, and perhaps also drew metaphorically to some extent on the conventional views of the South as a place in the nation that is feminine and other. It is important to consider what is at stake in Malcolm X's speeches when they make recourse to sexual ideologies that signify a degraded, deviant, inferior, and abject black masculinity. Furthermore, the scripts of the civil rights leadership as homosexual and inauthentic blacks who wanted to be white were often mutually constitutive.

While there is evidence to reveal Malcolm X's construal of the Uncle Tom as homosexual, it might be more accurate still to describe his formulation of the Uncle Tom as quintessentially bisexual. For Malcolm X paradoxically portrays the Uncle Tom as not only being identified with whiteness but also as having a ravenous sexual desire for white women, a claim that ironically invokes the historical stereotypes of the black male rapist in the South and that may well have been intended to fuel the panic in the United States about sex between white women and black men.[27] Such assertions were designed to raise anxieties about integration among whites, reflected the separatist philosophy of the Nation of Islam, and also implied the black male homosexual body to be threatening and sexually predatory. It invoked the paradigmatic historical imaging of black male sexuality as rapacious that was broadly disseminated in the film *Birth of a Nation*. This kind of "throwing off" also reinforced ironically, if inadvertently, the view propagated by southern reactionaries of the Civil Rights movement as grounded in sexual debauchery, with the main aim being to promote sex within genders and across races, which is evident in William Bradford Huie's novel *The Klansman*.

King was able to rise to prominence as a national spokesperson for the Civil Rights movement and to gain access to an audience that was ultimately international in reach in part because his seasoning within the African American sermonic tradition enabled him to cultivate a speaking style and a charisma that defied widespread conventional impressions of black men in the South as folksy, uneducated, and inarticulate.[28] The fact of his southernness informed the scripts that were produced of him within Malcolm X's speech repertoires. Martin Luther King's birth in the South and leadership in the southern-based Civil Rights movement, and Malcolm X's eventual urbanization that culminated in the assumption of a national leadership post in Harlem, were intricately linked to the philosophical dichotomy between the two men that the media gave continuing salience during the early 1960s. That King was so ubiquitously identified with the Civil Rights movement in the South and Malcolm X with the movement in the urban North helped make region a salient factor in Malcolm X's formulation of definitions of authentic blackness and masculinity. The "Uncle Tom" and the house Negro–field Negro binary, which was itself regionally and spatially inflected, provided a key mechanism for identifying the movement in the South as counterrevolutionary and, by extension, its male leadership as inadequate.

Because Malcolm X's speeches so assertively surrendered an epistemology on race and gender authenticity among African Americans, and given that King himself was southern, it is also important to recognize the extent to which Malcolm X's rhetoric held implications for the larger category of black men in the South. By marking them as feminine and homosexual and invoking the handkerchief-head as a sexually aberrant type, the speeches also in effect marked their bodies as pathological. They implied black men in the South to be "others" beyond the pale of black masculinity, who could in no way be "real" revolutionaries in the same sense as black men in the urban North. In effect, the speeches constituted a hierarchical and exclusionary script of black masculinity.

R. Bruce Brasell, John Howard, James T. Sears, Carlos L. Dews, and Carolyn Leste Law are just a few of the scholars who have disrupted the urban fixation in gay and lesbian and queer studies to consider southern or rural contexts in constituting racial, gender, class, and sexual identities.[29] The South has played an inordinate historical role in shaping taboos about interracial sex in the United States. As a novel such as Huie's illustrated, the South's discourse on interracial sex as perverse, along with assertive antimiscegenation sentiment, was frequently framed alongside its panic related to gay and lesbian sexuality. These fields have established critical foundations and methodologies for examining Malcolm X's rhetorical references to sex and sexuality at a deeper level. At this level, his project manifested the panic about homosexuality that became pervasive throughout 1960s black-liberation discourse, a panic that he at times seemed to grapple with through tacit invocations of a queer South.

As the autobiographies of Black Panther Party for Self-Defense co-founders Huey P. Newton and Bobby Seale reveal, Malcolm X's discourse had a strong impact on the organization's philosophy of self-defense.[30] Newton and Seale echo Malcolm X's rhetorical scripts of black men in the South as revolutionary misfits and Uncle Toms. These linkages seem particularly important when considering that the regional dialectics within the black-liberation movement of the 1960s have seldom been acknowledged, along with the unspoken philosophy that implied that if all black men were equal, some black men were more equal than others. Beginning in the first section of part 1 of his 1973 autobiography, *Revolutionary Suicide*, Newton indicates that his mother and father were born in the Deep South in Alabama and Louisiana, respectively, and met and married in Arkansas. After sharing this background, Newton begins to sketch a narrative that posits his father as an exceptional southerner and underscores how much his father differed from "typical" black men in the South:

> My father was not typical of southern Black men in the thirties and forties. Because of his strong belief in the family, my mother never worked at an outside job, despite seven children and considerable economic hardship. Walter Newton is rightly proud of his role as family protector. To this day, my mother has never left her home to earn money. (11–12)[31]

Here, Newton describes his father's effectiveness as a patriarch and uniqueness as a black southern man primarily in terms of an ability to keep his wife in the home and, implicitly, away from the proverbial sexual advances of white men, which might have been the result had she done domestic work.

Newton's heroic view of his father is ostensible when he expresses admiration for his father's preaching, and equally evident when he elaborates in the fourth chapter with a bit more specificity how his father differs from other black southern men:

> When I say that my father was unusual, I mean that he had a dignity and pride seldom seen in southern Black men. Although many other black men in the South had a similar strength, they never let it show around whites. To do so was to take your life in your hands. My father never kept his strength from anybody. (30)

Such reflections suggest that, ordinarily, "pride" and "dignity" are character-istics removed from black men in the South. In his son's eyes, Walter New-ton stood apart because of a lack of intimidation in the face of menacing white men in the South and fearlessness when it came to confronting them, whereas other black men in the region suppressed whatever radical spirits they may have had for the sake of survival. "My father," writes Newton, "was called 'crazy' for his refusal to let a white man call him 'nigger' or to play the Uncle Tom or allow whites to bother his family. 'Crazy' to them, he was a hero to us" (31). In Newton's eyes, Walter Newton's lack of intimidation in the face of armed white men distinguished him from other black southern men. Huey P. Newton suggests that his father, by exemplifying "strong" black manhood, helped make the development of his own revolutionary consciousness possible. A positioning of black southern men at the bottom of an implicit black male hierarchy is clear when Newton suggests that, ordinarily, black men in the South lack qualities of real men and manifest the obsequiousness of the proverbial Uncle Tom. Similarly, in recounting his discussions with inmates while incarcerated in a federal prison in St. Louis, Missouri, Bobby Seale relates black men in the South to the Uncle Tom stereotype and construes them as lacking political consciousness and courage in his autobiography, *Seize the Time*.[32] In these instances, the view of black men in the South as unmanly and cowardly reveals how geography constitutes authentic notions of black masculinity and demonstrates how some models of black masculinity are viewed as undesirable and inferior.

When examining Newton's comments in his autobiography in tandem with the inspiration that southern organizations such as the Lowndes County Freedom Organization provided for the establishment of their Oakland organization, we might conclude that he was somewhat ambiva-lent about the role that black southerners might play in black-liberation struggle. Even after he had been exposed to the organizing in the Alabama Black Belt under the rubric of the LCFO and had been so profoundly influenced by their philosophy of armed self-defense, when his autobiog-raphy was published in the early 1970s, he nevertheless described his father as a pure exception to the cowardice that he presumed to be ingrained in black southern men. Although, in his autobiography, Newton confesses that southern roots played an important role in his development as a black-revolutionary leader, it remains invested in a historically questionable nar-rative of black southerners as passive and counterinsurgent.[33]

These contradictions suggest the extent to which Newton's assertions about black southern masculinity were overly generalized and ahistorical. Such politics helped establish the groundwork for the urbanization of the black panther symbol and the Oakland organization's "exclusive claim" on it.[34] The LCFO, through such slogans as "One Man, One Vote," radical philosophy, iconography featuring guns, and symbols like the panther, helped establish foundations for the development of the masculinist image of black men that ultimately became so dominant in the mainstream media in the late 1960s. Yet the urbanization of the Black Panther symbol helps explain why black men in the South ironically remained marginal to and excluded from these constructs of black masculinity in popular and political contexts. While the critiques of the gender politics of the black-liberation movement of the 1960s have become familiar, it is also important to think more about the levels on which it produced ideologies of masculinity that were regional. That aspects of 1960s black nationalism ostensibly affirmed black southern and "folk" cultures by no means offset the hegemony of its prevailing urban aesthetics.

Malcolm X's speech repertoires set the stage for the misogynistic and homophobic bantering that became even more widespread in the late 1960s, such as Black Panther Eldridge Cleaver's references to Martin Luther King as "Martin Luther Queen." They anticipated tropes of white men as homosexual, effeminate, and impotent that were produced by black nationalists and performatively exemplified the masculinism that would come to characterize the black-liberation movement. Whiteness itself emerged in this political economy as a sexualized and gendered concept and translated into a marker of effeminacy. The black-liberation movement of the 1960s was an ideological context that expanded representations of black men in the South as incompatible with, and even inadequate for, the black-revolutionary movement.

As I hope to illustrate through an examination of Spike Lee's films in this chapter, the residual impact of the regional aspects of raced, sexed, and gendered black-liberation ideology were also evident in models of black masculinity in black popular culture of the 1990s. Several of Lee's films, which typically cast ideal black male revolutionaries as urban, clearly manifest geographical essentialisms about black masculinity in the South. They have frequently construed black men in the South as inferior and inauthentic, sometimes to the point of explicitly linking them to the Uncle Tom.

Furthermore, I aim to illustrate how Lee's films prioritize the urban in constructing models of black masculinity. My discussion highlights *School Daze* (1988), *Get on the Bus* (1996), *Crooklyn* (1994), and *Bamboozled* (2001). Taking my cue from such critics in southern studies as Jon Smith and Deborah Cohn, who have emphasized the utility of postcolonial approaches to the South, I draw mainly on postcolonial theory to illustrate ways in which Lee has produced an epistemology of southern space as different and other.[35] Lee's films feature what I call, drawing on Mary Louise Pratt, black southern contact zones.[36] Such spaces stress black southerners' alienation from notions of authentic blackness and masculinity and reinforce urban-centered definitions of black identity. In general, a clarification of the ways in which geography has recurrently inflected the models of blackness and masculinity offered in Lee's films seems necessary for understanding his complex formulations of gender, race, and sexuality.

When I Say " 'Bama," You Say "Fag"

In a January 1993 interview in the Paris African weekly *Jeune Afrique*, former Student Nonviolent Coordinating Committee (SNCC) chairman and Black Panther Party for Self-Defense member Kwame Ture (formerly Stokely Carmichael) minces no words in voicing his skepticism about Spike Lee's status as director of the film *Malcolm X*. Ture argues that "Spike Lee is incapable of making a film about Malcolm X" and describes the filmmaker as "a *petit bourgeois* who took the choice of selling his people for a fistful of dollars."[37] Ture invokes the scenario of Jewish "Zionists" making a film about Palestinian leader Yasir Arafat to suggest the impossibility of offering a fair portrayal of Malcolm X in a Hollywood-produced film.[38] Ture's comments echo those in an August 18, 1991, *Washington Post* interview with Amiri Baraka: "I was distressed he was taking up Malcolm and feared Malcolm would get the same treatment he had given the rest of black nationalism. . . . Malcolm X's life is not a commercial property. It can't be claimed by a petit bourgeois Negro who has $40 million."[39] Baraka was most vocal among the chorus of African American critics raising concerns about Lee's work on a film about Malcolm X. Baraka's criticism of Lee during this moment recalled his highly publicized opposition a decade earlier to the playwright Charles Fuller. Baraka's participation as a leader in the New York–based activist group the United Front to Preserve the Legacy of Malcolm X, which was assembled primarily as a reaction to Lee's project, was perhaps the most telling indicator of Baraka's concern. Extensive media focus on Baraka was sustained over the time spanning the announcement of Lee's directorship to the film's release.

As much as Lee attempts to identify with black-liberation movement history and to represent aspects of it in his films, such comments poignantly illustrate the ideological divisions between Lee and veteran black-liberation leaders. Both sets of comments emphatically apply the logic of black authenticity to Lee in ways reminiscent of the profuse mobilizations of such politics at varying points throughout Lee's own film career.[40] For instance, on Lee's part, we witnessed a similar critique of Norman Jewison, who had originally been chosen to direct the film on Malcolm X. As Lee famously commented, "I have a big problem with Norman Jewison directing 'The Autobiography of Malcolm X.' . . . That disturbs me deeply, gravely. It's wrong with a capital W. Blacks have to control these films."[41] This logic also shaped Lee's stipulation that all interviews about the Malcolm X project be conducted by black journalists. The questions about who was qualified to make a film about Malcolm X that a host of figures associated with the discourses of black nationalism debated were driven in part by a fear that the leader's life would be misrepresented as well as by an interest in protecting his legacy. Still, these debates about the film can also be understood as a reflection of deeper and more general anxieties about conserving conventional notions of black masculinity given Malcolm X's masculine iconicity in the African American context during his life as a leader and after his death. Baraka's concern that Lee would highlight Malcolm X's early years and obscure the ways in which Elijah Muhammad and the Nation of Islam so importantly shaped the leader's development might be understood, for instance, as a petition for the aspects of Malcolm X's persona aligned with notions of conventional black masculinity to receive fair play.

Malcolm X was released during a moment when Lee had high visibility in the media as a filmmaker. In more recent years, academic and media fascination with Lee has lessened, and the cultural authority that he singularly held as an African American filmmaker from the late 1980s and into the early 1990s—to the point of becoming what Wahneema Lubiano called a "totem"—seems to have diminished.[42] The title and tone of a 1996 *Newsweek* article by N'Gai Croal, "Bouncing off the Rim: Spike Lee Is Making a Career of Near Misses," was one of the earliest signals of a growing perception among some critics that there had been a decline in the quality and popular appeal of Lee's artistry. Croal notes that films after *Malcolm X* have failed to garner comparable box-office profits or to generate as much public interest. He also suggests, perhaps a bit too reductively, that the success Lee saw with his early films was attributable to how he "shrewdly courted controversy to maximize profit."[43] Moreover, such criticism often elides Lee's beginnings in independent film; furthermore, it seems somewhat unfair to rely on visibility and popularity in Hollywood as a measure of success. Todd Boyd has connected Lee's declining visibility as a filmmaker in more recent years to Lee's growing popularity within the "cult of celebrity."[44] Whatever his critics think of his status, Lee will go down in history as the most salient and influential African American filmmaker of the late twentieth century. This is one reason that it is perhaps especially important to continue to reflect on his repertoire of films, including those that were produced at the height of his career—a time when the very idea of an African American filmmaker still registered for some as an anomaly and novelty.

Lee's films are a useful site for critical analysis and reconsideration for me because of ways in which geography has saliently functioned in their construction of black masculinity. *Malcolm X* reinforced and extended the leader's rhetorical strategies of positing the urban as a necessary ingredient in fashioning black masculinity and notions of authentic blackness, logic that concomitantly cast black men in the South as alien to black-revolutionary activism and nationalism. However, it is useful to explore these strategies of representation in several of Lee's other films, where, I want to suggest, they are even more saliently evident. Lee's *School Daze*, which followed his first major film, *She's Gotta Have It* (1986), is set in an unspecified southern city and opens with an emphasis on Vaughn "Dap" Dunlap's campaign to raise consciousness among students and the administration at the historically black Mission College. His goal is to encourage the institution's divestment from apartheid South Africa. As the argument between Da Fellas and unemployed men hanging out at the Kentucky Fried Chicken in the community near the college reveals, geography is yet another source of conflict and division among issues that materialize as face-to-face confrontations between dichotomized groups or individuals throughout the film, such as light skin vs. dark skin, Greek vs. non-Greek, and African American vs. pan-Africanist. This film aligns urban subjectivity with the very possibilities for articulating and exemplifying an "authentic" black-revolutionary and nationalist masculinity and detaches authentic blackness from black men in the South to constitute the misogyny and homophobia so frequently discussed by the film's critics. It seems all the more crucial to recognize this problem because, as I have already argued, the familiar citations of black southerners as the epitome of racial authenticity in the African American context typically obscure ideological scripts of black southerners as undesirable.[45]

School Daze reveals its homophobia most explicitly in the infamous scene in which Dap leads Da Fellas in a call-and-response chant directed at the men of the fraternity Gamma Phi Gamma and mocks this group as "punks" and "fags" (i.e., "When I say 'Gamma' you say 'fag' "). This bantering helps authenticate the model of the urban black-nationalist revolutionary in which this film seems to be invested. It is significant that the homophobic scripting of Gamma is anticipated and paralleled in a scene almost immediately beforehand that marks black men in the South as feminine and perhaps also as gay. Invocations of sexuality, and references to homosexuality in particular, centrally drive the conflict between Da Fellas and "local yokels." It is when the leader of the latter group calls over to Da Fellas and asks, "Is it *true* what they say about Mission [limp-wristed] men?" in an effeminate voice that Dap leads Da Fellas out of the restaurant, forcing them to desert their barely touched chicken meals. Dap urges his group to leave presumably because he is trying to avoid what he anticipates will be an explosive and even violent confrontation in light of the character of this teasing. Once the group is in the parking lot, this man continues to refer to Dap and Da Fellas as "Missionaries" and "Missionettes." Dap's efforts to reason with the locals are exhausted when the leader of the group abruptly and insistently asks him, "Are you black?" Emphatically, Dap says that "I was gonna ask your country, 'BAMA ass why you got them drip, drip chemicals in you hair!" Two of Da Fellas chime in "And then come out in public with a shower cap on . . . like a fuckin' bitch!" while directing their gaze at the man standing beside him wearing a yellow plastic cap on his head. Here and throughout this scene, the camera emphasizes close-up shots of the two group leaders' faces to highlight the intensity of their emotions. The ready accessibility of gay identity for stereotyping and ridicule in the African American context is underscored in the recourse that men frequently make to accusations of gayness. Such politics conform to what Jacquie Jones has identified as the tendency within black popular film of the late 1980s to the early 1990s to assign gay identities and black females marked as "bitches" and "hos" to an "accusatory space" that "tried to codify words like 'punk' and 'faggot' in order to segment and control desire, and leave open spaces for blame."[46]

Hair functions as one of the main subjects of political conflict among blacks in the film, and "natural" hair is cited as a key marker of black authenticity. In light of Jones's observations, we can say that the invocation of "bitch" links the local man directly to an abject black femaleness. In the film, the association of hair processing with the feminine is reinforced by the fact that another group, the Wannabes, who wear their hair in long, teased-out, full-bodied curls, are mainly criticized for buying into Euro-American hair aesthetics. However, it is also conceivable that the local man is associated with the feminine in a misogynistic way and marked as objectionable by Dap and Da Fellas in light of their possible apprehension of the jerri curl hairstyle as part and parcel of an androgynous aesthetic. This hairstyle was dominant during the 1980s, the time period during which the film is set, and was sometimes associated with homosexuality.[47] While scholars have frequently considered feminizations of black masculinity in the United States, the politics of invoking the South in such formulations need more critical attention. The distinctions among these groups are heavily encoded in their bodies and dress. All the local men wear garish clothing styles. Dap and Da Fellas seem to be attaching an excessiveness to the leader's style, for instance, owing to both his hair and his white shoes. The attire of others in his group consists of tight-fitting polyester shirts with butterfly collars that recall 1970s fashions, cowboy boots, garish gold rings, and red "pleather." We should also examine why the character Dap invokes such terms as *country* and *'Bama* (i.e., Alabama) in pointing up what Kobena Mercer suggests have been prematurely deemed "slavish [white hairstyle] imitations" within African diasporan cultural discourse.[48] Ultimately, the character Dap makes recourse to southern geography to formulate what he intends to be a "diss" of this man and apprehends this man's southernness as something to make fun of.[49] Dap also calls him "'Bama" because of a perception of this man's clothing as tacky. It seems that wearing a jerri curl, and perhaps also being "country" and "'Bama," are implicitly qualities that make the "local" less "black" and imply him to be less capable of black leadership. This scene, particularly in light of the film's motto, "Uplift the Race," invokes historical ideologies of racial uplift in which folk people occupied a vexed or expendable place.

Jon Smith and Deborah Cohn point out that "perhaps U.S. Southern cultures and literatures seem so apt for postcolonial study precisely because the centralized terms of their experiences of exile and problematic identity are always already embedded in its disciplining discourse."[50] Historical social relations in the South, such as asymmetrical racial power relations, make postcolonial and colonialist studies indispensable frameworks for pondering the region's black and white identities, along with various other ethnic groups. Within postcolonial discourse, I draw on Mary Louise Pratt's notion of the "contact zone" to interpret Lee's strategies of representing black southern identities. According to Pratt,

> "Contact zone" is an attempt to invoke the spatial and temporal copresence of subjects separated by geographic and historical disjunctures, and whose trajectories now intersect. By using the term "contact," I aim to foreground the interactive, improvisational dimensions of colonial encounters so easily ignored or suppressed by diffusionist accounts of conquest and domination. A "contact" perspective emphasizes how subjects are constituted in and by their relations to each other. It treats the relations among colonizers and colonized, or travelers and "travelees," not in terms of separateness or apartheid, but in terms of copresence, interaction, interlocking understandings and practices, and often within radically asymmetrical relations of power.[51]

While the meanings for Pratt's term are multiple, I find it useful for my purposes to apply it to spaces where black southerners are encountered and marked as other (i.e., "feminine," "inferior," "not self"). Furthermore, I want to underscore that what I am describing as black southern contact zones are not merely contained within what have conventionally been categorized as southern geographies in the United States. As Inderpal Grewal has reminded us, contact zones are "everywhere" and "contained in particular discursive spaces that embody and control the narratives of encounters with difference."[52] Acknowledging the migratory aspects of the contact zone beyond the South is important for dismantling geographical essentialisms and points to the migratory status of southern subjectivity.[53] If the Kentucky Fried Chicken restaurant *is* the key site where the specificity of black southern identity is most explicitly addressed in the film, then it is not surprising that this is the location in the film where its geographically based politics also come to the fore.

By the time we come to this scene that highlights conflict between Da Fellas and the locals, the black southern contact zone that this Kentucky Fried Chicken restaurant and its parking lot exemplifies has already been twice-marked as counterrevolutionary and apolitical. First, Dap suggests his disdain for this space in his statement that a bus full of chicken has more potential to attract black people than his shantytown that symbolizes resistance to South African apartheid, which is virtually deserted. Second, the question that Da Fellas playfully pose to Dap—"What we want to know is, do revolutionaries eat Kentucky Fried Chicken?"—implies his view of this space as incompatible with black political consciousness. Even if the wisdom of the local men hits some nerves, Dap ultimately comes across as the wiser. He epitomizes black political consciousness in this film and, notwithstanding his sexism and homophobia, is endowed with the moral authority to give the resonant wake-up call that punctuates the end.

However, this scene is not the only one that makes recourse to the logic of authenticity in relation to blackness and masculinity. Dap's meeting with several Mission College administrators, President McPherson, and board of trustees head Cedar Cloud, which follows the film's characteristic formula of positioning subjects in face-to-face conflict, is similarly revealing. Ironically, Dap ends up in the president's office for being disruptive during the homecoming football game and not because of the shantytown vigils on campus. Once there, these administrators critique his protest methods and threaten him with expulsion for his activism. The extent to which they are incapable of understanding where he is coming from is underscored in his resolute silence in the face of McPherson's plea for him to "make us understand." Both McPherson and Cloud represent the long-standing tradition of the college and are aligned with the interests of white philanthropists who have been faithful supporters of the school. Furthermore, both men reveal themselves to be veterans of the Civil Rights movement who are strict adherents of the liberal tradition espoused by Martin Luther King. McPherson and Cloud condemn Dap's "all the way down, pro black nationalist image," to borrow the words of Dap's girlfriend Rachel, and fall into the category of what Dap has referred to in an earlier scene as "okey doke Negroes" and "foot shuffling, wanna be white Uncle Toms."

Indeed, McPherson's physical appearance as a senior black man with receding white hair even epitomizes the classic image of the Uncle Tom. In this scene, *School Daze* offers a dichotomous polarization of a southernized Uncle Tom with an urban rebel. Taken together as a composite, McPherson and Cloud fit the profile that Ralph Ellison's unnamed narrator in *Invisible Man* attaches to Dr. Bledsoe, the gatekeeping president of a black college in the South. It is not at all surprising that *School Daze* makes an explicit association between McPherson and whiteness. McPherson's fascination with whiteness also seems to be suggested in the lightness of his wife's skin. As we will see in the next section, however, Lee's attachments of the Uncle Tom to models of black masculinity in the South have sometimes been even more explicit and direct.

"Nigger Gingrich"

The October 18, 1995, Million Man March held in Washington, D.C., made history as the largest and most concerted assemblage of black men ever to take place on U.S. soil. It was a success notwithstanding the opposition of black feminists and various other sectors to its gender exclusion, its critique of welfare, and its organization by the controversial and reputedly anti-Semitic Minister Louis Farrakhan. The goals of what was in its entirety referred to as "The Million Man March and Day of Atonement, Reconciliation and Responsibility and Day of Absence" were spelled out in the official mission statement:

> Our priority call to Black men to stand up and assume this new and expanded sense of responsibility is based on the realization that the strength and resourcefulness of the family and the liberation of the people require it; that some of the most acute problems facing the Black community are those posed by Black males who have not stood up; that the caring and responsible father in the home; the responsible and future-focused male youth; security in and of the community; the quality of male/female relations, and the family's capacity to avoid poverty and push the lives of its members forward all depend on Black men's standing up; that in the context of a real and principled brotherhood, those of us who have stood up, must challenge others to stand also; and that unless and until Black men stand up, Black men and women cannot stand together and accomplish the awesome tasks before us.[54]

The march drew thousands of black men to the Capitol mall, men who had in many cases traveled cross-country in buses from faraway distances. The media's official head count of four hundred thousand has been regarded by some as a gross underestimate. The program included such featured speakers as Benjamin Chavis, Joseph Lowery, and Maya Angelou.

Released to mark the first anniversary of the march, the film *Get on the Bus*, whose screenplay was written by Reggie Rock Bythewood with Spike Lee as executive producer and director, revisits the event by highlighting the dynamics of a diverse group of black men who begin their journey to the Capitol in south central Los Angeles on a chartered bus. The film's financing through contributions by black men from the entertainment industry, including Robert Guillaume, Wesley Snipes, and Danny Glover, as well as other sectors, reflected the platform of the march. As Lee noted, "If we really wanted this film to come out correct, we had to do it ourselves."[55] The cross-country bus journey the film highlights is only one sign of the central role that geography plays in the film's formulation of blackness and masculinity. As I hope to illustrate, *Get on the Bus* suggests southern identity to be an undesirable ingredient in black masculine formation that substantially compromises possibilities for embodying authentic black masculinity. I am particularly fascinated by how it excludes a black southern man to mediate anxieties among black men based on gender and sexuality.

It is noteworthy that a cinematic tribute to a march promoting "atonement," "reconciliation," "responsibility," "brotherhood," and "unity" among black men stages as a climax the brutal ousting of a passenger who is black, male, and southern. For if "Get on the bus" is the welcoming command to board in LA for the cross-country trip to the nation's capitol, "Get *off* the bus" is equally resonant for the character Wendell Perry. In the end he is dramatically kicked off the bus by his fellow travelers, along with his bags. We even see a double play of his ousting that seems meant to dramatize the effect, which is comedic. Wendell comes across to the group as extremely materialistic, conservative, and self-serving. He indicates that he owns a car dealership in Memphis, drives a $74,000 Lexus SC400, and flashes a roll of cash. He quickly begins to spout rhetoric on the bus about the importance of black self-help. He shares his belief that to get ahead, blacks must work hard and get an education. A Phi Beta Kappa graduate of Vanderbilt University, he underscores that he never would have considered attending such historically black institutions as Fisk and Tennessee State, "nigger schools" where students "step and sing and sell fish sandwiches to buy textbooks." Passengers on the bus begin to lose patience with him for his criticisms of black leaders like Farrakhan, the march's raison d'être whom he calls "self-serving," as well as Elijah Muhammad and Jesse Jackson. Perry's example illustrates how even narratives of black men in the South as industrious and accomplished are easily construed as accommodationist, because of how accessible they can be to conservative agendas.

When asked about the extent to which he feels racism and discrimination are a problem for blacks, Wendell remarks that "racism is a figment of the black man's imagination. Brothers, we are moving into the next millennium. The year 2000 is here. Now we've got to move into the future. If I'm lying, how do you explain a man like Colin Powell? The white man never kept him down." Evan Sr.'s retort is that "Colin Powell made it in spite of racism and not because it doesn't exist, you Uncle Tom!" When Wendell requests that this be said more loudly, all men on the bus chime in together and yell "Uncle Tom!" They begin to call him names such as "Nigger Gingrich" to invoke Republican leader Newt Gingrich's controversial "Contract with America" of 1994, along with "Mark Fuhrman," the detective from the O. J. Simpson trial who became infamous for profusely using the word "nigger." An implicit linkage is also made between Wendell and the "Clarence Thomas tribe" that the driver, George, has invoked earlier in contrast to the implicitly authentic "Shaka Zulu tribe." Not being a Republican and supporting black leadership in the United States, along with O. J. Simpson, are the things that define black-nationalist consciousness and black authenticity on the bus in this scene. Wendell is separated from the series of names circulated and metaphorically attached to "authentic" black masculinity throughout the trip that evoke notions of transcendent black leadership, such as "Zulu warriors," "Kunta Kinte," "Hannibal," "Mandingo warrior," "Malcolm," "Martin," and "Moses." "Brother" circulates among the men on the bus as the ready and primary signifier of black male affinity and affirmation but registers as excessive and inappropriate when articulated by Wendell.

A tireless salesman, Wendell's cardinal offense on the bus is admitting that his only motive for attending the march is to network so that he can sell his cars among the many "niggers" who will be there. His references to the men on the bus with this term intensify as he points to them individually. The camera that the student filmmaker Xavier has had trained on him reinforces Wendell's centrality in this scene. Finally, Xavier stops his videotaping as Wendell talks because the statements are so disturbing. After Wendell has been thrown from the bus, the camera cuts to the passengers lined up under a blue sky on the side of the highway in what seems to be an idyllic setting raising clenched fists and yelling out the slogan "black power" in a show of solidarity. This legacy is implied to be incompatible with a man like Wendell. There is also an allusion to this discourse when Jeremiah, the most senior passenger, individually greets all the passengers who are already onboard the bus with the slogan as he takes his seat.

A southern background is the most obvious factor that sets Wendell apart from other men on the bus. Unlike them, he does not begin the trip in LA but literally begs and bargains to board in Memphis. Ultimately, the model of black southern male subjectivity foregrounded by the film is identified as the "enemy" and expunged from a community of black men bound for the Million Man March because of a perceived incompatibility with the neo-black-power sensibility they attach to the event. Furthermore, it is significant that the film ultimately attaches the Uncle Tom—a figure marked as apolitical and inimical to black cultural interests—to a black southern man.[56]

The tensions that ultimately erupt over issues of racial belonging within the category of blackness as related to Wendell—as well as the attribution of the Uncle Tom trope to him—are anticipated earlier in the film in the character Flip's accusation that the police officer Gary, because of a light complexion and interracial background, would have been a "House slave pimping around the big house" with privileges such as eating grits, potatoes, and chicken and sleeping with black women who were well groomed, as well as with white women, during the era of slavery. This is a clear allusion to the invocation of the house Negro–field Negro dichotomy in Malcolm X's speech discourse. Significantly, Jeremiah encourages acceptance of Gary's claim of black identity, pointing out that the house slave's diet typically consisted of corn mush and that a sexual liaison with a white woman might have resulted in lynching, which suggests the ahistoricism in Flip's accusations.

The interplay between Kyle and Randall, two gay passengers, provides a certain comic relief in keeping with what Marlon Riggs has referred to as the neominstrel politics of "Negro faggotry" animating many contemporary black film productions.[57] In this respect, we might consider the moment we witness Randall loudly and abruptly exclaim, "I mind that you're not man enough to admit you love me!" to his boyfriend Kyle, who is trying to be discreet about their relationship on the bus. However, the film also seems to be self-consciously invested in addressing the politics of gay exclusion in black communities. The staging of a fistfight between Kyle and Flip, who has taunted Kyle and Randall with such homophobic epithets as "sissies," "homos," "pussies," and "faggots" throughout the journey, while sometimes marking them as feminine, might be interpreted as part and parcel of such investments. Homosexuality and southernness come across on the bus as analogously abject in relation to authentic black masculinity. *Get on the Bus* makes the reclamation of gay black male identity contingent on Wendell's exclusion and mobilizes black gay identities to sustain its notions of authentic blackness by highlighting gay identities in arbitrating the conflict with Wendell. (Indeed, once the men arrive in Memphis, the film seems to make a punning and provocative correlation between homosexuality and the South in having Randall ask Jamal the question, "You ever been down South here before?" while standing at a public urinal, possibly alluding to oral sex.) Upon hearing that Kyle is gay and Republican, Wendell remarks, "You might be gay and you might be black, but as long as you're a Republican, you're all right. We are an endangered species." Here, his mention of black Republicans as an "endangered species" redirects a term that is frequently invoked to define black men as a group at risk, an issue also tacit in the name of the bus: *The Spotted Owl*. While they find a common bond in the conversation based on their shared party affiliation, Kyle soon criticizes Wendell for denying racism. It is at this point in the film that an ominous background tune begins playing to signal Wendell's impending ejection. When we consider that Flip—the actor who, in his interactions with various passengers, has voiced vile homophobic and misogynistic epithets throughout the journey—is even momentarily absolved and tacitly recuperated by the men on the bus to help in Wendell's ousting (Flip throws the bags out the door), the politics of black southern male exclusion in the film seem more apparent. Wendell alone is coded as being verbally negative to the point of being intolerable, and the threat that he represents based on his conservative politics ultimately supercedes that of homophobia and sexism in the film. At bottom, this scene invokes an undesirable model of black maleness from the South to displace the threat that gay identity represents to conventional masculinity on the bus.

The alignment of Wendell with Mark Fuhrman and Newt Gingrich recalls the ideological scripting of black southerners as covetous of whiteness. Wendell's marking as a channel for white southern racism finds further reinforcement in the later scene highlighting a drug search by a white southern state trooper, who stops the bus in the middle of the night and brings a dog onboard to search for drugs, refers to Jeremiah as "Uncle Remus," and categorically refers to men on the bus as "boys." This episode, like the encounter with Wendell, is disruptive to the harmony among black men on the bus. The scene also evokes the traumas faced by black men in the Jim Crow South, an era to which the bus's first stop in Little Rock, Arkansas, also seems to gesture. Jack E. White remarks in a *Time* review of the film that "Since in post–civil rights America this motley crew would have faced no greater danger than the boredom of a three-day bus ride, Lee concocts an anachronistic confrontation with two red-neck state troopers as the bus passes through the South."[58] Both the scenes with Wendell and the officer also accord with Lee's strategy of incorporating the South as "contact zones" in his films—encounters that seem to occur briefly and fleetingly yet at the same time are excessive. Ultimately, the film invokes southern identity as a factor that grossly forecloses any claims to authenticity for the black men within its black neonationalist and Afrocentric aesthetics. That the film foregrounds a pilgrimage to the nation's capitol in solidarity, while depicting a black man from the South as alien to and expendable within the formulation of authentic black masculinity, reveals its implicit investments in a scripting of "authentic" black masculinity as fundamentally urban. *Get on the Bus* well demonstrates geography's role in shaping discourses of blackness and masculinity in the African American context in the contemporary era.

Uncle Tom and the Alabama Porch Monkeys

Continuing the line of critique of Hollywood's narrow and limited representations of blacks that was established in such films as Robert Townsend's *Hollywood Shuffle* (1985) and Keenan Ivory Wayans's *I'm Gonna Git You Sukka* (1988), the film *Bamboozled* (2001), written and directed by Lee, offers a satire of black images in contemporary media that seems both timely and important. This production is relevant to my analysis because it reveals what has perhaps been the most assertive juxtaposition to date of the Uncle Tom trope and an urban black masculine revolutionary ideal within Lee's corpus. The film begins with a focus on the frustrations of Pierre Delacroix over black representations at CNS, the network where he is employed as a studio executive. When given the leeway to create a new show by Dunwitty, his white liberal boss, Delacroix formulates a neominstrel show that aims to satirize contemporary black media representations and to confirm that white audiences prefer to see degrading images of blacks in the media. Delacroix taps two homeless dancers whom he has seen performing in front of his building, Man Ray and Cheeba, to star in the show as "Man Tan of the Millennium" and "Sleep and Eat" in blackface, invoking black actors of the past such as Man Tan Morlon and Step N' Fetch It. Soon, Dunwitty expands the concept into *The Alabama Porch Monkeys*, a show with a plantation setting that will highlight Man Tan and Sleep and Eat, as well as such historical black stereotypes as Rastus, Mammy, and Topsy.

Bamboozled establishes Delacroix as the epitome of the Uncle Tom stereotype, well suggesting the continuing fascination with this image in Lee's film repertoire. The familiar stereotype of Uncle Tom as enraptured by and submissive to whiteness is most ostensibly addressed in the film when Delacroix is featured making a symbolic gift of his award for the success of *The Alabama Porch Monkeys* to Dunwitty, Delacroix's white liberal boss. This moment in the film alludes to the 1999 Golden Globe awards ceremony during which the actor Ving Rhames, who won the award for best actor, calls veteran actor Jack Lemmon, who had also been nominated in that category, on stage and attempts to hand over the award. It is significant that before Delacroix is shot by Sloan, his former assistant, the camera zooms in on and enlarges a plastic Uncle Mose salt shaker, one of the kitchen items manufactured and distributed along with an Aunt Jemima companion piece by F and F Mold and Die Works in Dayton, Ohio. The film's culmination in Delacroix's shooting death is anticipated several times in the mysterious spontaneous flipping of the coin mechanism on the bank on his desk. It fulfills the wish for genocide of the Uncle Tom that has been a recursive motif in African American cultural discourse, including several of Malcolm X's speeches.

While the reference to Delacroix's relationship with Sloan ostensibly adds to his scripting as heterosexual, there are elements in his portraiture in the film that imply him to be homosexual, which also allude to the specificity of Uncle Tom's ideological recastings as queer within aspects of the 1960s black-liberation movement. In this regard, we might consider the extent to which his lisping voice, hypercorrect articulation, and stilted mannerisms are meant to codify his sexuality. What seem to be queer resonances in Delacroix may take on added meaning for the film's viewers who recall "Blaine," the effeminate gay character portrayed by Damon Wayans on the Fox television series *In Living Color*, who frequently appeared in flimsy, garish outfits and flirted with " 'Toine," his fellow film reviewer and implied partner.

The images of a southern plantation on Delacroix's *Alabama Porch Monkey* feature, which tap into the implied nostalgia in the nation for the way of life in the "Old South," are signified in the film as the ones that most profoundly and problematically contradict and undermine authentic blackness. The film emphasizes ways in which they foreclose access to respectable and legitimate black subject formations. Notwithstanding his designation as an "Uncle Tom," Delacroix has no direct southern markings in the sense of Wendell Perry in *Get on the Bus* or the administrators in *School Daze*. However, when considering the model of the Uncle Tom he embodies, it is particularly fascinating that we have a juxtaposition of this figure with imagery of the South as emblematized in the *Alabama Porch Monkeys* show. This representation reinforces the investments of the Uncle Tom stereotype with a black southern specificity. This image further reveals the geographical logic that underpins Lee's construction of the ideal black male revolutionaries. We can ultimately recognize the validation of urban black masculinity as revolutionary in this film in the portrayal of the tap dancer Man Ray on the set taking a stand in resistance to the show and in his symbolic martyrdom as an assassin's victim. This narrative of the black urban male as revolutionary par excellence, and in contradistinction to an abject and other South, manifests the binary north-south logic evident in places in Malcolm X's speech corpus. The ostensible goal of the film is a satire of black minstrelized images. Yet the commentary that it makes, in electing to foreground the specificity of the South to epitomize regressive imagery in contemporary black culture, is telling, too. For the vast majority of images in contemporary black popular film and television that *Bamboozled* is invested in critiquing actually highlight black urban, not southern, life.

Though a black-nationalist sensibility seems to inflect the representations in Lee's films in light of this theme, it is noteworthy that *Bamboozled* extends its satire into its representation of the discourses of black nationalism as embodied in the Mau Mau group. The group is evocative of the reputed underground elements of the Black Panther Party. This allusion is sustained thorough the strong physical resemblance of its lone woman to Kathleen Cleaver. From its first appearance, the Mau Mau group is cast in dark, ominous shadows, a rendering that seems to foreshadow its murderous activities which punctuate the ending of the film. Julius, the group's most visible member, repeatedly reveals his lack of knowledge about black culture and history, inarticulateness, and misogyny, and the group's members come across as irrational and shortsighted. We are also led to believe that their malicious ambush of Man Ray stems from their lingering hostilities about having been turned down at the audition and hence their exclusion from possible opportunities for capitalist gain as aspiring rappers.

Girlz 'n the 'Burbs

Thus far, I have attempted to illustrate how and where Lee's film repertoire has codified black men in the South as emasculated, and sometimes as homosexual, an association that occurs partly in light of perceptions of the South as a feminine geography. The geographically inflected gender and racial formations that are discernible in *Crooklyn* also hold important implications for the analytical trajectory I am pursuing. We see an explicit association between gender-bending and black masculinity in the South in *Crooklyn* in a scene during which a transvestite prostitute, portrayed by RuPaul, dances seductively in a store with one of the Puerto Rican owners to a calypso song entitled "I'll Never Go Back Home to Georgia." It seems clear, too, that the metaphorical establishment of a correlation between the South and black female identity in this film, which ultimately reinforces a view of the South as feminine, does ideological work to the extent that it detaches the region from conventional notions of black masculinity.

More than one critic noted at the time of this film's release that Lee's scenes highlighting the South have the effect of adding life to a plot that is thin or nonexistent. Certainly, it seems that Lee represents the South as a geography primarily to highlight the redeeming qualities of Brooklyn and the urban North more generally. The film rehearses the familiar romantic narratives of the South as a place that provides a retreat for blacks from pressures of the urban North/inner city, for we learn that the girl protagonist Troy has been sent to the South because of her mother's cancer diagnosis. However, Troy's encounter with the South yields no feelings of endearment on her part. Her aversion for the South is on a par with that of Nella Larsen's protagonist Helga Crane in the novella *Quicksand* (1928).

Given Coco Fusco's acknowledgment of ethnographic cinema as a potentially colonialist medium, I want to further read this southern sequence in light of its overlap with the ethnographic film genre. It is true, of course, that

Lee's representations of blackness throughout his body of films might in fact be interpreted as ethnographic in character, if we consider the salience that he has recurrently given the black vernacular.[59] It seems, even, that much of the ideological force of Lee's films is encapsulated precisely where such codes are embedded. In this regard, we might think of the "country" Grady in *School Daze*, who, unlike the rest of Da Fellas, is completely reliant on forms of nonstandard English in his expression, and who tells a woman at the homecoming dance that her voluptuous body reminds him of collard greens and corn bread. However, the ways in which strategies of ethnographic cinema are mobilized to construct black southern geographies and identities in *Crooklyn* merit acknowledgment and analysis because of their undeniable specificity. To date, Fatimah Tobing Rony has provided one of the most illuminating definitions of ethnographic cinema. As she notes,

> In the popular imagination an "ethnographic film" is akin to a *National Geographic* special which purports to portray whole cultures within the space of an hour or two. The viewer is presented with an array of subsistence activities, kinship, religion, myth, ceremonial ritual, music and dance, and—in what may be taken as the genre's defining trope—some form of animal sacrifice. Like a classic ethnography which encapsulates a culture in one volume, an "ethnographic film" becomes a metonym for an entire culture.[60]

Rony's critical work is particularly useful where it highlights the racializing imperatives of this film genre. The visual play of switching to an anamorphic lens, which elongates images, most effectively marks off a black southern contact zone in the film. Inasmuch as this film technology reveals the discomfort Troy feels in the South, Lee's use of it dramatizes the difference she encounters and the contrastive value of the South with Brooklyn. Whereas the textures of late-1960s to early-1970s Brooklyn that are signified in Lee's film are constituted by hairstyles such as Afros and braids; African art; ethnic diversity; music by such artists as Sly and the Family Stone, the Staples Singers, and Curtis Mayfield; the athletic icon Julius Irwin; and such television shows as *Soul Train* and *The Partridge Family*, Troy encounters perfectly manicured suburban lawns, white televangelist programs, bedtime prayers with Aunt Song and Viola, and Viola's extensive Barbie doll collection. Following Rony's definition, the pronouncements of ethnographic cinema as related to this sequence become more obvious if we consider Troy's survey of mourning and prayer rituals, the birthday party, food, dress, and play over the course of her stay in the South. The comically rendered death of Aunt Song's dog, who, as it turns out, has been folded up inadvertently in a sofa bed, alludes to the typical animal sacrifice that Rony mentions in her definition. However, because of the levels on which it connotes scalping and thus invokes the proverbial "attack of the natives," we might read Aunt Song's willful straightening of Troy's hair as the climactic moment of ethnographic spectacle in the film: "Lord have mercy, child, you sure got one thick head of hair. You *need* a hot comb on these naps." "Who did that to your hair? . . . I knew she would," is Mrs. Carmichael's dismayed response to this straightened hair when Troy returns to Brooklyn. The smoke, dark clouds, and shadows that we see, along with scary sounds that we hear in a nightmare Troy has earlier in the film, during which her neighborhood's two young-adult glue sniffers chase and attempt to rob her, might even be interpreted as an eerie foreshadowing of her encounter with a South that threatens to rub off on her or to consume her.

The letter that Troy receives in Virginia on the occasion of her birthday and "reads" through her mother's narration, which shows us the family and neighbors at home—such as Troy's friend Mindy, who asks impatiently, "When will Troy be back from the South, Mrs. Carmichael?"—further establishes a Brooklyn/Virginia contrast, or a dichotomy between North and South in the film. Such logic recalls what Paul Gilroy has referred to as "the historic binary codes of American racial thought to which [Lee] subscribes," such as Straight and Nappy, Jigaboos and Wannabes, and black and white.[61] The Virginia that Troy samples for a month (again, the contact zone tends to be transitory) functions as a synecdoche for what is referred to as "the South" in the film. Even from her standpoint as a participant-observer, the gaze Troy directs at her southern relatives is unmistakably othering. Her reference to them as "these people" is thus quite telling. It also seems plausible to interpret the view that Troy directs at the South as "panoramic." "Panoramic views," Rony notes, "helped ground the representation of travel as penetration and discovery" in colonialist discourses.[62]

Ultimately, *Crooklyn* implicitly dissociates the South from black nationalism and, by extension, from notions of black authenticity. To the contrary, the film implies an intimacy between black-nationalist expressivity and the urban North, as focalized through Brooklyn. By extension, the film also locates authentic blackness in the urban North. If, as Anne McClintock points out, "Nations are frequently figured through the iconography of the familial and domestic space," then I would suggest that in *Crooklyn*, black nationalism is embodied through the Carmichael family specifically.[63] The relatives in the South are totally oblivious to black-nationalist thought and expressivity. As is the case in *School Daze*, the distinction between the urban North and the South in *Crooklyn* is mainly articulated through "black hairstyle politics."[64] Aunt Song makes Troy visibly uncomfortable by criticizing the coarse texture of Troy's hair, remarking, "You ain't got good hair like my baby," as well as by asking several times, "What y'all call that?" as a result of confusion about the braids and beads that Troy and her mother are wearing when they arrive. Significantly, it is Aunt Song's remark that Troy "was wearing them funny braids and beads and shells and things" that makes Troy, who never wanted to stay and who has been ready to leave for quite some time, angry, and compels her to insist on going home immediately. Once Troy returns to Brooklyn, the naturalized association of black-nationalist aesthetics with Brooklyn is underscored by the Afro Sheen commercial praising a black woman's natural hair that is playing when Troy flips on the television set and settles into her room in Brooklyn. Notably, Troy's final style is an Afro. Lee's representation of black southerners in this film has not evolved far from the prevailing tendency within black-nationalist thought of the 1960s to romanticize black southerners in order to claim an authentic black historicity and ancestry in the United States, while, paradoxically, constituting the urban as the site of the most vital and authentic contemporary locus of blackness.

Crooklyn distances black southerners from black nationalism through the implication that Aunt Song's family worships whiteness, which sustains the conventional stereotypes of black southerners as white-identified and also reinforces the scripting of the U.S. South *as* a "white" region. The investment of this family in the practice of white mimicry is suggested at various junctures in this sequence. Viola's large collection of white Barbie dolls, a Barbie record, and a Barbie poster in her room are perhaps the most revealing signposts of this white fixation. After the Carmichael family moves on to drop off Troy's brother in Tennessee and Troy's visit officially begins, the spinning Barbie record is the first thing revealed in a scene featuring Viola's room. The camera quickly cuts to a grouping of her Barbie dolls—which are all white and which are shown from three different angles—and, finally, to a large, white, blonde baby doll. The association the film makes between the Carmichael family and whiteness is reinforced through the portrayal of Viola interrupting play with Troy to sing along with the music on a white televangelist show with which Viola is obviously familiar, and the portrayal of Aunt Song coming in, looking on adoringly, and joining in. Aunt Song's white house and the depiction of someone in her neighborhood walking a white dog as the southern sequence begins also imply the obeisance that this family pays to whiteness. The film implies that the South is countermodern, notwithstanding the middle-class suburban lifestyle of Aunt Song's family. It is clear that the urban North, inflected with black-nationalist aesthetics (which may also be referencing the Afrocentrism of the early 1990s that was still influential at the time of the film's release), represents the "now" within the economy of the film. It is therefore not surprising that "slow" is the word that Troy uses to describe the South from which she is returning in a conversation with her Aunt Maxine and Uncle Brown. In *Crooklyn*, the South is construed as apolitical and feminine and ultimately implied to be discordant with notions of African American subjectivity. The film implies that Aunt Song's family internalizes and uncritically practices a way of life that is virtually indistinct from that of white southerners.

The representation of the black southern context as "slow" is also in keeping with how ethnographic cinema, as Rony notes, typically embeds its subjects in a "displaced temporal realm."[65] As Troy's brothers walk into Aunt Song's living room, they are ostensibly reacting to the refined decor of her house (one comments on its cleanliness). Nevertheless, their looks of amazement as they slowly take in the atmosphere, coupled with the introduction of the anamorphic lens at this juncture in the film, produces the effect that they are walking into an otherworldly kind of space, one radically different from any they have ever entered. Their expressions might be produced by walking through and seeing images of themselves in a house of mirrors, the kinds of images that have been produced by the anamorphic lens in reshaping their bodies on the screen. The difference and otherness that Troy relates to the South are also evident in her use of the term "funny" to describe the language of black southern relatives whom she has visited, and in her father's comments that "Aunt Song kind of weird, isn't she?" Lee's *Crooklyn* highlights ambivalence about the role of the South in African American subject formation and reveals the power relations among African Americans based on geography.

It is worth noting that, within Lee's film corpus, the symbolic wedding of the South and black female subjectivity has its most literal and effective realization in his landmark documentary film *Four Little Girls* (1996).

Four Little Girls tells the stories of Addie Mae Collins, Carole Denise Mc-Nair, Cynthia Wesley, and Carole Rosamond Robertson, who were killed by white supremacists in the September 15, 1963, 16th Street Baptist Church bombing in Birmingham, Alabama. The raced, sexed, and gendered representations of the South in Lee's films—along with my argument that his repertoire has been a salient popular site through which an urbanized conception of blackness and masculinity has been constituted in more recent years—may seem somewhat ironic to those who are familiar with the southern aspects of his background. Lee was born in Atlanta, Georgia, in 1957. He returned to the city to attend Morehouse College, where he frequently saw his grandmother Zimmie Sheldon, the financier of his undergraduate and graduate education and his first film. Furthermore, his father has roots in Snow Hill, Alabama, and his great-grandfather, William James Edwards, founded Snow Hill Institute, wrote a study entitled *Twenty-five Years in the Black Belt*, and was a student of Booker T. Washington. Still, while much of Lee's life has unfolded around a rural southern–urban northern dialectic, Lee has been mainly invested in the urban aspects of his identity. As Catherine Pouzoulet has noted, "Lee himself never fails to emphasize his Brooklyn roots. Brooklyn is where he grew up and still lives."[66]

There was no more poignant signal of how the discourses of Uncle Tom would undergo revision among African Americans during the 1960s black-liberation movement than James Baldwin's 1949 essay "Everybody's Protest Novel." This essay offers an unforgiving critique of the sentimental mode of writing through a consideration of Harriet Beecher Stowe's novel *Uncle Tom's Cabin*.[67] For Baldwin, Uncle Tom is purely exceptional in his capacity to signify a quintessential and unadulterated type of black masculinity in light of the Africanist physicality that is uniquely accorded him among the novel's primary male characters. Furthermore, that Uncle Tom's painstaking sanctification reflects the racialist Manichean logic at work for Stowe also makes him metaphorically emblematic of a broader economy of subjects identified as black, and the price that he pays for his redemption within her narrative schema, animated as it is by such a metaphysical crisis, is his unsexing and dehumanization. If this were true, we could even say that the processes by which Uncle Tom is enunciated as a spiritually transcendent being in the novel ironically replay the very mechanisms whereby his captive body, under the institution of slavery, is subjected and subordinated to the point that gender differentiation—as Hortense J. Spillers contends in her essay "Mama's Baby, Papa's Maybe: An American Grammar Book"—is precluded. For "in the historic outline of dominance, the respective subject-positions of 'female' and 'male' adhere to no symbolic integrity."[68]

Baldwin suggests that the sexed and gendered forms of unruliness that ultimately attach to the delineation of Uncle Tom are fundamentally infused with and constituted by ideologies of his abjection as a raced subject. We might understand revisionist representations of Uncle Tom and such related stereotypes as Aunt Jemima as militant in the black-liberation movement as an implicit response to and disavowal of the feminine qualities that have been inferred through Stowe's original sentimentalist narrative. Similarly, we might interpret purposeful masculinizations of the mammy figure in black-liberation-era art as a revision and reversal of aspects of her genealogy that have surrendered her as a model of white masculinity cross-dressed as female and donning blackface, as witnessed in *Birth of a Nation*. Uncle Tom's construction as homosexual and effeminate in Malcolm X's speeches was an outgrowth of the contestations over gender that have been endemic to the genealogy of Uncle Tom and a symptom of the homosexual panic that informed efforts toward a patriarchal black masculinity during the black-liberation era. The unruliness and irreducibility of Uncle Tom with regard to inscriptions of gender also continues to be apparent in the contemporary public sphere in light of the demasculinization of this stereotype, which is also frequently invoked in relation to women like Condoleezza Rice.

In general, we need to recognize that the black-liberation era, as constituted by a range of activist struggles in the United States and in international contexts, brought with it intensified contestation over definitions of black masculinity. One byproduct of the era was a shift from the valuation of what might be regarded as "genteel" models of black masculine leadership that emerged within the historical ideology of racial uplift, as invoked, for instance, in Sutton Griggs's Belton Piedmont in this book's introduction, to an increasing cultural fascination with and foregrounding of young, vocal black militants as the embodiment of "real" black masculinity, as we see in the construal of such a character as Garth in the film *The Klansman*. The use of profanity, à la Caliban's pedagogy on learning to "curse," became one important public rhetorical sign of black masculine authentication during this period. Evidence of this shift was clear during the era of black-liberation struggle in what Marlon Ross identifies as ways in which Amiri Baraka—at that time Leroi Jones—prioritized "the hipster arena affiliated with black men's foul mouthed, street smart dozens" over James Baldwin's "sophisticated sensibility."[69] The evolutionary aspect in black masculine formations in this sense is also the background against which it is necessary to interpret highly sexualized models of black masculinity that have been popularized in the contemporary hip-hop movement and epitomized by popular artists such as 50 Cent.

This shifting black masculine aesthetic was inaugurated by and most saliently emblematized in the conflicting leadership models provided by Martin Luther King and Malcolm X, for the defining signpost as this social and political milieu consolidated was their frequent juxtaposition in the media. One result of the formation of this new black masculine ideal was the advancement of ideologies marking southernness as an undesirable ingredient in black male subject formation. It produced a nationalist, and even arguably national, fantasy of black men in the South as inauthentically black, politically naïve, and counterrevolutionary. Geography played a role to some extent in debates about black masculinity that animated this period and in this era's revisionism in terms of black masculine aesthetics.

It is soberingly befuddling that Lee's remake of *Birth of a Nation* as a film student critiqued and revised the film in a way akin to William Bradford Huie's novel *The Klansman* and yet was met with criticism and resistance by his instructors, who revered the legacy of D. W. Griffith. This early moment in his film career anticipated his continuing artistic investment in critiquing stereotypes of black identity. His vision has sometimes been quite narrow and has reinforced the kinds of stereotypes that he has been most committed to critiquing: in his representations of black southerners and particularly in his raced and sexed representations of black masculinity. Malcolm X decisively shaped a nationalist project of black uplift in the mid-twentieth century that prioritized an urban grassroots community. Spike Lee typically presented an amalgam of the middle class and grassroots in his effort to redefine blackness in the late twentieth century. The definitions of blackness that emerged within both ideologies were urban-centered. They reveal the continuing role of geography in shaping notions of black identity and illustrate how foundational an interrogation of the U.S. South's ideological and racial discourse continued to be in the twentieth century in the effort to shape ideals of African American identity and black masculinity.

CHAPTER 5

Gangstas and Playas in the Dirty South

Something strange has happened in the rap industry in recent years, given the profusion of artists ostensibly marketing themselves as southern or identifying with "the dirty South." Such artists have gained increasing popularity in the hip-hop arena nationally and, in some cases, globally. This seems strange because when rap emerged in the mid-1970s, the East Coast was its undisputed epicenter of production. From the late 1980s into the early 1990s, the West Coast, which was then primarily known for gangsta rap, also became a force to be reckoned with in the rap industry. The idea of the South as a legitimate base and space for artists to produce rap, which has often been viewed as an inherently urban (and masculine) verbal art, had been virtually unthinkable until recent years. The success of many southern rap artists in the contemporary era should not obscure the reality that trying to get noticed in the rap industry was long the equivalent of attempting to squeeze water from a rock for many rappers from the South. There was a time not too long ago when the very idea of an MC or DJ from the South, if ever it crossed the minds of major producers or celebrated artists in the rap industry, was more likely to come across as amusing. I mean *amusing* here in the sense of how Samuel Johnson famously likened the phenomenon of a woman writing to a dog walking on its hind legs, the kind of thing that one takes note of out of amazement that it can be done at all. At worst, the idea of rappers from the South probably struck many in the rap industry as being ridiculous. A January 2004 article in *Ebony* magazine entitled "Southern-Fried Hip-Hop," with the tag line "Down-home lyrics and strong dance grooves are ingredients of a tasty menu," registers this long-held view of the South in the rap industry:

> Whether it's grubbing at a local barbecue spot in Memphis, bling-blinging
> while riding in a Caddy on Peachtree Street, or just kicking it at a joint
> on Bourbon Street, the Southern lifestyle has taken the hip-hop world
> by storm. Once the butt of jokes in the New York City/Los Angeles–
> dominated world of rap music, it's now cool to hail from below the Mason-
> Dixon line. . . . The "Dirty South" has joined the rap party, and rolling
> through the 'hood will never be the same.[1]

Indeed, the question that David Bry raises in a June 2002 cover story for *Vibe* magazine, one of many publications that has registered this sea change in the rap industry, seems quite appropriate: "Back during hip hop's much lauded 'golden era,' who would have thought that the entire country would be looking southward for stylistic cues?"[2]

I am amazed myself that southern rap is in a very different place now from where it was when I first noticed and began to track the development of the genre back in 1997 as a graduate student. Back then, it was obscure, unfamiliar, and seldom thought of by anyone at all. It was mentioned marginally in the media, if at all. While once virtual outsiders, southern artists have come to represent the vanguard of contemporary hip-hop. The South has moved from the margins to become the veritable new epicenter of rap production in the United States. Southern rap, including the "dirty South" variety, has become an established subgenre in rap, moved into its second decade of production, and produced numerous albums. Though few would have ever anticipated such a southern invasion, we have seen moments in recent years during which southern-based and southern-identified rappers such as Nelly, Ludacris, and David Banner, along with such groups as Outkast and Nappy Roots, have all dominated the hip-hop/R&B charts. These artists are among those from the South who have received extensive media exposure and achieved high levels of popular success. Furthermore, we have witnessed the emergence of a significant number of both female and white rappers identifying with the South. Many contemporary rap artists are emphasizing the immediacy and specificity of life in the South, including the rural South, and are constructing the South as an organic and viable here and now in the visual iconography and lyric content of their rap albums. The iconography along these lines has been central to the successful marketing of southern rap. The southern rap craze has created the context in which many contemporary singers and entertainers, even beyond rap, are highlighting southern roots, and slang terms associated with the southern scene, such as *crunk*, are very popular. What has happened for southern artists in the rap industry in recent years is nothing short of a major breakthrough and revolution.

The media has also been fascinated with such major groundbreaking producers in the genre as Master P (Percy Williams), the founder and CEO of No Limit Records (which is now known as the New No Limit), and Brian "Slim" Williams and Reggie "Baby" Williams, brothers and co-founders of Cash Money Records. In both instances, these producers stepped beyond the dominant East Coast–West Coast circuits of the rap industry to establish companies based in New Orleans for the purpose of providing creative outlets for youth living in the South. Their innovative strategies have paid off quite literally. They are "moguls" in the rap industry on par with Sean Puffy Combs (P. Diddy) of Bad Boy Entertainment and Russell Simmons of Def Jam Productions and featured on the pages of such magazines as *Forbes* and *Fortune* among the nation's youngest multimillionaires. The story of how these rap producers began to market and mainstream the sounds of artists who had developed an underground sound in the South that was distinct and innovative in its unique "bounce" rhythms, and how they made millions of dollars doing it, is also what has in part drawn increasing attention to the genre. The success of southern rap is in part attributable to its major producers. That is to say, one reason that southerners *can* rap nowadays is that their money talks. Rap has proliferated exponentially in the South in part because when it became a popular (and profitable) trend, many mainstream record companies with no prior investments in southern artists quickly sought a piece of the action and established southern branches.

The Florida-based group 2 Live Crew, which became the subject of national debates in the early 1990s following the arrest of the group leader "Luke Skyywalker" at a concert over the explicit content of lyrics on their album *As Nasty as They Wanna Be*, can be regarded as a major precursor to the contemporary profusion of rap in the South.[3] The same thing can be said of the Atlanta-based group Arrested Development, which was popular in the early 1990s. While it encompasses a range of styles, the current southern rap phenomenon as manifested in mainstream popular culture should also be recognized as an outgrowth of the gangsta rap movement that emerged on underground circuits in the South in the mid- to late 1990s. Indeed, what intrigues me even more than the contemporary popularity of southern rap—and has important implications for the analytical trajectory that I am pursuing in this study—is the space from which southern rap as a genre originally emerged in the 1990s. In the years before the genre became "cool," the assertive masculinist posturing of black southern rappers as "gangstas" and "playas" began to occur in part, I suggest, as a defensive response to the conventional exclusion of southern artists in the rap industry. This stance was on some levels an attempt to "represent the South" or a "dirty South" that had long lacked acknowledgment in rap. It is fascinating, for instance, that some of the earliest southern rap songs scripted in this vein not only acknowledged but also confronted stereotypes of black men in the South. One of the best examples is New Orleans rapper Joe Blakk's "Way Down South," which I examine in this chapter. Through its deft and witty verbal play and a binary construction of opposition between black men from a range of cities in the South and those from the East Coast, West Coast, and North, it emphasizes tensions and even potentially violent conflict among black men based on regional differences. At the same time, "Way Down South" confronts the historical exclusion of rappers in the South that was long the norm in the rap industry by attempting to dismantle perceptions that black southern rappers can't "bring it." This rap song is quite compelling for my purposes to the extent that its themes suggest that the South has remained a context of ideological formation in the African American context even into the contemporary era and confront the devaluation and stereotyping of black masculinity in the South. The import of Blakk's "Way

Down South" becomes even more apparent if we interpret it in relation to African American literary works that highlight geographical tensions among black men by such authors as Jean Toomer and Toni Morrison and in the foundational blues lyrics of W. C. Handy. Furthermore, I frame my examination of Blakk's song by an examination of the broader New Orleans scene of southern rap and its major producers and by an overview of some of the major themes in the genre. His piece is useful for my purposes in its critique of the dominant urban aesthetics in the African American popular context that have at times alienated or excluded black southerners and constituted distinctions and hierarchies among black men.

In her groundbreaking study on rap, Tricia Rose illustrates how the widely popular expressive form of rap as practiced by black female artists extends the spectrum of themes and issues that we might recognize in relation to black women's lives and acknowledges the marginal status of women in the rap industry.[4] It seems appropriate to punctuate a critical study of black southern masculinity with an engagement of contemporary rap in the South as a way of stepping beyond the texts in film and literature that I have considered thus far. I believe that we can better understand the diversity and complexity of black men's lives through rap's narratives, not only because many rap artists are male and sometimes come from a marginal class status, but also because their works speak to issues that are not addressed in the genres that have been salient in this study up to this point. This approach seems all the more useful when we recognize that the exclusion of southern rappers has been more seldom acknowledged than the concomitant marginality of female rappers.

As a genre, rap is often recognized as the quintessence of folk and vernacular aesthetics in the African American context. At the same time, rap has long been regarded as an inherently urban form. For the first time, southern rap has in effect crystallized a convergence of the folk aesthetics in the rap world with the historical regional context from which black vernacular forms are understood to have historically emerged in the United States. In a sense, the phenomenon resolves the perplexing paradox of rap, which has relied on its "vernacular" aspects to proclaim its authenticity as an African American form and acknowledged southern folk roots but devalued voices that might be classified as southern. Furthermore, southern identity is the central quality that authenticates and validates artists performing in this genre and authorizes them to speak or, to be more accurate, rap. The movement in some ways repackages the vexed folk fetishes that have conventionally identified the rural as most authentically black. Because of these dimensions, the southern rap genre is, of course, a useful framework in which we might consider debates over black authenticity. We must increasingly move beyond the critiques reflecting generational conflicts in the African American context regarding hip-hop, which can be somewhat shortsighted and reactionary. Still, hip-hop, and southern rap in particular, should not be immune to criticism. I readily admit that I am very troubled myself by the hegemony of hip-hop as a paradigm in contemporary African American music and African American culture. I am equally concerned by the ways in which African American youth are often monolithically categorized through sound bites like "the hip-hop generation" in such contexts as the political public sphere. Such logic obscures other areas that significantly impact the consciousness of African American youth that have nothing to do with hip-hop at all. In this chapter, I acknowledge some of the more problematic aspects of hip-hop and contemporary southern rap. Doing so is particularly urgent in light of its increasing dispersal in global and African diasporic contexts. That is to say, hip-hop is a form that is now global, and southern rap is increasingly mediating its globalization. In general, as is the case with almost any movement in popular culture, the emergence of southern rap as a commodity is a factor that has threatened to mitigate the genre's original subversive and oppositional content, which has existed alongside its more problematic qualities—such as misogyny, violence, and materialism—that mirror characteristics of mainstream rap. We might find value and inspiration in how many southern rappers have fought back in recent times and claimed a voice in the rap world. But the analytical trajectory that I have been pursuing in this study also clarifies some of the other issues in southern rap that deserve careful critical reflection. Within the framework of this study's larger thesis, it becomes clear, for instance, that southern rap's narratives of black men as "gangstas" and "playas" are intensely ironic. For, in some ways, they recast the historically raced and gendered pathologies of black men as criminal, violent, and overly sexualized that have roots in southern history.

New Orleans

A range of cities in the South have emerged over the past couple of decades as centers of southern rap production. Atlanta, Houston, and New Orleans have been the three major epicenters. In this chapter, I want to consider the

New Orleans foundations of southern rap specifically given the central role that the city played in Joe Blakk's formation as an artist. Also, it is the place where the major pioneering producers on the contemporary southern rap scene such as Master P and Brian and Reggie Williams got their start, men whose biographies alone are quite significant.

Russell Simmons, founder and CEO of Def Jam Records, is regarded as the "godfather" of hip-hop due to ways in which his pathbreaking entrepreneurial work as a producer in the music industry has made hip-hop music, dance, fashion, and speech familiar and accessible around the world. Master P, one of the earliest producers in the industry to put his finger on the pulse of southern "bounce" and to record and market this distinctive sound, can be regarded as having done substantial pioneering work to put the South on the map in the rap industry. This project began when he moved to Richmond, California, with his wife, Sonya, his high-school sweetheart, in the late 1980s to live near his mother. In doing so, he was also escaping the ravages of the Calliope housing project in New Orleans, a community in which he had experienced the death of one of his brothers at the hands of a drug addict and in which he had been a drug dealer himself. Soon after the move, he opened a record store called No Limits with ten thousand dollars of the money gained from a hospital malpractice suit over his grandfather's death. In a November 27, 1997, interview with *Rolling Stone*, Master P remarks that "[I left] because I knew that eventually, if I didn't get my life together, I'd probably go to jail or get killed." He goes on to say that "I had to decide to go on and chill by my mom's house and try to do something positive, because it was too hot at home. . . . Everybody was dying there. I wanted to try to start me a record company."[5] His business was successful, and Master P saw that its dividends, which averaged ten thousand dollars a month, were much greater than the ones that would have come from the car wash that he had originally thought about opening. Master P's incentives for giving up drug dealing not only had to do with the inherent dangers of the trade but also with the realization that there was much more money to be made in the music world than he could ever hope to make as a hustler on the street. Once he opened his store, he saw that while his customers were gaining exposure to such popular rap artists as Ice Cube, Tupac Shakur, and Ice-T, the unique bounce beats from home were getting no play. Consequently, Master P decided to try his hand in the music business and established No Limit Records, from which he released his debut album, *The Ghetto's Tryin' to Kill Me!*, in 1993. He peddled the album from city to city from the trunk of his car, ultimately selling over one hundred thousand copies. Using this same sales method, he sold twice as many copies of his second release, *Ninety-nine Ways to Die*.

After his initial success, Master P eschewed the conventional production sites for rap music on the East and West Coasts and opted to move the No Limit company back to his hometown, where he initially expanded the label by recruiting two of his brothers, Vyshonne/"Silkk the Shocker" and Corey/"C-Murder," to form a group called TRU, and by adding other artists such as Mia X and Mystikal. This move proved to be yet another strategic one on his part and eventually paid off. Rap artists the likes of C-Loc, Lil' Keke, Fiend, Young Bleed, Prime Suspects, Soulja Slim, Shull Durggery, and Lil Soldiers are among those whose careers were developed on the No Limit label after its inception. In 1998 No Limit Records sold 26 million records, exceeding sales of all other rap labels, with fifteen of the twenty-three albums it released going gold or platinum, and *Forbes* magazine listed Master P tenth among the highest-paid entertainers. That year the company had helped premier gangsta rapper Snoop Doggy Dog gain release from his recording contract with Suge Knight's controversial Death Row Records. In 1999 Master P was listed twenty-eighth on *Fortune*'s list of the Forty Richest Americans Under Forty and won an American Music Award for best rap/hip-hop artist. In 2001 the net worth of No Limit Records, along with a range of other successful companies that Master P developed, such as No Limit Real Estate, No Limit Sports, No Limit Films, a clothing line, Master P dolls, and a food and gas station, was estimated at $400 million.

The move to the South was just the first of several strategic and unprecedented moves in the rap industry that set Master P apart as a producer. For instance, he has been recognized widely for the unique marketing strategies that he utilized in building No Limit Records in the early days of the company. These strategies included keeping video production costs at a minimum; reducing advertising costs by incorporating sound bites from a range of artists on his label into the release of every individual No Limit CD; supersizing CDs to include fifteen or sixteen songs as opposed to the typical ten, which gave the label wide appeal among customers; and establishing "No Limit," with its soldiers' army tank symbol as a trademark with wide recognition through the marketing of clothing, films, sports, toys, and technology. However, perhaps the most important factor that made Master P exceptional among the entrepreneurial elite in the rap/hip-hop world was his rejection of "boutique label deals" from record companies that were eagerly recruiting him to cut a distribution deal in the wake of the three hundred thousand copies of his first two rap albums that he had sold independently, an arrangement that would have placed the majority of profits in the hands of the company.[6] Eventually, he successfully negotiated a deal with Priority Records that allowed the company to keep 15 percent of the profits with the remaining 85 percent going to No Limit Records in exchange for publicity and distribution and that allowed him to reserve full ownership of the master recordings. This is a setup that was unprecedented in the rap industry. In another atypical move among producers and recording artists, Master P had also refused to accept money from Priority Records up front. Because of his ingenuity, he is often called "the ghetto Bill Gates."[7]

Like Master P, the brother team Brian "Baby" Williams and Ronald "Slim" Williams launched their company, Cash Money Records, in New Orleans. Founded in 1992, the label has been home to a range of popular southern rap artists, including Juvenile, Lil' Wayne, and the Hot Boys. Baby and Slim were raised by their father in the Third Ward of New Orleans, a rough area located uptown. Their father operated a neighborhood grocery store and a lounge named the Gladys Bar after their mother, who died when Slim was nine and Baby was seven. This background allowed the boys to gain skills in bookkeeping. It was a loan from their father, who advised them not to change and to "show them what your town sounds like," that allowed them to launch their business.[8] In the beginning, Baby and Slim focused on developing local artists and, like Master P, sold CD's from the trunk of their car. Though they enjoyed some regional success, their original stars were unwilling to remain drug free and to devote time and energy to learning the protocols of the music business, such as interviewing, making media appearances, and signing autographs. Frustrated, the team opted to dismiss all of them with the exception of a young artist known as B. G. (Christopher Dorsey).[9] Cash Money's release of B. G.'s *Chopper City* in 1996, a track that combined the bounce sound with hardcore gangsta lyrics, signaled a turning point for the company, inaugurating a craze for bounce from New Orleans. With solo projects, Lil' Wayne, Turk, and Juvenile have also popularized the Cash Money label in recent years, and these artists, along with B. G., were part of the group the Hot Boys formed by the company. In 1998 the company signed a distribution deal with Universal Records. This arrangement gave it a nationwide distribution base for the first time, increasing its ability to market and publicize its artists and allowing Baby and Slim to retain full ownership. Cash Money's main strategy has been to keep production costs below fifty thousand dollars and to sell half a million records a month with very little overhead, tactics that maximize profits for both Cash Money and Universal. Slim, especially, has gained renown as a shrewd businessman in the record industry. In 1999 the combined album sales of Juvenile, Lil' Wayne, B. G., Turk, and the Hot Boys totaled 9 million and catapulted the southern style of rapping to the forefront of hip-hop.

Known for their flamboyance, their Bentleys, their love of partying, and their popularization of the "Bling Bling" concept symbolizing their love of gold and diamonds, the Cash Money team, often referred to as the "Cash Money Millionaires," is now a major force in the music industry. Baby and Slim, like Master P, are also well known for their charity work, particularly for their contributions to the Magnolia housing project community in New Orleans, identified in 1995 by the *Times Picayune* as the place where one was "most likely to be killed" in the city. Although the places from which they came, the Calliope project and the Magnolia, were rival communities, Master P and Cash Money have functioned less as competitors and more as mutual innovators in the rap industry. With Master P's move in 2002 from Priority to Universal to establish the New No Limit, which was primarily orchestrated so that he would be able to reach a global market, both companies now operate under the same major distributor.

Black Enterprise writer Tariq K. Muhammad has commented in light of the success of Master P and the Cash Money team that "the Louisiana bayou is an especially fertile ground for self-starting music entrepreneurs."[10] In setting up distribution deals that have given them relative autonomy and reserved company ownership, they have helped set new precedents in the music industry and have unsettled some of the formulas that many producers assumed were fixed in the past. As a result of their pioneering strategies, there is a possibility that the terms for negotiating with such major companies as Universal, Priority, and Time-Warner will be radically altered for producers in the future. These innovations seem especially significant during an age when many music artists complain of exploitation because they are denied royalties and have little to show financially for their success (due to low percentages on big profits from album sales), even as their large labels gross high profits.

In his 2001 autobiography entitled *Life and Def: Sex, Drugs, Money and God*, Russell Simmons sums up what makes these producers in the South pioneering, unique, and inspiring:

> When you have a hot company—a No Limit or Cash Money—all the majors can do is suck your dick. . . . These guys can't speak the king's English, but they can buy and sell most every white record executive in America. Master P, a man with a mouth full of gold, is one of the richest people in the country under 40. He owns his shit. The guys who run Cash Money own their own label. . . . I love the image of these Harvard guys sitting across from these southern boys with gold fronts in their mouths, having to give in because they want and need to be in business with them.[11]

Simmons's comments also acknowledge the ambivalence that persists concerning the success of these producers in the industry and how their southern-accented speech, style, and manner have shaped their perception. At times these qualities have led industry insiders to stereotype these producers as gullible, less intelligent, and vulnerable to exploitation. As Master P remarks, "People thought we was slow . . . probably thought I was ignorant 'cause of my slurring. But then that country slang really made people pay attention. People had to respect us for not changing our music, and for not trying to hide where we were from."[12] Similarly, Baby has commented that "people think we from the middle of nowhere, so they can take advantage of us. But we smart guys—we been studying this rap game. And we've worked harder than anyone just to earn the respect we got now."[13] It is quite telling for my purposes that these producers encountered similar politics of southern exclusion and stereotyping in their dealings in the music industry. As I will illustrate in more detail later on, these are the kinds of stereotypes that songs such as Joe Blakk's "Way Down South" forthrightly address.

Touré, a columnist for *Rolling Stone*, acknowledges how major southern rap producers sometimes very purposefully, through their flamboyant styles of dress and performance antics, turn southern stereotypes into a commodity. He remarks that Master P has turned "the South into hip-hop's land of dreams, inspiring scenesters all over the region to play up their loudest, liveliest cartoon visions of fame and fortune. . . . Along with his New Orleans neighbor Juvenile (of the Cash Money posse), P sells tons of records with no concessions to pop, R&B, or even the national hip-hop audience. These born-on-the-bayou ballers thrive on showing the world their asses, defiantly parading their down-home crudeness as a sign of freedom, and that crudeness is what gives their music its kick." Of Master P, Touré goes on to say that "his real sonic signature lies in those trademark No Limit choruses: male voices that chant maddeningly catchy singsong hooks, sliding in and out of tune. The choruses sound sloppy, almost painfully country, the musical equivalent of No Limit's brilliantly garish album covers, which look like they should have been painted on the side of a Chevy van in 1972. Upscale urbanites may gag, but that's the whole point—P loves to blow a big fat uunngh! [the No Limit trademark] in the face of West Coast jigginess and East Coast sophistication."[14] Similarly, David Bry has observed that "[Master] P's leadership and commercial acumen took southern rap music to new heights. His greatest legacy, though, may be the extent to which he undid commonly held stereotypes about southerners."[15]

While record companies in various regions eager to share in the profits from the genre are now producing southern rappers, New Orleans was a key city in which the genre underwent some of its earliest and most significant developments. In light of the phenomenal success of entrepreneurs like Baby, Slim, and Master P, the question that begs to be asked is, How and why did New Orleans in particular become a pioneering site in the production of southern rap? A rich history and a culture rich in cuisine, jazz, and architecture, as well as the annual Mardi Gras and such legendary areas as the French Quarter and sprawling boulevards, are qualities that have made New Orleans one of the most popular tourist attractions in the world. Nevertheless, this romantic culture is worlds apart from the everyday reality of many residents living in the city's less idyllic areas, such as the housing projects. To understand what made New Orleans a fecund site for the emergence of the southern rap that eventually took root there (initially under the banner of the gangsta style), it is important to recognize a variety of social, economic, and political factors. As was the case in many other cities at the outset of the 1990s, New Orleans was characterized by high rates of crime, violence, and drug trafficking. The city reigned as the nation's murder capital well into the decade. In the shadow of the Reagan-Bush era, an evaporating city budget and increased federal and state cutbacks had left New Orleans with a dwindling economy. Thriving oil and gas markets began to decline drastically in the 1980s, causing a recession, and tourism became the major source of revenue for the city. The jobs that were available paid little, and it was even commonplace for youth to leave the city to seek employment opportunities. Furthermore, an inadequate health-care system, rising taxes, poor public schools, and declining property values had lessened the quality of life in the city. Death and decay seemed to be the order of the day in New Orleans. These circumstances must be understood, too, in light of the crises that had ravaged the city in prior decades.

From the late 1980s and into the 1990s, New Orleans also experienced increasing racial polarization. The fault lines of the city were demarcated by race, with the vast majority of blacks concentrated in the inner city as whites fled to the suburbs en masse. Within this context, former neo-Nazi and Ku Klux Klan grand wizard David Duke, a state representative in Louisiana, received 57 percent of the white vote during his run for the U.S. Senate through a populist platform that attacked policies such as affirmative action and welfare. Black youth in the city made their disquietude over Duke known by attacking white onlookers and breaking storefront windows during the Martin Luther King parade. After the Senate race, Duke made it as far as the general election in a bid for governor in 1991, losing in the end due to concerted opposition from black voters and to the negative publicity that had been generated in the national media about his background as a white supremacist. Later on that year, the racial chasm in New Orleans widened more when city councilwoman Dorothy May Taylor, an African American, with the support of the African American mayor Sidney Bartheley, proposed an ordinance that encouraged the integration of all twenty-nine of the city's "krewes" so that anyone, irrespective of race, class, gender, sexuality, or ability, could be admitted. Many of these krewes, which sponsored elaborate parades in the city during Mardi Gras, were the exclusive province of wealthy white elites who met the threat of change with hostility and fought bitterly to conserve their time-honored organizations.[16] The racial and class disparities in the city have become more starkly apparent and the subject of national and global attention since the Hurricane Katrina tragedy in 2005, which occurred after several levees broke and the city flooded.

In *Louisiana Music*, journalist Rick Koster offers a comprehensive treatment of the development of various musical genres in Louisiana, such as jazz, creole, cajun, zydeco, R&B, gospel, blues, country, rock and roll, and rap. He acknowledges the diversity in musical styles that have developed in the state and its history as a fecund site of music production.[17] What is true about the state of Louisiana in terms of its musical richness is perhaps even truer for New Orleans as a city, for its music, of course, is one of the things for which New Orleans is best known historically. Though Mardi Gras and Carnival were the annual highlights, plays, balls, concerts, and parades made music an intimate part of life there during the antebellum period. Blacks in New Orleans established their own brass bands whose members studied with the French Opera House or orchestras in the city, sometimes even traveling to Paris for further instruction in music. This was a strategy that was particularly popular among Creoles, a privileged caste usually of a combination of white male paternity and black female maternity that set itself apart from the black community, and that nurtured its literacy in such areas as music, literature, and art. After 1894 the Creoles were forced to intermingle more intimately with the black population by mandate of a segregation ordinance based on the logic of hypodescent, which displaced them from the area downtown to the uptown district where blacks were concentrated and categorized them as wholly black, ignoring their mixed-race background. Further segregationist legislation in 1897 resulted in the establishment of a tenderloin district that eventually became known as Storyville.[18] This area drew both Creole and black musicians, and it was in this context that genres such as ragtime and jazz thrived. By the beginning of the twentieth century, dozens of brass bands proliferated, which also routinely followed the trend of apprenticeship with the city's most distinguished white musical venues such as the French Opera House. Jazz underwent some major developments in New Orleans early in the twentieth century under its practitioners such as William Manuel "Bill" Johnson, Edward "Kid" Ory, Sidney Bechet, Joseph "King" Oliver, and Louis Armstrong, who helped to birth a style that has come to be known as "New Orleans Jazz."[19]

That New Orleans would yield a version of "bounce" all its own, offer the emergent genre of southern rap many of its defining characteristics, and emerge as an epicenter of rap production in the contemporary era seems like a normal occurrence when considering the city's musically rich history. Koster has described the birth of bounce in New Orleans housing projects:

> It evolved in the St. Thomas project in 1989 when a young DJ, Kevin
> Tucker—a.k.a. MCT—improvised a series of street slogans in the fashion

of Mardi Gras Indian call-and-response chants, and an immediate crowd gathered. The result was a local scene that spawned dozens of "bounce" songs, all infectiously danceable, rap-pop fusions that glistened with summery possibility. Block parties sprang up with mobs of men, women, and kids choking the courtyards of housing projects, all exuberantly bouncin'— which requires the participant to bend forward, thrust ass proudly, and shimmy in appropriately rhythmic behavior.[20]

It is in the continuum of a New Orleans, which in prior eras yielded musical prodigies in such genres as jazz from impoverished communities where crime and violence were rampant, that we should also situate the profusion of talent that has emerged in the New Orleans inner city during the past few years. That New Orleans was economically devastated, drug- and crime-ravaged, and plagued by an escalating murder rate made the city fertile ground for the development of a genre like gangsta rap, which had emerged originally among young African American rappers in Los Angeles as both an artistic response to and imitation and reflection of postindustrial material conditions of the city such as gangs, drugs, and violence.[21] Moreover, rapping was one of the most accessible avenues of surviving and escaping the harshness and deprivation of life in inner city New Orleans, where good jobs were few and far between.

To understand more fully the important ways in which the South is reshaping the contours of the rap industry and the logic of black popular culture more generally, we need to recognize the marketing mastery that southern rap producers demonstrated and the corporate reforms they helped catalyze in rap music production. These developments are a direct outgrowth of their early work to promote various artists on the underground rap scene in the South. Recognizing these connections is particularly important because the southern origins of these producers have been more seldom acknowledged with the rise of their popularity in the mainstream.

Way Down South Where the Bounce Began

Notwithstanding a general umbrella term such as *southern rap*, it is necessary to avoid generalizations and to remember that this genre is diverse and ever evolving. It is no doubt as broad and wide-ranging in scope and thematic content as the large and diverse body of artists who have made contributions to its development over the past few years. The themes of southern rap songs frequently reflect those that can be found in the general body of rap music, such as boasts related to money and other material possessions such as cars, jewelry, and drugs or to the sexual conquest of women. These representations have become more popular as the genre itself has gained popularity, and the emphasis in album art is sometimes placed on cars, money, flashy jewelry, and scantily clad women. The 2004 controversy over Nelly that erupted at Spelman College in light of a scene in his music video for the song "Tip Drill," in which he swipes a credit card in a woman's buttocks, led students to protest a bone-marrow drive scheduled on campus, resulting in its cancellation, and indicates that some problems which have plagued rap more generally are also evident in southern rap. However, many southern rap narratives are distinct for their unique and subversive strategies of negotiating race, class, and masculinity. They frequently turn the conventional boast of rap on its head by assertively articulating the material realities of being young, male, and black and living in the contemporary South with limited resources and opportunities.[22] Eschewing fantasies of wealth that have often been dominant in rap, these rap songs claim their commercial currency and authority by their insistence on narrating "truths" about being poor and southern. Though some southern rap artists claim identities as "gangstas," "pimps," "ballers," and "playas," the speakers in many of their narratives admit to doing so in spite of not having a lot of money or other kinds of luxuries. The group Nappy Roots provides a classic example of this outlook in the track "Ballin' on a Budget" on their 2002 album *Watermelon, Chicken and Gritz*. The song mentions cars with rusted tailpipes, "baby mama drama," taking women to cheap hotels and the inability to afford contraceptives, going barefoot, smoking, and having alcohol but lacking cash for drugs like ecstasy. The refrain invokes "backwoods country folks" who have no access to cell phones and pagers. Images of the front porch on the album cover, a staple aspect of southern rap iconography, also allude to these dire material conditions.

While southern rappers invoke the concept of "representin'" that is so fundamental to rap, they have primarily used the concept to reflect their ongoing effort to make legible a South that has long been invisible in the rap industry. Album and song titles frequently invoke the South as a place directly or indirectly. Often, individual and group stage names directly or indirectly reference southern identity, as we see in the case of such artists as South Mob, Kotton Mouth, and Da Southern Soldier. On many albums, at least one anthem focuses on the South. We can also read the efforts of some of these artists to slur their speech and incorporate the black vernacular of the South into their lyrics as a strategy of subverting and distinguishing themselves from the prevailing aesthetics of rap that have ordinarily been associated with cities and with an urban style and voice. In many cases, artists are now, in fact, assertively claiming and celebrating the very qualities, attributes, and cultural practices that have conventionally contributed to the South's exclusion from rap.

The dialogism inherent to rap discourse is sometimes articulated in southern rap's narratives through rhetorical invocations of the East Coast and West Coast as well as through the establishment of intersubjectivity among southern geographies. For instance, an overview or "roll call" of southern cities, or of southern states, will often be incorporated into these songs. Southern rappers have also been interested in locating themselves within the general regional schema of rap in their roll calls. Da Southern Soldier mentions a down South–East Coast–West Coast–up North schema in their song "Goin' Home Wit' Somethin'." Furthermore, in some instances, southern rappers have attempted to diffuse the fabled rivalry in the rap industry between the East and West Coasts. This bicoastal feuding reached its worst realization in the conflict between the rappers Tupac Shakur and Biggie Smalls and their mysterious and violent deaths in 1996 and 1997, respectively. In "Reason for Rhyme," Eight Ball and M. J. G. chide East Coast and West Coast rappers for their warfare and underscore the South's separateness from this conflict. The 2002 hit duet entitled "Dilemma" by Nelly with Kelly Rowland of the group Destiny's Child also invokes a regional schema that acknowledges the South as a place where people are "bouncin'." However, some of the references to the East and West Coasts in southern rap have been more defensive. In these instances, southern rappers have invoked the East and West Coasts in defending themselves against assumptions and stereotypes about the South that they presume are prevalent in these areas. Addressing these sites in a tone that is at once confrontational and didactic, the goal is typically to inform the East Coast and West Coast about how things are done in the South or to warn these regions not to make assumptions about what goes on in the South. The direction of the line "If you don't know you'd better ask somebody" at the East Coast and West Coast is recurrent across a range of southern rap songs, from Joe Blakk's "Way Down South" to the Texas

Niggaz and Eses's "Execution" (2000). Dialogism has also been evident in the imprint of Mexican and Caribbean cultures on the southern rap genre, a factor that seems to reflect the increasing ethnic diversification of the South over the past decade. In this regard, we might consider the incorporation of Caribbean patois into the song "Da Land" (2000) by the group Dirty, which is a tribute to gangstas in Montgomery, Alabama. Similarly, the ways in which such Texas-based rappers as the Texas Niggaz and Eses have incorporated Spanish into their songs, as we see in "Million-Dollar Mexicans" (2000), reflect this syncretism.

Another prominent theme in the southern rap genre has been an engagement of southern history and symbolism, along with the South's white-supremacist racialist ideologies. References to historical white southern masculine formations are implicit in the song by the Geto Boys entitled "I'm Not a Gentleman" as well as in their ironic invocation of the Confederate rebel of the Civil War era in "Rebel Rap Family." That Lil' Jon and the East Side Boys appear on the cover of their *Put Yo' Hood Up* (2001) album flanked in burning Confederate flags suggests their wish to see the eradication and destruction of this symbol. Furthermore, their song alludes to factionalism based on neighborhood fault lines and to the continuing existence of the Ku Klux Klan. Nappy Roots invokes the historic "southern belle" ironically on their album in describing their trysts in hotels with women that do not result in marriage, along with summons for child-support payments. Possibly, the intention here is to boast of interracial sexual trysts. Lil' Wayne and Ludacris have developed personas within the rap industry that are ostensibly associated with historical qualities connoting southernness such as hospitality and charm. On *A Soldier's Diary* (2001), Da Southern Soldier includes a brief skit titled "I'm Goin' Undercover" that incorporates news footage mentioning the disappearance of civil rights activists Michael Schwerner, Andrew Goodman, and James Cheney in Mississippi in 1964 and mentions the activist examples of Martin Luther King and Rosa Parks in the song that follows. Most famously and controversially, the group Outkast was the object of a lawsuit for invoking civil rights veteran Rosa Parks in their 2000 song "Rosa Parks," which included profanity. It is particularly provocative that some artists rapping in the southern genre explicitly celebrate being "country" or call themselves "country boys," in effect resignifying the historically racialist implications of the term "boy" as a racial epithet deployed by white supremacists to denigrate black men in the South. At times the assertions of southern identity in southern rap actively subvert nostalgic white-supremacist celebrations of the region.[23]

The phrase "dirty South" has been one of the most salient and recurrent metaphors within the genre of southern rap, serving not only as a banner under which many artists posture but also as a catch phrase for invoking the South in a litany of songs. Alternatively, a "filthy South" is sometimes invoked, as is the case in the song "Hood Stuck," a track on Ludacris's album *Back for the First Time* (2000). The meanings of the term "dirty South" vary. Sometimes the connotations are explicitly sexual. The phrase has also often served as an assertive acknowledgment of the existence of a viable and coherent rap discourse in the South and, particularly, of the presence of "gangsta" economies in the South that are on a par with those on the East and West Coasts. "Dirty South" has in effect enabled many rappers in the South to assert a collective identity and has helped their effort to resist invisibility and exclusion in the rap industry, giving them legibility and a coherent way of being identified. The phrase ironically invokes and makes an attempt to celebrate and resignify attributes that have conventionally placed southerners on the margins of rap. In the phrase "dirty South," we are also reminded of the historical status of the South as an "abject" and "excluded" geography in the United States. Here I draw on the psychoanalytic meanings of these terms that have been offered by Julia Kristeva and David Sibley, respectively, which have been engaged in earlier sections of this study. The phrase "dirty South" is loaded with implications in terms of the South's history as a site of social, economic, legal, and political repression and disfranchisement for African Americans in the United States. Such meanings are invoked directly in the 2001 poem by Malcolm Ali entitled "The Dirty South (A Letter to Jim Crow)." Indeed, these references to the dirty South have sometimes had concomitant manifestations in African American literature. For instance, Colson Whitehead's novel *The Intuitionist* (2000) mentions a "dirty town" "down South."[24] Furthermore, it is significant that the preponderance of dirt metaphors in southern rap lies in the continuum with the recurrent invocations of dirt in southern women's literature that Patricia Yaeger has identified.[25] In rap, "Dirty South" attempts to unsettle the persisting view of black southerners as romantic in the African American context by underscoring the struggles and stresses of black life in the contemporary South, a site that has often been imagined as a retreat from and alternative to the violence and crime in the inner city.

In 1995 the Down South Hustlers, a New Orleans–based collective of rappers, released the CD *Bouncin' and Swingin': Tha Value Pack Compilation* on No Limit Records, with Master P as executive producer. This pioneering project was among the earliest albums that helped open a space for black southern rappers in the rap industry. Even more specifically, *Bouncin' and Swingin'*, which helped give salience to New Orleans bounce, made headway into a gangsta rap economy that was at the time dominated by West Coast artists and, in effect, heralded the outpouring of rap from the South that we have witnessed since the mid-1990s. Joe Blakk's track on the CD entitled "Way Down South" explicitly invokes the name of and seems to serve as an anthem for this larger collective. This track is particularly compelling for my interests in black southern masculine representational politics in light of the litany of allegations it makes about the stereotyping of black southern men by those from the East Coast, the West Coast, and the North who visit the region.

The song focuses its rhetorical energies on critiquing the impressions that black men from such urban cities as Brooklyn, Detroit, and Chicago allegedly have of the South. While call-and-response techniques are used throughout the song, Blakk, who wrote the lyrics, serves as the narrator. The first verse attempts to give outsiders in the South a sense of what they might conceivably encounter there. It establishes that the South is not a context immune to such issues as gang violence that are ordinarily associated with urban contexts. Instead, it insists that "drama" is almost all that goes on. Southern guys, the song suggests, carry weapons and are not afraid to fight or die.

In what seems to be an ironic invocation of romantic African American journeying to and through the South, the narrator goes from city to city in the climactic second verse, including New Orleans, Dallas, Little Rock, Baton Rouge, Jackson, and Knoxville, to catalog maladies that could potentially befall the unwitting traveler to these places at the hands of "country" men. This dimension recalls the use of the "roll call" in rap. The narrator issues a warning that is at bottom a threat to would-be travelers to the South from the East Coast, the West Coast, and the North. Indeed, instead of describing the South as a welcoming place, the song encourages regional outsiders who visit to get quick directions and get out. Blakk underscores that traveling into southern territories with arrogant, condescending, and preconceived notions of "country" men as fundamentally benign and non-threatening could get outsiders into a lot of unexpected trouble and even killed. The song suggests that the normally "bad" East Coast, West Coast, and northern guys who walk arrogantly into southern territories can expect to end up running scared in the end. Therein, the image evoked by the narrator is one of travelers dodging mysterious gunfire and running down the streets in a panic with their hats blowing off. Tre 8, who accompanies Blakk as a vocalist, claims that these travelers imagine that guys from the South ride on cows, live on farms, spit tobacco, pick cotton, play banjos, wear straw hats, and are poor, unstylish, and cowardly. Tre 8 frames Blakk's performance of the three main verses with repeated reminders that southern guys are in fact hip and with it in the sense that they, like the presumptuous travelers to the region, pimp, dress well, have money, and smoke in the bathroom. The song insists that men who travel to the South from the East Coast, the West Coast, and the North respect all this. The song underscores to them that the South is not "all country" like they think it is. It points out that life in the region is not like that depicted on popular 1960s shows that focused on the lives of rural southerners such as *Green Acres* and *The Beverly Hillbillies*. The song indicates that men in the South are presumed to be backward and dim-witted like many of the characters featured on these shows. Furthermore, the insistence that black guys in the region are not "bad seeds" is particularly provocative in light of the implication that degeneracy and inferiority are ordinarily related to men in this region because of this country-bumpkin stereotype. The narrator shrewdly reverses it, for he reminds travelers they are not as smart as they think they are and suggests that their perceptions of the South are wrong, misguided, and, in fact, just plain stupid. The song's message is that imagining the South as essentially agrarian and underestimating the extent to which southern males are participating in gangsta cultures could prove to be costly.

Blakk's song's third verse speaks to the issues that are manifest in his "'hood" but focuses on critiquing the specific prejudices that confront southern men who rap. Here he addresses the "drippin'" in rap contexts that suggests that men in the South can't rap. Here, "drippin'" refers to the general practice of rapping as "droppin' science" or spreading knowledge and sharing wisdom. This aspect of the song critiques rappers from other regions who "playa hate" against rappers from the South. From beginning to end, "Way Down South" assertively critiques stereotypes of black southern men. Overall, the song establishes that while men from other places might assume that southern guys are ignorant or backward, the latter are busy plotting schemes to make money in ways that are usually associated with "gangstas" in urban contexts.

The slang language invoked in the song enunciated alongside southern folk idioms and sayings intensifies, redirects, and even subverts the vernacular aspects of urbanized rap discourse. The patois singing style that punctuates the song's ending invokes the complex linguistic heritage of New Orleans, including its creole speech forms. The instrumental background of the song gives the lyrics an even stronger impact. From beginning to end, the final word of each line in the song typically packs the heaviest punch and emphasizes the assertive polemics of its narrative. Some word endings speak to the dominant issues that the song addresses, such as stereotypes. Others, such as "Mason Dixon," refer to place. Tre 8 echoes some of the lines as Blakk delivers them and interjects phrases that taunt or threaten regional outsiders. Their collaboration on the song even models the sense of solidarity attached by the song to guys throughout the South. Embedded alliteration and liberal puns add layers of meaning and deepen the linguistic texture of the song. Most significantly, perhaps, the profanity throughout "Way Down South" dramatizes the song's narrator's anger about ways in which black guys from the South are frequently perceived by those who are from outside the region. It uses this assertive speech, weaving in violent threats, as a strategy for confronting the ways in which southern guys are talked about, mocked, and ridiculed. Indeed, the misguided talk of outsiders, "Way Down South" alleges, functions as the primary means by which false perceptions of the South are circulated and sustained. It is fitting therefore that language is used as the primary means for confronting them as opposed to other forms of violence and aggression; this is a point that the song enacts at a performative level. The song recommends that guys from the East Coast, the West Coast, and the North not talk so much about the South. When they do, the narrator urges them to be sure they know what they are talking about.

The goal of "Way Down South" seems to be to assert that southern men can do all the criminal things that men in other regions are reputed to do. Ultimately, it becomes less subversive where it seems more invested in establishing similarities between southern guys and those from other regions as opposed to clarifying how such men are distinct. While it confronts the condescending attitudes of northerners, the message of "Way Down

South," which at bottom says that "we are just like you," in some ways concedes the superiority and exemplariness of northern models of black masculinity. The South emerges as a mere simulacrum by its logic.

Still, the message in the song that establishes continuities in the experiences of black southerners and those from other regions also helps disrupt, in effect, African American southern romance. That is to say, beneath the song's ostensible assertions of black southern male combativeness lies the suggestion that travelers to the South will not necessarily escape the problems that plague the inner city. To the contrary, they could meet the very same ones. Blakk's narrator acknowledges that dope dealers and dope fiends can be found in his neighborhood, that kidnapping and carjacking occur there, and that the South isn't different from Brooklyn or "Chi-town" (Chicago). In this respect, we might say that "Way Down South" provides a counternarrative to and an implicit critique of the scripting of the South as a safer and less stressful place for blacks than "the inner city," perceptions that I acknowledge in chapter 3. This narrative has often been instrumental in motivating African American return migrations to the region since the 1970s. Furthermore, we can interpret the narrator's assertion that there is no "love" in New Orleans for the black male travelers who come to the South from the East Coast, the West Coast, and the North, which is echoed emphatically by Tre 8, as a comment on ways in which aspects of African American cultural discourse have often scripted the South as a metaphorical black cultural "home" in the United States. Frequently, the South is perceived as a place that blacks can come to from other regions, such as the urban North, for nurturing and replenishment. These escapist narratives frequently obscure the range of social crises in the South and the challenges that black southerners face in negotiating aspects of day-to-day life. Indeed, in highlighting possibilities for less friendly and accessible encounters with black southern communities, we might even say that Blakk's rap concurs with postmodern perspectives on the African diaspora that have represented homelessness as a condition of black identity in the late twentieth century.

The "South" invoked by Blakk functions as a monolithic sign and as the opposite side of a homogenizing North-East-West triumvirate in the binary and geographically essentialist equation that he formulates. As is now typical of the burgeoning southern-based economy of rap in and beyond the gangsta genre, "Way Down South" invests itself in "representin' the South." Yet it is revealing that Blakk's narrator primarily references localities in urban cities in the South on the "tour" the song gives the men to whom the song is addressed. Blakk's highlighting of urban areas may in part account for the continuities that he finds in experiences in the South and those on the West and East Coasts and in the North. Even more specifically, the rhetoric of the song at this level illustrates the paradox of southern rap production. That is to say, even as many southern rap songs invoke the rural in album iconography, major cities in the South like Atlanta, New Orleans, and Houston have nevertheless served as the epicenters for the production of rap. The genre of southern rap itself is mainly a product of the urban South. Even so, Blakk acknowledges the potential of all southerners, wherever they are, to be pigeonholed by stereotypes of the region. He contests ways in which the region, notwithstanding its urban aspects, routinely gets coded as monolithically rural and country in the cultural imagination.

Michael Eric Dyson has pointed out that "gangsta rap is situated in the violent climes of postindustrial Los Angeles and its bordering cities. It draws its metaphoric capital in part from the mix of myth and murder that gave the western frontier a dangerous appeal a century ago."[26] Southern gangsta rappers have also in part drawn their "metaphoric capital" from the Old West. These linkages are explicitly evident in "Way Down South" when the narrator scripts black guys in the South from Texas as cowboys. Yet by rendering the South as a predatory and menacing site for black men, rappers in the "gangsta" genre also ironically invoke the Jim Crow South in which white supremacists practiced such vigilante terrors as lynching and other forms of violence that frequently annihilated the black male body.[27] This factor, along with a tacit compliance with black-on-black crime patterns of the contemporary era that have resulted in disproportionately high black-male homicide statistics, also drastically undercuts the subversive potential of their agenda. It is important to recognize that the southern gangsta postures invoked in Blakk's rap have in some instances been shaped, ironically enough, by migrants to the South from the East Coast and West Coast along with the urban North.

Gangsta rap has perhaps been one of the most controversial genres ever to emerge on the popular music scene. The salient invocations of this genre in the national public sphere in conversations on family values and censorship, in light of its association with violence, misogyny, and profanity, are likely memorable for some readers. Such critics as Rose, Dyson, and bell hooks have underscored the importance of recognizing the violence, money, and misogyny fetishized within gangsta rap cultures as a reflection of the obsession with capitalist gain in the dominant national culture, along with its sexism.[28] Gangsta rap was regarded by some critics as a rap fad that would soon pass—in much the same way that rap itself was heralded as an art form that would eventually lose its popular appeal. The form maintained its viability in the wake of the tragic deaths of its key practitioners such as Tupac Shakur and Biggie Smalls in part through the development of the genre in the South. Though the popularity of the genre has waned in recent years, its regional shift from the West to the South in the late 1990s helps explain why the current movement in southern rap was initially replete with references to "gangstas" and "playas."

It is important to recognize the references to "gangstas" and "playas" that were prevalent within the early hardcore, gangsta style of southern rap as a response among some artists to longstanding perceptions in broader rap discourse of such terms as being incompatible with black southern male identity. Blakk's efforts to cast the gangsta as southern, which mirror larger trends in the southern rap genre, are successful, it would seem, in helping to inscribe this type within a more diverse geography in the national context and to dislodge its significations that have been primarily associated with urban contexts. We can recognize the "gangsta" concept as a culturally indigenous example of black masculine fashioning. At a linguistic level, the term appropriates and revises "gangster," of course, a word primarily attached to white masculine organized crime and racketeering circuits in the nation's urban areas in the early decades of the twentieth century, which consolidated during Prohibition. In general, rap discourse's resignification of the "gangsta" recalls the related term "nigga," which attempts to revise and unsettle the historical racist epithet "nigger" while affirming friendship and community among black men. Furthermore, the gangsta recuperates the outlaw sensibility associated with the "bad Negro" in African American cultural history. Southernized, the "gangsta" helps reverse this type's characteristic urbanization that was typical in the twentieth century and revives its southern folk dimensions.

In light of the major concerns of this study, however, I want to suggest that the "gangsta" also subtends such classic ideological scripts of black masculinity as the Uncle Tom. Typically in rap discourse, the criminality and violence of the gangsta has been more fantasized than real and highly performative, as is evident in Blakk's "Way Down South." We need to recognize, however, that such images of violence and criminality place this type in a continuum with other egregious historical ideologies of black masculinity that originated in the South. On some levels, the "gangsta" resonates with the black rapist, a dominant fantasy in the southern cultural imagination that associated black men with violence and transgression. When we understand these linkages, we can recognize the "Uncle Tom" and the "gangsta" as two sides of the same coin. This is precisely one of the reasons for the juxtaposition of those terms in this study's subtitle. In similar fashion, we need to recognize that the hypersexuality and exploitative character of the "playa" also recasts historical black rapist mythology, which entailed scripts of black men as sexual predators. The internalization of the gangsta concept by black men in the South has had subversive aspects to be sure. Yet the question remains about the extent to which it can be detached from the salient epithets that have maligned black male subjectivity in the past and from the ones that are manifest in the present day.[29]

Perhaps more than anything, the violence and looting in the city of New Orleans that emerged after Hurricane Katrina points to the real-life consequences of gangsta posturing among some young black men, as do the high murder rates in the city, and reveal the harm they can do. It was, in fact, unconscionable and unthinkable that, in some cases, armed youth in the city were the ones who hampered desperate rescue efforts and attempts to save lives after the hurricane. In the aftermath, some critics' responses addressed the media's emphasis on the violence in the city and pointed out how these representations reinforced racial stereotypes in some instances, particularly of young black men. But they typically failed to acknowledge the serious threats that such bands of youth posed to human safety and to acknowledge the dire moral crisis that such behavior demonstrated. Furthermore, few efforts have been directed toward exploring strategies for bettering the lives of such youth and for showing them how they might redirect their energies more constructively and nonviolently. These concerns need to be on the agendas that are attempting to make meaningful and lasting interventions to remedy the material devastation of the city's landscape. The critical mass of rappers that has emerged from New Orleans is one telling indicator of the keen intellect and creativity among youth in the city, a creativity that needs to be recognized and nourished.

The tensions described by Blakk in "Way Down South" that have the potential to erupt in violence between male travelers from the East Coast, the West Coast, and the North, on one hand, and men living in the South, on the other, have notable literary antecedents in African American literary works that depict North-South conflicts between men. In the "Fern" sketch in Jean Toomer's *Cane* (1923), a "crusty numbness" is directed at the northern male traveler in the South by a man there because, the traveler speculates, "I was from up North and suspected of being prejudiced and stuck up." Later on in this sketch, the traveler, who has become enamored of the black southern beauty for whom the sketch is named, remarks that "I got one or two ugly looks from town men who'd set themselves up to protect her. In fact, there was talk of making me leave town. But they never did. They kept a watch-out for me, though. Shortly after, I came back North." Such tensions are also evident in the "Kabinis" sketch in which, in a sermon, Rev. Halsey directs the following comment at Ralph Kabinis: "You northern nigger, it's time fer y t leave. Git along now."[30] Similarly, in Toni Morrison's novel *Song of Solomon* (1977), we might consider the smug attitude that Milkman inadvertently manifests toward southern men in Shalimar when he suggests that he will just buy a new car for the ride home if no one is able to find a new belt for the one in which he is traveling. The novel's narrator describes their bitter reaction:

They looked with hatred at the city Negro who could buy a car as if it were a bottle of whiskey because the one he had was broken. And what's more, who had said so in front of them. He hadn't bothered to say his name, nor ask theirs, had called them "them," and would certainly despise their days, which should have been spent harvesting their own crops instead of waiting around the general store hoping a truck would come looking for mill hands or tobacco pickers in the flatlands that belonged to somebody else. His manner, his clothes were reminders that they had no crops of their own and no land to speak of either. Just vegetable gardens, which the women took care of, and chickens and pigs that the children took care of. He was telling them that they weren't men, that they relied on women and children for their food. And that the lint and tobacco in their pants pockets where dollar bills should have been was the measure. That thin shoes and suits and vests and smooth hands were the measure. That eyes that had seen big cities and the inside of airplanes were the measure. They had seen him watching their women and rubbing his fly as he stood on the steps. They had also seen him lock his car as soon as he got out of it in a place where there couldn't be more than two keys twenty-five miles around. He hadn't found them fit enough or good enough to want to know their names, and believed himself too good to tell them his. They looked at his skin and saw it was as black as theirs, but they knew he had the heart of the white men who came to pick them up in the trucks when they needed anonymous faceless laborers.[31]

Several of the men begin to joke that northern men have small penises and ask Milkman if "That's why they pants so tight. That true?" The ensuing slights that go back and forth between them, which on both sides are meant to be emasculating, culminate in a fight in which Milkman ends up getting his face, left hand, and "pretty beige suit" "slit." Two women who scream the name of one of his attackers keep him from getting his throat cut.[32] As is the case in this scene from *Song of Solomon* involving Milkman, and in the Kentucky Fried Chicken parking lot scene from Spike Lee's *School Daze* discussed in the previous chapter, southern rappers have often made recourse to questioning the heterosexuality of men from other regions, or marked them as feminine, as a way of belittling them and of avowing southern masculine authenticity and superiority.

The interfacings of "Way Down South" with American musical roots seem even more direct and deliberate than those in African American literature and reflect Blakk's deftness as a rap lyricist, a skill for which he has been praised. He specifically mentions a line from the folk song "Oh, Susanna." In doing so, Blakk mocks the stereotypes of southerners as simple folk people. Blakk seems to make implicit references to Geibel Adams's "Old Aunt Mandy's Chile," which was written around 1899, and to Lillian Rosedale Goodman's 1926 song entitled "Mammy's Precious Pickaninny." Both songs weave narratives centering on an infantile black male identity in the South. In doing so, he points to broader contexts beyond the East, North, and West for the stereotypes of black southern masculinity. Ultimately, these allusions imply stereotypes of black southerners to be an outgrowth of white racial discourses in the antebellum South. Allusions to such songs in Blakk's "Way Down South" suggest his investments in their critique. Significantly, however, Blakk makes a titular allusion to songs such as W. C. Handy's "Way Down South Where the Blues Began" (1932). In light of the ways in which "Way Down South" partially devotes itself to a critique of the impression in rap that guys from the South have no talent for this verbal art, we might interpret this allusion to Handy as a reminder that the South is the cultural site from which the majority of the predominant African American musical forms are traceable. It reiterates the South's status as a key source of the vernacular language forms that animate rap. Furthermore, the New Orleans home base of Blakk and other members of the Down South Hustlers, along with Blakk's emphasis on the qualities of his hometown, likely make it no coincidence that his rap song also invokes J. Layton Turner and Henry J. Creamer's 1922 song entitled "Way Down Yonder in New Orleans." (The singer Ray Charles has also recorded a version of this song.)

Unlike classic American folk songs, however, Blakk's rap is invested in a deromanticization of the South. His interplay with this folk musical archive is thus intensely ironic. While Blakk invokes several folk songs that in their content referenced and extended the plantation myth of the "happy slave" and obscured the brutal realities of Jim Crow, the content of his lyrics represent a radical departure from such conventional southern romanticism. Moreover, Blakk's "Way Down South" unsettles the images of "peace" and "love" that are explicitly attached to the South in Handy's song. Life in the South, his song suggests, is not so sweet. That Blakk's narrator describes the city where he lives as the "Swamps," a term that also metaphorically connotes spatial liminality, marginalization, and deprivation, also in effect unsettles conventional notions of southern romance.

A few other rappers have also spoken to the issue of southern disparagement in their songs in ways that are worth noting and address some of the themes that are manifest in a song such as Blakk's "Way Down South." The 9.17 Family remark the struggle of negotiating a southern identity as a new migrant to the city and evince an awareness of how much fun guys in the North make of them because of their slurs and unclear words on their 2001 album *Southern Empire*. This theme is also prominent throughout Gangsta Blak's 2001 album *Southern Flava*. The song "Somebody" speaks to a competition on the microphone that southern rappers win, notwithstanding the "haters" who are implicitly from outside the region. Similarly, his song "Cowardz in the South" ironically claims the stereotype of southern male fearfulness, asserting that those so-called cowards are not only crashing the club and receiving rewards for their artistry but also capable of defending themselves against their detractors from elsewhere. As is the case in Blakk's "Way Down South," a phrase echoes throughout the song that warns those from outside the region to be careful when talking about the South. We might interpret such lyrics in southern rap as an obvious response to stereotypes of southern men as cowardly, perceptions that construe them as alien from the "gangsta" concept. "World's Thickest Click" affirms the solidarity of southern rappers in the face of those who criticize them, and "South in Ya Mouth" acknowledges the widespread popularity and universality of southern rap as well as its growing audience. Lil' Troy's 1999 album *Sittin' Fat Down South* features a medley of rappers. In "Chop, Chop Chop," the Botany Boys, Lil' Troy, and Rasheed speak of the South as the "Third coast" that is taking over and warn those from outside the region about belittling southern men. Southern rap discourse also frequently reveals its internal tensions. For instance, on his 1999 album *Dirty South Gangsta Mix*, Mr. Quikk, who is a native of the Calliope area in New Orleans, mentions the Magnolia project derisively and refers to Baby and Slim as the "Cash Money Clowns" on the track "Sho Nuff."

In documenting the emergence of rap and its early contours, Tricia Rose defines rap music as "a black cultural expression that prioritizes black voices from the margins of urban America."[33] In more recent years, southern rap artists have helped expand the centers of rap music production, diversified its audiences, and encouraged a revision of its conventional definitions. Oftentimes, their artistry emerges from within sociocultural contexts that have been less legible and accessible in popular and public spheres. Contemporary southern rap has in effect begun to alter conventional presumptions about what black popular culture is, where it can be produced, and who can produce it. Furthermore, the genre has also begun to unsettle essentialist definitions of African American subjectivity and masculinity as "urban" that have been pervasive within hip-hop. The genre has also confronted narrow perceptions of what it means to be southern. The lively scene of rap production that has emerged in the South means there is more potential for talent in the region to be recognized. It means that southerners with an interest in rap will have their voices heard and be less likely to remain "black and unknown bards," to borrow the classic words of James Weldon Johnson.

Nowadays, their seeming dominance in the rap industry—to the point of having become "universal," in the words of southern artist Mystical—obscures some of the earlier struggles that many southern rap artists and producers faced before the genre gained widespread popularity and recognition.[34] Furthermore, it seems that the crossover into the popular mainstream and the market forces driving this process have come to increasingly shape the development of this genre, along with its narrative content. I value this genre, and consider it in this study, because I find it to be instructive and revealing where it speaks to the role that geography plays in the constitution of black male identities.

Lots of questions remain, and far more than I can treat here, however, about the southern rap genre: To what extent does the celebration of Master P and his fellow moguls in the rap industry obscure the repackaging and restructuring of forms of corporate dominance in blackface? Even if its tendency *is* to assert the South as an organic aspect of contemporary life, with front porches and soul-food motifs, how do aspects of the southern rap genre recast or commodify conventional discourses of black authenticity, southern romanticism, and "folk" ideologies? In light of the turn toward the South in the hip-hop arena and the emergence of the South as a production center in the rap industry, along with the global appeal of hip-hop as a form, what are some of the new ways in which the South is coming to shape cultural flows within transnational contexts, including the African diaspora? How does this "global" impact of the South differ from or overlap with the ways in which the South is developing as a neocolonial force in the contemporary period through the incursion of foreign industries that are drawn to the region by the promise of cheap labor? How do the politics of southern rap production extend such labor logic in the South when we consider the vast number of production companies that have sought a share in the southern rap enterprise because of its proven success? Given the dominance of hip-hop as a musical and cultural paradigm for the past quarter century, what *other* contexts and frameworks might be useful for interpreting southern rap? How does the persistence and spread of hip-hop as a general banner under which to categorize African American and other minority youth function as an ideology and reflect forms of corporate and capitalist hegemony, when we consider the interests of the major producers in sustaining the paradigm? How does southern rap align with, redefine, and resist this paradigm? Does southern rap, in fact, "represent" a paradigm shift?

CONCLUSION

When twenty-one-year-old Tiger Woods became the youngest Masters Tournament champion in history in Augusta, Georgia, in 1997, breaking the scoring record that had been in place for thirty-two years, golfing veteran Fuzzy Zoeller set off a firestorm of controversy when he made the following comments in a CNN interview: "That little boy [Woods] is driving well and he's putting well. He's doing everything it takes to win. So, you know what you guys [former champions] do when he gets in here? You pat him on the back and say congratulations and enjoy it and tell him not to serve fried chicken next year. Got it?" Zoeller snapped his fingers, walked away, and turned back. "Or collard greens or whatever the hell they serve."[1] These racially charged comments couched amid several backhanded compliments seem aimed more at cheapening and trivializing rather than commending Woods's golfing techniques. They anticipate in jest the menu that Woods, implicitly because of his racial background, will serve at the Champions Dinner the next year at the Augusta National Golf Club, where he as the neophyte champion will have the time-honored prerogative of selecting the menu. The comments suggest that by serving exotic soul food dishes, he will bring irreverence to an event that is ordinarily formal. By this logic, Zoeller imposes an essentialist and stereotypically "black" identification onto Woods, who prefers to acknowledge and respect his multiracial Chinese, African American, Native American, Dutch, and Thai heritage. Zoeller invokes such foods as collard greens and fried chicken, which were traditionally linked to the slave heritage of black southerners in the United States. These foods, alongside watermelon, were saliently imaged in racist caricatures of blackness. Zoeller evokes racist representational strategies that were popular in the Jim Crow era and relates minstrel imagery to Woods. His words construct an image of Woods in blackface, in effect, symbolically making him over as "black." The "they" says it all. Added to this, Zoeller boldly refers to Woods as a "boy," a word whose abusive uses in southern history to infantilize and emasculate black men makes these comments all the more demeaning. The racial differences between Zoeller, who is white, and Woods, who prefers to use the term "Cablinasian" as a neologism to describe his range of ethnic backgrounds, make all the difference and, in this case, cannot be ignored. Woods served cheeseburgers, chicken sandwiches, french fries, and milkshakes at the exclusive Champions Dinner in 1998.

Given that the tournament itself was held in Georgia, southern history looms even larger in this scenario. Like race, geography poignantly matters. This scenario demonstrates, once again, how easily the conventional racial logic of the South can reduce racial identities in the region to binary "black" and "white" categories while collapsing all signs of difference, including visible signs on the body that are ethnic or cultural. These condescending remarks reveal anxiety about a minority man's inroads into a sport conventionally dominated by white men. They were widely publicized, led to widespread outcry, and resulted in Zoeller's loss of endorsements with such enterprises as Kmart. In the aftermath, some critics felt that the incident was blown out of proportion, reflected Zoeller's character as a jokester in the golfing world, and viewed the outcry as a byproduct of what they perceived to be an obsession with political correctness. To his credit, Zoeller quickly apologized, remarking that "My comments were not intended to be racially derogatory, and I apologize for the fact that they were misconstrued in that fashion."[2] Whether he meant them in jest or not, the fact that he made them in the first place underscores one of the key points of *Black Masculinity and the U.S. South*. That is to say, this moment illustrates the persisting uses in the contemporary era of ideologies stemming from the U.S. South to constitute scripts of black male bodies as pathological and deviant. Furthermore, Zoeller's comments illustrate ways in which southern-based ideologies of black masculinity become nationalized and circulate in relation to a range of identities (Woods is a native Californian), very much in the vein of the ubiquitous Uncle Tom. Such comments speak well to the need to move beyond stereotypes, whether they are ostensibly pernicious or steeped in romance and nostalgia, in imagining black masculinity in relation to the U.S. South.

This study has aimed to illustrate how much we can enrich methods of analyzing complex racial contours of masculinity by expanding the range of factors recognized in masculine fashioning. One of my main goals has been to demonstrate that, even beyond salient identification categories of race, sexuality, class, nationality, and gender, critics are also sometimes slow or even resistant to examine and acknowledge such factors as geography, which are by no means incidental and play a role in shaping gender formations and in creating distinctions and hierarchies among black men. More broadly, they help shape discourses of race. This is not to suggest, however, that as we embrace more complex processes of masculine formation—and supplement what we know and continue to discover about how they work—we should dismiss the value in the integrative approaches to race and gender that have been foundational within the field that has been crystallizing as critical masculinities. It will be crucial, I believe, for critical and theoretical work on masculinity to respect and acknowledge the genealogies that have made its innovations conceivable and possible. In looking toward new theories and methods of critique within critical masculinity studies, it will not be very useful, for instance, to replicate the dismissive critiques of the "race, class, and gender" investigation within black and other woman-of-color feminist theory that was predominant in the 1970s and 1980s.[3]

Such methods of analysis within feminist scholarship were foundational for the kinds of integrative approaches to gender studies now conceivable that investigate a broader and more complex spectrum of gender formations, including masculinities.[4] Deborah E. McDowell's concluding chapter for Harry Stecopoulos and Michael Uebel's groundbreaking anthology *Race and the Subject of Masculinities* suggests black feminist theory as a vital genealogy and counterpoint for any theory of masculinity and speaks to the urgency of situating "the politics of sex and gender front and center" while acknowledging female subjectivity within this enterprise.[5] In *Black Masculinity and the U.S. South*, the aspects of the analysis in chapter 1 that examine the raced, sexed, and gendered politics of representing rape and lynching in the novel and film versions of *The Klansman*, while looking comparatively at white and black feminine representations within a broader critical dialogue on masculinity, demonstrate the utility of acknowledging these critical intersections. Similarly, chapter 2's look at the formation of black and white soldiers early in the twentieth century points to the importance of an integrative and comparative hermeneutics on race, gender, and region.

Black feminist scholarship has been particularly useful in its emphasis on how forms of black male subjection and oppression under white patriarchy are often manifested alongside hierarchies of gender within the African American context, within which masculine subjects are privileged, and internalize ideologies of male dominance that lead to violence, misogyny, and oppression against women, children, and others, including other black men. This study has aimed to demonstrate how recognition of hierarchies among black men based on such factors as geography, which can also be inimical and destructive, adds to this critical framework and might help move us toward a dialogue on gender that is more integrative and less essentialist. With this understanding, for instance, we might begin to recognize more of the obstacles to enlightened and inclusive antiracist discourses and develop more critical insights about racial-uplift ideologies while continuing the necessary struggle for civil and human rights.

This study has attempted to raise some questions about what is at stake in urban-centered models of black masculinity while making visible typically obscured gender hierarchies and stressing the salience of geography in constructing African American identities. It has aimed to show that hierarchies among black men that prioritize urban subjects—including and perhaps especially masculinist ones that have emerged within the discourses of black liberation—lie in a continuum with white-supremacist narratives of masculinity that privilege white masculine subjectivity and are contingent on the subordination and devaluation of black men and other men of color. The geographical distinctions among southern men like Sutton Griggs's Belton and the Mississippian, Charles Fuller's C. J. and Peterson, and Ralph Ellison's Trueblood and *Invisible Man* narrator, and particularly the role of the rural in creating such distinctions, suggests the importance of relating the gender hierarchies among southern black men to these larger race and gender frameworks. The representations of black men in the U.S. South as emasculated and unmanly, which, as I have argued in this book, were propagated in the contexts of slavery and Jim Crow, were crucially integral to constituting discourses of race both within and beyond the African American category. They played a vital role in consolidating racism and white supremacy in the U.S. South, along with a range of southern gender ideologies such as the southern belle and the southern gentleman, giving efficacy to notions of white male dominance and superiority within a patriarchal social order premised on fundamental and even mandatory divisions between such groups as men and women, blacks and whites, freed and enslaved, and wealthy and poor. Increasingly, and particularly if we are aiming for a more in-depth understanding of the intersection of race and masculinity, one must recognize that the binary formulas for pondering black and white categories in the U.S. South have also very much structured the approaches to masculine subject formations in the region and need to be deepened by a consideration of other racial and ethnic masculinities such as Asian, Indian, and Latino, among others. These methods will give recognition to the historical and continuing ethnic diversification of the U.S. South as a region. Furthermore, we need to pursue comparative studies of masculinity in diasporic and global frameworks.

Such hierarchical divisions that I have described in relation to the United States as a national context become all the more understandable, for instance, if we recognize their place in a continuum with representations of subordinated and emasculated colonized subjects in contradistinction to notions of white manliness that have been propagated within colonialism and imperialism. Such notions have been endemic to ideologies of white masculine dominance in the modern global arena. As a novel such as E. M. Forster's *A Passage to India* (1924) shows by the lack of resolution surrounding the question of whether the Muslim Dr. Aziz raped the Englishwoman Adela Quested on a visit to the Marabar caves, the rapist has dominated representations of masculine subjects in the cultural imaginary in colonial and imperial contexts in a way that is quite similar to how black men in the South have been constructed as rapists.

In some cases, the sad consequence and result of this black rapist myth has not only been the extreme violence of lynching or hasty pleas for capital punishment of men who were, in some cases, later proven innocent. The myth has also illustrated the lack of a genuine public and legal interest in such principles as truth and justice. John Singleton's 1997 film *Rosewood*—which is based on the historical race riot in a Florida town in 1923 and the violence and killing of blacks that ensued in the aftermath of a white woman's false charge that a black man had raped her, when, in fact, her assailant had really been white—poignantly illustrates these politics. Once the woman is brutally raped by her white assailant, she immediately establishes that "a nigger" did it. She seems to have no interest in catching or punishing her attacker, leaving him free to roam, and perhaps to rape again, in the community. Her husband, who becomes suspicious of her claims and snaps at her because there has been no success in finding her alleged black assailant after several days, feels obligated, nevertheless, to participate in the town's escalating mob activity. The film illustrates that because the black male population is collectively labeled as always already rapacious, any and all black scapegoats—men, women, and even children—are sufficient outlets on which to vent rage and anger, regardless of who, in fact, committed the heinous crime. Such random violence was very much in keeping with the characteristic ritualistic protocols of lynching. Similarly, Bebe Moore Campbell's novel *Your Blues Ain't Like Mine* (1992), which is based on the Emmett Till murder in 1955, reveals how in some cases propaganda and false accusations have fed this myth of the black rapist. Both works, through differing strategies, speak well to how some white men in the South who feel dubious and reluctant about participating in lynchings and accusations of rape have done so nevertheless to uphold their images as men in the face of pressures from their families and communities.[6] Alternatively, it has fueled the kind of curious white sexual voyeurism that James Baldwin describes in his short story "Going to Meet the Man" (1965): "He thought of the boy in the cell; he thought of the man in the fire; he thought of the knife and grabbed himself and stroked himself with a terrible sound, something between a high laugh and a howl, came out of him and dragged his sleeping wife up on one elbow. . . . He thought of the morning and grabbed her, laughing and crying, crying and laughing, and he whispered, as he stroked her, as he took her, 'Come on, sugar, I'm going to do you like a nigger, just like a nigger, come on sugar, and love me just like you'd love a nigger.'"[7]

In the contemporary era, there has been no more sobering a trace in the national context of the persistence of conventional southern narratives of black masculinity as inherently pathological than the news media's generalized portrayals of black male youth as rampaging rapists, looters, and criminals in the city of New Orleans after Hurricane Katrina in 2005. These reports described with some accuracy illegal activities that were rampant in the city in the wake of the storm and that, in some cases, were egregious and even unconscionable actions worthy of the harshest prosecution. Yet such generalizations were counterproductive and incendiary, as many critics have pointed out, to the extent that the salient emphasis on these groups of young black men obscured the levels on which other people in the city, including whites, looted and otherwise broke the law. Even in this millennial era, we continue to be haunted, it seems, by the lingering specter of the black rapist. It is clear too that the idea of the "bad Negro" shapes public and popular responses to black men, who are imagined to be inherently bad. Geography centrally shaped the Hurricane Katrina crisis, and the historical expendability of black southern bodies no doubt factored into the benign neglect of this population in the wake of the tragedy.

Whites are by no means the only ones who can conceivably internalize myths of black masculinity. Recently, on a bus with limited seats, I was sitting near the back and two young men, who were perhaps Latino, were loudly discussing the time they had spent in jail and the importance of keeping their women "in line," so to speak, to the point of beating them if necessary. The crowd emptied out a bit on the long route to Davis. As I looked up from my usual reading, I noticed that two Asian women who got on the bus bypassed several empty seats near the front that would have placed them next to middle-aged black men, who were likely workers in the Sacramento region. Instead, the women went all the way down the aisle to the very back of the bus and planted themselves right between those two guys. They presumed, I suppose, that those were the "safest" looking men, and so chose the two empty seats between them. I was stunned by the irony in their choice of seats. I wondered what they would have thought if they had boarded the bus minutes earlier.

An incident that I witnessed a few years ago is similarly telling. One day in 2002, as I was standing downtown in Baltimore, this time *waiting* for a bus, I also got a strong and visceral sense of the complexities of negotiating black masculinity. It was a moment that revealed the hidden consequences in the social world of these myths and stereotypes. Two black men were standing about ten yards from me talking to each other, and another black man, who was also waiting for the bus, was standing alone between them and me. A senior white woman, who was disabled, was sitting on the edge of a planter on the street, also waiting for the bus to come, in a position roughly parallel to the man standing alone. Accidentally, she dropped her cane down on the curb, and it rolled down to the street, beyond her reach. All of us saw this. The conversation between the two men ceased as they cast sideward glances at the cane. It would have been too risky and inconvenient for her to retrieve it herself. The man standing by himself, who was closest to her, seemed almost hypnotized by the sight of the cane bobbing back and forth as it came to a rest against the curb. He was the most logical and obvious candidate to pick it up and return it to her, the one who I presumed would do so. Yet the pause among him and the others was palpable. Though I was standing farthest away from her, and those three men were closest, I ended up taking the long walk down to pick it up and give it back to her. I could sense the gratitude and relief on their part that I got them off the hook by picking it up.

As a woman, I suppose that picking it up was not as much of a risk for me. They obviously wanted to do it but were hesitant. All of them, I sensed, were momentarily paralyzed on that busy Baltimore street by the thought of walking near a white woman to do something like pick up a cane, a scene that might easily translate into any number of things, including wielding a weapon and attempting to attack her. I sensed what they might have been thinking. What if she saw them and, misunderstanding their intentions, screamed? What if the police, or anyone else, who hadn't seen her drop the cane in the first place, saw one of them with it, holding it, even for a moment, and misunderstood what they were trying to do? Narratives of black men in and beyond the South whose quite innocent actions and intentions were misunderstood and, as a result, led to prison time or even death are quite familiar. These quiet and unspoken social and mental gymnastics over something as simple as picking up a cane reveal the hidden consequences of historical prejudices and myths about black men that inform simple actions (or nonactions) for some black men every day, whether people are willing to admit it or not.[8] Lingering racialist myths and stereotypes of black males as criminal, dangerous, or rapacious often preclude such men from doing the gentlemanly thing when they really want to, because the risks are far too high. That such experiences occurred in the midst of writing this book confirmed for me all the more what is at stake in its arguments. I can think of countless other incidents along these lines. Alice Walker's 1970 novel, *The Third Life of Grange Copeland*, documents the absurdity and high cost of such racial mythologies by depicting a young pregnant white woman who sinks to her death and drowns rather than grab the hand of a black man who is attempting to save her. We need to recognize, too, that while the contemporary emphasis on the more dire statistics about black masculinity in our time can point up areas where interventions are necessary and crucial, they can also performatively reinscribe the view of black men as pathological and obscure all the ways in which many black men are actually living (and loving) well.

Perhaps the greatest danger lies in blacks internalizing racialist myths themselves. These days, many African American men in and beyond the music world are posturing as gangstas, which serves in some instances as a strategy for acknowledging and confronting such racial myths or appropriating them for purposes of black masculine validation and affirmation. As I have indicated in this study, these postures are particularly provocative in the rap discourse of southern black men. While the gangsta may unsettle the docility that is frequently attached to black male subjectivity in the region, owing to such regionally based stereotypes as the Uncle Tom, it ultimately does not move us far beyond this prototype. The gangsta is a very limited and questionable representational formula for black masculine subjects and, I want to suggest, is in some ways quite regressive—far more regressive than it would appear to be on the surface. For it forecloses a broader and more diverse spectrum of black masculine representations. In this book, I have acknowledged the parallel genealogies of the Uncle Tom stereotype and the black rapist myth in the U.S. South as they have been dispersed from the U.S. South into the national context. In the contemporary era, it seems that aspects of mainstream entertainment media, in according such salience to rap artists posturing as "gangstas" while marginalizing or excluding altogether other performers, have in effect fused residual traces of the historical black rapist myth with the Uncle Tom and related minstrel stereotypes. That is to say, it is arguable that such artists, by performing an intensely fetishized and commercialized violent bravado within an entertainment-dominated culture, play a role for American audiences nowadays very similar to that of performers on the minstrel stage in early decades of the twentieth century. In this sense, the concert stage is not far from the minstrel stage and, in fact, feels far too close for comfort. The gangsta provocatively recasts the conventional southern strategies and signs for encoding and containing black masculinity but in some ways repeats them with very little difference.

As several sections of this book—and the final chapter in particular—have attempted to illustrate, work on the global South is an indispensable critical framework in our time for studying the U.S. South. Doing so will not only expand our understanding of this region but will also provide more methodologies for thinking about the continuities and discontinuities in how southern regions in various locations in the global context, including European, African, Asian, and Latin American, are constituted in relation to their respective Norths. This move seems necessary, for if one of my major concerns has been geography's neglect in considerations of identity and the South's role in shaping discourses of masculinity, it is also true that a great deal of geographical essentialism persists about what encompasses the South and even southern studies. The goal of this study has not been to urge an emphasis on the South as a place in line with conventional studies of the region or to promote a nostalgic or romantic look at its past. Rather, I have attempted to stress the importance of developing a better sense of how much the U.S. South, for better in some ways and for worse in others, is shaping the nation as well as the global arena and moving us toward the future.

Current statistics that frequently highlight an educational crisis in the South rarely allow us to forget the many ways in which the region lags behind the national averages in terms of intellectual achievement and can easily obscure its status as a vital site of not only cultural but also *intellectual* formation in the nation. Southern studies, in both its conventional and "new" manifestations, represents some of the best that the region has offered in the way of an enduring intellectual "tradition." I am increasingly perplexed by critical scholarship on the South that is written as if southern studies as a field does not exist. This elision even leads some critics to unwittingly rewrite or recast ideas that represent common knowledge in the field. In some cases, of course, this indifference has been understandable. The conventional failures to acknowledge race in southern studies, and the longstanding presumption that southern means "white," have been factors, for instance, that have made some scholars in black studies understandably indifferent to the field. Yet newer and more inclusive methodologies are changing the face and scope of southern studies scholarship. The best and most useful scholarship on the South should not ignore, exclude, or fail to confront the critical genealogies of the field. This study has revealed ways in which southern-based pathologies of black masculinity have variously infused white-supremacist sexual and racial propaganda, warped science, egregious military policies, and rap and black-revolutionary movement. Perhaps it is precisely because of this phenomenon that a closer critical look at black masculinity in the United States, and its complex regional contours, can serve as an exemplary basis for the examination of gender formations in a national and global perspective, for renewal and positive social change in the U.S. South, and for yet more revival in an ever-expanding and renewing southern studies.

NOTES

Introduction

1. Moses, *Black Messiahs and Uncle Toms*, 49.

2. Turner, *Celluloid Uncles*, 75. Also see Yarborough, "Strategies of Black Characterization."

3. See Wyatt-Brown, *Southern Honor*.

4. See Nelson, *National Manhood*.

5. Harper, *Are We Not Men?*, ix (emphasis in the original).

6. The conceptual limitations in this field were evident in its early years of development in the tendency to equate masculinity and whiteness and to generalize this model onto men of color. It was logic akin to the implicit and explicit equation of the category "woman" with whiteness in feminist work before the intervention of feminists of color, including black women, began to stress the importance of combining gender methodologically with other markers of difference such as race and class. See, for instance, Christian, *Black Feminist Criticism*; Angela Y. Davis, *Women, Race, and Class*; hooks, *Ain't I a Woman*; Michele Wallace, *Black Macho*; Cade, *The Black Woman*; Hull, Scott, and Smith, *All the Women Are White*; and Bell, Parker, and Guy-Sheftall, *Sturdy Black Bridges*.

7. The publication of a special issue of the journal *American Literature* in March 2005 (77.1) entitled "Erasing the Commas: RaceGenderClassSexualityRegion," which was introduced by Margo Crawford, encourages a more integrative treatment of region in precisely this sense. The ingenious formatting of the subtitle alone points to the importance of considering these terms in conjunction with one another.

8. Baker and Nelson, "Violence, the Body, and the South," 236.

9. See Yaeger, *Dirt and Desire*; and Jones and Donaldson, *Haunted Bodies*.

10. Griffin and Doyle, *The South as an American Problem*, 1.

11. See, for instance, Cummings, *The Dixification of America*; Carter, *From George Wallace to Newt Gingrich* and *The Politics of Rage*; and Applebome, *Dixie Rising*.

12. At the same time, it is necessary, of course, to unsettle logic that links southern identity to the production of scholarship on the South. We must do this as much as we must unsettle essentialist approaches to southern literature that rely on a southern birthplace in processes of canon formation. It is crucial to remember that a "southernist" and a "southerner" are very different things.

13. This is a turn in the field that has been most saliently advanced by Baker and Nelson. See their special issue of *American Literature* entitled "Violence,

the Body, and the South." Furthermore, in the introduction to *Critical Memory*, Baker points out that "a new Southern studies is long past due." In addition, he remarks that "searching revisionarily the geography, economics, race relations, and demographics of the United States at our turn-of-the-millennium moment is vital work, not only for an energetic new southern studies, but also for a new—and expansive—American cultural studies." Also see Baker's *Critical Memory*, 9, 10, and *Turning South Again*.

14. See Henderson, "'Where by the Way, Is This Train Going?'" 64.

15. See Fossett, Gussaw, and Richardson, "A Symposium," 598–600.

16. See Richardson, "Southern Turns."

17. Meeting Karla Frye, Karen Klossie, and Veronica Toombs at a conference in Liverpool, England, in 1997—they were also doing projects on the South—was a crucial moment for me and gave me my earliest sense of community in the field.

18. Moses, *Black Messiahs*, 52, 53.

19. Lefebvre, *The Production of Space*; and Soja, *Postmodern Geographies*.

20. Ching and Creed, *Knowing Your Place*, 7.

21. Sibley, *Geographies of Exclusion*; Gillian Rose, *Feminism and Geography*; Pile, *The Body and the City*; Massey, *Space, Place, and Gender*; and Duncan, *Body Space*.

Chapter 1. Lessons from Thomas Dixon to *The Klansman*

1. See Du Bois, *Black Reconstruction in America*; and Foner, *Reconstruction*.

2. Roberts, *From Trickster to Badman*, 189. Also see Bryant, *Born in a Mighty Bad Land*.

3. Wood, *Black Majority*.

4. Wright, *Native Son*.

5. My thinking here is informed by Patricia Hill Collins's discussion of the history of exploitation of black women's bodies through rape, prostitution, and pornography and by her acknowledgment of the pornographic dimension of displays of black women's bodies on the auction block during slavery. Collins, *Black Feminist Thought*, 168.

6. See "Violence Comes to a Southern Town: New Movie, *The Klansman* Examines the Anatomy of Black-White, White-White, Relationships," *Ebony* 30.2 (Dec. 1974): 148–154.

7. I am indebted to film scholar Mark Reid for sharing his recollections of the film's moment of release.

8. Vincent Canby, "Screening 'The Klansman': A Deep South Melodrama," *New York Times*, 21 Nov. 1974, p. 54; Roy Frumkes, "The Klansman," *Films in Review* 26.1 (June 1975): 46; A. D. Murphy, "The Klansman," *Variety* 276.13 (6 Nov. 1974): 20.

9. Keith Cohen, *Film and Fiction*.

10. Martha Huie, the widow of William Bradford Huie, was my source for this information.

11. See Huie's *He Slew the Dreamer, Did the F.B.I. Kill Martin Luther King?* and *Three Lives for Mississippi.*

12. Huie, *The Klansman.* All references in this chapter are to this edition and will be cited parenthetically in the text.

13. These implications are clear, for instance, in the following passage from the novel: "You heard Old Long Ears [President Lyndon B. Johnson] go on the television and get all hot in the collar about Ku Klux killing this pore innocent woman. But he didn't tell it all. He just told what suited him to tell. When we stripped this woman we took off a dress and a slip, and she was wearing some kinda little old girdle up here around her hips. But her crotch was bare as a possum's ass. She wasn't covered up between her legs like a decent white woman's supposed to be. She was bare-legged, bare-assed and bare-cunted, and she was in that car at night with a stiff-peckered, Freedom Now, black buck setting right up next to her" (10–11).

14. Jon Daniels, the white priest likely recalled here, was actually killed months later (August 1965) in Lowndes County, Alabama, shortly after President Lyndon B. Johnson signed the Voting Rights Act. Charles W. Eagles examines the life and death of Jon Daniels in *Outside Agitator.* For a similar biographical treatment of Viola Liuzzo, see Stanton, *From Selma to Sorrow.*

15. See Angela Y. Davis, *Women, Race, and Class,* 182. For additional perspectives on black women and rape, see Valerie Smith, *Not Just Race*; Pierce-Baker, *Surviving the Silence*; Giddings, *When and Where I Enter*; and Hine, "Rape and the Inner Lives of Black Women."

16. Giddings, "The Last Taboo," 443–444.

17. The novel describes such "rape shows" as a favored pastime in the county: "Well Lightning Rod has made money all his life by white boys getting him out in the woods, or behind lumber piles, and paying him to show 'em his long blacksnake. They still do it. And on a Saturday afternoon, in the woods, when a white gang is paid off and the boys start to drink a little before they go home to their wives, or down to Awful Annie's, they been known to have a little fun with Lightning Rod. They catch a nigger gal somewhere, or they hire one for a lay without telling her what's gonna happen then they form a circle in the woods, put the gal in the circle, and turn Lightning Rod in on her. I ain't never witnessed it, but the boys tell me it's a show better'n anything on TV" (63–64). This white male voyeurism is evocative of that in the "Battle Royal" of Ralph Ellison's *Invisible Man* (1952).

18. Valerie Smith offers perspectives on interracial rape in *Not Just Race.*

19. The film also appeared in the years after the release of Daniel Patrick

Moynihan's 1965 "Report on the Negro Family," which described black women as matriarchs who usurped the black male patriarchal role in the context of the family (Moynihan, *The Negro Family*).

20. To the contrary, the fate of Loretta in the novel is grim: "When he was a mile from the southernmost shacks, Breck saw firelight. From a quarter of a mile he saw that three shacks, including Loretta's, were wrapped in flames. From two hundred yards he saw the silhouette of a man between him and the flames. From a hundred yards he saw the front door of Loretta's shack open and Loretta come through the doorway with her mother in her arms. At the same instant Breck saw the man raise a gun and fire two shots at Loretta. From the back of the running horse Breck fired three shots at the man and saw him go down" (235–236). When Breck attempts a rescue, he discovers that all is for naught, for "Loretta was dead. The buckshot had struck her in the eyes and forehead, all but decapitating her" (236).

21. The reference here is to the white abolitionist John Brown who led the raid on Harpers Ferry, Virginia, in 1859. In the preface to his biography, W. E. B. Du Bois remarks him as "the man who of all Americans has perhaps come nearest to touching the real souls of black folk." See Du Bois, *John Brown*, xxxv.

22. For an overview of these movements, see Ture and Hamilton, *Black Power*. A slightly different edition was originally published by Random House in 1967. See also Carson, *In Struggle*.

23. See Newton, *Revolutionary Suicide*. Also see Robert F. Williams, *Negroes with Guns*.

24. Kelley, *Hammer and Hoe*, xiii. For additional perspectives on resistance among black southerners, see chapters 1–5 of Kelley's *Race Rebels*.

25. For an overview of tenets of the blaxploitation film genre, see James, *That's Blaxploitation*. Also see Koven, *Blaxploitation Cinema*. Ironically, as the *Ebony* article points out, "*The Klansman* didn't qualify for backing as a black exploitation film; the two main characters were white." See "Violence Comes to a Southern Town: New Movie, *The Klansman* Examines the Anatomy of Black-White, White-White Relationships," *Ebony* 30.2 (Dec. 1974): 149.

26. See Bogle, *Toms, Coons, Mulattoes*, 243.

27. The December 1974 *Ebony* feature story on the film makes an association between O. J. Simpson's career as a running back and his desperate run through the woods with Henry prior to the lynching scene.

28. See Diawara, "Black American Cinema," 3. For a comprehensive critical overview and general discussion of the film *Birth of a Nation*, see Lang, *The Birth of a Nation*. Among the other important treatments of the film in relation to the question of African American representation: Cripps, "The Reaction of the Negro"; Cripps, "The Year of *The Birth of a Nation*," in *Slow Fade to Black*;

Franklin, "*Birth of a Nation*"; Taylor, "The Re-birth of the Aesthetic in Cinema";
Jane Gaines, "*The Birth of a Nation* and *Within Our Gates*"; Dyer, "Into the Light";
and Linda Williams, *Playing the Race Card*.

29. Thomas Dixon Jr., *The Clansman*. All subsequent references are to this
edition.

30. Angela Y. Davis, *Women, Race, and Class*, 188.

31. See Wiegman, *American Anatomies*.

32. Among the most valuable resources on the topic of lynching are the
following: Wells-Barnett, *Southern Horrors*; Addams and Wells, *Lynching and
Rape*; Allen et al., *Without Sanctuary*; Dray, *At the Hands*; Gunning, *Race, Rape,
and Lynching*; Wexler, *Fire in a Canebrake*; Harris, *Exorcising Blackness*; Ginzburg,
One Hundred Years of Lynching; Walter White, *Rope and Faggot*; Litwack, *Trouble
in Mind*; and Patterson, *Rituals of Blood*.

33. We might compare the former comment to Walter White's report that a
prominent senator in the South once remarked that there is no such thing as a
"virtuous colored girl" beyond the age of fourteen. See *Rope and Faggot*, 66.

34. See McPherson, *Reconstructing Dixie*, 24–28.

35. Jane Gaines, "*The Birth of a Nation* and *Within Our Gates*," 185–188.

36. Eldridge Cleaver, *Soul on Ice* (New York: Dell, 1968).

37. See Toni Morrison's introduction to her anthology entitled *Birth of a
Nation'hood*, xxvii–xxviii.

38. Toomer, *Cane*, 7.

39. Wilson, *Our Nig*.

40. See Davis, *Women, Race, and Class*, 182.

41. See Frankenberg, *White Women*, 77.

42. Brody, *Impossible Purities*, 4–5.

43. Angelo Rich Robinson offers a compelling treatment of this intersection in
"Race Place, and Space."

44. See, for instance, Ignatiev, *How the Irish Became White*; Tuan, *Forever
Foreigners*; and Brodkin, *How Jews Became White Folks*.

45. As David Leverenz pointed out to me after a talk, it is also provocative to
wonder whether a photograph in the October 28, 1991, issue of *People* magazine
that showed Supreme Court nominee Clarence Thomas and his wife, Virginia,
sitting on a sofa with a Bible positioned between them also spoke to the historical
taboos against interracial sex by producing a sanitizing effect as much as it seemed
to suggest that Thomas was virtuous in the face of Anita Hill's sexual harassment
accusations during the hearings before the Senate Judiciary Committee. Wahneema
Lubiano has provided a revealing analysis of the photographic archive of this
cultural moment. See her "Black Ladies, Welfare Queens, and State Minstrels."

46. See DuCille, " Unbearable Darkness," 297–298.

47. On the other hand, black female identity—beyond its embodiments in O. J. Simpson's mother, Eunice Simpson; his daughter, Arnelle Simpson; and his ex-wife Marguerite Simpson-Thomas—remained invisible or marginal throughout the trial. This moment was no less generative in terms of the ideologies that it yielded in relation to black women, however, particularly in the condescending critiques of the intelligence of the predominantly black and female jurors who acquitted Simpson and in the feminist portrayal of black women as insensitive toward and uninformed about the issue of domestic violence in the aftermath of the trial. Traces of these stereotypes are evident in a 1999 critical piece in the journal *Critical Inquiry*, in which James A. W. Hefferman remarks that black women have "an unusually high tolerance for spousal abuse." Hefferman goes on to argue that the view of the jurists, as well as that of black women in the United States who widely supported Simpson, was shaped by the specter of lynching, and that they ultimately failed to empathize with Nicole Brown because rather than the cry of a battered woman in the 911 tapes, they heard "the voice of a white woman aiding and abetting the voices of a police force whose record of racist contempt and brutality . . . evoked the merciless cries of a lynch mob." This argument is shortsighted in its simplistic casting of black women as uncritical supporters of black men in crisis and as women who, in light of the details of historical memory, are led to prioritize, in a knee-jerk and reactionary way, matters of race over gender. My own misgivings about Simpson's innocence emerged early on and remained throughout the trial and in the aftermath of the verdict.

Assumptions of black female complacency in the face of spousal abuse also fail to recognize how a culturally specific rhetoric on domestic violence sometimes shapes the view of the issue among some black women. This rhetoric, which overstates black female strength and agency (i.e., to fight back) in the face of domestic violence, was evident, for instance, in Marguerite Simpson-Thomas's comment in an interview that if O. J. Simpson had ever attempted to hit her, she would have knocked him out with a frying pan. An excellent example of the phenomenon I am describing is illustrated also in Steven Spielberg's film *The Color Purple* in a scene in which the character Sophia (Oprah Winfrey), who is known for her strength, courage, and fighting spirit, tells Celie (Whoopi Goldberg), "Girl you better bash Mr.'s head in and think about heaven later!" Furthermore, while Sophia and her husband are perceived by their community to be "fighting" and "beating on" each other, the reality is that she is a victim of domestic violence, which ultimately ends her marriage. See Hefferman, "The Simpson Trial and the Forgotten Trauma of Lynching," 806. This piece addresses a 1997 essay by Shoshana Felman, "Forms of Judicial Blindness." Also see John Leland, "How Terry Got Her Groove," *Newsweek*, 29 April 1996, 76–80.

48. Richard Combs, *Monthly Film Bulletin* 42.497 (June 1975): 139.

49. By this I mean that it is useful to consider Toni Morrison's introduction to *Birth of a Nation'hood* in relation to her larger conversation about the politics of race in the American literary canon in such works as *Playing in the Dark: Whiteness and the Literary Imagination.* Examining the development of the concept of citizenship beginning in the antebellum period, Dana Nelson points out that white manhood "worked symbolically and legally to bring men together in an abstract but increasingly functional community that diverted their attention from differences between them—differences which had come alarmingly into focus in the post-Revolutionary era." See Nelson, *National Manhood*, 6.

50. Brent Davis has offered the most thoroughgoing examination of Huie's life and career in the 1997 documentary titled *I'm in the Truth Business: William Bradford Huie*, which was produced by the University of Alabama Center for Public Television. The William Bradford Huie Papers are available at Ohio State University.

51. I received this information from Martha Huie.

Chapter 2. Charles Fuller's Southern Specter

1. William Faulkner, *Soldiers' Pay* (New York: Liveright, 1997). All further references to this work are to this edition and will be cited parenthetically in the text.

2. Thadious Davis, *Faulkner's "Negro,"* 1–7.

3. Wolcott, "Mediums, Messages, and Lucky Numbers."

4. Sibley, *Geographies of Exclusion*, 11. Steve Pile and Gillian Rose are other cultural geographers who have combined geography and psychoanalysis. See Rose, *Feminism and Geography*; and Pile, *The Body and the City*.

5. Dixon, *Ride out the Wilderness*, xi.

6. See Wray and Newitz, *White Trash*.

7. Houston A. Baker Jr. has steered the dialogue in this direction by outlining a broader theoretical nexus for thinking about the interrelations of the South, masculinity, and race, all of which are important concepts to remember in interpreting Fuller's play. See Baker, *Turning South Again.*

8. See Baraka, "The Descent of Charlie Fuller."

9. This white masculine anxiety to which I refer was culturally manifest in print and news media beginning in the 1980s and helped constitute the concept of reverse discrimination and the backlash against affirmative action. The decade's popular culture offered one of the most poignant treatments of this panic in the 1983 John Landis film *Trading Places*, which starred Dan Aykroyd and Eddie Murphy. Therein, white masculine usurpation by black men is illustrated comically in the

situation of Winthrop (portrayed by Aykroyd), who realizes in a key scene that he has lost everything—his house, his job, and perhaps even his girlfriend—to Billy Ray, a black homeless petty thief (portrayed by Murphy). These circumstances occur due to the cruel machinations of Winthrop's wealthy corporate bosses as they attempt to settle a one-dollar bet on the relative roles of race and environment in determining behavior.

10. Charles Fuller, *A Soldier's Play* (New York: Noonday Press, 1981). Further references to this source are to this edition and will be cited parenthetically in the text.

11. Harriott, *American Voices*, 110.

12. Stanley Crouch, "Talent, Luck and the Sleeping Yo-yo of American Social Progress: A Conversation with Charles Fuller," *Vogue*, October 1982, 186.

13. See Edith Oliver's review of *A Soldier's Play* in the *New Yorker*, 7 Dec. 1981, 112; see Joe Cunneen's review of the play in *Christian Century* 31 (Mar. 1982): 378–380.

14. See, for instance, Olaniyan, *Scars of Conquest*; Hay, *African American Theatre*; and Benston, *Performing Blackness*.

15. Harry Stecopoulos and Michael Uebel have advanced the critical and theoretical dialogue on race and masculinity in their anthology *Race and the Subject of Masculinity*. Other literary studies on the relationship between race and masculinity, with a focus on black masculinity, include Harper, *Are We Not Men?*; Blount and Cunningham, *Representing Black Men*; Carby, *Race Men*; Awkward, *Negotiating Difference*; Reid-Pharr, "Tearing the Goat's Flesh"; and Maurice O. Wallace, *Constructing the Black Masculine*. Among other useful studies of black masculinity are Ross, *Manning the Race*; Carbado, *Black Men*; and Hine and Jenkins, *A Question of Manhood*.

16. Fuller, quoted in N. Graham Nesmith, "Charles Fuller Steadfast: A Decade Offstage Hasn't Changed the Pulitzer-winning Playwright's Objectives," *American Theatre* 16 (Oct. 1999): 100.

17. The fantasy of racial harmony in the military has been sanctioned even more in recent years by the fashioning of General Colin Powell, an African American, as a national hero for his performance in the Persian Gulf War, by the rumors of Powell's interest in running for president that began to circulate in the mid-1990s, and by his appointment as secretary of state in the administration of President George W. Bush. See Slotkin, "Unit Pride." For more on blacks in military history, see Barbeau and Henri, *The Unknown Soldiers*; Astor, *The Right to Fight*; Ulysses Lee, *United States Army*; Nalty and MacGregor, *Blacks in the Military*; Nalty, *Strength for the Fight*; Cooper, *Hell Fighters*; Scott, *American Negro*; McGuire, *Taps for a Jim Crow Army*; Motley, *The Invisible Soldier*; Segars, Rosenburg, and Barrow, *Black Confederates*; Bergeron et al., *Black Southerners in Gray*; Higginson,

Army Life; W. E. B. Du Bois, *The Gift of Black Folk* and *Black Reconstruction in America*; and Buckley, *American Patriots*.

18. Fuller, quoted in Herbert Mitgang, "Playwright Traces the Long Road to a Hit," *New York Times*, 11 Jan. 1982, 13; and Carol Lawson, "Charles Fuller 'Stunned' on Winning Pulitzer," *New York Times*, 13 Apr. 1982, 11.

19. In *A Soldier's Play*, military officials' lockdown of men in the 221st Chemical Smoke Generating Company to prevent racial rioting in the wake of the news of the murder invokes this Brownsville incident.

20. See Brown, *The Negro*. William Wells Brown, as some readers may recall, was also the first African American dramatist. Also see Brooks, *A Street in Bronzeville*; Killens, *And Then We Heard*; Junius Edwards, *If We Must Die*; John A. Williams, *Captain Blackman*.

21. Anderson, "Disposal of the Colored Drafted Men"; reprinted in Barbeau and Henri, *Unknown Soldiers*, 191–193.

22. Kristeva, *Powers of Horror*, 208.

23. Notwithstanding the multifaceted ideological deployments of the term *white trash* in the contemporary era, here I refer to the embrace of this concept in the nineteenth century among white planters of the southern elite to identify poor whites, the class of subordinate whites that helped maintain slave society in the South and aligned with ruling-class interests in the region during and after Reconstruction to help disenfranchise African Americans legally, politically, and economically.

24. Barbeau and Henri, *Unknown Soldiers*, 90.

25. See, for instance, Angela Y. Davis, *Are Prisons Obsolete?*

26. See Higginson, *Army Life*, 195.

27. Here, I invoke the critical and theoretical sense defined by subaltern studies, which considers the agency of peasant groups that have conventionally been perceived as powerless to effect social and political change. See, for instance, Guha, *Elementary Aspects* and *Dominance without Hegemony*; also see Guha and Spivak, *Selected Subaltern Studies*; and Guha, *Subaltern Studies Reader*. Brent Hayes Edwards has stressed the importance of remembering the specificity of the original contexts of subaltern studies in "wondering whether it is possible to speak of a subaltern studies or a 'colonial studies'—to use the phrase employed by the men themselves—that is elaborated among *colonial* intellectuals *in the metropole*, a possibility that may seem either anathema or oxymoron when juxtaposed with the relatively 'pure' oppositionality of Subaltern Studies in India." I bear these observations in mind even as I find it provocative to ponder continuities between the Indian peasant class that is the referent of subaltern studies and the insurgency of slaves in the South during the Civil War era, especially in light of how Du Bois also links this slave class to the origins of the larger labor movement in the United

States. See Edwards's "The Shadow of Shadows," 13–14. Nahum Dimitri Chandler has made linkages between the discourse of W. E. B. Du Bois and subaltern studies. See, for instance, "Originary Displacement."

28. See Astor, *The Right to Fight*, 126–127.

29. Lee, *United States Army*, 89.

30. James H. Jones, *Bad Blood*, 1.

31. See Baker, *Blues, Ideology, and Afro-American Literature*; and Gates, *The Signifying Monkey*.

32. Richards, "Writing the Absent Potential," 65.

33. See Levine, "Race, Sex, and Colonial Soldiery in World War I."

34. Linard, "Secret Information," quoted in Barbeau and Henri, *Unknown Soldiers*, 114–115.

35. Archer-Shaw, *Negrophilia*. Also see Berliner, *Ambivalent Desire*.

36. Michel Fabre, *From Harlem to Paris*, 2.

37. See Brent Hayes Edwards, *The Practice of Diaspora*.

38. Gates, *Colored People*, 83–84.

39. See Kevin K. Gaines, *Uplifting the Race*, 6.

40. Lavie and Swedenberg, *Displacement*, 1.

41. Farah Jasmine Griffin provides an insightful discussion of these issues in *"Who Set You Flowin'."*

42. See Pile, *The Body and the City*, 91.

43. See Kristeva, *Powers of Horror*, 1–2.

44. Sibley, *Geographies of Exclusion*, 8.

45. Sibley, *Geographies of Exclusion*, 15.

46. In *Dirt and Desire*, Patricia Yaeger notes the recurrence of dirt in southern literature. The haze in which C. J. appears with a ghostlike aura, which marks his absence, is mirrored in the smoky material product generated by the 221st Chemical Smoke Generating Company formed in the wake of his death. While C. J. sees the dust as an essential instrument of his protection in a way that recalls the powers associated with the biblical Samson's hair ("jes' a pinch'll make you strong as a bull," C. J. tells Peterson [44–45]) and its loss as a sign of coming death, for Cobb, C. J.'s invocation of the Farmer's Dust registers as a sign of mental illness.

47. Park and Wald, "Native Daughters," 624.

48. Wiegman, *American Anatomies*, 13.

49. Naylor, *Bailey's Café*, 86, 88.

50. For a revealing discussion of these issues, see Smith and Godlewska, "Critical Histories of Geography."

51. Smith and Cohn, *Look Away!*

52. Patricia Yaeger, introduction to *The Geography of Identity*. For a treatment of the haunting theme in literary narration, see Gordon, *Ghostly Matters*.

53. In the flashbacks, it is also clear that the character was losing voice even before his death. We hear C. J.'s voice most assertively and articulately in the soliloquy that he presents prior to his death during Cobb's visit to the stockade, a moment that, if revealing on the one hand, seems all the more aberrant, on the other, in light of C. J.'s resolute silence during the prior encounter with Waters.

54. Derrida, *Specters of Marx*, 11 (emphasis in the original).

55. Harriott, *American Voices*, 108.

56. Fuller's allusion to the "caged bird" of Paul Laurence Dunbar's 1899 poem "Sympathy" links a broken spirit and a feeling of dehumanization to imprisonment and the loss of freedom. However, the irony is that C. J.'s cage is one in which he loses his ability and will to sing, notwithstanding the "bird" in his blood.

57. Pauline Kael, review of *A Soldier's Story* in the *New Yorker*, 26 Nov. 1984, 118.

58. Baraka, "The Descent of Charlie Fuller," 51–54. While Smalls and Peterson are still alive in prison, they are also symbolically dead and perhaps even undergoing an experience akin to C. J.'s in the stockade.

59. Pile, "Masculinism," 260, 261.

60. The film also introduces a broader range of characters like Colonel Nivens, who is mentioned but never seen in the play. The colonel feasts and reads a newspaper at a lavish breakfast table on a side porch with his elegant blonde wife while coolly dialoguing with Davenport. This scene further brings into relief the racialist aspects of the hierarchical military and links Nivens's privileges as an officer to his status as a wealthy southern elite. The film gives us the added advantage of viewing the active fieldwork of the 221st Chemical Smoke Generating Company as well as the complex layout of the base. Finally, in contrast to the play's grim ending, *A Soldier's Story* ends on an upbeat note with a festive parade that shows the company members joyous in the wake of the military's integration and eager to go overseas to fight. Taylor and Davenport are shown amid the fanfare riding together in a jeep, a scene that affirms their equality and implies a truce.

61. Fuller, quoted in Harriott, *American Voices*, 115.

62. George Goodman, "Black Theater: Must It Appeal to Whites?" *New York Times*, 10 Jan. 1982, 1.

63. These dimensions are further evident where Smalls manifests classic symptoms of hysteria, a psychic phenomenon whose relation to male subjectivity has been compellingly clarified by David Eng. When we see Smalls initially he is withdrawn, inconsolable, and virtually immobilized over the news of Waters's death. As we learn later, Smalls was literally sickened by the murder of Waters and has been suffering from sleeplessness. He seems to be in denial of his role in the

murder up to his final session with Davenport. The flashback sequences provided by Peterson, Wilkie, Smalls, and Cobb even conform to some extent to techniques of psychodrama, developed by Viennese psychiatrist J. L. Moreno, that entail acting out conflicts individually or in a group to achieve an emotional discharge. See Eng, *Racial Castration*.

64. "Larry Riley's Smartest Move Was Deciding to Play Dumb," *People*, 22 Nov. 1984, 85.

65. Ginsberg, *Passing*, 3.

66. Demastes, "Charles Fuller," 53.

67. Here, Fuller seems to allude to the scene in *The Narrative of the Life of Frederick Douglass* (1845) in which Sandy offers the young Frederick a protective and empowering root prior to the pivotal fight with Covey.

68. In the film, the dirt that Waters throws in Peterson's face during the fight reinforces these signs of abjection.

69. Jack Hamann's *On American Soil: How Justice Became a Casualty of World War II* revisits several salient cases in which black soldiers were unfairly accused or court-martialed during the war.

70. See Joseph L. Galloway, "A Half-Century Later, Seven Black Heroes Have Been Nominated for a Medal of Honor," *U.S. News & World Report*, 6 May 1996, 28.

71. Peter A. Bailey, "Introducing Adolph Caesar: Veteran Actor Wins Critical Acclaim in *A Soldier's Story*," *Ebony*, Dec. 1984, 60–62; Ralph Blumenthal, "Howard Rollins Is Dead at 46; Star in TV's 'Heat of the Night,'" *New York Times*, 10 Dec. 1996; and "Larry Riley, 39, Actor on 'Knot's Landing,'" *New York Times*, 10 June 1992.

72. In 2005 Fuller's play received its first major revival in New York, starring Taye Diggs, Anthony Mackie, James McDaniel, and Steven Pasquale with Jo Bonney as director.

Chapter 3. Ralph Ellison's Rural Geography

1. Larsen, *Quicksand*, 116, 119.

2. As some critics have observed, the novella's forthright engagement of black women's sexuality departs from the silence that had typically impacted such representations in African American writing. Furthermore, it disrupts the idealized marriage plot that dominated African American fiction in the nineteenth century, heralding critiques of marriage in black women's writing that emerged in conjunction with a modernist aesthetic, such as Zora Neale Hurston's 1937 novel, *Their Eyes Were Watching God*. See, for instance, DuCille, *The Coupling Convention*.

3. Gray, *The Tuskegee Syphilis Study*, 83; also see James H. Jones, *Bad Blood*; and Reverby, *Tuskegee's Truths*.

4. Harding, *The Racial Economy of Science*, 7–8.

5. Gilman, *Difference and Pathology*, 211.

6. Cohen, *The Boundaries of Blackness*, 119–148.

7. Ralph Ellison, *Invisible Man* (New York: Vintage, 1995). All further references to this work are to this edition and will be cited parenthetically in the text.

8. See, for instance, Wray and Newlitz, *White Trash*; Billings et al., *Confronting Appalachian Stereotypes*; Hsiung, *Two Worlds in the Tennessee Mountains*; and J. W. Williams, *Hillbillyland*.

9. Du Bois, *Black Reconstruction in America*.

10. Danbom, *Born in the Country*, xi.

11. Larson. *Sex, Race, and Science*, 1.

12. Carby, *Cultures in Babylon*, 182. This is an itinerary of thought that Carby first inaugurated in the late 1980s by questioning the view of black rural folk as romantic, critiquing their citation as the bearers of history and preservers of African American culture in the effort to constitute a "tradition" of black women's fiction writing (see Carby's *Reconstructing Womanhood*). Concomitantly, Carby has remarked the cottage industry of criticism surrounding Zora Neale Hurston as symptomatic of this folk emphasis in light of this writer's literary oeuvre on black, rural, southern identities and raises objections to and adduces as a problem the prioritization of the black vernacular in the work of scholars positioned at the vanguard of African American literary theory such as Henry Louis Gates Jr. and Houston A. Baker Jr. See Carby, *Cultures in Babylon*, 147.

13. Carby, *Cultures in Babylon*, 9. Some others who have offered useful critical treatments of black folk identities in recent years include Favor, *Authentic Blackness*; Maxwell, "'Is It True What They Say about Dixie?'"; Nicholls, *Conjuring the Folk*; and Duck, "'Go There Tuh Know There.'"

14. See Stack, *Call to Home*.

15. Carby, *Reconstructing Womanhood*, 175.

16. Carby, *Cultures of Babylon*, 148.

17. Baker, *Blues, Ideology, and Afro-American Literature*, 172–197.

18. O'Meally, *The Craft of Ralph Ellison*, 2. We might even say that conversations related to the use of folk forms in Ellison have by now come to represent a distinct subgenre of criticism on the author. See, for instance, Kent, "Ralph Ellison and Afro-American Folk and Cultural Tradition"; Neal, "Ellison's Zoot Suit"; Bluestein, *The Voice of the Folk*; Clipper, "Folkloric and Mythic Elements in *Invisible Man*"; O'Meally, "Riffs and Rituals"; and Whyte, "Invisible Man as a Trickster Tale."

19. Ellison, *Going to the Territory*, 240–241.

20. Warren, *So Black and Blue*, 59.

21. Lawrence Jackson's 2002 biography of Ellison, which is the first written on

the author, seems assertively psychoanalytic where Jackson postulates the three-year-old Ellison's loss of his thirty-nine-year-old father as one of the impetuses behind the quest for literary success that climaxes for Ellison at age thirty-nine in 1953, the year in which he receives the National Book Award. This year is therefore seen by Jackson as a fitting and symbolic point to conclude treatment of Ellison's early life. This approach is also very much in keeping with popular tenets of the biography genre.

22. Ellison, *Going to the Territory*, 131.

23. Cloke et al., *Writing the Rural*, 1.

24. Cloke and Little, *Contested Countryside Cultures*, 1–2.

25. Some of the works in black British cultural studies that have most significantly contributed to my understanding of the field include Carby, *The Empire Strikes Back*; Diawara, "Englishness and Blackness"; Gilroy, *There Ain't No Black in the Union Jack*; Mercer, *Welcome to the Jungle*; and Baker et al., *Black British Cultural Studies*.

26. See Gilroy, *Small Acts*, 221.

27. For more perspectives on the relation of Britain and the U.S. South, see Ward et al., *Britain and the American South*.

28. See the introduction to Ching and Creed's *Knowing Your Place*, 1–38.

29. See Spillers, "'The Permanent Obliquity of an In(pha)llibly Straight,'" 133.

30. Cloke and Little, *Contested Countryside Cultures*, 1.

31. Simpson, *Academic Postmodern*, 138–139.

32. Brunskill, *Illustrated Handbook of Vernacular Architecture*; and Grow, *Old House Book*.

33. Grow, *Old House Book*, 39.

34. Douglass, *Narrative*, 92.

35. Toomer, *Cane*, 3–4.

36. Incidents that I witnessed during my high school years in Montgomery, Alabama, in the mid- to late 1980s at the Catholic and historically black St. Jude Educational Institute underscored for me how much even those living in small or medium-sized towns and cities in the South (by no means urban in the conventional sense) often alienate identities perceived as rural. I always found intriguing the jokes that some students regularly leveled at commuters from rural Alabama. The irony of these jokes was never lost on me, and it would immediately come to mind whenever I heard such bantering, for I was very aware of ways in which people from other regions in the United States sometimes stereotyped and mocked places like Montgomery. Although these jokes were always told in good fun and never in malice, in retrospect I can say that they were fully indicative of how much ideology inflects the view of rural identities in a variety of contexts, including towns, cities, and metropolitan areas of the South. And of course such

outlandish views of the rural well suggest the extent to which these communities are imagined, fantasized, and invented in ways that have little to do with the reality of lives lived in these contexts.

37. One of the other fascinating places where Ellison references the Bible occurs in the scene with the young white liberal Emerson, during which the narrator discovers the content of Dr. Bledsoe's malicious letter of recommendation; here, the novel invokes the story of Uriah the Hittite, the husband of Bathsheba: "I had seen the letter and it had practically ordered me killed. By slow degrees . . ." (194).

38. Ching and Creed, *Knowing Your Place*, 4.

39. Miller, "Social Science, Social Policy," 260–261.

40. Toni Morrison, *The Bluest Eye* (New York: Plume, 1994), 18.

41. Maurice O. Wallace, *Constructing the Black Masculine*, 135.

42. Baker, *Blues, Ideology, and Afro-American Literature*, 183.

43. hooks, *Black Looks*.

44. George Hughes, *Reading Novels*, 131.

45. Stewart, *A Space*, 38.

46. Stewart, *A Space*, 37.

47. Stewart, *A Space*, 32 (emphasis in the original).

48. Stewart, *A Space*, 31.

49. Stewart, *A Space*, 33–34.

50. Bachelard, *Poetics of Space*, 8.

51. Bachelard, *Poetics of Space*, 5, 8.

52. See Spillers, *Black, White, and in Color*; Lane, *The Psychoanalysis of Race*; Cheng, *The Melancholy of Race*; and Claudia Tate, *Psychoanalysis and Black Novels*.

53. Bachelard, *Poetics of Space*, 11.

54. Jean Hill, "Back to the Land," *Essence* 34.4 (August 2003): 158–162.

55. See Duck, "'Go There Tuh Know There.'"

56. As Robin D. G. Kelley has pointed out, in pondering clothing and dance styles among African American youth in 1943, Ellison may have provided the linchpin for understanding the possibilities for the emergence of Malcolm X's political radicalism. See Kelley, "The Riddle of the Zoot."

Chapter 4. Spike Lee's Uncle Toms and Urban Revolutionaries

1. See Perry, *Malcolm*, 28–29, 75–78.

2. The cover of the original paperback edition of *The Autobiography of Malcolm X* (New York: Grove, 1966) states that Malcolm X "rose from hoodlum, thief, dope peddler, pimp . . . to become the most dynamic leader of the Black Revolution. He said he would be murdered before this book appeared."

3. Rampersad, "The Color of His Eyes," 131.

4. Lee's stated rationale for this strategy was that he aimed to make the film

appropriate for all viewing audiences. It is tempting still to infer that this approach reflected anxieties about exogamy in Malcolm X's sexual history. Skepticism about interracial sex and love was quite evident in Lee's 1991 film, *Jungle Fever*. Lee was very concerned about how Malcolm X's widow, Betty Shabazz, and their daughters would respond to the film. These anxieties perhaps impacted Lee's decision not to incorporate the kinds of sex scenes in the film *Malcolm X* that he had highlighted in some of his other films. Furthermore, at the time, Denzel Washington was noted for his reluctance to perform nude scenes and to kiss white women in films.

5. Kipnis, "The Stepdaughter's Story," 59–73.

6. Ross, "Camping the Dirty Dozens," 291.

7. This image of Malcolm X initially gained widespread popularity through Ossie Davis's eloquent eulogy casting the leader as a "shining black prince" and as the "manhood" of black people in the United States.

8. Patricia J. Williams, "Clarence X, Man of the People."

9. Malcolm X, *The Autobiography of Malcolm X*, as told to Alex Haley (New York: Ballantine Books, 1992). All subsequent references are to this edition of the text and will be cited parenthetically.

10. See Kelley, "The Riddle of the Zoot," 156.

11. Majors and Billson, *Cool Pose*.

12. Jeffries, "Toward a Redefinition of the Urban," 159.

13. White and White, *Stylin'*.

14. Imam Benjamin Karim, introduction to *Malcolm X*, 8, 9–10.

15. See Ching and Creed, *Knowing Your Place*, 28.

16. Of course, Lee's film's focus on comically rendering the zoot suit also obscures, in effect, the political significance of this attire, in light of the zoot suit riots in 1943 that scholars from Robin D. G. Kelley to Graham White and Shane White have revealingly examined, in which armed American servicemen in several cities such as Detroit and Harlem attacked young black and Mexican men on the street who wore this attire. The loitering of these populations was viewed as a lack of support for the war effort, and in a time when fabric was being rationed, their wearing of these suits was viewed as unpatriotic.

17. See Archie Epps, *Malcolm X: Speeches at Harvard*, 58. This is not to say that Malcolm X identified as rural per se. A closer reading of Malcolm X's speeches also seems useful because only a few scholars have offered sustained and focused analysis of the complex imagery that Malcolm X uses in his speech repertoires, which are a component of the sermonic tradition in African American literary and cultural history. Fredrick Sunnemark's work points to the importance of examining the rhetorical devices of black-liberation movement leaders more extensively. See Sunnemark, *Ring Out Freedom*.

18. Malcolm X, from "Message to the Grassroots," in *Malcolm X Speaks*, 10–12.

19. See *Malcolm X: The Last Speeches*, 40.

20. On his trip to Africa in 1964, Malcolm X would later rethink black nationalism as an organizing principle in the black-liberation movement.

21. The use of the term *Negro* to signify a more authentic blackness in such moments was highly provisional, as indicated by his typical prefacing of the term with "so-called." This strategy was also likely as much a reflection of Nation of Islam philosophies about black nomenclature in the United States. Phillip Brian Harper provides a useful analysis of the use of the term *nigger* to suggest lack of authenticity within the category "black." See Harper, *Are We Not Men?*, 69–71.

22. Robin D. G. Kelley discusses the use of the house Negro–field Negro dichotomy to critique the black middle class in his essay "House Negroes on the Loose." Critiqued more broadly through these metaphors is the philosophy of nonviolence, and its Christian influences in particular. Malcolm X highlights a double standard wherein blacks (and men specifically) participate in violence on behalf of the United States on foreign soil out of patriotic duty but at the same time neglect to defend themselves, and black women and children, from violent attacks within the nation. Furthermore, he deploys the metaphors to critique racial integration as an objective of the Civil Rights movement.

23. In the seminal study *Black Messiahs and Uncle Toms: Social and Literary Manipulations of a Religious Myth*, Wilson Jeremiah Moses acknowledges that Malcolm X's militancy and philosophy of self-defense had distinct appeal among black men in the urban North in comparison to King's: "They were proud of the integration movement and of King, but they found both the man and the movement difficult to understand. They did not see how it would be possible for any self-respecting black man to live in the South without carrying a gun and using it at least once a day" (209).

24. See Malcolm X, *Malcolm X: The Last Speeches*, 35.

25. See Malcolm X, *By Any Means Necessary*, 170.

26. Malcolm X, *Malcolm X Speaks*, 31.

27. Malcolm X, "Twenty Million Black People," in *Malcolm X: The Last Speeches*, 31–32.

28. I borrow this point about King's rhetorical style from historian Clarence Walker.

29. See, for instance, Brasell " 'The Degeneration of Nationalism' "; Howard, *Men Like That*; Sears, *Rebels, Rubyfruit, and Rhinestones*; and Dews and Law, *Out in the South*.

30. Newton, *Revolutionary Suicide*, 113; and Seale, *Seize the Time*, 3. It is notable that the Black Panther Party platform and program, which includes ten points and was devised by Newton and Seale in 1966, also draws on the ten propositions of the Nation of Islam.

31. Newton, *Revolutionary Suicide*. All references are to the Writers and Readers edition and will be cited parenthetically in the text.

32. Seale, *Seize the Time*, 313–314.

33. Still, the reality has been that the South, perhaps like no other place in the United States, was a seasoning ground for armed resistance among blacks. This is a point that Newton and some others who were members of the Black Panther Party, such as Kathleen Cleaver and David Hilliard, have readily acknowledged. David Hilliard has remarked, "Partly, this proclivity to violence is, I think, a southern trait. Down south, everybody is armed, whites and blacks. (When I arrive in California, the locals are amazed I carry a knife.)" See Hilliard, *This Side of Glory*, 40–41. Similarly, in reflecting on how exposure to the culture of violence in the South conditioned her and many of her comrades for membership in the Black Panther Party and its self-defense agenda, Kathleen Cleaver shares the following comments in a 1999 interview: "Let's get straight to it: this was California. This was the Wild West. And many of the people who joined the Black Panthers—their families had moved from rural areas of the South that are very violent. Huey was born in Louisiana, Bobby Seale was born in Texas, Eldridge was born in Arkansas. They came from families that were used to having guns, and were wary of being attacked by racists." She goes on to remark that "I came from Alabama. Everybody had guns. I learned how to shoot when I was a little kid, going out hunting. Racial violence is definitely your backdrop in the South. You don't even question it, it's like part of the universe." See Linfield, "The Education of Kathleen Neal Cleaver," 184.

34. See Pearson, *The Shadow of the Panther*, 97. The ownership of the symbol by the Oakland organization consolidated for a variety of complicated reasons. We should consider, for instance, the allure that Newton and Seale's organization held for blacks in urban contexts in the 1960s, rioting in cities across the nation that gave issues in black urban contexts increasing importance on black-liberation agendas, the "Free Huey" campaign that began in 1967 in the wake of Newton's imprisonment for allegedly murdering a police officer that gave the Oakland organization wider recognition and brought thousands of new members, J. Edgar Hoover's categorization of the Black Panther Party as the top threat to national security in the United States, and the surveillance and brutal assaults that were a part of the FBI's Counterintelligence Program (COINTELPRO) designed to neutralize the organization, and the Oakland group's emergence as a commodity in light of media fascination with the stylization and revolutionary nationalism of the members. Furthermore, the gradual shift in focus in SNCC from grassroots projects in the rural South to an increasing focus on urban contexts during the organization's final years of existence, and Stokely Carmichael's concomitant rise as a black militant leader for urban contexts in the wake of increasing factionalism

that emerged within SNCC during the late 1960s (along with his brief membership in the Oakland Black Panthers), enabled this organization's eventual conflation with the black panther symbol.

35. Smith and Cohn, *Look Away!*

36. Pratt, *Imperial Eyes*, 7.

37. This interview, made available through Reuters, is quoted in the 1 January 1993 edition of the *Los Angeles Times*. See "Carmichael Blasts Lee on '*Malcolm.*'"

38. An allusion to the biblical Esau, who sold his birthright to his younger brother Jacob for a mess of pottage, is also clear. In light of the invocation of the term "sell out," we might infer a reference to the discourses of Uncle Tom.

39. See Jacqueline Trescott, "The Battle over Malcolm X—Spike Lee vs. Amiri Baraka: Who Should Immortalize the Man on Film, and How?" *Washington Post*, 18 Aug. 1991. Lee reports his budget for the film to have been $25 million.

40. These vociferous critiques also underscore the ideological ruptures that separate black nationalisms produced within the 1960s and 1990s and the superficiality of the continuities that have often been posited in recent years for the purpose of linking those eras. Gerald Horne surely identifies one of the most egregious symptoms of positing in the contemporary period superficial continuities between 1960s and 1990s black nationalisms by pointing out how black youth in the 1990s, to advance a myth of "contemporary black unity," recast "narrow nationalists" from the 1960s as "ideological descendants" of the "progressive nationalists" who had been their contemporaries, when in reality, the former had often been agents in the deaths of many of the latter. Horne's most telling example of this phenomenon is the constitution of ideological linkages by some blacks in the 1990s between Malcolm X and forces who have been implicated in the leader's death, such as the Nation of Islam and the Minister Louis Farrakhan. Such an analysis provides an apt illustration of the futility in attempts to establish univocality where black nationalisms are concerned for the purpose of promoting notions of black community; suggests what is at stake in the constitution of fantasies of a monolithic black nationalism within black culture; and reminds us that unity in black nationalisms was an impossibility within prior eras and that the possibilities for uniformity among black nationalisms are no greater in the contemporary period. See Horne, "Myth and the Making of '*Malcolm X*,'" 444. Within Lee's corpus, the disparate and conflicting negotiations of black nationalism across his range of films, including the more recent *A Huey P. Newton Story* (2001), the film adaptation of Roger Guenveur Smith's play, well imply the elusiveness of narratives of consensus in discourses of black nationalism within the contemporary era.

41. See Trescott, "The Battle over Malcolm X." Predictably, some critics highlighted the ways in which these criticisms of Jewison by Lee were ironically

paralleled in the outcry over Lee's directorship of the Malcolm X film that I have referenced here.

42. See Lubiano, "But Compared to What?" 174.

43. N'Gai Croal, "Bouncing off the Rim," *Newsweek*, 22 April 1996, 75.

44. See Boyd, *Am I Black Enough for You?*, 29.

45. The most immediate reaction to *School Daze*, as some readers may recall, was outcry over Spike Lee's decision to "air dirty linen" by highlighting skin-color hierarchies among African Americans. The film was more favorably linked, however, to the resurgence of enrollments at historically black colleges in the years after its release and to the revitalization of black sororities and fraternities. The film's release occurred not only during an era in which black nationalism was being revived in urban centers among African Americans alongside an emergent Afrocentrism but also in the midst of a growing international movement against the apartheid system in South Africa. The traces of an Afrocentric sensibility are particularly manifest in the Gamma Phi Gamma fraternity display during the homecoming parade, which features Gamma queen Jane Toussaint emerging from a pyramid flanked by four Gamma members who fan her with feathers. This fascination with ancient Egypt, given the Gamma Phi Gamma fraternity's indifference to the contemporary issue of apartheid, is telling.

46. Jacquie Jones, "The Accusatory Space," 95–96.

47. While the film makes an explicit association between the jerri curl and lower-class status, the reality is that if this style appealed primarily to many men in this sector, it was also embraced by black men across a range of class categories, including those positioned within black celebrity cultures, such as Michael Jackson, Prince, several members of New Edition, and El Debarge.

48. Mercer, *Welcome to the Jungle*, 114.

49. It is the local man's jerri curl cap, and especially his wearing of it in public, that mainly contributes to his marking as "country" and "'Bama" by Da Fellas. (One of Da Fellas metaphorically refers to the local man as "the jerri curl," as if to suggest him as a walking embodiment of this hairstyle.)

50. Smith and Cohn, *Look Away!*, 10.

51. See Pratt, *Imperial Eyes*, 7.

52. Grewal, *Home and Harem*, 4.

53. I borrow this concept from Davies, *Black Women, Writing, and Identity*.

54. Members of an executive council that included such figures as Benjamin Chavis (now Benjamin Muhammad), Ron Daniels, Minister Louis Farrakhan, Maulana Karenga, Haki Madhubuti, and Rev. Willie Wilson drafted this statement. See Karenga, "The Million Man March / Day of Absence Mission Statement," 3–4.

55. Jack E. White, "In the Driver's Seat: Inspired by Its Message, Black Men Finance Spike Lee's Film about the Million Man March," *Time*, 21 Oct. 1996, 78.

56. It is possible to read Jeremiah, in light of issues that are discussed in the introduction, as a reformed Uncle Tom whose redemption on the bus (i.e., as evidenced in the moral authority that he wields) has lain in making the transformation to identification with the rhetoric of black power. Significantly, he says he is attending the march because of a desire to be "first in line at the revolution" but once "didn't believe in trouble makers and rabble rousers" when he was working at a company to which he once begged to be reinstated after being laid off and that fired him after thirty-three years of dedicated work.

57. Riggs, "Black Macho Revisited," 306–307.

58. Jack E. White, "In the Driver's Seat," 78.

59. Wahneema Lubiano has acknowledged Lee's frequent uses of the vernacular: "If Lee's strength is a certain ability to document some of the sounds and sights of African American culture—its style focus—that vernacularity cannot guarantee counter-hegemonic cultural resistance. One can be caught up in Euro-American hegemony within the vernacular, and one can repeat the masculinism and heterosexism of vernacular culture. Vernacular language and cultural productions allow the possibility of discursive power disruptions, of cultural resistance, but they do not guarantee it. The particular politics of the specifics of vernacular culture that Lee represents are problematic. The films' presentation of and the critics' acceptance of these politics without a challenge encourages audiences to consider these representations as African American essences." See Lubiano, "But Compared to What?," 183–184. We might relate the kinds of black vernacular cultural specificities to which Lubiano refers to what Greg Tate describes as Lee's "black in-jokes and semiotic codes," which have included not only representations of Malcolm X but also citations of such personas as Zora Neale Hurston, musical forms like jazz and hip-hop, the history of Reconstruction, the jerri curl hairstyle, and drugs. See Greg Tate, *Flyboy in the Buttermilk*, 208. We could extend Tate's list a bit more by adding Lee's references to historically black colleges, gospel and spiritual traditions, soul food, and hair pressing, among other things.

60. Rony, *The Third Eye*, 7.

61. Gilroy, *Small Acts*, 186.

62. See Rony, *The Third Eye*, 7.

63. McClintock, " 'No Longer in a Future Heaven,' " 90.

64. Mercer, *Welcome to the Jungle*, 97–128.

65. Rony, *The Third Eye*, 7.

66. Catherine Pouzoulet, "The Cinema of Spike Lee: Images of a Mosaic City," in Reid, *Spike Lee's* Do the Right Thing, 33.

67. Baldwin, "Everybody's Protest Novel," 498.

68. Spillers, "Mama's Baby, Papa's Maybe," 455.

69. See Ross, "Camping the Dirty Dozens," 293.

Chapter 5. Gangstas and Playas in the Dirty South

1. "Southern-Fried Hip-Hop: Down-home Lyrics and Strong Dance Grooves Are Ingredients of a Tasty Menu," *Ebony*, Jan. 2004, 74.

2. David Bry, "Song of the South," *Vibe*, June 2002, 94.

3. For critical perspectives on this controversy, see Henry Louis Gates Jr., "2 Live Crew, Decoded," *New York Times*, 19 June 1990; Baker, *Black Studies, Rap, the Academy*; and Kimberlé Williams Crenshaw, "Beyond Racism and Misogyny: Black Feminism and 2 Live Crew," *Boston Review*, 6 Dec. 1991, 30–32.

4. Tricia Rose, *Black Noise*, 153–154.

5. Fred Schruers, "Survival of the Illest: New Orleans' Master P Builds a Hip-Hop Empire from the Underground Up," *Rolling Stone*, 27 Nov. 1997, 22.

6. This proposed arrangement has been part and parcel of a longstanding strategy in the rap industry. As Tricia Rose has pointed out, "In the 1980s, after rap spurred the growth of new independent labels, the major labels moved in and attempted to dominate the market but could not consolidate their efforts. Artists signed to independent labels, particularly Tommy Boy, Profile, and Def Jam, continued to flourish, whereas acts signed to the six majors [CBS, Polygram, Warner, BMG, Capitol-EMI, and MCA] could not produce comparable sales. It became apparent that independent labels had a much greater understanding of the cultural logic of hip-hop and rap music, a logic that permeated decisions ranging from signing acts to promotional methods. Instead of competing with smaller, more street-savvy labels for new rap acts, the major labels developed a new strategy: buy the independent labels, allow them to function relatively autonomously, and provide them with production resources and access to major retail distribution." These forms of corporate negotiation in the rap industry are consistent with the record company dealings to which pop artist Prince brought widespread public attention in the mid-1990s by changing his name to "The Artist Formerly Known as Prince" and painting the word "slave" on the side of his face. His goal was to protest the slim profits that his company, Paisley Park, was receiving from Warner Brothers, a company that had also refused to pay him royalties for his earlier albums (Rose, *Black Noise*, 7).

7. Master P has since relocated from Louisiana to Hollywood, California.

8. Jason Fine, "Cash Money's Midnight Ride," *Rolling Stone*, 8 June 2000, 88.

9. Fine, "Cash Money's Midnight Ride," 84.

10. Tariq K. Muhammad, "Hip-Hop Moguls: Beyond the Hype," *Black Enterprise*, Dec. 1999, 78.

11. Simmons, *Life and Def*, 208–209.

12. Bry, "Song of the South," 98. Here, Master P points to the strategies of disguising aspects of southern identity, such as voice, that I mention in this book's introduction and chapter 2.

13. See Fine, "Cash Money's Midnight Ride," 82.

14. See Touré, "Juvenile, P and Biggie Rule Hardcore from the South and from the Beyond," *Rolling Stone*, 20 Jan. 2000, 59.

15. Bry, "Song of the South," 98.

16. See Flake, *New Orleans*; and Gill, *Lords of Misrule*.

17. Koster, *Louisiana Music*.

18. Southern, *The Music of Black America*, 341–342. Also see Blassingame, *Black New Orleans*.

19. Broven, *Walking to New Orleans*.

20. Koster, *Louisiana Music*, 293.

21. See Kelley, *Race Rebels*, 183–227.

22. In general, I want to emphasize the importance of not conflating the romantic, ancestral, and nostalgic urban fantasies for black southern "folk" of an earlier group such as Arrested Development with the themes that have emerged among contemporary rap artists. Whereas the former sensibility is one that this group popularized in black popular culture in the early 1990s, one major difference is that for the latter movement, the South is *not* "another place" that has to be rediscovered and returned to for purposes of self-discovery in the sense that Arrested Development's hit rap song "Tennessee" describes the region. But the rap of contemporary southern artists typically describes the South as a place that is here and now and as where they live.

23. The complex history of race relations in the South has also played out in the social lives of some southern rap artists in instances. For instance, a 1998 article in the *New Republic* titled "Baton Rouge Dispatch: Gate Crashers" describes the outcry over Master P's relocation, along with fellow rappers Snoop Doggy Dog, Mystikal, Silkk the Shocker, and C-Murder, into an exclusive gated community called Country Club of Louisiana in Baton Rouge, in which homes range in price from $300,000 to $3 million. While reactions to the arrival of this group were mixed, the article reports that "in a state where many citizens proudly wore their Confederate gray until the end of World War I, the successful assimilation of flamboyant rap musicians into a gated white subdivision—'They're just like the other Country Club residents,' says one Baton Rouge civic leader—has to be counted as a kind of progress." See Scott Stossel, "Baton Rouge Dispatch: Gate Crashers," *New Republic*, 30 Aug. 1999, 18–22. The video for the 2001 song "Bad Boy for Life" by Sean "Puffy" Combs (now P. Diddy) on the album *P. Diddy and the Bad Boys Family* points to these kinds of tense social dynamics, which

entailed Master P's denial of membership in the golf club. The video begins by highlighting homes in a suburban neighborhood with well-manicured lawns on a quiet and peaceful morning. The camera flashes to a senior white male clad in a bathrobe going into his front yard to retrieve his morning paper, and to another front yard where a younger white male is clipping the hedges, and then to a "For Sale" sign in the front yard of the adjacent house. The men turn their heads in slow motion as a long black tour bus pulls up to the curb and stops. A long stream of women and men clad in black exit and begin to move large pieces of black leather furniture. The camera then zooms in on the word "Sold" on the "For Sale" sign. A white woman who has joined the young man on the front yard to gawk at the spectacle—likely his wife—faints. The new residents begin to ride scooters up and down the street, play basketball games, and perform motorcycle stunts in which various neighbors participate. Also embedded in the video is a skit, sans musical background, in which a white male neighbor knocks on the door of P. Diddy, who portrays himself in the video, and warns the rapper not to knock any more golf balls through windows on the block. The new neighbors have a major concert block party. The next morning, P. Diddy is shown in his white bathrobe and cap going to retrieve his morning paper and is greeted by four white youth across the street who are wearing "punk" outfits and spiked hair. Ironically, he proclaims "There goes the neighborhood" to himself as he greets them. Finally, we hear the voice of the woman next door, presumably the same one who fainted, calling over to greet him and him speaking back to her and jokingly remarking that "I saw you enjoying the party last night, Mrs. Jennings, and shaking that ass." We might further interpret the video as a critique of notions of white racial purity and homogeneity, a thematic element that seems to be reinforced through the use of the colors black and white as the central symbols therein. On some levels, we might also say that this video acknowledges the widespread panic in many suburban communities over the popularity of gangsta rap among young white teenagers, who, statistics say, represent 80 percent of gangsta rap's consumers.

24. Whitehead, *The Intuitionist*, 78.

25. Yaeger, *Dirt and Desire*.

26. See Dyson, *Between God and Gangsta Rap*, 184–185.

27. Such linkages are apparent in the 1994 film *Jason's Lyric*, which is set in Texas. The character Joshua fails to show up on time to help the crime ring to which he belongs pull off a bank robbery. As a consequence, they make off with no cash. In the end, the only loot they have to show for the elaborate caper is an expensive watch that Joshua steals at the last minute from a customer in the bank. This makes him the last one to the waiting getaway car that is eager to flee police

sirens. After the unsuccessful heist, we see Joshua's bloody, shirtless body strung up in a garage by a chain. With other members of the ring looking on, Antoine, the leader, tortures him by cutting into his flesh with a chainsaw. That Joshua blames his tardiness on Antoine's sister Lyric, who told Joshua's brother Jason about the robbery, and that Jason has been dating her, feeds Antoine's fury. This scene clearly evokes the specter of lynching. The character Treach of *Naughty by Nature*, who plays the role of Antoine, forges linkages with rap discourse.

28. hooks, *Outlaw Culture*; Dyson, *Between God and Gangsta Rap*; and Rose, *Black Noise*.

29. Michael Awkward, drawing on the work of Hortense Spillers, has offered critical perspectives on some of the more contemporary epithets that are specific to black masculinity, including "Lazy Shiftless Nigger," "Rapist," "Ghetto Blaster," "Affirmative Action," and "Car Jacker." See Awkward, *Negotiating Difference*. Also see Spillers, "Mama's Baby, Papa's Maybe."

30. Toomer, *Cane*, 17, 19, 110.

31. Morrison, *Song of Solomon*, 269.

32. Morrison, *Song of Solomon*, 271.

33. See Rose, *Black Noise*, 2.

34. Quoted in David Bry, "Song of the South," 98.

Conclusion

1. Zoeller's comments were quoted widely in the media. See, for instance, Glenn Sheeley, "Zoeller's Remarks Meet with Disbelief: Veteran Refers to Woods as 'Little Boy,'" *Atlanta Journal and Constitution*, 21 April 1997.

2. "Zoeller Apologizes for Ill-Chosen Words," *Fayetteville (N.C.) Observer*, 22 April 1997.

3. In more recent years, this critical and theoretical motif has been cited frequently, and in some instances even mocked, as a "holy trinity" of sorts that has been, thankfully, knocked from its sacred and mighty throne by critics who now know better what a limiting and stifling framework it was.

4. One distinct byproduct of the "race, class, gender" motif was the concept of "intersectionality" that legal scholar Kimberlé Williams Crenshaw developed within the fields of critical race theory and feminism, which emphasized that the categories must be looked at together, for forms of black women's oppression have not been legible within conventional approaches to race or gender discrimination. See Crenshaw, "Demarginalizing the Intersection of Race and Sex."

5. Deborah E. McDowell, "Pecs and Reps: Muscling in on Race and the Subject of Masculinities," in *Race and the Subject of Masculinities*, ed. Harry Stecopoulos and Michael Uebel (Durham: Duke University Press, 1997), 369.

6. One work that grapples with the ambivalence that I am describing is Paul Laurence Dunbar's short story entitled "The Lynching of Jube Benson" (1907).

7. James Baldwin, "Going to Meet the Man," in *Going to Meet the Man*, 249.

8. In *Critical Memory*, Houston A. Baker Jr. poignantly theorizes such moments in black male experience by examining the reluctance of Richard Wright as a black male to report that he has seen the cook at the café where he is working spitting in the food. Although in the North the specter of southern racial attitudes and prejudices and the reprisals that he anticipates hold him back, Wright confides in one of his black female co-workers, who eventually tells the white boss (3–6).

BIBLIOGRAPHY

Adams, Rachel, and David Savran, eds. *The Masculinity Studies Reader*. London: Blackwell, 2002.

Addams, Jane, and Ida B. Wells. *Lynching and Rape: An Exchange of Views*. Ed. Bettina Aptheker. New York: American Institute for Marxist Studies, 1977.

Alexander, Robert. *I Ain't Yo' Uncle: The New Jack Revisionist "Uncle Tom's Cabin."* In *Colored Contradictions: An Anthology of Contemporary African-American Plays*. Ed. Harry J. Elam Jr. New York: Penguin, 1996. 21–90.

Allen, James, et al. *Without Sanctuary: Lynching Photography in America*. Santa Fe, N.M.: Twin Palms, 2000.

Anderson, E. D. "Disposal of the Colored Drafted Men." National Archives. RG 165, Item 8142–50. Reprinted in Barbeau and Henri, *Unknown Soldiers*, 191–193.

Applebome, Peter. *Dixie Rising: How the South Is Shaping American Values, Politics, and Culture*. New York: Harvest Books, 1997.

Archer-Shaw, Petrine. *Negrophilia: Avant-Garde Paris and Black Culture in the 1920s*. New York: Thames & Hudson, 2000.

Astor, Gerald. *The Right to Fight: A History of African Americans in the Military*. New York: Da Capo Press, 1998.

Awkward, Michael. *Negotiating Difference: Race, Gender, and the Politics of Positionality*. Chicago: University of Chicago Press, 1995.

Bachelard, Gaston. *The Poetics of Space: The Classic Look at How We Experience Intimate Places*. Boston: Beacon Press, 1969.

Baker, Houston A., Jr. *Black Studies, Rap, the Academy*. Chicago: University of Chicago Press, 1993.

———. *Blues, Ideology, and Afro-American Literature: A Vernacular Theory*. Chicago: University of Chicago Press, 1984.

———. *Critical Memory: Public Spheres, African American Writing, and Black Fathers and Sons in America*. Athens: University of Georgia Press, 2001.

———. *Turning South Again: Rethinking Modernism / Re-Reading Booker T.* Durham: Duke University Press, 2001.

Baker, Houston A., Jr., and Dana D. Nelson. "Violence, the Body, and the South." *American Literature* 73 (June 2001): 231–244.

Baker, Houston A., Jr., et al., eds. *Black British Cultural Studies: A Reader*. Chicago: University of Chicago Press, 1996.

Baker, Houston A., Jr., with an introduction by Margo Crawford. "Erasing the Commas: RaceGenderClassSexualityRegion." *American Literature* 77.1 (March 2005).

Baldwin, James. "Everybody's Protest Novel." In *Uncle Tom's Cabin*. Ed. Elizabeth Ammons. New York: W. W. Norton, 1994. 495–501.

———. *Going to Meet the Man*. New York: Vintage, 1993.

Bammer, Angelika, ed. *Displacements: Cultural Identities in Question*. Bloomington: Indiana University Press, 1994.

Baraka, Amiri. "The Descent of Charlie Fuller into Pulitzerland and the Need for African American Institutions." *Black American Literature Forum* 17 (Summer 1983): 51–54.

Barbeau, Arthur E., and Florette Henri. *The Unknown Soldiers: African-American Troops in World War I*. New York: Da Capo Press, 1996.

Bell, Roseann P., Bettye J. Parker, and Beverly Guy-Sheftall. *Sturdy Black Bridges: Visions of Black Women in Literature*. New York: Anchor Books, 1979.

Benston, Kimberly W. *Performing Blackness: Enactments of African American Modernism*. New York: Routledge, 2000.

Bergeron, Arthur W., et al. *Black Southerners in Gray: Afro-Americans in Confederate Armies*. Mechanicsburg, Penn.: Stackpole Books, 1997.

Berlant, Lauren. "National Brands / National Body: *Imitation of Life*." In *Comparative American Identities: Race, Sex, and Nationality in the Modern Text*. Ed. Hortense Spillers. New York: Routledge, 1991. 110–140.

Berliner, Brett A. *Ambivalent Desire: The Exotic Black Other in Jazz-Age France*. Amherst: University of Massachusetts Press, 2002.

Bhabha, Homi. *The Location of Culture*. New York: Routledge, 1993.

Billings, Dwight B., et al., eds. *Confronting Appalachian Stereotypes: Back Talk from an American Region*. Lexington: University of Kentucky Press, 2001.

Blake, Susan L. "Ritual and Rationalization: Black Folklore in the Works of Ralph Ellison." In *Ralph Ellison: Modern Cultural Views*. Ed. Harold Bloom. New York: Chelsea House, 1986. 121–136.

Blassingame, John W. *Black New Orleans, 1860–1880*. Chicago: University of Chicago Press, 1973.

———. *The Slave Community: Plantation Life in the Antebellum South*. New York: Oxford University Press, 1972.

Blount, Marcellus, and George P. Cunningham, eds. *Representing Black Men*. New York: Routledge, 1996.

Bluestein, Gene. *The Voice of the Folk*. Amherst: University of Massachusetts Press, 1972.

Bogle, Donald. *Toms, Coons, Mulattoes, Mammies and Bucks: An Interpretive History of Blacks in American Films*. New York: Continuum, 1989.

Boles, John B., ed. *Shapers of Southern History: Autobiographical Reflections*. Athens: University of Georgia Press, 2004.

Bordo, Susan. *The Male Body: A New Look at Men in Public and Private*. New York: Farrar, Straus & Giroux, 1999.

Boyd, Todd. *Am I Black Enough for You? Popular Culture from the 'Hood and Beyond.* Bloomington: Indiana University Press, 1997.

Brasell, Bruce. "'The Degeneration of Nationalism': Colonialism, Perversion, and the American South." *Mississippi Quarterly* 56 (Winter 2003): 33–54.

Brodkin, Karen. *How Jews Became White Folks and What That Says about Race in America.* New Brunswick, N.J.: Rutgers University Press, 1999.

Brody, Jennifer DeVere. *Impossible Purities: Blackness, Femininity and Victorian Culture.* Durham: Duke University Press, 1998.

Brooks, Gwendolyn. *A Street in Bronzeville.* New York: Harper and Bros., 1945.

Broven, John. *Walking to New Orleans: The Story of New Orleans Rhythm and Blues.* Gretna, La.: Pelican, 1978.

Brown, William Wells. *The Negro in the American Rebellion.* New York: Mnemosyne, 1997.

Brunskill, R. W. *Illustrated Handbook of Vernacular Architecture.* New York: Universe Books, 1970.

Bryant, Jerry. *Born in a Mighty Bad Land: The Violent Man in African American Folklore and Fiction.* Bloomington: Indiana University Press, 2003.

Buckley, Gail. *American Patriots: The Story of Blacks in the Military from the Revolution to Desert Storm.* New York: Random House, 2001.

Cade, Toni. *The Black Woman.* New York: Signet, 1970.

Cameron, James. *A Time of Terror.* Milwaukee, Wis.: T D Publications, 1982.

Carbado, Devon W., ed. *Black Men on Race, Gender and Sexuality: A Critical Reader.* New York: New York University Press, 1999.

Carby, Hazel. *Cultures in Babylon: Black Britain and African America.* London: Verso, 1999.

———. *The Empire Strikes Back: Race and Racism in Seventies Britain.* London: Hutchinson, 1982.

———. *Race Men.* Cambridge, Mass.: Harvard University Press, 1998.

———. *Reconstructing Womanhood: The Emergence of the Afro-American Woman Novelist.* New York: Oxford University Press, 1987.

Carmichael, Stokely (later Kwame Ture), with Ekwueme Michael Thelwell. *Ready for the Revolution: The Life and Struggles of Stokely Carmichael (Kwame Ture).* New York: Scribner, 2003.

Carson, Clayborne. *In Struggle: SNCC and the Black Awakening of the 1960s.* Cambridge, Mass.: Harvard University Press, 1981.

Carson, Clayborne, et al., eds. *The Eyes on the Prize Reader: Documents, Speeches, and Firsthand Accounts from the Black Freedom Struggle.* New York: Penguin, 1991.

Carter, Dan. *From George Wallace to Newt Gingrich: Race in the Conservative Counterrevolution, 1963–1994.* Baton Rouge: Louisiana State University Press, 1999.

————. *The Politics of Rage: George Wallace, the Origins of the New Conservatism, and the Transformation of American Politics*. 2nd ed. Baton Rouge: Louisiana State University Press, 2000.

Chandler, Nahum Dimitri. "Originary Displacement." *Boundary 2* 27 (Fall 2000): 249–286.

Chase, C. Thurston. *A Manual on School-houses and Cottages for the People of the South*. Washington, D.C.: Government Printing Office, 1868.

Cheng, Anne. *The Melancholy of Race*. New York: Oxford University Press, 2000.

Ching, Barbara, and Gerald W. Creed, eds. *Knowing Your Place: Rural Identity and Cultural Hierarchy*. New York: Routledge, 1997.

Christian, Barbara. *Black Feminist Criticism: Perspectives on Black Women Writers*. New York: Pergamon Press, 1985.

Clarke, John Henrik, ed. *Malcolm X: The Man and His Times*. Trenton, N.J.: Africa World Press, 1990.

Cleaver, Eldridge. *Soul on Ice*. New York: Dell, 1968.

Clipper, Lawrence J. "Folkloric and Mythic Elements in *Invisible Man*." *CLA Journal* 13 (1970): 229–241.

Cloke, Paul, et al. *Writing the Rural: Five Cultural Geographies*. London: Paul Chapman, 1994.

Cloke, Paul, and Jo Little, eds. *Contested Countryside Cultures: Otherness, Marginalisation, and Rurality*. London: Routledge, 1997.

Close, Stacey K. *Elderly Slaves of the Plantation South*. New York: Garland, 1997.

Cobb, James C. *The Most Southern Place on Earth: The Mississippi Delta and the Roots of Regional Identity*. New York: Oxford University Press, 1992.

Cohen, Cathy J. *The Boundaries of Blackness: AIDS and the Breakdown of Black Politics*. Chicago: University of Chicago Press, 1999.

Cohen, Keith. *Film and Fiction: The Dynamics of Exchange*. New Haven: Yale University Press, 1979.

Collins, Patricia Hill. *Black Feminist Thought: Knowledge, Consciousness, and the Politics of Empowerment*. New York: Routledge, 1991.

Connor, Marlene Kim. *What Is Cool? Understanding Black Manhood in America*. Chicago: Agate, 2004.

Cooper, Michael. *Hell Fighters: African American Soldiers in World War I*. New York: Lodestar Books, 1997.

Crenshaw, Kimberlé Williams. "Demarginalizing the Intersection of Race and Sex: A Black Feminist Critique of Antidiscrimination Doctrine, Feminist Theory and Antiracist Politics." *University of Chicago Legal Forum*, 1989, 139–167.

Cripps, Thomas. "The Reaction of the Negro to the Motion Picture *Birth of a Nation*." *Historian* 25 (May 1963): 344–362.

—————. *Slow Fade to Black: The Negro in American Film, 1906–1942*. New York: Oxford University Press, 1977.

Cummings, Stephen. *The Dixification of America: The American Odyssey into the Conservative Economic Trap*. New York: Praeger, 1998.

Danbom, David B. *Born in the Country: A History of Rural America*. Baltimore: Johns Hopkins University Press, 1995.

Davidson, Cathy N., and Jessamyn Hatcher, eds. *No More Separate Spheres: A Next Wave in American Studies Reader*. Durham: Duke University Press, 2002.

Davies, Carole Boyce. *Black Women, Writing, and Identity: Migrations of the Subject*. New York: Routledge, 1994.

Davis, Angela Y. "Afro-Images: Politics, Fashion, and Nostalgia." *Critical Inquiry* 21 (Autumn 1994): 37–45.

—————. *Are Prisons Obsolete?* New York: Seven Stories, 2003.

—————. *Women, Race, and Class*. New York: Vintage, 1983.

Davis, Thadious. *Faulkner's "Negro": Art and the Social Context*. Baton Rouge: Louisiana State University Press, 1983.

Dawson, Graham. *Soldier Heroes: British Adventure, Empire and the Imaginary of Masculinity*. New York: Routledge, 1994.

Demastes, William. "Charles Fuller and *A Soldier's Play*: Attacking Prejudice, Challenging Form." *Studies in American Drama* 2 (Summer 1987): 42–56.

Derrida, Jacques. *Specters of Marx: The State of the Debt, the Work of Mourning, and the New International*. Trans. Peggy Kamuf. Durham: Duke University Press, 1994.

Dews, Carlos, and Carolyn Leste Law, eds. *Out in the South*. Philadelphia: Temple University Press, 2001.

Diawara, Manthia. "Black American Cinema: The New Realism." In *Black American Cinema*. Ed. Manthia Diawara. New York: Routledge, 1993. 3–25.

—————. "Englishness and Blackness: Cricket as Discourse on Colonialism." *Callaloo* 13 (1990): 830–844.

Dixon, Melvin. *Ride out the Wilderness: Geography and Identity in Afro-American Literature*. Urbana: University of Illinois Press, 1987.

Dixon, Thomas, Jr. *The Clansman*. Lexington: University of Kentucky Press, 1970.

Douglass, Frederick. "Lynch Law in the South." *North American Review* 155 (July 1892): 17–24.

—————. *Narrative of the Life of Frederick Douglass*. Ed. Houston A. Baker Jr. New York: Penguin, 1986.

Dray, Phillip. *At the Hands of Persons Unknown: The Lynching of Black America*. New York: Random House, 2002.

Du Bois, W. E. B. *Black Reconstruction in America, 1860–1880.* New York: Free Press, 1998.

———. *The Gift of Black Folk: The Negroes in the Making of America.* Millwood, N.Y.: Kraus-Thomson, 1975.

———. *John Brown.* Ed. David Roediger. New York: Modern Library, 2001.

DuCille, Ann. *The Coupling Convention: Sex, Text, and Tradition in Black Women's Fiction.* New York: Oxford University Press, 1993.

———. "The Unbearable Darkness of Being: 'Fresh' Thoughts on Race, Sex, and the Simpsons." In Morrison, *Birth of a Nation'hood,* 293–338.

Duck, Leigh Anne. "'Go There Tuh Know There': Zora Neale Hurston and the Chronotope of the Folk." *American Literary History* 13.2 (2001): 265–294.

Duncan, Nancy, ed. *Body Space: Destabilizing Geographies of Gender and Sexuality.* London: Routledge, 1996.

Dyer, Richard. "Into the Light: The Whiteness of the South in *The Birth of a Nation.*" In *Dixie Debates: Perspectives on Southern Cultures.* Ed. Richard H. King and Helen Taylor. Washington Square, N.Y.: New York University Press, 1996. 165–176.

Dyson, Michael Eric. *Between God and Gangsta Rap: Bearing Witness to Black Culture.* New York: Oxford University Press, 1996.

Eagles, Charles W. *Outside Agitator: Jon Daniels and the Civil Rights Movement in Alabama.* Chapel Hill, N.C.: University of North Carolina Press, 1993.

Early, Gerald. *The Culture of Bruising: Essays on Prizefighting, Literature, and Modern American Culture.* Hopewell, N.J.: Ecco, 1994.

Edwards, Brent Hayes. *The Practice of Diaspora: Literature, Translation, and the Rise of Black Internationalism.* Cambridge, Mass.: Harvard University Press, 2003.

———. "The Shadow of Shadows." *Positions: East Asia Cultures Critique* 11.1 (2003): 11–49.

Edwards, Junius. *If We Must Die.* Washington, D.C.: Howard University Press, 1984.

Ellison, Ralph. *Going to the Territory.* New York: Vintage, 1995.

———. *Invisible Man.* New York: Vintage, 1995.

Eng, David. *Racial Castration: Managing Masculinity in Asian America.* Durham: Duke University Press, 2001.

Epps, Archie, ed. *Malcolm X: Speeches at Harvard.* New York: Paragon House, 1991.

Fabre, Geneviève. "The Free Southern Theatre, 1963–1979." *Black American Literature Forum* 17 (1983): 55–59.

Fabre, Michel. *From Harlem to Paris: Black American Writers in France, 1840–1980.* Urbana: University of Illinois Press, 1991.

Faulkner, William. *Soldiers' Pay.* New York: Liveright, 1997.

Favor, J. Martin. *Authentic Blackness: The Folk in the New Negro Renaissance.* Durham: Duke University Press, 1999.

Felman, Shoshana. "Forms of Judicial Blindness, or the Evidence of What Cannot Be Seen: Traumatic Narratives and Legal Repetitions in the O. J. Simpson Case and in Tolstoy's *The Kreutzer Sonata.*" *Critical Inquiry* 23 (Summer 1997): 738–788.

Flake, Carol. *New Orleans: Behind the Masks of America's Most Exotic City.* New York: Grove, 1994.

Foner, Eric. *Reconstruction: America's Unfinished Revolution, 1863–1877.* New York: Harper & Row, 1988.

Fossett, Judith Jackson, Adam Gussaw, and Riché Richardson. "A Symposium: New Souths." *Mississippi Quarterly* 55 (2002): 569–612.

Frankenberg, Ruth. *White Women, Race Matters: The Social Construction of Whiteness.* Minneapolis: University of Minnesota Press, 1993.

———, ed. *Displacing Whiteness: Essays in Social and Cultural Criticism.* Durham: Duke University Press, 1997.

Franklin, John Hope. "*Birth of a Nation:* Propaganda as History." *Massachusetts Review* 20 (Autumn 1979): 417–434.

Friend, Craig Thompson, and Lorri Glover, eds. *Southern Manhood: Perspectives on Masculinity in the Old South.* Athens: University of Georgia Press, 2004.

Fuller, Charles. *A Soldier's Play.* New York: Noonday Press, 1981.

Gaines, Ernest J. *A Gathering of Old Men.* New York: Vintage, 1983.

Gaines, Jane. "*The Birth of a Nation* and *Within Our Gates:* Two Tales of the American South." In *Dixie Debates: Perspectives on Southern Cultures.* Ed. Richard H. King and Helen Taylor. Washington Square, N.Y.: New York University Press, 1996. 177–192.

Gaines, Kevin K. *Uplifting the Race: Black Leadership, Politics, and Culture in the Twentieth Century.* Chapel Hill: University of North Carolina Press, 1996.

Gates, Henry Louis, Jr. *Colored People: A Memoir.* New York: Alfred A. Knopf, 1994.

———. *The Signifying Monkey: A Theory of African-American Literary Criticism.* New York: Oxford University Press, 1988.

Gerster, Patrick, and Nicholas Cords, eds. *Myth and Southern History: The New South.* 2nd ed. Vol. 2. Urbana: University of Illinois Press, 1989.

Gibson, Donald. "Chapter One of Booker T. Washington's *Up From Slavery* and the Feminization of the African American Male." In *Representing Black Men.* Ed. Marcellus Blount and George P. Cunningham. New York: Routledge, 1996. 95–110.

Giddings, Paula. "The Last Taboo." In Morrison, *Race-ing Justice, En-gendering Power,* 441–465.

————. *When and Where I Enter: The Impact of Black Women on Race and Sex in America*. New York: Bantam, 1984.

Gill, James. *Lords of Misrule: Mardi Gras and the Politics of Race in New Orleans*. Jackson: University Press of Mississippi, 1997.

Gilman, Sander. *Difference and Pathology: Stereotypes of Sexuality, Race, and Madness*. Ithaca: Cornell University Press, 1985.

Gilroy, Paul. *Small Acts: Thoughts on the Politics of Black Culture*. New York: Serpent's Tail, 1993.

————. *There Ain't No Black in the Union Jack*. London: Hutchinson, 1987.

Ginsberg, Elaine K., ed. *Passing and the Fictions of Identity*. Durham: Duke University Press, 1996.

Ginzburg, Ralph. *One Hundred Years of Lynching*. Baltimore: Black Classic Press, 1962.

Glissant, Edouard. *Caribbean Discourse: Selected Essays*. Trans. J. Michael Dash. Charlottesville: University Press of Virginia, 1989.

Goings, Kenneth. *Mammy and Uncle Mose*. Bloomington: Indiana University Press, 1994.

Goldfield, David. *Region, Race and Cities: Interpreting the Urban South*. Baton Rouge: Louisiana State University Press, 1997.

Gordon, Avery. *Ghostly Matters: Haunting and the Sociological Imagination*. Minneapolis: University of Minnesota Press, 1997.

Gray, Fred D. *The Tuskegee Syphilis Study: An Insider's Account of the Shocking Medical Experiment Conducted by Government Doctors against African American Men*. Montgomery: New South Books, 1998.

Grewal, Inderpal. *Home and Harem: Nation, Gender, Empire, and the Culture of Travel*. Durham: Duke University Press, 1996.

Griffin, Farah Jasmine. *"Who Set You Flowin'": The African American Migration Narrative*. New York: Oxford University Press, 1995.

Griffin, Larry J., and Don H. Doyle, eds. *The South as an American Problem*. Athens: University of Georgia Press, 1995.

Griggs, Sutton. *Imperium in Imperio: A Study of the Negro Race Problem: A Novel*. North Stratford, N.H.: Ayer, 2001.

Grossman, James R. *Land of Hope: Chicago, Black Southerners, and the Great Migration*. Chicago: University of Chicago Press, 1991.

Grow, Lawrence. *The Old House Book of Cottages and Bungalows*. Pittstown, N.J.: Main Street Press, 1987.

Guha, Ranajit. *Dominance without Hegemony: History and Power in Colonial India*. Cambridge, Mass.: Harvard University Press, 1997.

————, ed. *Elementary Aspects of Peasant Insurgency in Colonial India*. Durham: Duke University Press, 1999.

————, ed. *Subaltern Studies Reader, 1986–1995*. Minneapolis: University of Minnesota Press, 1997.

Guha, Ranajit, and Gayatri Chakravorty Spivak, eds. *Selected Subaltern Studies*. New York: Oxford University Press, 1988.

Gunning, Sandra. *Race, Rape, and Lynching: The Red Record of American Literature, 1890–1912*. New York: Oxford University Press, 1996.

Guy-Sheftall, Beverly. *Daughters of Sorrow: Attitudes Toward Black Women, 1880–1920*. Brooklyn, N.Y.: Carlson, 1990.

Hale, Grace Elizabeth. *Making Whiteness: How White People Profit from Identity Politics*. Philadelphia: Temple University Press, 1998.

Hamann, Jack. *On American Soil: How Justice Became a Casualty of World War II*. Chapel Hill: Algonquin Books, 2005.

Harding, Sandra. *The Racial Economy of Science: Toward a Democratic Future*. Bloomington: Indiana University Press, 1993.

Harper, Phillip Brian. *Are We Not Men? Masculine Anxiety and the Problem of African-American Identity*. New York: Oxford University Press, 1996.

Harriott, Esther. *American Voices: Five Contemporary Playwrights in Essays and Interviews*. Jefferson, N.C.: McFarland, 1988.

Harris, Trudier. "Ellison's 'Peter Wheatstraw': His Basis in Black Folk Tradition." *Mississippi Folklore Register* 9 (1975): 117–126.

————. *Exorcising Blackness: Historical and Literary Lynching and Burning Rituals*. Bloomington: Indiana University Press, 1984.

————. *From Mammies to Militants: Domestics in Black American Literature*. Philadelphia: Temple University Press, 1982.

————. *The Power of the Porch: The Storyteller's Craft in Zora Neale Hurston, Gloria Naylor, and Randall Kenan*. Athens: University of Georgia Press, 1996.

Hay, Samuel A. *African American Theatre: An Historical and Critical Analysis*. New York: Cambridge University Press, 1994.

Hefferman, James A. W. "The Simpson Trial and the Forgotten Trauma of Lynching: A Response to Shoshana Felman." *Critical Inquiry* 25.4 (Summer 1999): 801–806.

Henderson, Mae Gwendolyn. "Toni Morrison's *Beloved*: Re-Membering the Body as Historical Text." In *Comparative American Identities: Race, Sex, and Nationality in the Modern Text*. Ed. Hortense Spillers. New York: Routledge, 1991. 62–86.

————. " 'Where by the Way, Is This Train Going?': A Case for Black (Cultural) Studies." *Callaloo* 19 (Winter 1996): 60–67.

Hernton, Calvin. *The Sexual Mountain and Black Women Writers: Adventures in Sex, Literature, and Real Life*. New York: Anchor Books, 1987.

Higginson, Thomas Wentworth. *Army Life in a Black Regiment*. Boston: Beacon Press, 1962.

Hilliard, David. *This Side of Glory: The Autobiography of David Hilliard and the Story of the Black Panther Party*. New York: Lawrence Hill Books, 1993.

Hine, Darlene Clark. "Rape and the Inner Lives of Black Women in the Middle West: Preliminary Thoughts on the Culture of Dissemblance." In *Unequal Sisters: A Multicultural Reader in U.S. Women's History*. Ed. Ellen Du Bois and Vicki L. Ruiz. New York: Routledge, 1990. 272–297.

Hine, Darlene Clark, and Earnestine Jenkins, eds. *A Question of Manhood: A Reader in U.S. Black Men's History and Masculinity*. Vol. 1. Bloomington: Indiana University Press, 1999.

hooks, bell. *Ain't I a Woman: Black Women and Feminism*. Boston: South End Press, 1981.

———. *Black Looks: Race and Representation*. Boston: South End Press, 1992.

———. *Outlaw Culture: Resisting Representations*. New York: Routledge, 1994.

———. *Reel to Real: Race, Sex and Class at the Movies*. New York: Routledge, 1996.

———. *Talking Back: Thinking Feminist, Thinking Black*. Boston: South End Press, 1989.

———. *We Real Cool: Black Men and Masculinity*. New York: Routledge, 2004.

Horne, Gerald. "Myth and the Making of 'Malcolm X.'" *American Historical Review* 98 (1993): 440–451.

Howard, John. *Men Like That: A Southern Queer History*. Chicago: University of Chicago Press, 1999.

Hsiung, David C. *Two Worlds in the Tennessee Mountains: Exploring the Origins of Appalachian Stereotypes*. Lexington: University of Kentucky Press, 1997.

Hughes, George. *Reading Novels*. Nashville: Vanderbilt University Press, 2002.

Hughes, Linda K., and Howard Faulkner. "The Role of Detection in *A Soldier's Play*." *Clues* 7 (1986): 83–97.

Huie, William Bradford. *Did the F.B.I. Kill Martin Luther King?* Nashville, Tenn.: Thomas Nelson, 1977.

———. *He Slew the Dreamer: My Search with James Earl Ray for the Truth about the Murder of Martin Luther King*. New York: Delacorte, 1970.

———. *The Klansman*. New York: Delacorte, 1967.

———. *Three Lives for Mississippi*. New York: Whitney Communications, 1965.

Hull, Gloria T., Patricia Bell Scott, and Barbara Smith. *All the Women Are White, All the Blacks Are Men, but Some of Us Are Brave: Black Women's Studies*. New York: Feminist Press, 1982.

Hunter, Tera W. *To 'Joy My Freedom: Southern Black Women's Lives and Labors after the Civil War*. Cambridge, Mass.: Harvard University Press, 1997.

Ignatiev, Noel. *How the Irish Became White*. New York: Routledge, 1995.

Jackson, John. *Race, Racism, and Science: Social Impact and Interaction*. Santa Barbara, Calif.: ABC-Clio, 2004.

Jackson, Lawrence. *Ralph Ellison: Emergence of Genius*. New York: John Wiley & Sons, 2002.

James, Darius. *That's Blaxploitation: Roots of the Baadasssss 'Tude (Rated X by an All' Whyte Jury)*. New York: St. Martin's, 1995.

Jeffries, John. "Toward a Redefinition of the Urban: The Collision of Culture." In *Black Popular Culture: A Project by Michele Wallace*. Ed. Gina Dent. New York: New Press, 1992. 153–163.

Johnson, James Weldon. *Lynching, America's National Disgrace*. New York: National Association for the Advancement of Colored People, 1924.

Johnson, Michael K. *Black Masculinity and the Frontier Myth in American Literature*. Norman: University of Oklahoma Press, 2002.

Jones, Anne Goodwyn, and Susan V. Donaldson, eds. *Haunted Bodies: Gender and Southern Texts*. Charlottesville: University of Virginia Press, 1998.

Jones, Jacqueline. *Labor of Love, Labor of Sorrow: Black Women, Work and the Family from Slavery to the Present*. New York: Vintage, 1985.

Jones, Jacquie. "The Accusatory Space." In *Black Popular Culture*. Ed. Gina Dent. New York: Routledge, 1991. 94–98.

Jones, James H. *Bad Blood: The Tuskegee Syphilis Experiment*. Rev. ed. New York: Free Press, 1993.

———. "The Tuskegee Syphilis Experiment: 'A Moral Astigmatism.'" In *The Racial Economy of Science: Toward a Democratic Future*. Ed. Sandra Harding. Bloomington: Indiana University Press, 1993. 275–286.

Kaplan, Amy, and Donald Pease, eds. *Cultures of United States Imperialism*. Durham: Duke University Press, 1993.

Kaplan, Caren. *Questions of Travel: Postmodern Discourses of Displacement*. Durham: Duke University Press, 1996.

Karenga, Maulana. "The Million Man March / Day of Absence Mission Statement." *Black Scholar* 25 (1995): 2–11.

Karim, Imam Benjamin, ed. *Malcolm X: The End of White World Supremacy*. New York: Arcade, 1971.

Kelley, Robin D. G. *Hammer and Hoe: Alabama Communists during the Great Depression*. Chapel Hill: University of North Carolina Press, 1990.

———. "House Negroes on the Loose: Malcolm X and the Black Bourgeoisie." *Callaloo* 21 (1998): 419–435.

———. *Race Rebels: Culture, Politics, and the Black Working Class*. New York: Free Press, 1994.

———. "The Riddle of the Zoot: Malcolm Little and Black Cultural Politics during World War II." In *Malcolm X: In Our Own Image*. Ed. Joe Wood. New York: Doubleday, 1992. 155–182.

Kent, George. "Ralph Ellison and Afro-American Folk and Cultural Traditions." In *Speaking for You: The Vision of Ralph Ellison*. Ed. Kimberly W. Benston. Washington, D.C.: Howard University Press, 1987. 95–124.

Kern-Foxworth, Marilyn. *Aunt Jemima, Uncle Ben, and Rastus: Blacks in Advertising, Yesterday, Today and Tomorrow*. Westport, Conn.: Greenwood, 1994.

Killens, John Oliver. *And Then We Heard the Thunder*. Washington, D.C.: Howard University Press, 1984.

Killens, John Oliver, and Jerry Ward, eds. *Black Southern Voices: An Anthology of Fiction, Poetry, Drama, Nonfiction, and Critical Essays*. New York: Penguin, 1992.

Kipnis, Laura. "The Stepdaughter's Story: Scandals National and Transnational." *Social Text* 58 (Spring 1999): 59–73.

Koster, Rick. *Louisiana Music: A Journey from R&B to Zydeco, Jazz to Country, Blues to Gospel, Cajun Music to Swamp Pop to Carnival Music and Beyond*. Cambridge: Da Capo Press, 2002.

Koven, Mikel J. *Blaxploitation Films*. New York: Trafalgar Square Books, 2001.

Kristeva, Julia. *Powers of Horror: An Essay on Abjection*. Trans. Leon S. Roudiez. New York: Columbia University Press, 1982.

Lane, Christopher, ed. *The Psychoanalysis of Race*. New York: Columbia University Press, 1998.

Lang, Robert, ed. *The Birth of a Nation*. New Brunswick, N.J.: Rutgers University Press, 1994.

Larsen, Nella. *Quicksand*. New York: Penguin, 2003.

Larson, Edward J. *Sex, Race, and Science: Eugenics in the Deep South*. Baltimore: Johns Hopkins University Press, 1995.

Lavie, Smadar, and Ted Swedenberg, eds. *Displacement, Diaspora and Geographies of Identity*. Durham: Duke University Press, 1996.

Lee, Spike, and Lisa Jones. *Uplift the Race: The Construction of School Daze*. New York: Simon & Schuster, 1998.

Lee, Ulysses. *The United States Army in World War II, Special Studies: The Employment of Negro Troops*. Washington, D.C.: Center of Military History, the United States Army, 1994.

Lefebvre, Henri. *The Production of Space*. Trans. Donald Nicholson-Smith. Cambridge, Mass.: Blackwell, 1991.

Lemann, Nicholas. *The Promised Land: The Great Migration and How It Changed America*. New York: Vintage, 1991.

Lerner, Gerda. *Black Women in White America*. New York: Vintage, 1973.

Levine, Philippa. *Prostitution, Race and Politics: Policing Venereal Disease in the British Empire*. New York: Routledge, 2003.

————. "Race, Sex, and Colonial Soldiery in World War I." *Journal of Women's History* 9 (Winter 1998): 104–130.

Lewis, Samella, ed. *Black Artists on Art*. Los Angeles: Contemporary Crafts, 1969.

Lhamon, W. T., Jr. *Raising Cain: Blackface Performance from Jim Crow to Hip Hop*. Cambridge, Mass.: Harvard University Press, 1998.

Linard, Colonel. "Secret Information Concerning Black American Troops." Quoted in Barbeau and Henri, *Unknown Soldiers*, 114–115.

Linfield, Susie. "The Education of Kathleen Neal Cleaver." *Transition* 77 (2000): 172–195.

Litwack, Leon F. *Trouble in Mind: Black Southerners in the Age of Jim Crow*. New York: Alfred A. Knopf, 1998.

Long, Margaret. "Black Power in the Black Belt." *Progressive* 30 (Oct. 1966): 23.

Lorrigio, Francesco. "Regionalism and Theory." In *Regionalism Reconsidered: New Approaches to the Field*. Ed. David Jordan. New York: Garland, 1994. 3–27.

Lubiano, Wahneema. "Black Ladies, Welfare Queens, and State Minstrels: Ideological War by Narrative Means." In Morrison, *Race-ing Justice, Engendering Power*, 323–363.

————. "'But Compared to What?': Reading Realism, Representation, and Essentialism in *Do the Right Thing*, *School Daze*, and the Spike Lee Discourse." In *Representing Black Men*. Ed. Marcellus Blount and George Cunningham. New York: Routledge, 1996. 173–204.

Majors, Richard, and Janet Mancini Billson. *Cool Pose: The Dilemmas of Black Manhood in America*. New York: Simon & Schuster, 1992.

Manring, M. M. *Slave in a Box: The Strange Career of Aunt Jemima*. Charlottesville: University Press of Virginia, 1998.

Marks, Carole. *Farewell—We're Good and Gone: The Great Black Migration*. Bloomington: Indiana University Press, 1989.

Massey, Doreen. *Space, Place, and Gender*. Minneapolis: University of Minnesota Press, 1994.

Maxwell, William J. "'Is It True What They Say about Dixie?': Richard Wright, Zora Neale Hurston, and Rural/Urban Exchange in Modern African-American Literature." In *Knowing Your Place: Rural Identity and Cultural Hierarchy*. Ed. Barbara Ching and Gerald W. Creed. New York: Routledge, 1997. 71–104.

McClintock, Anne. "'No Longer in a Future Heaven': Gender, Race and Nationalism." In *Dangerous Liaisons: Gender, Nation, and Postcolonial Perspectives*. Ed. Anne McClintock, Aamir Mufti, and Ella Shohat. Minneapolis: University of Minnesota Press, 1997. 89–112.

McDowell, Deborah E. "Pecs and Reps: Muscling in on Race and the Subject of Masculinities." In *Race and the Subject of Masculinities*. Ed. Harry Stecopoulos and Michael Uebel. Durham: Duke University Press, 1997. 361–385.

McGuire, Phillip. *Taps for a Jim Crow Army: Letters from Black Soldiers in World War II.* Santa Barbara, Calif.: ABC-Clio, 1983.

McPherson, Tara. *Reconstructing Dixie: Race, Gender, and Nostalgia in the Imagined South.* Durham: Duke University Press, 2003.

Mercer, Kobena. *Welcome to the Jungle: New Positions in Black Cultural Studies.* London: Routledge, 1994.

Miller, Andrew T. "Social Science, Social Policy, and the Heritage of the African-American Family." In *The "Underclass" Debate: Views from History.* Ed. Michael B. Katz. Princeton, N.J.: Princeton University Press, 1993. 254–292.

Mitchell, Elvis. "Spike Lee: The *Playboy* Interview." In *Spike Lee Interviews.* Ed. Cynthia Fuchs. Jackson: University Press of Mississippi, 2002. 155.

Moraga, Cherríe, and Gloria Anzaldúa, eds. *This Bridge Called My Back: Writings by Radical Women of Color.* New York: Kitchen Table / Women of Color Press, 1981.

Morrison, Toni. *The Bluest Eye.* New York: Plume, 1994.

———. *Song of Solomon.* New York: Alfred A. Knopf, 1977.

———, ed. *Birth of a Nation'hood: Gaze, Script, and Spectacle in the O. J. Simpson Case.* New York: Pantheon, 1997.

———. *Playing in the Dark: Whiteness and the Literary Imagination.* New York: Vintage, 1993.

———, ed. *Race-ing Justice, En-gendering Power: Essays on Anita Hill, Clarence Thomas, and the Construction of Social Reality.* New York: Pantheon, 1992.

Morton, Patricia. *Disfigured Images: The Historical Assault on African American Women.* New York: Praeger, 1991.

Moses, Wilson Jeremiah. *Black Messiahs and Uncle Toms: Social and Literary Manipulations of a Religious Myth.* University Park: Pennsylvania State University Press, 1982.

Moynihan, Daniel P. *The Negro Family: The Case for National Action.* Washington, D.C.: n.p., 1965.

Murray, Albert. *The Omni-Americans: New Perspectives on Black Experience and American Culture.* New York: Avon, 1971.

Nalbantoglu, G. B., and C. T. Wong, eds. *Postcolonial Space(s).* New York: Princeton Architectural Press, 1997.

Nalty, Bernard. *Strength for the Fight: A History of Black Americans in the Military.* New York: Free Press, 1986.

Nalty, Bernard C., and Morris J. MacGregor, eds. *Blacks in the Military: Essential Documents.* Wilmington, Del.: Scholarly Resources, 1981.

Naylor, Gloria. *Bailey's Café.* New York: Vintage, 1992.

Neal, Larry. "Ellison's Zoot Suit." In *Ralph Ellison: A Collection of Critical Essays.* Ed. John Hersey. Englewood Cliffs, N.J.: Prentice Hall, 1970. 58–79.

Nelson, Dana D. *National Manhood: Capitalist Citizenship and the Imagined Fraternity of White Men.* Durham: Duke University Press, 1998.

Newton, Huey P. *Revolutionary Suicide.* With the Assistance of J. Herman Blake. New York: Writers and Readers, 1995.

Nicholls, David G. *Conjuring the Folk: Forms of Modernity in African America.* Ann Arbor: University of Michigan Press, 2000.

Olaniyan, Tejumola. *Scars of Conquest / Masks of Resistance: The Invention of Cultural Identities in African, African-American, and Caribbean Drama.* New York: Oxford University Press, 1995.

O'Meally, Robert. *The Craft of Ralph Ellison.* Cambridge, Mass.: Harvard University Press, 1980.

―――. "Riffs and Rituals: Folklore in the Work of Ralph Ellison." In *Afro-American Literature: The Reconstruction of Instruction.* Ed. Dexter Fisher and Robert B. Stepto. New York: MLA, 1979. 153–169.

Park, You-me, and Gayle Wald. "Native Daughters and the Promised Land: Gender, Race, and the Question of Separate Spheres." In *No More Separate Spheres.* Ed. Cathy N. Davidson. *American Literature* 70 (Fall 1998): 607–633.

Patterson, Orlando. *Rituals of Blood: Consequences of Slavery in Two American Centuries.* New York: Basic Books, 1998.

Patton, Phil. "Mammy: Her Life and Times." *American Heritage,* Sept. 1993, 78–87.

Pearson, Hugh. *The Shadow of the Panther: Huey Newton and the Price of Black Power in America.* Reading, Mass.: Perseus Books, 1994.

Perry, Bruce. *Malcolm: The Life of a Man Who Changed America.* New York: Station Hill Press, 1991.

Pierce-Baker, Charlotte. *Surviving the Silence: Black Women's Stories of Rape.* New York: W. W. Norton, 1998.

Pile, Steve. *The Body and the City: Psychoanalysis, Space, and Subjectivity.* New York: Routledge, 1996.

―――. "Masculinism, the Use of Dualistic Epistemologies and Third Spaces." *Antipode* 26 (Fall 1994): 255–277.

Powell, Richard J. *Black Art and Culture in the Twentieth Century.* London: Thames & Hudson, 1997.

Pratt, Mary Louise. *Imperial Eyes: Travel Writing and Transculturation.* New York: Routledge, 1992.

Rampersad, Arnold. "The Color of His Eyes: Bruce Perry's *Malcolm* and Malcolm's *Malcolm.*" In *In Our Own Image.* Ed. Joe Wood. New York: Anchor Books / Doubleday, 1992. 117–133.

Reed, Adolph. *Stirrings in the Jug: Black Politics in the Post-Segregation Era.* Minneapolis: University of Minnesota Press, 1999.

Reid, Mark, ed. *Spike Lee's* Do the Right Thing. New York: Cambridge University Press, 1997.

Reid-Pharr, Robert. "'Tearing the Goat's Flesh: Homosexuality, Abjection and the Production of a Late Twentieth-Century Black Masculinity." *Studies in the Novel* 28 (Fall 1995): 372–394.

Reverby, Susan M. *Tuskegee's Truths: Rethinking the Tuskegee Syphilis Study*. Chapel Hill: University of North Carolina Press, 2000.

Richards, Sandra L. "Writing the Absent Potential: Drama, Performance, and the Canon of African American Literature." In *Performance and Performativity*. Ed. Andrew Parker and Eve Kosofsky Sedgwick. New York: Routledge, 1995. 64–88.

Richardson, Riché. "Southern Turns." *Mississippi Quarterly* 56 (2003): 555–579.

Riggs, Marlon T. "Black Macho Revisited: Reflections of a SNAP! Queen." In *Black Men on Race, Gender and Sexuality: A Critical Reader*. Ed. Devon Carbado. New York: New York University Press, 1999. 306–311.

Roberts, Diane. *The Myth of Aunt Jemima: Representations of Race and Region*. New York: Routledge, 1994.

Roberts, John W. *From Trickster to Badman: The Black Folk Hero in Slavery and Freedom*. Philadelphia: University of Pennsylvania Press, 1989.

Robinson, Angelo Rich. "Race, Place, and Space: Remaking Whiteness in the Post-Reconstruction South." *Southern Literary Journal* 35 (Spring 2002): 97–107.

Rony, Fatimah Tobing. *The Third Eye: Race, Cinema, and Ethnographic Spectacle*. Durham: Duke University Press, 1996.

Rose, Gillian. *Feminism and Geography: The Limits of Geographical Knowledge*. Minneapolis: University of Minnesota Press, 1993.

Rose, Tricia. *Black Noise: Rap Music and Black Culture in Contemporary America*. Hanover, N.H.: Wesleyan University Press, 1994.

Ross, Marlon. "Camping the Dirty Dozens: The Queer Resources of Black Nationalist Invective." *Callaloo* 23 (2000): 290–312.

———. *Manning the Race: Reforming Black Men in the Jim Crow Era*. New York: New York University Press, 2004.

Rubin, Louis D. "Uncle Remus and the Ubiquitous White Rabbit." *Southern Review* 10 (1974): 787–804.

Russo, Peggy A. "Uncle Walt's Uncle Remus: Disney's Distortion of Harris's Hero." *Southern Literary Journal* 25 (Fall 1992): 19–32.

Scott, Emmett. *The American Negro in the World War*. Chicago: Homewood, 1919.

Seale, Bobby. *Seize the Time: The Story of the Black Panther Party and Huey P. Newton*. Baltimore, Md.: Black Classics Press, 1991.

Sears, James. *Rebels, Rubyfruit, and Rhinestones: Queering Space in the Stonewall South*. New Brunswick, N.J.: Rutgers University Press, 2001.

Segars, John H., R. B. Rosenburg, and Charles Kelly Barrow, eds. *Black Confederates*. Gretna, La.: Pelican, 2001.

Sibley, David. *Geographies of Exclusion: Society and Differences in the West*. New York: Routledge, 1995.

Silverman, Kaja. *Male Subjectivity at the Margins*. New York: Routledge, 1992.

Simmons, Russell. *Life and Def: Sex, Drugs, Money, and God*. New York: Three Rivers Press, 2001.

Simpson, David. *The Academic Postmodern and the Rule of Literature: A Report on Half-Knowledge*. Chicago: University of Chicago Press, 1995.

Singa, Mrinalini. *Colonial Masculinity: The "Manly Englishman" and the "Effeminate Bengali" in the Late Nineteenth Century*. Manchester, UK: Manchester University Press, 1995.

Slotkin, Richard. "Unit Pride: Ethnic Platoons and the Myths of American Nationality." *American Literary History* 13 (Fall 2001): 469–498.

Smith, Barbara, ed. *Home Girls: A Black Feminist Anthology*. New York: Kitchen Table / Women of Color Press, 1983.

Smith, Jon, and Deborah Cohn, eds. *Look Away! The U.S. South in New World Studies*. Durham: Duke University Press, 2004.

Smith, Neil, and Anne Godlewska. "Critical Histories of Geography." In *Geography and Empire*. Oxford, UK: Blackwell, 1994. 1–8.

Smith, Valerie. *Not Just Race, Not Just Gender: Black Feminist Readings*. New York: Routledge, 1998.

Soja, Edward. *Postmodern Geographies: The Reassertion of Space in Critical Social Theory*. London: Verso, 1989.

————. *Third Space: Journeys to Los Angeles and Other Real and Imagined Places*. Cambridge: Blackwell, 1996.

Southern, Eileen. *The Music of Black America: A History*. 2nd ed. New York: W. W. Norton, 1971.

Spillers, Hortense. *Black, White, and in Color: Essays on American Literature and Culture*. Chicago: University of Chicago Press, 2003.

————. "Changing the Letter: The Yokes, the Jokes of Discourse, or, Mrs. Stowe, Mr. Reed." In *Uncle Tom's Cabin*. Ed. Elizabeth Ammons. New York: W. W. Norton, 1994. 501–522.

————. "Mama's Baby, Papa's Maybe: An American Grammar Book." In *Within the Circle: An Anthology of African American Literary Criticism from the Harlem Renaissance to the Present*. Ed. Angelyn Mitchell. Durham: Duke University Press, 1994. 554–581.

————. " 'The Permanent Obliquity of an In(pha)llibly Straight': In the Time of the Daughters and the Fathers." In *Changing Our Own Words: Essays on*

Criticism, Theory, and Writing by Black Women. Ed. Cheryl Wall. New York: Routledge, 1989. 127–149.

Stack, Carol. *Call to Home: African Americans Reclaim the Rural South.* New York: Basic Books, 1996.

Stanton, Mary. *From Selma to Sorrow: The Life and Death of Viola Liuzzo.* Athens: University of Georgia Press, 1998.

Stecopoulos, Harry, and Michael Uebel, eds. *Race and the Subject of Masculinity.* Durham: Duke University Press, 1996.

Steiner, Michael, and Clarence Mondale. *Region and Regionalism in the United States: A Source Book for the Humanities and Social Sciences.* New York: Garland, 1988.

Stewart, Kathleen. *A Space on the Side of the Road: Cultural Poetics in an "Other America."* Princeton, N.J.: Princeton University Press, 1996.

Storhoff, Gary. "Reflections of Identity in *A Soldier's Story.*" *Literature-Film Quarterly* 19 (1991): 21–26.

Stowe, Harriet Beecher. *Uncle Tom's Cabin.* Ed. Elizabeth Ammons. Norton Critical Edition. New York: W. W. Norton, 1994.

Sunnemark, Fredrick. *Ring Out Freedom! The Voice of Martin Luther King, Jr., and the Making of the Civil Rights Movement.* Bloomington: Indiana University Press, 2004.

Tate, Claudia. *Psychoanalysis and Black Novels: Desire and the Protocols of Race.* New York: Oxford University Press, 1998.

Tate, Greg. *Flyboy in the Buttermilk: Essays on Contemporary America.* New York: Simon & Schuster, 1992.

Taylor, Clyde. "The Re-birth of the Aesthetic in Cinema." *Wide Angle* 13.3–4 (July–Oct. 1991): 12–30.

Terry, Jennifer, and Jacqueline Urla, eds. *Deviant Bodies: Critical Perspectives on Difference in Science and Popular Culture.* Bloomington: Indiana University Press, 1995.

Thomas, Kendall. "'Ain't Nothing Like the Real Thing': Black Masculinity, Gay Sexuality, and the Jargon of Authenticity." In *Representing Black Men.* Ed. Marcellus Blount and George P. Cunningham. New York: Routledge, 1996. 55–69.

Tillich, Paul. *The Courage to Be.* New Haven: Yale University Press, 1952.

Toomer, Jean. *Cane.* Ed. Darwin T. Turner. Norton Critical Edition. New York: W. W. Norton, 1988.

Trotter, Joe William. *The Great Migration in Historical Perspective: New Dimensions of Race, Class and Gender.* Bloomington: Indiana University Press, 1991.

Tuan, Mia. *Forever Foreigners or Honorary Whites? The Asian Ethnic Experience Today.* New Brunswick, N.J.: Rutgers University Press, 1999.

Ture, Kwame (formerly Stokely Carmichael), and Charles V. Hamilton. *Black Power: The Politics of Liberation.* New York: Vintage, 1992.

Turner, Patricia A. *Celluloid Uncles and Ceramic Mammies.* New York: Anchor Books, 1994.

"Violence Comes to a Southern Town: New Movie, *The Klansman* Examines the Anatomy of Black-White, White-White Relationships." *Ebony* 30.2 (Dec. 1974): 149.

Wallace, Maurice O. *Constructing the Black Masculine: Identity and Ideality in African American Men's Literature and Culture, 1775–1995.* Durham: Duke University Press, 2002.

Wallace, Michele. *Black Macho and the Myth of the Superwoman.* New York: Dial Press, 1978.

———. "*Uncle Tom's Cabin:* Before and After the Jim Crow Era." *Drama Review* 44 (Spring 2000): 137–156.

Ward, Joseph P., et al. *Britain and the American South: From Colonialism to Rock and Roll.* Jackson: University Press of Mississippi, 2003.

Warren, Kenneth W. *So Black and Blue: Ralph Ellison and the Occasion of Criticism.* Chicago: University of Chicago Press, 2003.

Wells-Barnett, Ida. *Southern Horrors: Lynch Laws in All Its Phases.* New York: Age Print, 1892. Reprint, Arno Press and *New York Times*, 1969.

Wexler, Laura. *Fire in a Canebrake: The Last Mass Lynching in America.* New York: Scribner, 2003.

White, Deborah Gray. *Ar'nt I a Woman? Female Slaves in the Plantation South.* New York: W. W. Norton, 1985.

White, Shane, and Graham White. *Stylin': African American Expressive Culture from Its Beginnings to the Zoot Suit.* Ithaca: Cornell University Press, 1998.

White, Walter. *Rope and Faggot: A Biography of Judge Lynch.* New York: Alfred A. Knopf, 1929.

Whitehead, Colson. *The Intuitionist.* New York: Anchor Books, 2000.

Whyte, Philippe. "*Invisible Man* as a Trickster Tale." In *Ralph Ellison's Invisible Man: Modern Critical Interpretations.* Ed. Harold Bloom. Philadelphia: Chelsea House, 1999. 61–80.

Wiegman, Robyn. *American Anatomies: Theorizing Race and Gender.* Durham: Duke University Press, 1995.

Williams, John A. *Captain Blackman: A Novel.* Garden City, N.Y.: Doubleday, 1972.

Williams, J. W. *Hillbillyland: What the Movies Did to the Mountains and the Mountains Did to the Movies.* Chapel Hill: University of North Carolina Press, 1995.

Williams, Linda. *Playing the Race Card: Melodramas of Black and White from Uncle Tom to O. J. Simpson.* Princeton, N.J.: Princeton University Press, 2001.

Williams, Patricia J. "Clarence X, Man of the People." In *In Our Own Image*. Ed. Joe Wood. New York: Anchor Books / Doubleday, 1992. 190–202.

Williams, Robert F. *Negroes with Guns*. Detroit: Wayne State University Press, 1998.

Wilson, Harriet. *Our Nig*. Ed. Henry Louis Gates Jr. New York: Vintage, 1983.

Witt, Doris. *Black Hunger: Food and the Politics of U.S. Identity*. New York: Oxford University Press, 1999.

Wolcott, Victoria W. "Mediums, Messages, and Lucky Numbers: African American Female Spiritualists and Numbers Runners in Interwar Detroit." In *The Geography of Identity*. Ed. Patricia Yaeger. Ann Arbor: University of Michigan Press, 1996. 273–306.

Wood, Peter. *Black Majority: Negroes in Colonial South Carolina from 1670 to the Stono Rebellion*. New York: Alfred A. Knopf, 1974.

Woodward, C. Vann. *The Burden of Southern History*. Baton Rouge: Louisiana State University Press, 1960.

———. *The Strange Career of Jim Crow*. New York: Oxford University Press, 1955.

Wray, Matt, and Annalee Newlitz, eds. *White Trash: Race and Class in America*. New York: Routledge, 1996.

Wright, George C. *Racial Violence in Kentucky, 1865–1940: Lynchings, Mob Rule and Legal Lynchings*. Baton Rouge: Louisiana State University Press, 1990.

Wright, Richard. *Native Son*. New York: Harper & Row, 1989.

———. *Uncle Tom's Children*. New York: Harper & Row, 1989.

Wyatt-Brown, Bertram. *Southern Honor: Ethics and Behavior in the Old South*. New York: Oxford University Press, 1982.

X, Malcolm. *The Autobiography of Malcolm X*. As told to Alex Haley. New York: Grove Press, 1966. Reprint, New York: Ballantine, 1992.

———. *By Any Means Necessary*. Ed. George Breitman. New York: Pathfinder, 1992.

———. *Malcolm X: The Last Speeches*. Ed. Bruce Perry. New York: Pathfinder, 1989.

———. *Malcolm X Speaks: Selected Speeches and Statements*. Ed. George Breitman. New York: Grove/Weidenfeld, 1990.

———. *Malcolm X Talks to Young People: Speeches in the U.S., Britain and Africa*. Ed. Steve Clark. New York: Pathfinder, 1991.

Yaeger, Patricia. *Dirt and Desire: Reconstructing Southern Women's Writing, 1930–1990*. Chicago: University of Chicago Press, 2000.

———, ed. *The Geography of Identity*. Ann Arbor: University of Michigan Press, 1996.

Yarborough, Richard. "Strategies of Black Characterization in *Uncle Tom's Cabin* and the Early Afro-American Novel." In *New Essays on* Uncle Tom's Cabin. Ed. Eric Sundquist. New York: Cambridge University Press, 1986. 45–84.

INDEX

abjection: and blackness, 64, 128; and blacks in nation, 24; bodily, 151; and C. J. in *A Soldier's Play*, 106, 112; and geography, 100; and Julia Kristeva, 8, 85, 100, 139, 215; within psychoanalysis, 8; racial, 140; rural, 136, 146, 151; southern, 8, 13, 14; and World War II, 85

activism, black, 52

affirmative action, 78

African American: agrarian life, 129; culture and rap, 202; "folk," 126, 132; folklore, 33; gangsta rap, 211; identity, 5, 9–10, 90, 141; literary criticism, 129; literary history, 33; literary studies and *A Soldier's Play*, 82, 89, 90; masculinity, 14; national culture, 128; in urban context, 17, 95

Afrocentricity, 134

AIDS, 17, 154; and absence of African Americans in research studies, 122

Alabama Porch Monkeys, The (fictional show), 187–88

Alexander, Robert: *I Ain't Yo' Uncle*, 15

antebellum era, 24, 25, 32, 49, 56, 58

Aunt Jemima, 3, 168, 187, 195. *See also* stereotypes

authenticity, black racial: and African American identity, 5, 6; and black masculinity, 36; and black southern folk romanticism, 83, 227; and black-nationalist consciousness, 183; and *Crooklyn*, 191; and southern

rap, 202; and southerners, 177; and Spike Lee, 175. *See also* black masculinity

Autobiography of Malcolm X, 161

Baldwin, James: "Everybody's Protest Novel," 194–95, 196; "Going to Meet the Man," 234

Bamboozled (dir. Lee), 186–89

Baraka, Amiri, 195; on Charles Fuller, 78, 79, 82, 110, 174; and Spike Lee, 174–75

Birth of a Nation, The (dir. Griffith, 1915): and Christianity, 46; and Dixon's *The Clansman*, 19, 20, 24, 37–39, 43, 45, 62, 69, 71, 72; and Emancipation and Reconstruction, 57, 59; and film history, 55–56; and Huie's *The Klansman*, 43, 62, 71, 72; and Lee's "The Answer," 196; and masculinizations of the mammy figure, 195; as national cinema in U.S., 56; representation of black men in, 88; and sexual and stereotypical excessiveness, 54, 169

Black Belt, 172; and association with past, 142; as detriment to uplift ideology, 137; and geography, 138; and *Invisible Man*, 143, 145, 155. *See also* racial uplift

black femininity, 60, 61, 189, 231; as pathological, 71, 178

black feminism: and critical race theory, 8, 231

black liberation: Aunt Jemima as
militant during, 195; and *Birth of a
Nation*, 39; and black masculinity, 36,
156, 160; and black men, 52, 173; and
black power, 20, 50; and black racial
authenticity, 83; and discourse, 5, 15,
171, 232; gender politics of, 52, 63,
173; and Huey P. Newton, 172; and
Malcolm X, 159; and Spike Lee, 175;
and Uncle Tom, 187
black masculinity, 2, 3, 4, 5, 6, 14, 19,
237–38; as abject, 17, 20, 65, 119, 146,
167; and African American identity,
196; asexual, 50; and authenticity,
36, 182, 185; and "bad Negro,"
35–36; and black liberation, 195; and
class ideology, 6; as criminal, 72;
desexualized, 50, 60; and exclusion of
black southerners, 82; feminization
of, 178; and geography, 39, 82, 91,
119, 160, 161, 167, 176, 196; and Huey
P. Newton, 172–73; as hypersexual,
63; ideal, 147; and *The Klansman*
(1974), 53; and Malcolm X, 158, 159,
163, 169, 196; and *Malcolm X*, 176;
and *The Marrow of Tradition*, 28;
and Martin Luther King, 196; and
militancy, 15, 51, 53; and the military,
20, 73; northern models of, 219;
and pathology, 5, 20, 65, 71, 73, 122,
154, 234, 236, 238; patriarchal, 195;
perceptions of, 163; as pornographic,
36; as rapacious, 130; and region,
35; rural, 123–24, 131, 146, 149, 163;
and scholarship, 8; and Sean Puffy
Combs, 67–68; and sexuality, 3,
4, 8, 122, 154, 196; and space, 145;
and Uncle Tom, 181, 194, 221; in
United States, 18; urban, 15, 21, 33,
54, 83, 156, 232; as violent, 64; and

white femininity, 68. *See also* black
liberation; white masculinity
black men: anxieties about, 182; as
"beasts," 30; and black liberation,
173; as "bucks," 36; elite, 75; and
family values, 18; as folksy, 169;
as gangstas, 65, 202, 236–37; and
geography, 232; images of, as rapists,
4, 30, 33, 42, 45; and lynching, 29,
37, 58; as lustful, 36; masculinist
images of, 173; middle-class, 19; in
the military, 108; northern, 163; as
pathological, 88, 202, 236; as "playas,"
202; and rap, 201; and sexuality, 20,
182; in the South, 8, 18, 21, 22, 35, 86,
147, 159, 170, 171, 172, 173, 176, 177,
183, 184, 189, 196, 216, 222, 232, 236;
suffering police brutality, 35; in white
southern imagination, 25, 53. *See also*
stereotypes
black nationalism, 159, 183, 257n40; and
blackness, 167; in *Crooklyn*, 191, 192;
and *Malcolm X*, 175; and Mau Mau
group, 188–89; urban, 164, 177, 191,
193
black neonational movement, 134
Black Panther Party for Self-Defense,
50–51, 171, 173, 174, 188, 256n33; and
black rural southern specificity, 52;
and Nation of Islam, 255n30
black power, 20, 38, 49, 50, 51, 52, 53
black racial uplift, 2, 6
black rapist myth: and Brian Nichols,
69–70; emergence of, after Civil
War, 19; and "gangsta," 222; and
interracial sex, 142; and the Ku Klux
Klan, 58; and lynching, 233; and the
military, 93; as racial propaganda,
36; and Shirfin's *The Klansman*, 20,
64; and *A Soldier's Play*, 91; and the

South, 36; and white supremacy, 5. *See also* Uncle Tom: and black rapist

black revolution, 63

black studies, 13, 14, 16. *See also* southern studies

black women: and domestic violence, 244n47; as "emasculating," 49; as promiscuous, 45; and rape, 53. *See also* stereotypes

blackness, 14; African American as dominant term in, 134; authentic, 168, 170, 176, 188; and black nationalism, 167; desirable, 90; and diaspora, 127; and *Get on the Bus*, 182, 184; and masculinity, 174, 180; as modern signifier, 93; and Paris, 94; as pathological, 65, 121–22; rural, 131, 142, 146, 155; and sexual perversion, 142; and the South, 155; and southern identities, 82; Spike Lee's representations of, 190; and the urban North, 96–97, 191, 194, 196

Blakk, Joe, 21, 203; and American folk songs, 225; Down South Hustlers, 216, 225; "Way Down South," 200–201, 207, 213, 216, 217, 218–22, 225

blaxploitation, 20, 38, 53, 54, 242n25

body: black female, 45, 48, 119; black feminine, as asexual, 3; black, in global context, 13; black, in white southern imagination, 24; black, infected, 122; black male homosexual, 169; black southern male, 2, 4, 106, 220; and geography, 66; as hypersexed or pathological, 4, 5, 6, 36, 44, 88, 91, 92, 93, 119–20, 123, 130, 143, 160, 230; juxtaposition of black and white, 150; subjection of black, in medicine and science, 123; vulnerable black, 70; white female, 58; and white

southern men, 59; white voyeurism of black, 143. *See also* stereotypes

Brown, William Wells, 84

Brown v. Board of Education, 9

Cane (Toomer), 66, 141–42, 223

Carmichael, Stokely, 174

Cash Money Records, 199, 205, 206, 207

Chestnutt, Charles, 26–28, 37; and class, 28; and status of blacks, 23

citizenship: and democracy for white men, 154; exclusionary notions of, 131

civil rights, 15, 18, 124; activism, 40; and African Americans, 80; black, 9, 42; and masculinity, 169; and sex, 41. See also *Klansman, The* (Huie, 1967)

Civil Rights era: and Civil War era, 58; post–, 71; and post-Reconstruction era, 45

Civil Rights movement: and *Birth of a Nation* and *The Clansman*, 72; and Martin Luther King, 169, 170, 180; southern reactionaries of, 169; and white southern anxiety, 41

Civil War: and Civil Rights era, 58; and preference for black southern soldiers, 87; and violence against black southerners, 25

Clansman, The (Dixon): and Christianity, 46; and Griffith's *Birth of a Nation*, 19, 20, 24, 37–39, 43, 45, 62, 69, 71, 72; and Huie's *The Klansman*, 61

class: anxiety, 167; black bourgeois professional or elite black men, 32, 75, 90; black intellectual, 126; black middle, 45, 78, 167; blacks as subordinate, 75; distinctions in uplift ideologies, 100; poor or black

102; and constitution of African Americans, 77, 78, 105, 131, 132, 232; and gender, 90, 230; and identity, 133, 134, 137; and incest, 142; and interracial tension, 90; and *Invisible Man*, 128; and masculinity, 106, 110, 115, 165; notions of, after Hurricane Katrina, 234; *Quicksand*, 118; and race, 115, 165, 230–31; relations of African Americans based on, 193; rural, 21, 119, 132, 136, 139, 143, 151; and *School Daze*, 180; and *A Soldier's Play*, 82; southern, 179; tensions around, 201; Tuskegee Syphilis Study, 120; urban-centered, 104, 139; and white supremacy, 86

Get on the Bus (dir. Lee): blackness and masculinity in, 182–83, 185–86; and geography, 182, 186; homophobia in, 185; homosexuality and southernness in, 185; and model black southern male subjectivity, 184; South as contact zone in, 186; and southern identity, 182, 188

Geto Boys, 214

ghosts. *See* specter

globalization, 14, 17; and the South, 94

Gone with the Wind (Mitchell/dir. Fleming), 24–25

Great Migration, 16, 70, 77, 86, 148

Griffith, D. W. (*Birth of a Nation*), 10, 19, 38, 196

Griggs, Sutton (*Imperium in Imperio*), 1, 2

Harlem, 77, 163; after Great Depression, 129; in *Invisible Man*, 144, 145; and Paris, 93–94; and racial uplift, 94

Harlem Renaissance, 83

hip-hop, 14; and African American culture, 202; as global, 202, 227; and Russell Simmons, 203; South in, 227; and urban bias, 226. *See also* rap

Huie, William Bradford (*The Klansman*), 11, 37, 39, 45, 71, 72

Hurston, Zora Neale, 250n2, 251n12

identity: African American, 5, 196, 232; black diasporic, 127; black female, 189, 244n47; black gay, 185; black southern rural, 124, 127, 134, 145, 149, 154, 224; black urban, 174; collective, in South, 215; elite notions of African American, 155; and geography, 133, 134, 227; psychoanalysis to black, 152; rural, 124, 135, 145, 154; southern, 182, 201, 215, 239n12; and space, 141

incest. See under *Invisible Man*

interracial sex. *See* sex, interracial

Invisible Man (Ellison): 21, 123, 133, 181; and "folk," 128, 154; and geography, 128, 135, 139, 143, 149; Harlem in, 144, 145; and incest, 131, 136–38, 142, 146, 149, 150–52; and interracial sex, 142; pathological black masculinity in, 122, 156; race and gender in, 146; and racial abjection, 140; as regional masterpiece, 130; and repercussions of slavery, 130; and rural geography, 132, 143, 145, 147, 149, 151, 154; and sexual pathology, 138; and spatiality, 153; and status of black men, 145; and temporality, 142, 149, 150, 151, 152, 154; Trueblood in, 122–23, 131, 136–40, 142–43, 145–52, 232; and undesirability of the rural, 131, 139, 140, 144; and urban geography, 155

168, 170, 173, 195; and Martin Luther
  King, 168; and memories of Ku Klux
  Klan, 164; and Nation of Islam, 158,
  162, 164–65, 257n40; and region, 170;
  and rural background, 163, 164, 165,
  254n17; and sexuality, 159, 169, 254n4;
  on the South, 165, 170; stereotype of,
  157; and Uncle Tom references, 21,
  167–68, 169, 170, 171, 195; and uplift,
  196; and urban North bias, 165, 167,
  170; and urbanization, 163
Malcolm X (dir. Lee), 158, 160, 164,
  174; and authentic blackness, 176;
  and black masculinity, 176; and black
  nationalism, 175; and urban bias, 176
mammy, 3, 168, 187; and *Birth of a
  Nation*, 195. *See also* stereotypes
Marrow of Tradition, The (Chesnutt),
  26–28, 34, 60; and Dr. Miller,
  28–30; and interracial sex, 26; and
  Josh Green, 28–30, 32–33. *See also*
  stereotypes
masculinity: authentic, 170; and
  blackness, 174, 180, 182, 194; and
  diasporic subject, 233; and geography,
  237; in *Get on the Bus*, 182; and Josh
  Green, 29; and Malcolm X, 175;
  and race, 21, 77, 82, 154, 156; and the
  South, 232; and southern rap, 212; as
  urban, 226. *See also* black masculinity
Master P, 22, 199, 203, 206, 207, 227,
  261–62n23; as the "ghetto Bill Gates,"
  205; and No Limit Records, 199,
  203–4, 208, 216
military: and black masculinity, 20,
  73–74; and black rapist myth, 93;
  desegregation in, 102; hierarchies
  in, 107; interracial and interethnic
  harmony in, 83; and lynching, 77;
  mixing blacks from rural South and

urban North, 94; and race, 89, 92;
  segregation in, 83, 84, 88, 93; and
  Soldiers' Pay, 75; and *A Soldier's Play*,
  89, 91; and South's racial social order,
  74; and white supremacy, 92; and
  World War I, 5, 74. *See also* soldiers
Million Man March, 181
minstrelsy, 3, 24, 92, 99, 148, 188; and
  "gangstas," 237; and Tiger Woods,
  229
miscegenation, 45, 58, 62, 71. *See also*
  racial intermixture
Mississippi Freedom Democratic Party
  (MFDP), 51
Mitchell, Margaret, 24–25
Morrison, Toni, 99, 201; *Birth of a
  Nation'hood*, 64, 72, 245n49; *The
  Bluest Eye*, 144–45; *Song of Solomon*,
  223–24

Nappy Roots, 212, 214
Nation of Islam: and Black Panther
  Party, 255n30; and Elijah Muhammad, 161, 175; homophobia in, 168;
  and Malcolm X, 162, 164–65, 257n40;
  and separatist philosophy, 169;
  sexuality and gender in, 158
National Association for the Advance-
  ment of Colored People (NAACP),
  37
New Negro, 26. *See also* racial uplift
New Orleans: blacks in, 210; and
  bounce sound, 210, 216; and French
  Opera House, 210; and Hurricane
  Katrina, 222, 234; jazz in, 211; racial
  and class disparities in, 208–9; rap,
  203, 205, 207–8, 216, 218; in "Way
  Down South," 219
Newton, Huey P., 171–73
Nichols, Brian, 69

Our Nig (Wilson), 66
Outkast, 214

Parks, Gordon (*Shaft*), 53
Parks, Rosa, 214
passing, 113
performativity, 99
Perry, Bruce (biography of Malcolm X), 157–58
Plessy v. Ferguson, 25, 26, 99
politics, white liberal, 78

queerness, 159
Quicksand (Larsen): and geography, 118; Helga's interracial body in, 119; and rural South, 118, 128, 189

race: and masculinity, 154, 156; psychoanalysis, 152; and southern rap, 212
racial intermixture, 4, 41, 67, 71, 92, 118, 169, 170, 214. *See also* sex, interracial
racial uplift, 95, 97, 100, 101, 195; and Black Belt blacks, 137; and black intellectual and middle classes, 126; and Harlem, 94; rural, 146; and *School Daze*, 179; and Urban League, 77; and urban North, 80
rap: and African American subjectivity, 226; and black authenticity, 202; and black female artists, 201; and black men's lives, 201; and bounce sound, 205, 210, 216; as commodity, 202; and *crunk*, 199; and "dirty South," 12, 21, 197–98, 215; East Coast/West Coast, 213, 215, 217; elite in, 205; excluding South from, 213; female and white artists identifying with South, 199; "folk" and vernacular in, 201, 218; in global and diasporic contexts, 202;

industry, 212; and Jim Crow, 220; questioning heterosexuality of men, 223; and region, 213, 223; "roll call" in, 216; southern, 12, 16, 21; as urban and masculine verbal art, 197; urban forms of, 201; West Coast artists, 216; and white supremacist racial ideologies, 214. *See also* gangsta rap; New Orleans: rap
rape: black male of white woman, 19, 33, 42, 47, 50, 57, 59, 62, 63; interracial, 48, 60; and Ku Klux Klan, 44; and lynching, 38, 46, 48, 54, 57, 62, 63, 91, 231; public perceptions of, 37; and violence against black body, 37; white male of black woman, 26, 37, 45, 47, 62, 63
Reconstruction, 87, 124, 160; backlash against, 9, 24; Emancipation and, 57; end of, 25; and Ku Klux Klan, 37; politicians, 160; post-, 33, 45; slavery and, 67; and white supremacy, 32, 45, 100; white women and black men during, 130; and whites, 23, 32, 59
resistance: nonviolent as feminine, 169
Rice, Condoleezza, 7, 195
Rosewood (dir. Singleton), 233
rural: as abject, 136; black identity, 127; black masculinity, 124, 146, 149, 163; black men, 147; black southerners, 124, 125, 126, 153, 155; blackness, 125, 131, 142, 146, 155; bodies, 143; as dispensable, 128; geography, 119, 132, 136, 139, 145, 151; identity, 135, 145, 154; Malcolm X and, background, 163, 164, 165, 254n17; migration, 162; and national belonging, 133; as pathological, 144; and queer studies, 170; race, 135; sentimental attachment to, 135; South, 118, 120, 124, 153, 154,

155, 220; studies, 130, 133, 134; in transnational framework, 135; and urban, 161

South (*continued*)

practices in, 86–87; and Ellison, 129; ethnic diversification of, 214, 233; as feminine, 169, 189; in global context, 14, 94, 134, 237–38; Jim Crow, 35; and Malcolm X, 165; and masculine subject formation, 232; and masculinity and femininity, 10, 78; migration to, 70; and military, 74; and nation, 9, 56; and North binary, 159, 167, 189, 194; and poor whites, 125; post-Emancipation, 121; as "problem," 9; queer, 171; in *Quicksand*, 118; and race problems, 70, 261n23; as racially monolithic, 124; and rap artists, 198, 215, 217; as regressive, 129; rural, 112, 114, 118, 120, 124, 134–35, 144, 147, 148, 153, 154, 155, 220; as scene of trauma and terror, 97; and slavery, 132; as "slow," 193; in *A Soldier's Play*, 82; and white men, 75, 172; and whiteness, 67, 155. *See also* rap

southern literature, 11, 12, 13, 22, 26, 72, 82, 115, 129–30. *See also* southern studies

southern studies, 13, 14, 130, 237; and African American literature, 13; global, 12, 94, 104, 238; new, 11, 13, 72, 238; and postcolonial studies, 179; and queer studies, 12; race in, 238. *See also* southern literature

space: black masculine, 145; and black southerners, 179; cabin, 137, 141–42, 145–46; cottage, 141; and rural identities, 145. See also *Invisible Man*

specter, and C.J., 104, 106, 248n46, 249n53. See also *Invisible Man*

stereotypes, 47; Aunt Jemima, 3, 168, 187, 195; "bad Negro," 28, 29, 33–36, 64, 70, 221, 234; "'Bama," 178; "beasts," 30; bestial, 47, 58, 92; "bitch," 178; "bucks," 36; "country," 178; "field Negro," 166–67, 170; "house Negro," 159–60, 165–68, 170; "Jim Crow," 9, 76, 99; "monkey," 99; "nigga," 221; Old Black Joe, 3; "playas," 200, 202, 221; in post–Civil War era, 24; Rastus, 187; southern, 93, 114, 193, 213; southern rap responding to, 225–26; Topsy, 187; tragic mulatto, 118; Uncle Mose, 187; Uncle Remus, 3, 186; "white trash," 85–86, 125. *See also entries for specific stereotypes*

stereotypes, of blacks: identity, 53, 196; masculinity, 6, 50, 51, 52, 72, 154, 196, 200, 222, 232, 234–35; men, 82, 91, 177, 189; men as lustful, 36, 57, 63, 103, 122, 169; northerners, 167; as rapist, 25, 30, 35, 36, 37, 42, 45, 57, 58, 92, 142, 169, 222, 233, 234; southerners, 83, 88, 92, 95, 101, 113, 167 (*see also* stereotypes, of southern: rural blacks); women, 45, 49, 60, 62, 119

stereotypes, of southern: gentleman, 28, 56, 75; lady, 28, 56, 214; rural blacks, 125, 128, 142, 144, 168

stereotypes, of whites, 62, 160, 173

Stowe, Harriet Beecher (*Uncle Tom's Cabin*), 3, 60, 194–95

Stuart, Charles, 4

Student Non-Violent Coordinating Committee (SNCC), 51, 174, 256–57n34

subaltern studies, 247n27

temporality: in *Invisible Man*, 142, 149, 150, 151, 152

Texas Niggaz and Eses, 213–14

theater, 89

Thomas, Clarence, 15, 161, 243n45; and
Anita Hill, 7, 243n45
Tre 8, 217, 218
Tupak Shakur, 221
Ture, Kwame (Stokely Carmichael), 174
Turner, Nat, 14–15, 31. *See also* slavery;
stereotypes
Tuskegee Institute, 124
Tuskegee Syphilis Study, 88, 119, 121,
122, 123; and black male body, 4, 21;
and geography, 120
2 Live Crew, 200

Uncle Tom, 21, 49, 91, 148, 156, 184,
221, 222; as bisexual, 169; and black
liberation, 187; and black male body,
5, 58; and Black Panther Party, 172;
and black rapist, 3, 4, 7, 16, 18, 160,
169, 237; as homosexual or queer,
168, 169, 187, 195; and Malcolm X,
21, 167–68, 170, 171; Martin Luther
King Jr. as, 159, 166; and Nat Turner,
14–15; and Pierre Delacroix, 188;
revision of, discourse, 194–95; and
School Daze, 180–81; and Spike
Lee, 173, 181; and whiteness, 169,
181. *See also* stereotypes; Thomas,
Clarence
urban, 80, 83, 134, 226; in academia,
14, 16, 126; bias or fetishism, 19,
127, 135, 165, 174, 176, 188, 232;
black male revolutionary, 51–52,
186; black nationalism, 164, 192,
193; distinctions with rural, 114,
161; North and blackness, 96, 102,
154; North and rural South, 54, 83,
94, 100, 135, 145, 155, 162; North as
superior site of African American
masculine formation, 109, 191; rap,
201, 213

Van Peebles, Melvin (*Sweet Sweetback's
Badasssss Song*), 53

Walker, Alice, 103
Walker, David, 30–32
Wallace, Governor George, 41
Washington, Booker T., 7, 15, 194; and
Tuskegee Institute, 121
Wells, Ida B., 15
white femininity, 67–69, 231; exalted,
58–59, 61, 66
white masculinity, 5, 51, 78, 102; and
panic, 42, 245n9; and *Soldiers' Pay*,
75; in South, 28, 130. *See also* black
masculinity
white men, 75, 172–73
white sexuality, 5
white studies, 17
white supremacy, 5, 45, 92, 238; and
black sexuality, 123; and David
Duke, 209; and depictions of black
men, 20; and geography, 86; and
The Klansman (1967), 46; and *The
Klansman* (1974), 47, 48, 53, 56,
65; and lynching, 58, 220; and
masculinism, 130; and rap, 214; and
Reconstruction, 32, 45, 100; and *A
Soldier's Play*, 96, 97, 101. *See also*
Reconstruction
white womanhood, 4, 5, 58
whiteness, 67, 69, 155; antebellum, 125;
black southerners as covetous of, 186;
and Uncle Tom, 169
Williams, Brian "Slim," 22, 203; and
Cash Money Records, 199, 205, 206
Williams, Ronald "Baby," 22, 203; and
Cash Money Records, 199, 205, 206,
207
Wilmington Riot of 1898, 26
Woods, Tiger, 71, 229–30

World War I: African American men in, 76, 80, 116; and *Birth of a Nation*, 56; black soldiers as inferior in, 5, 88, 92; and *Soldiers' Pay*, 75; and white women, 92

World War II, 85

Wright, Richard, 33–34, 35, 264n8

Young, Terence: *The Klansman*, 19

Zoeller, Fuzzy, 229–30

Made in the USA
Monee, IL
11 November 2020

47172762R00184